EVA® AND VALUE-BASED MANAGEMENT

EVA® AND VALUE-BASED MANAGEMENT

A Practical Guide to Implementation

S. DAVID YOUNG

STEPHEN F. O'BYRNE

McGraw-Hill

New York   San Francisco   Washington, D.C.   Auckland   Bogotá
Caracas   Lisbon   London   Madrid   Mexico City   Milan
Montreal   New Delhi   San Juan   Singapore
Sydney   Tokyo   Toronto

Library of Congress Cataloging-in-Publication Data

Young, S. David
    EVA and value-based management : a practical guide to implementation / by S. David
Young and Stephen F. O'Byrne.
        p.   cm.
    ISBN 0-07-136439-0
    1. Economic value added.   2. Corporations—Valuation.   3. Capital
investments—Decision making.   4. Managerial economics.   5. Industrial management.   I.
O'Byrne, Stephen F.   II. Title.

HG4028.V3 Y68 2000
658.15—dc21
00-055007

McGraw-Hill

A Division of The **McGraw·Hill** Companies

  9 0 FGR/FGR   6 5

0-07-136439-0

*The sponsoring editor for this book was Catherine Schwent, the editing supervisor was Ruth W.
Mannino, and the production supervisor was Tina Cameron. It was set in 11/13 Times Roman by
Pro-Image Corporation.*

Printed and bound by Quebecor World/Fairfield

This publication is designed to provide accurate and authoritative information in regard
to the subject matter covered. It is sold with the understanding that neither the author nor
the publisher is engaged in rendering legal, accounting, or other professional service. If
legal advice or other expert assistance is required, the services of a competent professional
person should be sought.

    —From a Declaration of Principles jointly adopted by a Committee of the American Bar
    Association and a Committee of Publishers.

EVA® is a registered trademark of Stern Stewart & Co.

This book is printed on recycled, acid-free paper containing a
minimum of 50% recycled de-inked fiber.

CONTENTS

v

Chapter 3

Implementing EVA 79

Chapter 4

Management Compensation 113

Chapter 6

EVA   205

Chapter 7

Value Drivers   269

PART THREE

CONCLUSIONS

Chapter 11

Lessons Learned, and the Future of Economic Value Added   467

PREFACE

We were motivated to write this book partly because of our frustration with the EVA and VBM publications already available. Several of these publications have made important, even seminal, contributions to the topic of value-based management, and we have learned a lot from them. However, the literature in general is, in our view, unsatisfying. No earlier book has really assessed the experience of EVA/VBM companies in the 1990s—a period during which EVA/VBM implementation increased dramatically. Nearly all the widely cited references on EVA or value-based management are advocacy books that avoid discussion of implementations that have failed. Also, even the more recently written works fail to discuss, in detail, the numerous technical innovations in EVA/VBM implementation that have occurred in recent years. Another shortcoming of the existing literature is the failure to recognize that there are two quite distinct audiences interested in EVA and VBM: the general management reader who wants a strategic overview and assessment and the more technically minded reader who demands practical detail and supporting evidence. In our view, nearly all of the earlier works are either impenetrable for the general management reader or lack the technical detail needed to guide implementation.

In writing this book, we have striven to provide a fair and balanced assessment of EVA/VBM implementation, covering failures as well as successes. We also provide a strategic overview for the general management reader and a full and complete discussion of technical methodologies for professionals tasked with managing the actual implementation process. The book is not intended to be a "teaser," which tries to tell you just enough to whet your appetite so if you want to know more you will have to hire us as your consultants. We aim to be as comprehensive in our treatment of the subject as possible. There are limits to what we can tell you, mainly because of client confidentiality and the fact that some of the industry-specific nature of our experiences would not be of interest to a wide audience, but for the most part, the secrets of the trade as we understand them are revealed here. We try to hold nothing back.

This book is organized in three parts. In Part I, we lay out the basic concepts of EVA and value-based management. Our perspective is a broad one, approaching the subject with a company CEO or board member in mind. In short, the first part of this book presents what a senior, nonfinancial executive needs to know about EVA and how to use it.

In Part II, we revisit key topics addressed in Part I, but from a more technical perspective. For example, we address the topic of management compensation in both parts, but while the focus of our discussion in Part I is mainly strategic and conceptual, Part II shows, in detail, how an EVA-linked bonus plan actually works. Part II addresses a number of other technical issues as well, including the cost of capital, accounting adjustments to EVA, and alternative value-based measurement approaches such as CFROI. Part II is intended to answer the questions that we often encounter from finance specialists, accountants, and value-based management professionals. We don't pretend that all technical concerns will be answered, but we are confident that we have gone much further than any other published materials on the subject in dealing with complicated implementation issues in a forthright and comprehensive fashion.

In the final part of the book, Part III, we present our conclusions, including some practical tips on making EVA work. We also share our thoughts on the future of EVA and value-based performance measurement.

S. David Young

Stephen F. O'Byrne

EVA® AND VALUE-BASED MANAGEMENT

PART ONE

Understanding EVA

CHAPTER 1

The Shareholder Value Revolution

A security analyst once described his father's transport company to us. For this small businessman, growth and investment decisions were usually no more complicated than "should I buy another truck?" Unlike his son, who had an MBA from a leading British business school, he knew nothing of economic value added, discounted cashflow, or any of the tools of modern corporate finance. Back-of-the-envelope calculations provided the answer. He knew that if he got it wrong, he would burden the business with debt it could not afford.

"If I buy another truck," he asked, "how much extra profit do I have to earn to pay for it? Will the investment make me better off or not?" All successful small-business owners have this intuitive sense of value creation, even if they cannot express the process with the rigor of a business school graduate.

Top managers of large companies have this intuition too. They can nevertheless go badly off track, sometimes destroying billions of dollars of wealth in the process. What separates the senior executive of a large publicly traded company from the owner-manager of a small transport company? It's tempting to think that successful small-business owners possess some sort of folk wisdom that eludes their big business counterparts. Our popular culture extols the virtues of these Davids, doing battle against slower Goliaths. The truth, however, is less romantic.

3

Quite simply, senior corporate executives are too often paid to worry about things other than creating value. When managers don't own the companies they manage, or own only a small percentage of the outstanding shares, it's hardly surprising if value creation is not their top priority, because the value they may create belongs to others. As a result, value is destroyed, not intentionally, but because managers pursue other goals that sometimes conflict with the creation of value, such as market share, volume growth, customer satisfaction, jobs, stakeholders, or the old standby, "strategic" reasons.

It's not that these goals are undesirable. Value-creating companies, however, pursue them not for their own sake but because long-term value creation for their shareholders is not possible otherwise. The problem is that the need to earn competitive returns on capital, a precondition to sustained success in any business enterprise, sometimes gets obscured in large, complex companies. Corporate bureaucracies can insulate managers, leading them to believe that capital comes from budgets and not from the capital markets.

More top managers now recognize the problem. Pressures in deregulated capital markets to deliver ever-increasing profits have led hundreds of large companies around the world to adopt new performance metrics to track management's success in creating value for shareholders and to motivate employees throughout the firm to make their work consistent with the overarching goal of value creation.

In recent years, corporate managers have been bombarded by consultants with a plethora of acronyms, such as EVA, RONA, and CFROI.[1] Although proponents of a particular measure assert its superiority over its competitors, all such metrics are organized around the same basic principle: To create value for their shareholders, companies must earn returns on invested capital that exceed the cost of capital. Each metric may have its own distinctive advantages and disadvantages, and each is expressed in its own distinctive way. Yet at their most basic level, they are all designed to measure management's success in achieving this aim.

---

1. EVA is a registered trademark of Stern Stewart & Company. RONA stands for return on net assets. CFROI is cashflow return on investment.

In this book, we compare EVA, or economic value added, with RONA, CFROI, and other financial performance metrics. We also discuss how it fits in a comprehensive value-based approach to business management. EVA measures the difference, in monetary terms, between the *return* on a company's capital and the *cost* of that capital. It is similar to conventional accounting measures of profit, but with one important difference: EVA considers the cost of *all* capital. The net income figures reported in company income statements consider only the most visible type of capital cost—interest—while ignoring the cost of equity.

Although estimating the cost of equity is a subjective process, measures of performance that ignore such costs cannot reveal how successful a company has been in creating value for its owners. We will see later that another difference between EVA and conventional profit figures is that EVA is not constrained by generally accepted accounting principles (GAAP).

The basic ideas behind EVA are not new. EVA is essentially a repackaging of sound financial management and corporate finance principles that have been around for a long time. Yet EVA *is* an innovation, and an important one at that, because it has made modern finance theory, and the managerial implications of this theory, more accessible to corporate managers who are not well trained in finance or never thought they had to be. The ideas may not be original, but in form there is content, especially in a business world populated by managers who are often instinctively hostile to finance. EVA helps managers to better understand financial goals, and in so doing, it helps them achieve these goals.

WHY SHAREHOLDER VALUE, AND WHY NOW?

Investors have always cared about stock returns, but profound changes have emerged in corporate boardrooms in the last 20 years, first in the United States and more lately spreading to Europe, Latin America, and Asia. A confluence of factors and circumstances have led boards of directors and senior executives to rethink their roles and those of their companies, especially as regards value creation.

The growing predominance of the shareholder wealth culture is largely a consequence of several major developments:

+ The globalization and deregulation of capital markets
+ The end of capital and exchange controls
+ Advances in information technology
+ More liquid securities markets
+ Improvements in capital market regulation
+ Generational changes in attitudes toward savings and investment
+ The expansion of institutional investment

A generation ago, capital markets were both highly seg-mented and highly regulated. Limits on capital flows, combined with low liquidity in most of the world's securities markets, meant that capital resources tended to stay put. Corporate managers liked it that way, because pressures for performance were re-strained. Even when companies underperformed, senior managers were rarely fired.

Despite the absence of capital market pressure, many com-panies fared well, making a lot of money for their investors, thanks largely to robust economic growth. Remember that in the 30 years after World War II, growth rates of 4 percent, 5 percent, or even higher were common in several Western economies. In such a world, companies didn't have to be especially good to be profitable; they only had to be there. Connections were important; ties to the political, commercial, and financial elite of the day were often more critical to corporate success than strategic vision or managerial excellence.

But this state of affairs underwent profound changes in the 1970s and early 1980s, beginning with free-floating exchange rates in currency markets, and followed by the OPEC oil crisis, the end of fixed brokerage commissions in the United States, a growing climate of deregulation that forced its way into many sectors of the economy, the elections of Margaret Thatcher and Ronald Rea-gan, and the start of a massive worldwide wave of privatization. The General Agreement on Tariffs and Trade, or GATT, played an important role too, as did the gradual strengthening of the Euro-pean Economic Community (later the European Community and now the European Union).

Moreover, the 1980s saw a staggering increase in the power and accessibility of computing technology, while the growth of investment capital brought on several years of solid, worldwide economic expansion. Meanwhile, stock exchanges, eager to promote the interests of local companies in increasingly competitive global markets, strove to improve the attractiveness of these companies to foreign investors by lifting restrictions on foreign brokers, adopting technologically advanced trading systems, and boosting the depth and liquidity of the exchanges to reduce transaction costs. Regulation was taken seriously, but not the kind of regulation that stifles markets. Rather, regulation that makes securities trading a fairer game was welcomed—such as insider trading constraints and corporate disclosure requirements.

As these developments took shape, a new generation of young investors began to emerge, flush with surplus income and possessed as well of more favorable attitudes toward stock markets than earlier generations. Their parents grew up in the Great Depression or in the war years. As economies grew in the post-War era, and people had money in their pockets, they socked it away in bank accounts or built up equity in their homes; stocks were for rich people or gamblers.

Their children think differently. Aided by a seemingly endless bull market (interrupted by the odd crash or two) and solid evidence that with a long enough investment horizon a person is almost certainly better off investing in the stock market than in government bonds or bank accounts, millions of people whose parents never even thought about buying stocks have taken the plunge and become shareholders. This trend was accelerated by privatization campaigns in Great Britain, France, and elsewhere that sought to ensure the permanence of private ownership by encouraging dispersion of the shares of newly privatized companies among a large cross section of citizens.

Interest in stocks, and in investing generally, has grown in ways unimaginable to finance professionals as recently as the 1970s. The result is a veritable worldwide explosion in mutual funds, unit trusts, and other forms of institutional investment. Not only do many more people have a financial stake in companies, typically through mutual funds or pension funds, but of particular importance to corporate managers is that these funds are run by professional managers who care only about performance and delivering the highest returns possible to the people who hired them. There is little doubt that the explosion in pension fund investing

since the 1960s, and the growth of professional money management that came with it, is the single greatest factor behind the
emphasis on shareholder value creation in American companies.

When these capital market developments are taken together,
the principal lesson to corporate managers should be clear: Capital
has attained a degree of mobility that is unprecedented in human
history, and it will go where it is most appreciated. In other words,
capital isn't "sticky" anymore; capital can move. And move it will,
whenever investors believe their capital will be more productively
employed somewhere else.

In this new world, companies must not only be competitive
in commercial markets, but they must also be competitive in capital markets. Otherwise, their cost of capital will be higher than
their competitors', a problem that is corrected either by improved
performance or by takeover. In the worst cases, companies will go
bankrupt. All managers understand that for their companies to
survive and grow they must be competitive in terms of operating
costs—such as labor, materials, or administrative costs. What has
changed is that survival also requires competitive *capital* costs, a
reality still not fully appreciated by many corporate managers.

A CASE IN POINT: EUROPE AND THE SHAREHOLDER VALUE REVOLUTION

Because the impact of these capital market developments was felt
first in the United States, observers sometimes make the mistake
of assuming that this change process is driven by the United States
and the powerful American investment banks. The reality is very
different, however. In the 1980s, American corporate executives
often resisted the performance demands imposed by capital markets with all the ferocity of European and Asian managers in the
1990s. These changes began in the United States, but when they
arose in other countries, it was for the same reasons as in the
United States—not because American investment bankers sought
to impose their hegemony on new markets. Crediting (or blaming)
American investment houses for the spread of the shareholder
value revolution is to confuse cause and effect.

To illustrate, consider recent developments in Europe. Until
the 1980s, most European countries heavily protected their national champions from American and Japanese competitors. However, with growing European integration and a secular, worldwide

trend toward freer trade, European companies have been subjected to an unprecedented degree of competition, both from non-
Europeans and from each other. Liberalized trade gives customers
choices they did not have before.

In this environment, companies either deliver value to their
customers or they lose market share and fail. As a result of deregulation in the world's capital markets, investors too can go
elsewhere whenever companies fail to deliver. The end of most
capital controls, more liquid currency and securities markets, advances in information technology, and the growing importance of
institutional investors have all played a role in creating massive
pools of investment capital that can flow from one market to the
next practically in an instant. Other important developments have
occurred as well. Securitization has turned otherwise illiquid instruments into tradable commodities; derivatives offer powerful
tools for hedging the risks of investing in new markets; privatization has turned thousands of former state enterprises into competitors for risk capital; and investors have become better informed and more demanding.

These developments have led to the gradual erosion of "re-
lational" capitalism in which many business activities are conducted according to "old school ties" or other devices for social
and cultural cohesion, which place little emphasis on value creation and more on the preservation of privilege and the *status quo*.
For example, French *noyaux durs* (of large, stable shareholders)
and German universal banks have been notoriously undemanding
of their holdings because of long-standing business practices and
strong personal relations between shareholders and company
managers.

Europe's impressive response to the challenges of free trade,
evidenced by the strong export performance of many European
companies, offers some hope that it can make similar strides in
the capital markets. The French, for example, have responded to
increased commercial competition by becoming world-class retailers and luxury-brand managers.

But just as Europeans have learned to cope with deregulated
commercial markets in the last 15 years, in the next 15 years they
must learn to cope with deregulated *capital* markets and the re-
lentless demands from shareholders and their representatives for
performance. They must learn to communicate with and satisfy
the demands of their capital providers, just as they have learned

to communicate with their customers. EVA and similar value-based metrics are emerging as important tools for European managers, and for managers everywhere, to cope with the dramatic changes taking place in corporate finance.

This trend will only be intensified by what may be the most important development in European capital markets: the growth of capitalized pension funds. With aging populations and an unsustainable safety net, a growing number of Europeans now recognize that underfunded social security programs will be unable to serve the retirement needs of today's workforce. In France, for example, the ratio of active workers to retirees went from 4.69 in 1960 to just 2.10 in 1990. INSEE, the French statistical office, estimates that by 2010 there will only be 1.65 workers for every recipient of social security.[2] Demographic trends in Germany and Italy are even more discouraging.

To provide for the needs of an aging population, and to stimulate savings and corporate investment, many countries have implemented or are planning to implement tax-advantaged pension and savings plans that are already beginning to channel unprecedented amounts of equity capital to Europe's stock exchanges. These funds are invested by professional portfolio managers, competing aggressively against each other for the right to manage pension assets. Such money managers are interested only in performance, because that is how they are judged by their clients. The *noyaux durs* of stable, undemanding shareholdings that have characterized so much of French corporate governance are coming under enormous pressure, as professional money managers "vote with their feet" and withdraw support from any company that does not offer the prospect of competitive returns. German companies, which until recently enjoyed the relaxed performance standards imposed by Deutsche Bank and its sister institutions, are finding themselves under similar pressure.

The trend toward ever greater institutional investment has been intensified by profound changes in the savings behavior of individuals. In the United States, more people than ever participate in equity markets, mainly through mutual funds and personal pensions. And, unlike past participation in stock markets by

---

2. "Retraite: Évaluez vos besoins," *Le Figaro Patrimoine*, November 13, 1998, p. 28.

middle-class investors, stakes often run into the hundreds of thousands of dollars, or more. Attitudes among young European professionals have changed too. Their parents, many of whom suffered through two world wars and periods of hyperinflation, traditionally put their savings in the safest vehicles they knew— mainly bank accounts, government bonds, and sometimes under their mattresses. But today's young investors are more sophisticated about markets and have a better understanding of the risks and rewards of stock market investing. The result is an enormous growth in demand for mutual funds and similar investment vehicles. Indeed, many of the largest American fund managers are now aggressively promoting their services all over the world, especially in Western Europe.

The advent of the Euro, the European Union's common currency, is also playing an important role in changing corporate attitudes. With one currency in place of several, it is now easier to compare the performance of companies in different countries. If, for example, a Danish company is underperforming compared to peers in other countries, its poor performance will be more apparent to investment professionals. These money managers will express their displeasure, and the firm's share price will fall. As investors in European equities increasingly make their decisions irrespective of national boundaries, companies will be driven to change.

Dozens of large European companies have already undergone profound transformations. Nowhere is this change more obvious than in the firms that are listed on the New York Stock Exchange. A case in point is Veba, a diversified German company with sales of over $45 billion, which now proclaims in advertisements in the world's business press that "enhancing shareholder value over the long term is our sole objective."

Similar changes are taking place in France. In 1996, the economic adviser to the country's prime minister, after deciding that he wanted a career change and despite a lack of relevant experience, used his connections to secure appointment as the chief executive of Credit Industriel & Commercial (CIC), a large bank that was then under state control (and later privatized). Usually, such an arrangement would have generated little notice, as elites from the French civil service have often moved into top management posts in the private sector. But the appointment created such an uproar within the bank that the government was forced to back down and appoint a professional banker instead.

As an observer wrote:

> [The civil servant's] ambition collided with the market forces that are re-shaping Europe. Privatization, deregulation, globalization, and closer integration are rewriting the rules of European business. Professionalism, profits, return-on-equity, and corporate governance are in; size for the sake of size, cross-shareholdings that shield management, and political patronage are out.[3]

While France's old-boy network still functions, it is no longer possible to be parachuted into a chief executive's position in a large enterprise after just a few years in government service. Going to the right schools still counts for more in France than it does in the United States, but at least today candidates for top management posts are expected to have a suitable track record in business.

The pressure throughout Europe for improved financial performance has led to unprecedented levels of CEO turnover. Until recently, poor share price performance was unlikely to get a chief executive fired. An appointment as CEO came with a sense of entitlement. But globalization means that public companies everywhere are starting to play by the same rules.

Important differences still persist between the corporate governance regimes of European industry and those of their American competitors, but the convergence in corporate accountability is unmistakable and irreversible. Until the very recent past, hostile takeovers were viewed as a uniquely American phenomenon, but a wave of hostile bids began to sweep Europe in early 1999. Olivetti's attack on Telecom Italia, BNP's proposed takeover of Paribas and Société Générale, and LVMH's struggle to gain control over Gucci would all have been unthinkable not too long ago. Quite simply, the shareholder value revolution is gripping the continent.

Unfortunately, while large global companies in Europe seem to be getting the message, smaller players are either oblivious to the new realities or act as if they were. Lacking the management

---

3. T. Kamm, "Market Forces Push France's Elite Corps Out of Top Sinecures," *Wall Street Journal Europe*, May 7, 1998, pp. 1, 8.

systems and thinking needed to compete in global, deregulated capital markets, these companies are in for a rude awakening when these realities hit home.

VALUE CREATION AND STAKEHOLDERS

While managers are feeling increased pressure to deliver value, they often lack the necessary diagnostic tools. Moreover, they lack the *language* of value creation—that is, a means of persuading capital providers that funds will be productively and profitably employed in their companies. Managers who fail in this task will find their companies at a competitive disadvantage in the race for global capital resources. They must learn to navigate the rough seas of competitive capital markets, or they will find themselves replaced by managers who can.

Still, there is widespread resistance, especially in Europe, to the idea that creating value for shareholders should be management's top priority. Value-based management is often criticized on the grounds that it ignores important constituencies other than the firm's shareholders, such as employees, customers, suppliers, the environment, and the local community. Yet a growing body of evidence in Europe and North America shows that companies with good reputations in terms of (1) product and service quality, (2) the ability to attract, develop, and retain talented people, and (3) community and environmental responsibility tend to outperform stock market averages.

This evidence suggests that firms deliver value to shareholders only when they deliver value to their other constituencies. If customers are not satisfied, they buy from competitors. If employees feel their talents are unappreciated and undervalued, they too go elsewhere.

In its 1995 annual report, Coca-Cola, one of the world's top value creators, makes the claim: "Coca-Cola provides value to everyone who touches it." What the statement means is that every constituency that comes in contact with Coke and its products has somehow been enriched for the experience. Whether it is customers who take comfort from the brand, employees who work in a stimulating and rewarding environment, bottlers who enjoy attractive profit margins, or most important, shareholders who are wealthier because of the company's strong financial performance, everyone is better off because Coke exists. While this statement may seem egregiously immodest to some, it reflects an important philosophical attitude among Coke's managers. Their number one job is to create shareholder value, a task that is achieved only by delivering value to everyone else.

Yet even Coca-Cola sometimes forgets this fundamental truth, as its recent problems in Europe testify. The company's tardy response to product contamination in Belgium in 1999 rocked its share price, despite Belgium accounting for only a tiny percentage of worldwide sales. Troubles with antitrust authorities in France and Italy, and a reputation (deserved or otherwise) for sharp competitive practices were further reminders to Coke management that the cost of failing to address the legitimate concerns of regulators and the general public are ultimately borne by shareholders.

Nevertheless, while these experiences point out the importance of satisfying all important constituencies, Coca-Cola's approach to value creation should not be confused with "stakeholder" capitalism, in which all the firm's stakeholders are viewed as having "claims" on the company. In the view of Coke's managers, and correctly in our view, shareholders *always* come first. The most important difference between this value-based approach to management and the stakeholder view is that value-based managers do not think of their companies as entities with claims against them, but rather as engines for the creation of value. Such managers view their role as using corporate resources to create a bigger pie, while those taking the stakeholder view seem more concerned with dividing a pie that's already on the table. In the stakeholder view, shareholders have no greater claim on the company's resources than any other group and, indeed, are sometimes outranked by other stakeholders.

Managers who encourage such an attitude may be using stakeholder claims as a smokescreen to obscure what is really their inability to deliver value to the company's shareholders. In an increasingly competitive world, such companies will be at a distinct disadvantage in capital markets and, ultimately, will be unable to sustain the benefits they extend to stakeholders at the expense of shareholders.

Put another way, the stakeholder view imposes an implicit tax on equity capital. However, unlike taxes imposed by governments, this tax is easily avoided by the simple expedient of investing in another company. Still, the high wages, comfortable and stimulating work environments, high-quality products, and other contributions that corporations offer to the world are sustainable only when the investors who make such contributions possible are given competitive returns on their scarce capital. Otherwise, they will put their money somewhere else, and the company will fail, with devastating consequences to all stakeholders.

Despite its logical shortcomings, stakeholder capitalism has gained a growing number of adherents in recent years. Ironically, one reason for its growing popularity is the failure of socialism. With the socialist dream in tatters, critics of capitalism have been forced to come to terms with the market's obvious superiority in promoting economic efficiency. Rather than directing their wrath at the entire capitalist system, they target their criticisms toward one particular form of capitalism—the Anglo-American variety. In this view, the virtues of the market economy must be harnessed to social goals, such as job protection and social welfare, in contrast to the dog-eat-dog version of capitalism, which characterizes the perceptions held by most Europeans (and leftists everywhere) of the way the American economy works. A gentler, kinder, more humane form of capitalism is called for that balances society's interests with individual self-interest. Companies are urged to pursue social goals that go beyond the mere investor-driven vision of wealth maximization.

In short, stakeholder theory suggests that in their dealings with employees, suppliers, and local communities, companies should not be bound solely by contractual relationships. These constituencies are more than just parties to a contract; they are also, as the theory goes, vital cogs in the corporate machinery. Although most people accept that successful companies don't treat constituents in purely contractual terms, stakeholder theory goes much further. Its advocates urge that employees, local communities, and other interested parties should be given substantial consultative and even decision-making input into important corporate activities. Otherwise, their interests will not be properly represented, and they will be made to suffer for the benefit of investors.

However, is it true that companies that put shareholders at the top do so at the expense of other stakeholders? The evidence says no.

Every year *Fortune* publishes a ranking of America's most admired companies. *Fortune* has also published the Stern Stewart 1000, a ranking of publicly traded companies in the United States according to the total amount of value created. Eleven of the top 20 value creators in the 1996 ranking were also in the top 20 (out of 431) of the most admired companies. Moreover, 7 of the top 10 value creators were among the 10 most admired companies. At the other end of the scale, 17 of the bottom 20 value creators (i.e., the greatest value destroyers) were also ranked in the most admired survey, and 12 of those were among the bottom 20 percent.

Of course, companies are admired, or not admired, for their financial performance, but *Fortune* uses eight criteria for its most admired companies, five of which are nonfinancial: innovation; quality of management; community and environmental responsibility; the ability to attract, develop, and keep talented people; and the quality of products or services.

Complementary results can be found outside the United States. A Boston Consulting Group (BCG) study of German companies reveals a strong link between investing in employees and stock market performance.[4] It finds that companies with relatively high "employee focus" produced higher long-term returns for shareholders than industry peers. This research examines 10 industrial sectors from 1987 to 1994. Employee focus is defined in two ways: traditional human resources (HR) policies and "intrapreneurship." Traditional HR policies include training expenditures per employee, the number of layoffs relative to the industry average, and the extent to which the contribution of employees is reflected in corporate mission statements and publications. Intrapreneurship, a notion similar to empowerment, is defined in terms of flexible working hours, the prevalence of teams, the independence of working units, opportunities for employees to learn skills in new areas, and pay for performance.

---

4. L. Bilmes, K. Wetzker, and P. Xhonneux, "Value in Human Resources," *Financial Times*, February 10, 1997, p. 10.

In every industry, the companies that score highest on these criteria produced better shareholder returns than their competitors. In addition, the employee-focused companies also created the most jobs. This finding turns conventional wisdom in Europe on its head. It is widely assumed that companies deliver superior stock market returns by sacrificing the interests of their employees. Nevertheless, BCG finds that more than three-quarters of the companies with above-average shareholder returns produced a net increase in jobs over the observation period. Contrast this record with the rest of German industry, and it becomes plain that shareholder returns need not put millions of people out of work.

The example of Bilfinger + Berger, a large German construction company, is particularly instructive. In the late 1980s, in response to years of mediocre performance, the company embarked on a radical change program. Operations were decentralized, with employees down to the level of site foreman sharing in project risks and rewards. The company invested heavily in training and in the development of work teams. Compensation, performance reviews, and promotion policies were also overhauled. As a result, the company's sales grew at an annual rate of more than 20 percent, and share price performance was dramatically reversed. Bilfinger + Berger's performance in the next seven years placed it at the very top of its industry.

On deeper reflection, the fact that companies with solid financial performance also do well on key nonfinancial indicators, including human resources, is hardly surprising. Unlike other perspectives on the firm, the value perspective is unique in that it is the *only* one that incorporates all information about a company, including the following:

 • Sales and growth in market share
 • Customer satisfaction
 • Product liability
 • Relations with suppliers
 • Labor productivity and labor relations
 • Taxes
 • Regulatory or judicial action taken by governments for environmental damage, tax evasion, or securities fraud
 • Interest and principal payments to lenders

♦ Reputation with banks and other lenders
♦ Return on invested capital

The reason why value encompasses all these factors is simple: Shareholders are *residual* claimants on the company. They get paid last. Not only do conventional measures of a company's operating performance influence value, but so also do the claims held by all the company's other constituencies, including its customers, employees, managers, suppliers, local communities, and national governments. In short, companies that neglect these constituencies cannot deliver value to their shareholders.

A BRIEF WORD ON VALUE-BASED MANAGEMENT VERSUS EVA

There is much confusion these days between value-based management (VBM) and EVA. VBM is normally viewed as a broader concept than EVA, although some practitioners use the terms interchangeably. VBM, as one observer writes, "instills a mind-set where everyone in the organization learns to prioritize decisions based on their understanding of how those decisions contribute to corporate value."[5] This means that all key processes and systems in a company must be oriented to the creation of value. For example, the creation of shareholder value must be the paramount goal in managing a company's supply chain or developing new products. A comprehensive VBM program should consider each of the following elements:

♦ Strategic planning
♦ Capital allocation
♦ Operating budgets
♦ Performance measurement
♦ Management compensation
♦ Internal communication
♦ External communication (with the capital markets)

As we will see in Chapter 2, EVA is based on the notion of economic profit (also known as *residual income*), which states that

5. James A. Knight, *Value-Based Management*. New York: McGraw-Hill, 1998.

wealth is created only when a company covers all operating costs *and* the cost of capital. In this narrow sense, EVA is really just an alternative way of viewing corporate performance. We think this formulation is far too narrow, however, because it misses the vital contribution that EVA can make to the management of a value-driven firm.

At its most basic, EVA is a measure of performance, but it would be a mistake to limit its role in this way. It can also serve as the centerpiece of a strategy implementation process linked to each of the major functions listed above. As we will show, when managers formulate strategy, they should do so with the aim of maximizing the company's stream of future EVAs. Capital allocation too benefits from the use of EVA because, when linked to management pay, EVA provides strong incentives for managers to seek out and implement value-creating investments. In fact, much of our approach to EVA centers on its use in management compensation. One of EVA's great virtues is that targets can be devolved to operating divisions and departments (sometimes in the form of EVA drivers, instead of EVA itself). In this way, a company's operating budgets, even those for units deep in the organizational hierarchy, can be directly linked to the requirements of the capital markets. Finally, EVA is a highly effective communication tool, both for making value creation concepts accessible to the line managers who ultimately drive performance in companies and for contacts with the capital markets.

Throughout this book, we show how EVA, if used properly, can help companies to implement a comprehensive VBM program. When EVA is viewed in this all-inclusive manner, it converges with the concept of VBM.

Still, there is much hype in the world of EVA. Unfortunately, some consultants are prone to overpromise the benefits of EVA and VBM. Many of the criticisms leveled against EVA in the business press and by consultants with competing approaches are reactions to extravagant claims that cannot be supported on the basis of evidence (and sometimes on the basis of logic). One of our purposes in writing this book is to lay out the right way to think about and implement EVA, while always striving to avoid making claims that we cannot defend.

CHAPTER 2

Value Creation and Economic Value Added

The Basics

Accepting value creation as the paramount corporate goal is only a start. Managers must also be able to measure their progress in achieving it. Determining the measurement criteria that will be used and establishing guidelines for interpreting the results is important in the early stages of designing and implementing EVA. Only then can measures be tied to management compensation in the interest of aligning the goals of managers and shareholders. In this chapter, we will discuss how to measure value creation and the role that EVA plays in promoting value-creating behavior.

VALUATION PRINCIPLES

Suppose you want to buy a business. How much would it be worth to you, and how would you determine that? When we invest in businesses, or any asset for that matter, we commit capital. Or more precisely, we commit *cash*.[1] Why commit cash today, whether it's for an asset, a capital project, or an entire business? Because we believe, rightly or wrongly, that we will receive a lot more cash in the future. After all, if we did not believe this, why

---

1. The argument does not change just because we acquire an asset with shares or other non-cash assets. These other assets have value, and therefore can be used to acquire other assets, precisely because the owner can convert them into cash.

would we ever, from an economic point of view, invest in anything? When we think of investment in these terms, valuation becomes a straightforward exercise, at least conceptually.

Discounted Cashflow

The key question we should always be asking ourselves whenever we think of investing is how much the right to the future cashflow stream from the investment is worth to us today. This value is a function of just three major factors: the *magnitude*, the *timing*, and the *degree of uncertainty* of the future cashflows.

By *magnitude* we mean that, all else being equal, the greater the cashflow, the better. Yet, the magnitude or size of the cashflow tells us surprisingly little about how much it is worth to us today unless we also know its *timing*. Cash has a time element, which means that we would rather have it today than have to wait for it. Therefore, the earlier we expect to receive a cashflow, the more valuable that cashflow is to us today.

Even at that, size and timing are still not the whole story. Because the cashflow in question is a *future* cashflow, there is always the risk that it will not materialize as planned. Sometimes this risk is negligible, as when we invest in the bonds of stable governments, and sometimes the risk is substantial, as when we invest in a start-up venture. If we have two investment alternatives with the same expected cashflows in both magnitude and timing, but one investment is low-risk and the other high-risk, which would we prefer? The less risky one, of course. Therefore, the *degree of uncertainty* or riskiness regarding a future cashflow, not just its size and timing, will determine how much we are willing to pay for it today.

These insights are captured in the discounted cashflow (DCF) approach to valuation. With this approach, we project expected future cashflows, then "discount" them at an interest rate, or rate of return, that reflects the perceived riskiness of the cashflows. The discount rate reflects both the time value of money (namely, that investors would rather have cash today than tomorrow and must therefore be paid to wait) and a risk premium that reflects the incremental return investors require to compensate them for the risk that the cashflow might not materialize. This approach is summarized in the formula:

$$\text{Value} = \sum_{t=1}^{t=n} \frac{\text{CF}_t}{(1 + r)^t}$$

where n is the economic life of the asset or investment (usually expressed in years), CF_t is the expected cashflow in period t, and r is the discount rate that reflects the perceived riskiness of the cashflows.

This equation tells us that the value of any asset is equal to the sum of discounted future cashflows, with the discounted value of each cashflow a function of (1) the nominal amount, (2) risk, and (3) when receipt of the cashflow is expected. The discount rate is the investor's cost of capital, which indicates the return that the investor would expect to receive if the cash were invested elsewhere in assets, capital investments, or portfolios of similar risk.

As an illustration of the DCF approach, consider an example:

♦ We can invest $2500 today in a capital project: $1000 for a tangible asset that is expected to last for five years, and $1500 for the working capital requirement (WCR).[2]

♦ The working capital requirement is expected to be constant over the five-year investment horizon. At the end of year 5, the working capital will be released, and we can reclaim the cash.

♦ The cost of capital (discount rate) for the investment is 10 percent.

♦ The tax rate is 0.

♦ Net operating profits, before depreciation, are expected to be $600 in the first year, growing by $50 a year through the fifth and final year of the project. This figure is sometimes known as *Earnings before Interest, Taxes, Depreciation, and Amortization*, or EBITDA.

♦ Tangible assets are depreciated over a five-year period using the straight-line method.

Before discounting, we estimate the expected cashflows using the "free cashflow" model. The logic behind this model is simple:

2. The working capital requirement equals short-term operating assets (such as inventories and receivables), net of short-term operating liabilities.

Because investments tie up cash, their *value is based on the amount of future cashflows that will accrue to investors.* Free cashflow can be thought of as the amount of cashflow left over from the company's operating activities after expected investments have been made. It is from this residual cashflow that companies can then return cash to their capital providers. In brief, free cashflow makes it possible for companies to make interest payments, pay off the principal on the loans, pay dividends, and buy back shares. These are the four ways that companies return cash to their capital providers, and therefore, the expectations of such cashflows will be the ultimate determinant of a company's value from a capital market perspective.

The free cashflow for any period is calculated as follows:

	EBITDA
−	Depreciation and amortization
−	Taxes
=	Net operating profit after tax (NOPAT)
+	Depreciation and amortization
−	Capital expenditures
−	Changes in the working capital requirement (WCR)
=	Free cashflow

Although depreciation and amortization are not cashflows, we subtract them from EBITDA because of their effect on corporate taxes (depreciation acts as a tax shield). After taxes have been calculated, depreciation and amortization are added back.

In the example shown in Table 2–1, where the working capital requirement does not change over the life of the project, taxes are zero, and no further capital investments are required, the EBITDA in years 1 through 4 and the future cashflows must be the same. Year 5 is the one year in which EBITDA does not equal free cashflow, because the release of working capital provides an additional cashflow of $1500. Also, because EBITDA does not include any depreciation expense, there is no need to add it back to estimate the free cashflows. Finally, because the tax rate is 0, there is no depreciation tax shield.

T A B L E   2–1

Free Cashflow Where Working Capital Requirement Is
Stable over Life of Project

		Year 1	Year 2	Year 3	Year 4	Year 5
EBITDA		$600	$650	$700	$750	$ 800
Capital expenditures	($1000)					
Changes in the WCR	($1500)					1500
Free cashflow	($2500)	$600	$650	$700	$750	$2300

The present value of the free cashflows, or the *net present value* (NPV) of the project, equals the present value of the cash *in*flows in years 1 through 5, minus the initial investment. These present values are calculated by multiplying each future cashflow by a present value factor that equals $1 \div (1 + r)^N$, where N is the number of periods in the future. For example, the present value of the $650 cashflow in year 2 is $650 $[1 \div (1 + 0.10)^2]$, $650 × 0.82645, which equals $537.19. The present values are then summed to reveal the NPV of the project:

$$NPV = -\$2500 + \$600/1.1^1 + \$650/1.1^2 + \$700/1.1^3 + \$750/1.1^4 + \$2300/1.1^5$$

which equals $1049. This means that undertaking the project creates $1049 of wealth for shareholders. The positive NPV indicates that the investment is expected to earn a return greater than the cost of its capital. Superior returns in this form are the source of corporate value creation.

While this is an example of valuing an individual capital project instead of an entire business, the same attributes that give rise to value for any asset or investment—namely, its ability to provide investors with future free cashflows—is equally true for businesses. The value of a business, like the value of a capital project, is a function of how much future free cashflow is expected, with the cashflows discounted at the opportunity cost of capital. (The opportunity cost of capital is the rate of return that a company's capital providers would have expected had they invested their capital in other investment opportunities of similar risk.)

There is one important difference to consider in valuation at the business level. Any excess cash that the company already possesses must be added to the present value of the future free cashflows. (Operating cash is not included here because it is already included in the working capital requirement, as we will shortly discuss, and is thus reflected in the cashflow estimates.) In other words, we value the company's ability to generate future free cashflows, ignoring cash that the company has already generated, and then add the cash to get the value of the firm.

Internal Rate of Return

Instead of using net present value (NPV) to choose which capital investments to undertake, most companies prefer an alternative DCF approach to valuation, *the internal rate of return* (IRR). The IRR is the true interest yield expected from an investment and is thus expressed as a percentage. NPV by contrast is expressed in monetary terms (dollars or other currencies). Because it uses percentages, IRR is widely viewed as easier to understand than NPV. Also, it can be calculated without having to estimate a cost of capital. For these reasons, and because corporate executives think it is easier to compare projects of different size when using IRR, they prefer it to NPV.

There are serious flaws with this thinking, as we will explore later, but at least IRR gives the same go/no-go decision as the NPV rule. When IRR is used to evaluate investments, the common practice is to select projects whose IRR exceeds the cost of capital (sometimes called the *hurdle rate* when used in this context) and to reject projects whose IRR is less than the cost of capital. The IRR for any project simply equals the discount rate that equates the present value of future net cash inflows with the initial investment required for the project.

In the $2500 investment example shown in Figure 2–1, $2500 is invested today, in exchange for expected cashflows of $600, $650, $700, $750, and $2300, in years 1, 2, 3, 4, and 5, respectively. The IRR for this project—that is, the interest rate for which the present value of the cashflows in years 1 through 5 equals $2500 (the initial investment)—is approximately 22 percent. Even before calculating the IRR, we knew that it would have to be greater than 10 percent, because when the future cashflows are discounted at that rate, the NPV of the project is positive.

F I G U R E   2-1

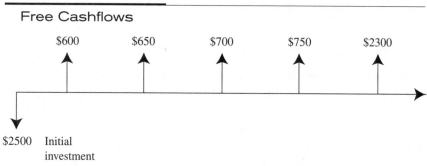

Free Cashflows

$600 $650 $700 $750 $2300

$2500   Initial
        investment

The IRR criterion leads to the same conclusion as the NPV rule, assuming that the hurdle rate is the same as the discount rate used to calculate NPV. Indeed, it must. If the IRR is higher than the discount rate (i.e., the company's cost of capital), the NPV must be positive. In either case, the decision is obvious: Make the investment.

One important drawback of this approach is that if management focuses on maximizing IRR and not NPV, there is a significant risk in companies or divisions where return on investment is greater than the *weighted-average cost of capital* (WACC) that managers will forgo investment in projects expected to earn greater than the WACC but less than the return on existing assets. The aim for the value-oriented manager should be to invest in any positive NPV project, and this means any project where the expected IRR is greater than the cost of capital. The goal is *not* to maximize IRR or return on investment, but to maximize NPV.

Another problem with IRR is the implicit assumption that all cashflows received over the investment horizon will be reinvested at the IRR itself. When the IRR is substantially higher than the company's cost of capital, this assumption is highly unrealistic. For example, if IRR is estimated to be 20 percent, all cashflows received over the life of the investment are expected to be reinvested and earn 20 percent, even if the company's WACC is, say, only 8 percent. A more realistic assumption is that interim cashflows will earn only 8 percent, or the cost of capital. A mathematical adjustment to the IRR formula can take this into account, but most companies do not bother to make it. As a result, the IRRs reported for particular capital projects are often overstated.

MARKET VALUE ADDED AND
EXCESS RETURN

Firms create value for their shareholders when they invest in projects, products, technologies, or strategies that are expected to earn returns greater than the cost of capital. In other words, shareholders become richer whenever companies undertake positive NPV projects. In valuing prospective capital projects to determine whether NPV is positive or negative, companies can use the free cashflow model we just discussed. But there is a problem.

The free cashflow model is forward-looking. It's based on expectations of the future, not on what a company has delivered in the past. This makes perfect sense, of course, because when investors contribute capital to the firm, they do so on the promise of cashflow in the future. However, value-creating behavior requires more than the proper methodology for valuing capital investments. It also requires performance measurement and incentive compensation systems that make managers responsible for seeking out and implementing positive NPV projects, as well as for realizing the economic benefits promised by those projects.

The problem is that performance measures, and the rewards given to managers on the basis of these measures, are based on the past, not the future. Managers are evaluated on and paid for the results they have already delivered, not for the results they may deliver in the future. Very simply, while capital markets value companies and investments on the basis of expectations of the future, performance measures and incentive compensation, by their very nature, must be based on the past. If companies do not choose performance measures wisely (and in our experience, many don't), they run a huge risk of paying managers to do the wrong things. In short, managers may be paid, unknowingly, to engage in behaviors that actually destroy shareholder value, even if wealth creation is proclaimed as the company's primary mission. To reduce this risk, and to increase the likelihood that managers will make decisions and undertake actions that promote shareholder value, a growing number of companies throughout the world have turned to value-based metrics. The idea behind such metrics is simple: Companies should adopt performance measurement techniques that are conceptually linked with the free cashflow model of valuation. In other words, corporate managers should be evaluated in a manner that is consistent with the way that the capital markets will evaluate their firms.

Market Value Added

One such metric is *market value added* (MVA). MVA is the difference between the market value of the firm (including equity *and* debt) and the total capital invested in the firm:

$$MVA = \text{market value} - \text{invested capital}$$

Many VBM practitioners consider MVA to be the most important of all value-based metrics. We disagree, but before elaborating on our reasons for this position, let's consider the appeal of MVA.

Market value is the "enterprise value" of the firm, namely, the sum of the market value of *all* capital claims held against a company by the capital markets as of a particular date. More simply, it's the sum of the market value of debt and the market value of equity. Invested capital is the amount of capital invested in the company by its capital providers as of that same date. How do we know if a company is a value creator? Its market value, which is a function of capital market expectations of future free cashflows, discounted at the cost of capital, exceeds invested capital. In other words, MVA is positive.

Investors contribute capital to firms in anticipation of managers investing it productively. Market value reflects the market's verdict on how successful managers have been in investing the capital entrusted to them, in transforming it into something bigger. And the higher the MVA, the better. Negative MVA means that the value of the investments undertaken by management is less than the capital contributed to their companies by the capital markets. This means that wealth has been destroyed.

The aim of the firm's managers should be to create as much MVA as possible. Note that when we say that management should seek the highest MVA possible, the aim is *not* to maximize the value of the firm, which is accomplished easily enough by investing ever-increasing amounts of capital. For example, if a company raises $20 million in capital and invests the capital in projects that are expected to earn the cost of capital, both total value and total capital increase by $20 million and MVA is unchanged.

MVA increases only when invested capital earns a rate of return greater than the cost of capital. When newly raised capital is invested in value-creating projects (i.e., those with a positive net present value), MVA increases. When that capital is invested in value-destroying projects (i.e., those with a negative net present value), MVA is reduced.

By emphasizing MVA, we see that growth for its own sake does not create value. We can grow the firm, but the growth does not necessarily create value. When Coca-Cola's former CEO, the late Roberto Goizueta, said, "The curse of all curses is the revenue line," he meant that an obsession with growing sales is the surest route to value destruction. Growth creates value only when the growth strategy's incremental value exceeds the incremental capital invested.

Although it's hard to disagree with the logic expressed thus far, there is a fundamental conceptual flaw with MVA as a cumulative measure of performance. To illustrate this problem, assume that a company is formed at the end of 1994 with $100 million of equity capital. The company has no debt. Let's assume that the cost of capital is 12 percent and remains at that level. It is now five years later, and the market value of the equity is $140 million. For this firm:

$$MVA = \$140 \ M - \$100 \ M = \$40 \ M$$

The obvious conclusion to draw from the MVA figure is that the company has created $40 million in wealth for its shareholders. But wait.

Suppose that $100 million had been invested elsewhere five years ago, in another company of comparable risk. The 12 percent cost of equity implies that such an investment would be expected to earn 12 percent a year. This means that at the end of the five years, an investor would expect

$$\$100 \ M \times (1.12)^5 = \$176.23 \ M$$

But our company is worth only $140 million. Is it correct to say that this company is a value creator? Clearly not, especially if such an investment should be worth $176.23 million. Our intuition should be telling us that instead of creating $40 million of wealth, this firm actually *destroyed* over $36 million of wealth. The problem here is that MVA neglects the opportunity cost of the capital invested in the company.

There is another problem with MVA. To illustrate, suppose two firms, ABC and XYZ, each have a market value of $10 billion and invested capital of $8 billion. Both companies have an MVA of $2 billion and would appear to be equivalent in their abilities to create shareholder value. But MVA is a "snapshot" indicator, measuring the difference between market value and invested capital on a particular date. Imagine that ABC has paid no dividends in its history and has yet to buy back any of its shares, while XYZ has been systematically returning cash to its shareholders for many years. Would you still consider the performance of the two companies to be identical? Certainly not. XYZ has clearly produced more wealth for its shareholders than ABC. While it is still true that the higher the MVA, the better (all else being equal), conventional MVA measurement fails to take into account previous cash returns to shareholders.

Excess Return

We have a solution to these problems with MVA: *excess return*. Unlike MVA, excess return charges a company for the capital it has used since it was founded (or at least since the beginning of a measurement period), while crediting companies for the returns their shareholders should have earned from distributions, such as dividends and share buybacks, reinvested in the market. Excess return, not MVA, is the true measure of a company's cumulative wealth creation.

Excess return is defined as the difference between actual wealth and expected wealth at the end of the measurement period:

$$\text{Excess return}_N = \text{actual wealth}_N - \text{expected wealth}_N$$

When a single investment is made at the start of the measurement period, expected wealth is simply the future value of the initial investment, $I_0 (1 + c_e)^N$, where I_0 is the initial investment (made at time 0), c_e is the cost of equity, and N is the number of periods over which the excess return is measured. Actual wealth

is the future value of the cashflows received over the measurement
period:

$$
\begin{aligned}
\text{Actual wealth}_N = & \\
& \text{Dividends}_1\,(1 + c_e)^{N-1} \\
+ \quad & \text{Dividends}_2\,(1 + c_e)^{N-2} \\
+ \quad & \text{Dividends}_3\,(1 + c_e)^{N-3} \\
& \qquad\quad . \\
& \qquad\quad . \\
& \qquad\quad . \\
+ \quad & \text{Dividends}_N\,(1 + c_e)^{N-N} \\
+ \quad & \text{Price}_N
\end{aligned}
$$

where dividends are any cash distributions made to shareholders
(including share buybacks), and price$_N$ is the value of equity at
the end of the measurement period. We can now express the excess return of the company from time 0 to time N as follows:

$$
\begin{aligned}
& \text{Dividends}_1\,(1 + c_e)^{N-1} \\
+ \quad & \text{Dividends}_2\,(1 + c_e)^{N-2} \\
+ \quad & \text{Dividends}_3\,(1 + c_e)^{N-3} \\
& \qquad\quad . \\
& \qquad\quad . \\
& \qquad\quad . \\
+ \quad & \text{Dividends}_N\,(1 + c_e)^{N-N} \\
+ \quad & \text{Price}_N \\
- \quad & \text{Price}_0\,(1 + c_e)^{N}
\end{aligned}
$$

On a practical level, the calculation of excess return is complicated by the fact that between time 0 and time N, the paid-in
capital of the company can change because of new share issues
and share repurchases. But this complication is easily dealt with.

To illustrate, let's return to our earlier example. In addition
to investing $100 million at the end of 1994, the company also
pays dividends, buys back shares, and issues new equity:

Dividends (1995)	$ 2 M
Dividends (1996)	$ 2 M
Dividends (1997)	$ 2.5 M
Dividends (1998)	$ 3 M
Dividends (1999)	$ 3 M
Share buybacks (end of 1995)	$10 M
Share buybacks (end of 1996)	$12 M
New share issue (end of 1998)	$25 M

Expected wealth at the end of 1999 is the sum of $176.23 million (the expected value of the $100 million invested five years earlier) and $25 million $\times$ 1.12 (the expected value of the $25 million invested one year earlier), or $204.23 million.

Actual wealth at the end of 1999 is the sum of the market value of equity on that date ($140 million) and the end-of-1999 value of all distributions made to the shareholders over the five years, including dividends and share buybacks:

Dividends (1995)	$ 2 M $\times$ 1.12^4	= $ 3.15 M
Dividends (1996)	$ 2 M $\times$ 1.12^3	= $ 2.81 M
Dividends (1997)	$ 2.5 M $\times$ 1.12^2	= $ 3.14 M
Dividends (1998)	$ 3 M $\times$ 1.12	= $ 3.36 M
Dividends (1999)	$ 3 M $\times$ 1.00	= $ 3.00 M
Share buybacks (end of 1995)	$10 M $\times$ 1.12^4	= $ 15.74 M
Share buybacks (end of 1996)	$12 M $\times$ 1.12^3	= $ 16.86 M
Value of equity (end of 1999)		$140.00 M
Total actual wealth (end of 1999)		$188.06 M

Therefore, excess return equals $188.06 million − $204.23 million, or −$16.17 million.

Although maximizing excess return should be the ultimate goal of the value-based firm, excess return has important weaknesses in terms of motivating and evaluating managers. First, excess return is unlikely to be effective in motivating managers below the top management ranks, because it can be calculated only for publicly traded entities. Operating divisions do not have share prices, and thus it is not possible to observe actual shareholder wealth. This problem applies equally to MVA. In other words, excess return and MVA can be observed only at the corporate level; they are not observable for operating divisions. For subordinate managers, the relationship between their actions and excess return is too remote for excess return to effectively motivate them to create value or to serve as a reliable indicator of their contribution to shareholder value.

Taken collectively, however, the impact that such managers have on a company's share price and its excess return is profound. The actions of all company employees—especially managers one, two, and three levels below the executive board—ultimately determine the company's ability to deliver value to its shareholders systematically and create lots of excess return. After all, top managers may provide strategic direction for the company, but they don't produce or sell anything. Rather, their subordinates actually produce the company's products and services, and interact most closely with the company's customers.

Excess return and MVA are plagued by still another problem. Both are wealth or "stock" measures. A *stock measure* is a term used by economists to denote the wealth that has been accumulated as of a certain date. It's a snapshot measure that by itself says nothing about performance or the creation of value over a period of time. The problem is that managerial performance must be evaluated over periods of, say, three months, six months, or a year. We need flow measures, not stock measures.

What we need, therefore, are measures of performance that

1. Can be calculated at divisional levels, thus providing line of sight for divisional managers.
2. Are flows, not stocks, and thus are amenable to performance evaluation over periods of time.
3. Promote the creation of shareholder wealth.

EVA IS THE SOLUTION

To achieve these measures of performance EVA is brought into play. EVA is calculated as follows:

	Net sales
−	Operating expenses
=	Operating profit (or earnings before interest and tax, EBIT)
−	Taxes
=	Net operating profit after tax (NOPAT)
−	Capital charges (Invested capital × Cost of capital)
=	EVA

where EBIT = earnings before interest and tax, NOPAT = net operating profit after tax, and capital charges = invested capital × cost of capital.

Unlike market-based measures, such as excess return and MVA, EVA can be calculated at divisional levels. If NOPAT, which measures the after-tax profit the company has generated from its ongoing operations, invested capital, and the WACC are known, EVA can, in theory, be calculated for any entity, including divisions, departments, product lines, geographic business segments, and so on. The entity in question does not have to be publicly traded. Therefore, EVA can restore the line of sight at divisional levels that is lost when using excess return or MVA.

EVA also satisfies our second criterion, namely, that we want a flow measure for performance measurement, not a stock measure. EVA is a flow, because it is a measure of profit. All profit measures, by definition, are flows. As we will see, EVA is a means of turning the stock measure of excess return into a flow. The principal difference between EVA and more conventional profit measures is that EVA is an "economic" as opposed to an "accounting" profit. It is based on the idea that for a business to earn what economists call "rents" (i.e., abnormal returns on investment), revenues must be sufficient to cover not only all operating costs but also all capital costs (including the cost of equity finance). Without the prospect of economic profits, there can be no wealth creation for investors.

The notion of economic profit confirms EVA's relation to shareholder wealth, the final condition required of a value-based metric. But we can draw an even more explicit link between the two. Remember that the goal of the value-oriented firm is to maximize excess return.

To understand this relationship, we should first note that

Market value = invested capital + present value of future EVAs

We will prove this equivalency later in the chapter, but for now, the key point is that the value of the firm on any particular date (such as the beginning of the excess return measurement period) is a function of the capital market's expectations of future EVA. The higher these expectations are, the higher the value of the firm.

Future EVAs come from two sources: a continuation of the performance levels already achieved and EVA improvement. When invested capital is added to the capitalized value of current EVA (EVA/WACC), we have the *current operations value* (COV) of the firm. This is what the market value of the firm would be if the capital markets expect the same EVA performance into perpetuity as the company has achieved in the most recent year. COV equals the sum of invested capital and the capitalized value of current EVA. The capitalized value of current EVA equals the current level of EVA divided by the cost of capital.

The capitalized value of EVA improvement is known as *future growth value* (FGV). Therefore:

Market value = current operations value + future growth value
                = invested capital + capitalized value of current
                EVA + future growth value

In short, FGV is the capitalized value of *expected* EVA improvement over all future periods. To put it another way, it equals the present value of expected EVA improvement in all future years, discounted at the cost of capital. It can easily be estimated by subtracting the COV from the firm's market value. Because of these expectations a company can increase EVA from one year to the next and share price actually declines. The market may simply have been expecting greater improvement. We can now restate the market value of the firm as follows:

Market value = invested capital
                + capitalized value of current EVA
                + capitalized value of expected EVA
                improvement

What this also means is that for a company's share price to

rise, it must do either or both of two things: exceed EVA expectations in the current year and/or create excess FGV.

Excess EVA improvement means doing better than the capital markets expected (or not as badly as feared) in a given year. Excess FGV means that FGV at the end of the excess return measurement period is higher than what the capital markets would have expected it to be at the beginning of the period. For example, if FGV at the beginning of 1999 is $50 million, and shareholders expect FGV to remain constant, an end-of-year FGV of $62 million means that excess FGV of $12 million has been created.

To see these concepts at work, assume that a company's market value at the beginning of the year is $500 million. Its EVA in the previous year was $20 million, invested capital at the beginning of the current year is $140 million, the WACC is 10 percent, and the company has no debt. Current operations value at the beginning of the current year is $340 million, $140 million + ($20 million/0.10) (the capitalized value of current EVA). Therefore, FGV is $160 million ($500 million − $340 million). This means that investors are expecting substantial EVA improvement in future years.

The $160 million of FGV implies that the market anticipates improvement in EVA. We can actually estimate how much improvement is required in the coming year. To keep things simple, we assume that the expected change in FGV is 0 (an assumption we relay in Chapter 8). The required return on the FGV, based on a WACC of 10 percent, is $16 million ($160 million × 10 percent). Each dollar of EVA improvement contributes $1 of cash to investors, plus $10 of additional COV ($1 ÷ 0.10), or $11 in total. To get the required $16 million of return on the FGV, we need $1.45 million, $16 million ÷ 11, of EVA improvement. In other words, an EVA increase in the following year of $1.45 million should result in $16 million, or $1.45 million × 11, of return to investors. We can infer from this analysis that investors expect EVA in the following year to be $21.45 million, the current year's EVA ($20 million) plus the expected EVA improvement.

Now suppose that the company's EVA in the current year is $31 million, exceeding expectations by $9.55 million. Meanwhile, the market value of the firm has grown to $610 million. Invested capital remains at $140 million.

The current operations value is now $450 million, the invested capital of $140 million plus the capitalized value of EVA

[($31 million ÷ 0.10), or $310 million]. Therefore, FGV is $160 million ($610 million − $450 million).

The excess return is the actual ending wealth minus expected ending wealth. We know that the actual ending wealth is the sum of ending market value of equity ($610 million) and any cash distributions made to investors in that year (assuming no cash payments in previous periods). If EVA is $31 million, and invested capital is $140 million, NOPAT must be $45 million ($31 million plus $14 million of capital charges, assuming a 10 percent cost of capital). If invested capital remains at $140 million, which we assume in this example, all of this NOPAT must be distributed to shareholders. Therefore, ending shareholder wealth is $610 million plus $45 million, or $655 million. Ending expected wealth is $550 million, the beginning wealth of $500 million × (1 + WACC), or $500 million × 1.10. This gives us an excess return of $105 million ($655 million − $550 million).

In this example, the excess return is also equal to the capitalized value of excess EVA improvement, $9.55 million × 11 (assuming that each dollar of EVA improvement translates into $11 of additional value), because the actual FGV ($160 million) equals expected FGV. If market value had been greater than $610 million, the actual FGV would exceed the expected FGV by the difference. For example, if market value had been $620 million, FGV would be $170 million instead of $160 million. Because of the higher market value, excess return would also be higher ($115 million, reflecting the $10 million of additional shareholder wealth, instead of $105 million).

To summarize:

Excess return = capitalized future value of excess EVA
improvement + excess future growth value

Very simply, as companies outperform or underperform EVA expectations, and as they create excess FGV, investors convert these surprises into value.

To further prove this crucial point, we use another example. A company is formed at the beginning of 1994, with $100 million in invested capital. It earns NOPAT of $10 million in 1994, $40 million in each year from 1995 through 1998, and $10 million in 1999. Invested capital remains at $100 million throughout the observation period. The company has no debt and has a policy of paying out NOPAT, in its entirety, as dividends in the year in which it is earned. The market value of equity is $100 million at the end of 1999 (although it fluctuates during the observation period), exactly equal to invested capital. In other words, MVA at the end of 1999 is 0. The cost of equity (and, therefore, the WACC, because the company is an all-equity firm) is 10 percent. For the sake of simplicity, we will assume that expected EVA improvement in any year is 0. Therefore, any improvement or deterioration from the previous year will be considered excess EVA improvement. Finally, our example assumes no excess FGV.

Table 2–2 shows what happens to excess return, EVA, and other key measures. First, note that EVA equals NOPAT, less capital charges. Because invested capital and WACC are constant throughout the observation period, capital charges are constant too ($10 million in each year, or $100 million of invested capital × the 10 percent WACC). As a result, EVA goes from 0 in 1994, to $30 million in each of the next four years, reverting to 0 in 1999. Because we assume that expected EVA improvement is 0, excess EVA improvement is $30 million in 1995, a *negative* $30 million in 1999, and 0 in all other years.

T A B L E   2–2

In Millions of Dollars	1994	1995	1996	1997	1998	1999
NOPAT	10	40	40	40	40	10
Invested capital	100	100	100	100	100	100
EVA	0	30	30	30	30	0
Excess EVA improvement	0	30	0	0	0	-30
FV of excess EVA improvement	0	30	33	36.3	39.93	13.923
Capitalized future value	0	330	363	399.3	439.23	153.153
Dividends	10	40	40	40	40	10
Future value of dividends	10	51	96.1	145.71	200.281	230.309
Market value of equity	100	175	152	127	100	100
Actual shareholder wealth	110	226	248.1	272.71	300.281	330.309
Expected shareholder wealth	110	121	133.1	146.41	161.051	177.156
Excess return	0	105	115	126.3	139.23	153.153
MVA	0	75	52	27	0	0

The first step in calculating the excess return is to calculate the future value of the excess EVA improvements. We do this for each year by multiplying the prior-year future value by 1.10 (1 + the WACC of 10 percent) and then adding the current-year excess EVA improvement. For 1995, the future value of excess EVA improvement is $30 million, the excess EVA improvement achieved in that year. For 1996, the future value of excess EVA improvement is the prior-year future value, $30 million, multiplied by 1 + WACC, or $33 million, plus the excess EVA improvement for 1996, $0 million, for a total of $33 million. For 1999, the future value of excess EVA improvement is the prior year future value, $39.93 million, multiplied by 1.10, or $43.923 million, plus the excess EVA improvement for 1999, −$30 million, or $13.923 million.

We calculate the capitalized future value of excess EVA improvement by multiplying the future value by $(1 + WACC)/WACC$. This gives us, at the end of 1999, $13.923 × (1.10/.1), or $153.153. We multiply the future value of excess EVA improvement by $(1 + WACC)/WACC$ because every dollar of unexpected EVA improvement contributes $1 to cash and $1/WACC to current operations value. (Note that $1 + $1/WACC equals ($1 + WACC)/WACC.)

Note that this figure is exactly equal to the excess return for the period. Excess return equals the sum of the future value of dividends and the market value of equity, less expected shareholder wealth. Both dividends and expected wealth grow each year by an amount equal to the WACC. For example, the value of dividends as of the end of 1995 ($51 million) equals the dividends paid out in the previous year ($10 million) times (1 + WACC), plus the dividends paid in 1995 ($40 million). The assumption behind this calculation is that any dividends received by shareholders in the previous year would have been reinvested, earning the cost of capital. Expected shareholder wealth at the end of 1999 ($177.156 million) equals the invested capital at the beginning of the observation period ($100 million) times 1.10^6.

Although in the example we make a few simplifying assumptions, such as no expected improvement in EVA, our results would hold even in more complex, real-life scenarios in which nonzero EVA improvements are embedded in share price. In other words, it must always be true that excess return, the ultimate measure of a company's cumulative success in creating shareholder wealth, equals the capitalized future value of excess EVA improvement plus excess future growth value (if any). It is for this reason that we place so much emphasis on EVA improvement, especially when we lay out the principles and working mechanics of value-driven compensation programs. That is, tying management bonuses to EVA improvement, and therefore encouraging improvement that exceeds capital market expectations, is our way of motivating managers to maximize excess return.

In this example, MVA at the end of 1999 is 0, while excess return is $153.153 million. The smaller figure for MVA is the result of its failure to credit the company for the substantial dividends returned to shareholders over the six-year observation period. Quite simply, MVA does not distinguish between a company that earns and distributes nothing from a company that earns and distributes plenty. If the company in our example had earned no profits and paid no dividends from 1994 to 1999, but its market value and invested capital were $100 million, MVA would still be 0.

Yet MVA does have its uses. First, managers can seek to maximize *current* MVA in full confidence that as they are doing so excess return is also being maximized. It can be shown (as we prove later in this chapter) that

Market value added =   present value of future EVAs

When companies make investments or adopt strategies that are expected to deliver a more valuable stream of future EVAs than before, the effect is a simultaneous increase in MVA and excess return. The problems with MVA emerge only when performance is measured at the end of a period or when period-based goals are set. It is perfectly appropriate to say that in choosing, say, one strategy over another, we choose the one that is expected to deliver the higher current MVA. It is not appropriate, however, to proclaim that our goal over the next five years is to maximize MVA. Because of MVA's failure to adjust for the opportunity cost of invested capital, or for the returns that shareholders can earn on cash distributions, it is not the correct benchmark for measuring performance. Only excess return satisfies this criterion.

To summarize, as long as the maximization of MVA is expressed as a goal for a proposed investment or strategy made at a *point* in time, and not as a goal over a *period* of time, it is entirely equivalent to the maximization of excess return.

Also, MVA can, under a restrictive set of assumptions, be made to equal excess return. If all positive EVAs are treated as distributions (i.e., reductions) of invested capital, and all negative EVAs as contributions (i.e., additions) to capital, MVA at the end of the observation period will equal excess return. This point can be proven by returning to the last example.

We now recalculate MVA, treating the positive EVAs earned from 1995 onward as reductions in invested capital (see Table 2–3). For example, the $30 million of EVA in 1995 reduces end-of-year capital to $70 million (the starting invested capital of $100 million minus that year's EVA). As a result of this capital reduction, capital charges in 1996 are only $7 million ($70 million × 10 percent) instead of $10 million ($100 million × 10 percent), as before.

EVA for 1996 becomes $33 million, $3 million higher than the unadjusted figure, reducing invested capital still further to $37 million (end-of-1995 capital of $70 million, minus EVA for 1996). This process brings adjusted invested capital to nearly zero in 1997. By the end of 1998, capital turns negative, becoming even more negative in the following year (–$53.153 million). By the end of 1999, MVA equals the market value of the firm minus adjusted invested capital, in other words, $100 million – (–$53.153), or $153.153 million, exactly the same as excess return.

T A B L E   2–3

In Millions of Dollars	1994	1995	1996	1997	1998	1999
NOPAT	10	40	40	40	40	10
Unadjusted invested capital	100	100	100	100	100	100
Unadjusted EVA	0	30	30	30	30	0
Adjusted invested capital	0	70	37	0.7	−39.23	−53.153
Unadjusted capital charges	10	10	10	10	10	10
Adjusted capital charges	10	10	7	3.7	0.07	−3.923
Adjusted EVA	0	30	33	36.3	39.93	13.923
Excess return						**153.153**
Market value added						**153.153**

CALCULATING EVA

As mentioned, EVA equals NOPAT, less capital charges. (You will recall NOPAT is the company's operating profit, net of tax, and measures the profits the company has generated from its ongoing operations.) Capital charges equal the company's *invested capital* (also called *capital* or *capital employed*) times the weighted-average cost of capital. The WACC equals the sum of the cost of each component of capital—short-term debt, long-term debt, and shareholders' equity—weighted for its relative proportion, at market value, in the company's capital structure.

Invested capital is the sum of all the firm's financing, apart from short-term, non-interest-bearing liabilities, such as accounts payable, accrued wages, and accrued taxes. That is, invested capital equals the sum of shareholders' equity, all interest-bearing debt, both short-term and long-term, and other long-term liabilities.

How does EVA relate to NPV? The present value of future EVAs equals NPV.

With this in mind, we can estimate the NOPAT for each year in the forecast period:

	Year 1	Year 2	Year 3	Year 4	Year 5
EBITDA	$600	$650	$700	$750	$800
− Depreciation	200	200	200	200	200
= NOPAT	$400	$450	$500	$550	$600

Invested capital decreases each year because the tangible assets are depreciated. Thus, the invested capital, $2500 at the beginning of year 1, decreases by $200 a year. Capital charges in each period will equal 10 percent of beginning invested capital:

	Year 1	Year 2	Year 3	Year 4	Year 5
Tangible assets	$1000	$ 800	$ 600	$ 400	$ 200
+ WCR	1500	1500	1500	1500	1500
= Invested capital	$2500	$2300	$2100	$1900	$1700

We can now calculate expected EVAs:

	Year 1	Year 2	Year 3	Year 4	Year 5
NOPAT	$400	$450	$500	$550	$600
− Capital charges	250	230	210	190	170
= EVA	$150	$220	$290	$360	$430

When discounted at the 10 percent cost of capital, the present value of the future EVAs equals $1049, exactly the same as the present value of the free cashflows. Therefore, EVA provides valuations identical to those of the DCF approach. This occurs because the present value of the depreciation and capital charges equals the initial investment of $2500 minus the present value of the working capital recovered at the end of year 5. This equality will hold in all cases, regardless of depreciation policy.

In fact, EVA valuations must be identical to DCF valuations and therefore provide equivalent results to the most popular DCF approaches such as the McKinsey valuation model and the shareholder value analysis approach associated with the LEK/Alcar Consulting Group. These cashflow approaches, however, have an important advantage over EVA because they forecast expected cashflows in each future period. The future EVAs that emerge from the valuation model are *not* cashflows and cannot be used, for example, to prepare a cash budget or to determine cash needs.

The balance sheets shown in Figure 2–2 clarify how capital is defined in EVA. The balance sheet on the left is a normal balance sheet. On the right we see an EVA balance sheet in which short-term non-interest-bearing liabilities are netted against short-term operating assets—inventories, receivables, and prepaid expenses. The left side of this balance sheet is referred to as "net assets"; "invested capital" appears on the right side.

We deduct short-term, non-interest-bearing liabilities from other current assets (i.e., all current assets, except cash) from invested capital. Although nearly all liabilities are to some extent interest bearing (if they weren't, suppliers extending credit in competitive markets would go bankrupt), digging out the interest

Regular versus EVA Balance Sheet
(NIBL = non-interest-bearing liabilities;
WCR = working capital requirement)

Regular Balance Sheet   The EVA Balance Sheet

component of accounts such as trade payables is seldom worth the effort. In addition, the entire cost of goods and services bought in from suppliers, including any interest component, is reflected in either cost of sales or selling, general, and administrative expenses. Therefore, the company is charged, albeit indirectly, for these interest costs.

As long as the return generated from the use of "net" assets (that is, the sum of cash, working capital requirement, and fixed assets) exceeds the cost of the invested capital, EVA is positive. The return on net assets (RONA) is calculated as follows:

$$RONA = NOPAT \div \text{net assets}$$

When RONA is greater than WACC, EVA is positive, and when RONA is less than WACC, EVA is negative, because

$$EVA = (RONA - WACC) \times \text{invested capital}$$

When EVA is framed in this way, an important question emerges: Why not use RONA by itself? What does EVA offer us that RONA does not? The risk to companies of using RONA to the exclusion of EVA is that divisional managers might bypass value-creating projects because they would reduce RONA (a risk whenever RONA is greater than WACC), or they might undertake value-destroying projects because they would increase RONA (which can happen when RONA is less than WACC). Either way, reliance on RONA alone can lead to suboptimal behavior.

The latter problem is a serious risk today in Japanese companies. Few large Japanese firms have earned large RONAs in recent years, and with the country's recent economic downturn, the situation has worsened. The average RONA in 1997 for large publicly traded Japanese companies was practically zero. Still, growing capital market pressure has led several of these companies to adopt RONA or return on equity (ROE) as a measure of corporate performance. If managers of these companies are evaluated on RONA, and RONA is significantly lower than WACC—which it is for most large Japanese companies—managers might be tempted to invest in capital projects that will earn less than the WACC as long as they are expected to earn more than the existing RONA. The result is that value-destroying Japanese companies may invest ever-increasing amounts of capital in value-destroying activities, digging themselves, and the Japanese economy, into an ever-deeper hole.

A few years ago, Apple Computer faced a very different problem. Its managers, too, were evaluated on the basis of RONA. Moreover, as recently as the early 1990s, the company's RONA was 30 percent, among the highest of any large American business. This high RONA made management reluctant to make further investments, passing up opportunities with expected returns of 20 percent despite the fact that these returns far exceeded the company's cost of capital. The result is that Apple systematically underinvested, contributing to the massive problems that brought the company to the brink of collapse in 1997. A stronger company might have overcome the problems caused by focusing on the wrong metric. However, as former Apple CEO Gil Amelio describes, there was much in the way Apple was run, especially in terms of its corporate culture, that was dysfunctional and contributed to the gradual erosion of its once-strong position in the computer industry. Choosing the wrong measure to focus on certainly didn't help.[3]

Before the early 1980s, Coca-Cola also focused on percentage, not monetary, returns. Although they enjoyed the world's most powerful brand name, Coca-Cola managers were reluctant to leverage it for fear that additional products (such as a diet version of the flagship product) would not earn the same high returns the company was used to achieving. This problem was corrected under the leadership of Roberto Goizueta, a chemical engineer by training, who soon learned after becoming CEO that the key to success was not maximizing RONA but maximizing EVA.

A company that focuses on RONA while ignoring EVA is like a basketball team that tries to maximize its field goal percentage to the exclusion of all other goals, such as total points. After one slam dunk, that particular measure has been optimized, yet the team loses because it doesn't try to score again. Shooting percentage is important, of course, but the best players understand that the key to winning is to "play the percentages" by taking shots they are capable, if not certain, of making.

Businesses too must play the percentages. The business equivalent of a slam dunk does not come along very often, which means that if we want to play the game and win, we must shoot every time the percentages are in our favor. In other words, we invest whenever the returns are expected to exceed the cost of capital.

Still, RONA is a major improvement over the measures that companies have normally relied on to measure performance. We learned this lesson firsthand from work with a well-known German manufacturer. This company had invested heavily over a

3. G. Amelio, with W. Simon, *On the Front Line*, New York: HarperBusiness, 1998.

period of several years in new plant and equipment. Senior managers congratulated themselves on the resulting improvements in employee productivity, proudly citing charts that showed steady growth in output per employee. To these managers, this meant that the company had achieved huge efficiency gains. Yet they were puzzled by the company's mediocre financial performance. On closer inspection, it became clear that what the company had really accomplished was the substitution of labor with new but capital-intensive technologies. Output per employee grew, but the company's output charts conveniently ignored the huge increase in capital that made the output gains possible. Employees had become more "efficient," but only at the expense of lower asset (and capital) efficiency.

An important virtue of RONA is that it not only captures any productivity gains achieved by the company's workforce, but it also considers the assets the workforce uses to achieve its output. Although it does not explicitly measure capital charges, it does remind managers that there is a cost to acquiring and holding assets.

THE WORKING CAPITAL REQUIREMENT

When calculating EVA, taking into account the working capital requirement, or WCR, of a company is essential. Net assets, which are, as mentioned, the sum of cash, the working capital requirement, and fixed assets—are investments for which the firm's capital providers expect, and managers must deliver, a competitive return. Although everyone understands fixed assets and cash, some explanation is needed for the working capital requirement.

Consider a typical manufacturing company. As we see in Figure 2–3, the operating cycle begins with the acquisition of the materials, parts, and components that are used in the company's products. These materials are then transferred from materials warehouses to the factory, where workers and various elements of manufacturing overhead (such as public utilities, maintenance, and depreciation) combine to convert the materials into the finished product.

The Operating Cycle

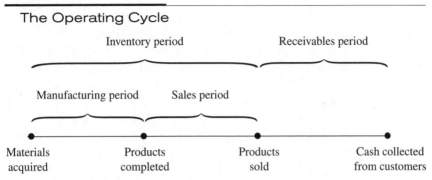

The time it takes to go from acquisition of materials into a finished product is the *manufacturing period*, or "cycle time." Products must then be sold, which typically requires a *sales period* of several days or weeks after the manufacturing process is complete. Until the product is sold, it stays within the company as inventory of some form—materials, work-in-process, or finished goods. Therefore, the sum of the manufacturing period and the sales period equals the *inventory period*.

The operating cycle does not end with the sale of the product, however. Most companies extend credit to their customers. The *receivables period* indicates the length of time it takes for the company to collect cash from customers after a sale has taken place. The length of a company's operating cycle is thus the sum of its inventory period and its receivables period. We call this a "cycle" because a portion of the cash collected from customers is used to pay suppliers and acquire more materials, which in turn enables the process to repeat itself.

For our discussion here, the key point to note about this cycle is that it requires investment. The most obvious manifestations of that investment are the amounts that a company ties up in inventory and receivables. However, there may be other types of investment as well. For example, suppose a company needs additional space to store finished products because of recent market growth. It acquires this additional capacity by leasing a warehouse. When it signs the lease contract, it hands the landlord a check for $150,000, giving the company exclusive rights to use the warehouse for the next 12 months. Accountants treat this transaction as a *prepaid expense*, which is classified as a current asset. This prepaid expense is clearly related to the operating cycle, and it represents a further investment that the company has made.

Companies may also have other working capital items, such as *nontrade receivables* (money owed by employees, for example). Finally, companies may need to maintain a particular level of cash to support their day-to-day operations. For example, retailers need to keep some cash in the register. We call this type of investment *operating cash* to distinguish it from more discretionary balances, or *excess cash*.

Therefore, we can think of the total investment in a company's operating cycle as

Inventories + receivables
 + prepaid expenses and other current assets + operating cash

It is crucial to note, however, that this amount does not represent the company's own investment in the cycle, but rather the total investment made by the company and others. What others? Its suppliers, employees, and the government, for starters. The extent to which other parties invest in the company's operating cycle is the extent to which the company itself, and by extension its shareholders, does not have to.

When suppliers grant credit to a company, they are really investing in its operating cycle. The same can be said for employees when they have not yet been paid for work already performed, for the government, in the form of owed but unpaid taxes, and for customers when they make advance payments. We can estimate the company's (and its shareholders') *net* investment in the operating cycle by subtracting the sum of accounts payable (supplier finance), accrued expenses (which include unpaid wages and taxes), and advance payments from the *total* investment in the operating cycle. We call this net investment the *working capital requirement* (WCR):

$$WCR = \text{(inventories + receivables}$$
$$+ \text{ other current assets + operating cash)}$$
$$- \text{ (accounts payable + accrued expenses}$$
$$+ \text{ advances from customers)}$$

EVA measurement compels management to generate returns on this investment, just as it does for excess cash and fixed assets.

A CASE STUDY OF MVA/EVA CALCULATIONS

In this section, we show how MVA and EVA are calculated using the example of Harnischfeger, an American manufacturer of mining equipment and pulp and papermaking machinery. Table 2–4 shows the financial statements of Harnischfeger. Table 2–5 provides the template we use for estimating EVA. This template is designed to provide a "first-pass" approximation of EVA that can be calculated quickly and easily from public financial disclosures. (In Chapter 6, we explore more complicated approaches to EVA measurement.)

We begin by estimating the total investment in Harnischfeger's operating cycle. If we assume Harnishfeger needs operating cash balances equal to 1 percent of total sales (which were $2.888 billion in fiscal year 1996), operating cash is $28.88 million. The total investment in the company's operating cycle is thus:

$$\$667.786 \text{ M (receivables)}$$
$$+ \$547.115 \text{ M (inventories)}$$
$$+ \$158.413 \text{ M (other current assets)}$$
$$+ \$28.88 \text{ M (operating cash)}$$
$$= \$1{,}402.194 \text{ M}$$

Simply put, about $1.4 billion was tied up in Harnischfeger's operating cycle. Remember that the WCR equals (inventories + receivables + other current assets + operating cash) − (accounts payable + accrued expenses + advances from customers).

Harnischfeger's WCR as of the end of fiscal year 1996 is as follows:

T A B L E   2–4

Harnischfeger Industries, Inc. Consolidated Balance Sheet for Year Ended October 31, 1996*

	1996	1995
Assets		
Current assets		
Cash and cash equivalents	$ 36,936	$239,043
Accounts receivable—net	667,786	499,953
Inventories	547,115	416,395
Businesses held for sale	26,152	—
Other current assets	132,261	57,999
Total	1,410,250	1,213,390
Property, plant, and equipment		
Land and improvements	48,371	31,571
Buildings	301,010	233,788
Machinery and equipment	776,332	676,546
Total	1,125,713	941,905
Accumulated depreciation	(491,668)	(454,249)
Total	634,045	487,656
Investments and other assets		
Goodwill	512,693	147,943
Intangible assets	39,173	66,796
Other assets	93,868	124,982
Total	645,734	339,721
Total Assets	$2,690,029	$2,040,767
Liabilities and Shareholders' Equity		
Current liabilities		
Short-term notes payable	$ 49,633	$ 22,802
Trade accounts payable	346,056	263,750
Employee compensation and benefits	160,488	100,041
Advance payments and progress billings	155,199	154,401
Accrued warranties	50,718	43,801
Other current liabilities	315,033	138,508
Total	1,077,127	723,303
Long-term obligations	657,765	459,110

T A B L E   2–4

Continued

	1996	1995
Other liabilities		
Liability for postretirement benefits	78,814	101,605
Accrued pension and related costs	39,902	52,237
Other liabilities	14,364	20,820
Deferred income taxes	54,920	34,805
Total	188,000	209,467
Minority interest	93,652	89,611
Shareholders' equity		
Common stock	51,407	51,118
Capital in excess of par value	615,089	603,712
Retained earnings	148,175	53,560
Cumulative translation adjustments	(37,584)	(42,118)
Less stock employee compensation trust	(61,360)	(60,483)
Less treasury stock	(42,242)	(46,513)
Total	673,485	559,276
Total	$2,690,029	$2,040,767
Sales		$2,887,570
Cost of sales		2,166,775
Product development, selling, and administrative expenses		433,776
Restructuring charge		43,000
Operating income		244,019
Interest income		6,505
Interest expense		(68,763)
Income before taxes and minority interest		181,761
Provision for income taxes		(63,600)
Minority interest		(3,944)
Net income	$114,217	

* In thousands of dollars.
Source: Harnischfeger's 1996 Annual Report.

T A B L E   2–5

Template for Calculating Economic Value Added

   Operating income
+ Interest income
+ Equity income (or − equity loss)
+ Other investment income
− Income taxes
− Tax shield on interest expense
= Net operating profit after tax (NOPAT)

   Short-term debt
+ Long-term debt (including bonds)
+ Other long-term liabilities (deferred taxes and provisions)
+ Shareholders' equity (including minority interest)
= Invested capital (IC)
   Average IC = $(IC_{Beg} + IC_{End}) \div 2$

   NOPAT
− Capital charges (average IC × cost of capital)
= EVA

($547.115 M + $667.786 M + $158.413 M + $28.88 M)
  − ($346.056 M + $526.239 M + $155.199 M = $374.70 M)

Note that

Invested capital = excess cash + WCR + fixed assets

The excess cash is the difference between the balance in cash and cash equivalents, $36.936 million, and operating cash, $28.88 million, or $8.056 million. Fixed assets, which include all the company's long-term assets, amount to $1,279.779 million ($634.045 million for net property, plant, and equipment, and $645.734 million for other long-term assets, including goodwill). Total invested capital for Harnischfeger, as of October 31, 1996, is as follows:

$8.056 M + $374.70 M + $1,279.779 M = $1,662.535 M

We can arrive at the same answer by netting short-term, non-interest-bearing liabilities ($1,027.494 million) against total assets ($2,690.029 million), *or* by summing short-term debt ($49.633 million), long-term debt ($657.765 million), provisions for pensions and other long-term liabilities ($133.08 million), deferred taxes ($54.92 million), minority interest ($93.652 million), and share-holders' equity ($673.485 million). This can be summarized as follows:

Invested capital

= excess cash + WCR + fixed assets

= total assets − short-term, non-interest-bearing liabilities

= short-term debt + long-term debt + other long-term liabilities + shareholders' equity

Defining capital as the sum of excess cash, WCR, and fixed assets is called the *operating approach*, while summing up the different forms of finance is called the *financing approach*. The important point here is that while it does not matter which definition is used, at least at the companywide level, our measure of invested capital (and, therefore, of EVA) should be the same.

Harnischfeger's MVA

Harnischfeger had 47,598,340 shares of common stock outstanding, selling for $40 per share, at the end of fiscal year 1996. This yields a capitalized market value for equity of $1,903.934 million. The market value of the firm equals the market value of all claims against the company's assets, including equity, minority interest, and debt (including other long-term liabilities such as deferred taxes and provisions). Because Harnischfeger does not report market values for its debt, we will use book values. If the terms of the debt are known (or, more specifically, the pattern of future cashflows), market values can be approximated by discounting the future cashflows at prevailing interest rates. Otherwise, book values will have to suffice.

For corporate users of EVA, the market value of debt can be estimated, even in the absence of a secondary market, by discounting future cashflows (interest and principal payments) at prevailing interest rates. Analysts outside a company will probably have to rely on book values for debt, unless the debt is publicly traded, if they cannot determine the company's current interest rate and the timing of future debt service payments. For minority interest (the stake outsiders hold in the company's subsidiaries), we will also use book value as a proxy for market value. Therefore, the market value of the company on October 31, 1996, is as follows:

	Common shares	$1,903.934 M
+	Minority interest	93.652 M
+	Short-term debt	49.633 M
+	Long-term debt	657.765 M
+	Other long-term liabilities	188.000 M

which equals $2,892.984 million, or about $2.9 billion.[4] We can now calculate MVA:

$$MVA = \text{market value} - \text{invested capital}$$

$$= \$2,892.984 \text{ M} - \$1,662.535 \text{ M}$$

$$= \$1,230.449 \text{ M}$$

This figure means that as of October 31, 1996, Harnischfeger had a market value that was about $1.23 billion greater than the amount of capital contributed to the company by investors. Because MVA is the present value of future EVAs, discounted at the company's cost of capital, the MVA can be taken as an indication that the market expects Harnischfeger's management to generate positive EVAs in the future.

Harnischfeger's EVA

Although calculating EVA can be complex, especially when potential adjustments are considered, we begin by taking the simplified "shortcut" approach summarized in Table 2–5. This approach produces an easy, credible estimate of EVA for the overwhelming majority of companies.

---

4. Including other long-term liabilities (e.g., deferred taxes and provisions) in the market value of the firm is controversial. Some practitioners would argue that these items do not represent claims by capital market players in the same way as interest-bearing debt. However, because these miscellaneous liabilities are included in invested capital, by adding them to the market value of the firm, we neutralize their effect on MVA. In other words, any amount that is added to market value for these liabilities is then subtracted when MVA is calculated.

Operating profit equals sales, net of operating expenses, including cost of sales and selling, general, and administrative expenses. The tax shield equals 35 percent (Harnischfeger's corporate tax rate) times the interest expense of $68.763 million. Net operating profit after tax (NOPAT) is calculated as follows:

Operating profit	$244.019 M
Interest income	6.505 M
−Income taxes	(63.600 M)
−Tax shield on interest	(24.067 M)
NOPAT	$162.857 M

Capital charges equal the company's invested capital times the weighted-average cost of capital. Harnischfeger estimates its WACC to be 12 percent.[5] Interest income is included in NOPAT because cash is included in invested capital. (Remember that cash is included in net assets, and because net assets must equal invested capital, it is also embedded in the latter.) If capital charges are imposed on all invested capital, management should also be credited with any returns earned on cash. Of course, any returns generated from bank deposits or government bonds (a typical destination for excess cash) will be far lower than the capital charges imposed on the cash balances, so that the net impact of including cash in EVA measurement will always be negative. When EVA is measured at divisional levels, cash is typically excluded from invested capital because surplus cash is nearly always managed centrally by the corporate treasurer. In such cases, interest income should also be excluded from NOPAT.

We already know invested capital at the end of fiscal year 1996, but to calculate capital charges for the year, we also need to know invested capital at the beginning of the year (i.e., the end of the previous fiscal year). We can calculate it by subtracting short-term non-interest-bearing liabilities, $700.501 million, from total assets, $2,040.767 million, which equals $1,340.266 million. This figure yields average invested capital for the year of

---

5. From Harnischfeger's 1996 Annual Report.

$1,501.401 million (beginning invested capital of $1,340.266 million + ending invested capital of $1,662.535 million, divided by 2). Assuming a 12 percent cost of capital:

NOPAT	$162.857 M
−Capital charges	180.168 M
EVA	($17.311 M)

Harnischfeger's financial costs exceeded its operating profits by about $17.3 million, hence the EVA is *negative*. Some analysts prefer to calculate EVA on the basis of beginning invested capital instead of the average invested capital for the year. In this case, capital charges for 1996 equal $160.832 million ($1,340.266 million multiplied by the 12 percent WACC), yielding a marginally *positive* EVA of $2.025 million. In this case, the choice of which invested capital figure to use determines whether EVA is negative or positive.

This analysis suggests that Harnischfeger's operating performance was approximately value-neutral in 1996, which contrasts sharply with its $1+ billion MVA. The figures indicate that the market is expecting the company's future EVAs to be much higher than the 1996 amount. In other words, the market's verdict on Harnischfeger's management and its ability to deliver shareholder value is favorable, despite near-zero EVA performance in 1996. These results are not the least bit contradictory, because EVA is a single period measure of performance, while MVA reflects capital market expectations of performance in all future periods. As we will see later in this chapter, many well-known publicly traded companies in the United States and in Europe have a strongly positive MVA despite a low or even negative EVA.

COMPARING EXCESS RETURNS, MVA, AND EVA: EVIDENCE FROM THE UNITED STATES AND EUROPE

In Tables 2–6 through 2–9, we show the excess returns, MVA, and EVA for selected companies in the United States, the United King-

T A B L E 2-6

Excess Returns, MVA, and EVA for Selected U.S. Companies

In Millions of Dollars	Data Period	Excess Return	Excess Return Per Initial $1	MVA	1998 EVA	1998 WACC
Microsoft	1989–98	313,289	90.303	326,912	2,899	0.116
General Electric	1989–98	256,129	6.861	294,792	1,239	0.104
Intel	1989–98	176,662	36.434	173,199	3,064	0.124
Coca-Cola	1989–98	147,431	10.103	156,787	2,419	0.099
Pfizer	1989–98	140,045	14.965	152,941	848	0.100
Wal-Mart Stores	1989–98	130,183	7.400	160,006	1,917	0.093
Merck	1989–98	129,276	5.491	161,282	2,934	0.117
Cisco Systems	1990–98	124,999	283.320	137,920	679	0.117
Philip Morris	1989–98	110,202	4.945	113,837	2,446	0.097
Lucent Technologies	1996–98	105,086	4.970	139,188	−10	0.095
Dell Computer	1989–98	95,554	348.224	90,738	1,178	0.128
Exxon Mobil	1989–98	94,585	1.729	133,798	1,201	0.080
Procter & Gamble	1989–98	94,174	6.369	110,095	1,932	0.107
Bristol Myers Squibb	1989–98	84,490	3.920	125,484	2,204	0.103
Johnson & Johnson	1989–98	77,303	5.506	99,142	1,314	0.106
Home Depot	1989–98	74,386	36.238	81,540	810	0.090
Schering-Plough	1989–98	73,023	13.618	77,326	1,245	0.117
Eli Lilly	1989–98	69,305	5.901	93,013	1,370	0.109
BellSouth	1989–98	67,516	3.454	81,146	1,546	0.081
Abbott Laboratories	1989–98	59,387	6.108	68,573	1,670	0.089
America Online	1992–98	59,109	323.540	67,545	2	0.128
SBC Communications	1989–98	56,208	3.853	92,288	2,371	0.077
Warner-Lambert	1989–98	49,794	9.355	58,159	762	0.102
Compaq Computer	1989–98	47,959	17.597	56,307	−1,013	0.129
American Home Products	1989–98	47,208	3.611	64,372	1,207	0.097
MCI Worldcom	1989–98	42,038	293.403	83,184	−3,450	0.105
PepsiCo	1989–98	44,721	4.359	53,726	651	0.101
EMC	1989–98	38,766	186.614	39,485	396	0.122
Oracle	1989–98	36,772	26.349	37,450	987	0.085
Time Warner	1989–98	34,554	1.374	64,079	−1,694	0.089
Chevron	1989–98	33,121	2.209	37,127	−460	0.073
Gillette	1989–98	31,856	9.112	48,389	358	0.097
Medtronic	1989–98	31,702	28.106	39,817	157	0.108
McDonalds	1989–98	30,360	3.598	42,622	314	0.089
Gap	1989–98	29,779	21.312	30,529	645	0.089

T A B L E   2–6

Continued

In Millions of Dollars	Data Period	Excess Return	Excess Return Per Initial $1	MVA	1998 EVA	1998 WACC
DuPont	1989–98	28,672	1.511	46,401	−529	0.090
Bell Atlantic	1989–98	27,333	1.541	70,856	706	0.079
Sun Microsystems	1989–98	26,883	17.408	28,707	403	0.111
IBM	1989–98	26,186	0.638	149,685	3,000	0.112
GTE	1989–98	25,962	1.451	54,154	1,221	0.075
Hewlett-Packard	1989–98	24,391	1.701	52,445	511	0.123
Safeway	1990–98	23,879	17.280	26,796	490	0.070
Xerox	1989–98	23,702	3.788	33,893	−489	0.081
Amgen	1989–98	23,061	33.798	24,060	620	0.099
Carnival	1989–98	21,726	9.585	24,296	458	0.084
Tyco International	1989–98	21,227	5.471	38,118	434	0.102
AT&T	1989–98	54,527	1.276	107,313	2,077	0.085
Yahoo	1989–98	20,197	22.579	23,041	N/A	0.101
Disney	1989–98	19,989	2.262	42,742	−817	0.097
Texas Instruments	1989–98	19,899	4.934	26,925	−557	0.121
Colgate-Palmolive	1989–98	19,897	5.885	25,121	390	0.110
Campbell Soup	1989–98	20,799	5.181	23,766	451	0.086
Sara Lee	1989–98	15,432	3.205	24,154	−1,088	0.100
Honeywell	1989–98	14,545	3.252	19,450	526	0.097
Anheuser-Busch	1989–98	14,924	1.914	27,061	600	0.082
Texaco	1989–98	11,742	0.920	16,896	−534	0.068
Enron	1989–98	10,808	4.885	11,965	−16	0.069
Emerson Electric	1989–98	10,866	1.596	20,709	372	0.104
Nike	1989–98	9,303	9.751	8,116	84	0.097
Avon Products	1989–98	9,237	7.608	11,331	242	0.095
Heinz	1989–98	9,133	1.588	18,533	114	0.091
Kimberley-Clark	1989–98	9,318	1.896	25,304	609	0.085
Bestfoods	1989–98	8,522	2.211	14,134	443	0.085
General Dynamics	1989–98	7,008	4.107	5,256	74	0.100
Ford Motor	1989–98	34,621	0.951	63,500	3,673	0.060
Harley-Davidson	1989–98	6,311	26.792	6,215	101	0.089
Raytheon	1989–98	5,086	1.197	7,078	−329	0.074
Minnesota Mining	1989–98	6,125	0.423	22,651	400	0.086
General Mills	1989–98	7,342	1.730	11,654	363	0.087

T A B L E   2–6

Continued

In Millions of Dollars	Data Period	Excess Return	Excess Return Per Initial $1	MVA	1998 EVA	1998 WACC
Lexmark	1995–98	4,698	3.812	6,004	172	0.099
Southwest Airlines	1989–98	4,652	7.970	5,141	24	0.114
Gannett	1989–98	4,599	0.965	14,016	543	0.081
Biogen	1989–98	4,160	19.436	5,388	55	0.116
Schlumberger	1989–98	3,055	0.444	17,208	69	0.094
Fedex	1989–98	2,766	0.638	8,625	−67	0.101
McGraw-Hill	1989–98	2,671	0.843	8,489	109	0.100
Analog Devices	1989–98	2,458	3.977	3,901	−44	0.112
Waste Management	1989–98	2,297	16.570	23,987	−1,416	0.089
Ingersoll Rand	1989–98	2,290	1.227	5,060	20	0.096
Sherwin Williams	1989–98	2,195	2.027	3,308	33	0.090
Circuit City	1989–98	2,192	2.552	3,209	1	0.072
Caterpillar	1989–98	1,237	0.209	11,300	687	0.075
Maytag	1989–98	1,160	0.684	5,046	147	0.088
Corning	1989–98	968	0.313	8,912	177	0.072
Kellogg	1989–98	918	0.036	12,931	271	0.080
TRW	1989–98	878	0.300	4,081	195	0.078
Nucor	1989–98	685	0.714	1,705	35	0.090
Humana	1993–98	459	0.417	1,296	−119	0.083
Eaton	1989–98	337	0.201	3,011	64	0.078
Bausch & Lomb	1989–98	198	0.191	2,547	−110	0.088
New York Times	1989–98	−7	−0.231	4,768	60	0.082
Quaker Oats	1989–98	663	0.230	7,901	148	0.099
Seagram	1989–98	−74	−0.041	3,875	−477	0.083
Ralson Purina	1989–98	1,233	0.377	8,515	143	0.083
Stanley & Works	1989–98	−662	−0.477	1,794	22	0.097
Deere	1989–98	−688	−0.231	3,557	259	0.088
Whirlpool	1989–98	−868	−0.389	2,212	47	0.082
Knight-Ridder	1989–98	−1,291	−0.514	2,343	77	0.078
Cummins Engine	1989–98	−1,580	−1.743	91	−253	0.081
Penney	1989–98	−1,733	−0.224	5,025	−348	0.067
Crown Cork & Seal	1989–98	−1,966	−0.530	1,145	−251	0.061
Goodrich	1989–98	−2,060	−1.430	1,068	0	0.090
Weyerhaeuser	1989–98	−2,213	−0.419	5,586	−478	0.081
Thermo Electron	1989–98	−2,229	−0.488	436	−38	0.067

TABLE 2–6

Continued

In Millions of Dollars	Data Period	Excess Return	Excess Return Per Initial $1	MVA	1998 EVA	1998 WACC
Goodyear	1989–98	−2,244	−0.720	4,120	106	0.097
Owens Corning	1989–98	2,692	0.748	3,058	−833	0.065
Delta Airlines	1989–98	−2,434	−1.012	3,800	196	0.087
Georgia Pacific	1989–98	−333	−0.139	1,858	−442	0.072
Dow Jones	1989–98	−3,308	−1.095	3,917	−81	0.087
Boise Cascade	1989–98	−3,473	−2.099	401	−225	0.073
International Paper	1989–98	−3,484	−0.595	4,860	−1,277	0.079
Mead	1989–98	−3,616	−1.474	733	−167	0.079
Grace	1989–98	4,238	1.859	969	−354	0.082
Polaroid	1989–98	−4,013	−2.315	432	−136	0.076
Champion International	1989–98	−4,170	−1.376	775	−296	0.064
Hilton	1989–98	−4,312	−1.414	4,805	−121	0.081
Tandy	1989–98	−4,606	−1.100	3,234	−23	0.076
Navistar	1989–98	−4,715	−2.984	1,122	73	0.084
Newmont Mining	1989–98	−4,946	−1.620	1,612	−451	0.069
USX-Marathon	1991–98	−2,084	−0.337	4,980	−132	0.082
Times Mirror	1989–98	−3,940	−0.904	3,492	−109	0.078
Reynolds Metal	1989–98	−6,120	−1.868	1,202	−310	0.086
Eastman Kodak	1989–98	−481	−0.057	19,253	730	0.073
Union Pacific	1989–98	−1,403	−0.068	3,758	−2,147	0.068
Unisys	1989–98	−8,321	−2.247	8,740	142	0.112
Occidental Petroleum	1989–98	−9,285	−1.239	2,748	−365	0.075
General Motors	1989–98	−6,668	−0.386	31,891	−3,971	0.054
ITT Industries	1989–98	5,659	1.032	2,515	−318	0.076
CBS	1989–98	−10,639	−1.627	13,597	−1,674	0.107
Toys R Us	1989–98	−10,653	−2.261	621	−493	0.073
Dow Chemical	1989–98	−11,340	−0.730	12,612	132	0.079
Apple Computer	1989–98	−11,444	−2.383	4,043	170	0.068
K Mart	1989–98	−13,913	−1.932	1,575	−45	0.073
Dun & Bradstreet	1989–98	−7,727	−0.773	5,580	221	0.071
Nabisco	1991–98	−21,587	−1.941	1,840	−2,114	0.075
Sears Roebuck	1989–98	2,070	0.209	10,233	−481	0.092

Note: Excess returns as of December 31, 1998. MVA as of December 31, 1998. WACC = weighted average cost of capital.

T A B L E   2–7

Excess Returns, MVA, and EVA of Selected British Companies

In Million of Pounds	Data Period	Excess Return	Excess Return Per Initial £1	MVA	1998 EVA	1998 WACC
Glaxo Wellcome	1989–98	50,840	5.038	73,069	1,502	0.101
Smithkline Beecham	1989–98	25,304	4.027	45,893	400	0.095
Vodafone Airtouch	1989–98	21,363	8.171	29,656	560	0.112
British Telecom	1989–98	19,995	1.045	44,903	1,931	0.082
BP Amoco	1989–98	19,375	1.224	47,583	590	0.096
Astra Zeneca	1989–98	16,504	2.808	22,679	476	0.098
Unilever	1989–98	9,247	2.729	21,347	−96	0.103
Reuters	1989–98	5,193	2.000	8,703	275	0.108
British Aerospace	1989–98	5,034	1.795	7,275	546	0.084
Boots	1989–98	4,502	1.975	7,697	−158	0.103
National Grid	1989–98	4,099	1.189	5,639	847	0.093
Tesco	1989–98	3,499	1.142	7,431	188	0.092
Kingfisher	1989–98	2,809	1.768	6,739	197	0.098
Cadbury Schweppes	1989–98	2,462	0.576	8,768	178	0.094
Thames Water	1990–98	2,205	1.938	1,970	146	0.091
British Sky Broadcasting	1995–98	1,603	0.366	8,246	267	0.089
Invensys	1989–98	1,429	1.854	7,217	−225	0.094
Pearson	1989–98	1,287	0.548	6,523	350	0.079
Granada	1989–98	1,132	−0.249	8,388	383	0.089
Cable & Wireless	1989–98	582	0.098	13,244	634	0.099
Whitbread	1989–98	−290	−0.150	1,262	−4	0.092
Safeway	1989–98	−505	−0.200	1,344	36	0.085
Rolls-Royce	1989–98	−751	−0.536	2,133	97	0.089
Sainsbury	1989–98	−825	−0.097	4,787	227	0.080
British Airways	1989–98	−1.062	−0.169	1,016	−194	0.075
Reckitt Benckiser	1989–98	−1,161	−0.708	2,347	40	0.096
Marks & Spencer	1989–98	−1,548	−0.256	7,041	−157	0.096
Carlton Communications	1989–98	−2,310	−1.638	3,017	163	0.091
Bass	1989–98	−3,081	−0.895	4,804	281	0.098
EMI	1989–98	−4,288	−1.557	4,105	166	0.091
Hilton	1989–98	−4,731	−2.010	1,589	87	0.079
BAT	1989–98	−6,602	−0.713	8,384	−1,028	0.082
Allied Domecq	1989–98	−6,671	−1.574	4.026	87	0.093
ICI	1989–98	−13,941	−1.721	3,867	90	0.072
Hanson	1989–98	−16,206	−1.820	1,679	219	0.066

Note: Excess returns as of December 31, 1998. MVA as of December 31, 1998. WACC = weighted average cost of capital.

T A B L E   2-8

Excess Returns, MVA, and EVA of Selected German Companies

In Millions of Deutsche Marks	Data Period	Excess Return	Excess Return Per Initial DM1	MVA	1998 EVA	1998 WACC
Deutsche Telekon	1996–98	46,977	0.499	103,250	−1,187	0.077
SAP	1989–98	41,098	30.152	40,577	708	0.086
Veba	1989–98	24,639	1.881	27,593	−549	0.079
RWE	1989–98	16,080	2.096	20,054	1,714	0.155
Volkswagen	1989–98	14,814	1.681	24,658	181	0.091
Viag	1989–98	12,511	2.543	14,288	207	0.075
BMW	1989–98	7,643	0.952	19,012	−614	0.094
Preussag	1989–98	5,784	2.262	9,140	219	0.096
Henkel	1989–98	4,314	0.987	7,047	152	0.088
Schering	1989–98	4,283	1.195	10,266	548	0.150
Audi	1993–98	3,991	2.543	4,171	262	0.063
Bayer	1989–98	3,792	0.112	26,664	173	0.090
BASF	1989–98	3,747	0.180	15,642	1,159	0.115
Axel Springer	1989–98	1,331	0.768	3,737	279	0.091
Hugo Boss	1989–98	544	1.809	661	76	0.080
Grohe	1993–98	206	0.583	74	57	0.061
Jil Sander	1990–98	−189	−1.396	−4	1	0.059
Wella	1994–98	−913	−0.487	1,214	20	0.090
Salamander	1989–98	−996	−1.608	153	−28	0.078
Villeroy & Boch	1990–98	−1,468	−1.607	−451	−33	0.068
Continental	1989–98	−2,278	−1.040	2,816	90	0.076
Degussa	1989–98	−2,293	−0.804	5,918	121	0.087
Daimler Chrysler	1989–98	−2,642	−0.209	135,443	−1,436	0.087
Hochtief	1989–98	−3,467	−1.005	1,899	−102	0.080
Thyssen Krupp	1989–98	−4,294	−1.404	1,842	160	0.073
Philipp Holzmann	1989–98	−4,591	−1.993	654	−134	0.055
Linde	1989–98	−5,096	−1.089	4,152	27	0.092
Metallgesellschaft	1989–98	−8,702	−2.507	2,905	390	0.155
Siemens	1989–98	−16,452	−0.626	35,988	608	0.127

Note: Excess returns as of December 31, 1998.
MVA as of December 31, 1998.
N/A = not available.
WACC = weighted average cost of capital.
COE = cost of equity.
DM = Deutsche mark.

T A B L E   2–9

Excess Returns, MVA, and EVA of Selected French Companies

In Millions of French Francs	Data Period	Excess Return	Excess Return Per Initial FF1	MVA	1998 EVA	1998 WACC
France Telecom	1997–98	200,869	0.920	343,475	2,591	0.085
L'Oréal	1989–98	199,429	7.820	240,729	767	0.099
Carrefour	1989–98	130,454	8.055	138,238	1,242	0.084
Pinault-Printemps-Redoute	1989–98	94,019	7.100	105,185	1,533	0.089
Total Fina	1989–98	58,800	3.988	80,221	67	0.083
Sanofi-Synthelabo	1989–98	51,174	2.506	79,148	−220	0.086
Suez Lyonnaise des Eaux	1989–98	32,864	−0.010	160,709	−7,257	0.079
Sodexho	1989–98	26,405	6.395	34,309	−147	0.075
St Microelectonics	1989–98	18,509	0.539	58,638	12	0.094
Air Liquide	1989–98	13,378	0.419	56,479	746	0.074
Casino Guichard-Perrachon	1989–98	11,492	0.293	30,678	136	0.072
Cap Gemini	1989–98	11,081	−0.314	49,441	596	0.079
Danone	1989–98	11,048	0.178	111,774	−2,348	0.085
Legrand	1989–98	10,411	1.358	23,688	347	0.084
Valeo	1989–98	6,643	0.741	34,234	−424	0.082
Lagardere	1991–98	6,294	0.594	27,132	−822	0.081
Canal Plus	1989–98	−1,686	−0.287	37,692	−1,999	0.076
Accor	1989–98	−3,001	−0.662	25,897	38	0.071
Bouygues	1989–98	−3,843	−0.803	21,698	−28	0.066
Renault	1989–98	−4,528	−0.112	16,298	16,289	0.059
Schneider	1989–98	−4,771	−2.750	28,151	106	0.104
Lafarge	1989–98	−29,212	−1.320	25,059	1,010	0.075
Thomson-CSF	1989–98	−39,424	−1.512	25,678	−2,989	0.116
Michelin	1989–98	−46,572	−2.308	5,015	937	0.087
Saint-Gobain	1989–98	−48,271	−1.336	13,722	2,036	0.078
Alcatel	1989–98	−58,514	−0.916	125,819	−2,611	0.093
LVMH	1989–98	−60,139	−1.173	57,147	−1,116	0.079
PSA-Peugeot Citroën	1989–98	−61,974	−1.680	−9,650	−2,029	0.061

Note: Excess returns as of December 31, 1998.
MVA as of December 31, 1998.
WACC = weighted average cost of capital.
FF = French franc.

dom, Germany, and France.[6] Our survey is limited to businesses that are not primarily in financial services, such as banks and insurance companies. We include estimates for each company's WACC, and the excess return per dollar of initial shareholder wealth. This measures the excess return per dollar of initial investment for a shareholder who invests at the start of the period and makes no additional investments. The excess return per dollar (pound sterling, deutsche mark, or franc) of initial investment can be negative when the aggregate excess return is positive, e.g., Suez Lyonnaise des Eaux and Cap Gemini. This means that the company raised additional equity and the positive excess returns of the new equity holders exceeded the losses of the original shareholders.

---

6. Although the EVA template shown in Table 2–4 provides a highly useful, first-pass approximation of EVA for most companies, the EVA figures reported in Tables 2–6 through 2–9 include some adjustments not shown in Table 2–4. For companies without finance subsidiaries, we calculate the implicit interest on other long-term liabilities and add it back to income. Our assumption is that these liabilities, like Harnischfeger's pension and postretirement benefits, are reported on a present value basis, but that the implicit interest is buried in an operating expense, such as pension expense. For companies with finance subsidiaries, we exclude short-term debt and other long-term liabilities from capital and treat the related interest expense as an operating expense. The practical effect of these adjustments was to report the results of the company as they would have been had the finance subsidiary been accounted for under the equity method of accounting. Under the equity method, only the equity investment in the subsidiary is reported in the parent's balance sheet (and, hence, in its invested capital), while the income statement (or, in this case, the NOPAT) effect is limited to the parent's share of the subsidiaries' profits. Our review of the financial statements of companies with large finance subsidiaries shows that short-term debt is the principal source of finance for finance-subsidiary receivables (the principal source of income for such businesses). In addition, most of the parents' long-term non-interest-bearing liabilities (reported by most American companies as "other liabilities") are finance-subsidiary related. Therefore, by removing both short-term debt and other, long-term liabilities from invested capital, we remove all capital invested in the finance subsidiary apart from the parent company's equity investment. And by subtracting the interest paid on the short-term debt and leaving the implicit interest on other long-term liabilities as an operating expense, the net effect on the parent's NOPAT of the finance subsidiary's operations is the difference between income on the latter's receivables and the interest expense on the loans that financed those receivables. In other words, after the adjustments, the parent's NOPAT reflects only its profit from the finance subsidiary, much as it would have had the equity method, instead of full consolidation, been used to account for the subsidiary.

The excess return per dollar of initial investment is included to adjust for the size of the initial capital endowment. This adjustment is important because similar excess returns can arise from huge returns on a small asset base (e.g., Dell Computer) or from modest returns on a huge asset base (e.g., Exxon). Excess return may be the best measure of cumulative benefit to shareholders, but excess return per initial dollar of wealth (as of the beginning of the excess return measurement period) may be a better measure of management skill. While Dell delivered $348 of excess return for every dollar of initial wealth, Exxon delivered less than $2 over the same period.

For most companies, excess returns are measured for the 10 years ending December 31, 1998. However, the excess return period is shorter for several companies either because the companies did not exist in 1989 or were not yet publicly traded. MVA is calculated as of the end of 1998, while EVA is measured for the year 1998.

As expected, companies with high excess returns also have high MVAs. Our research shows that the correlation between excess returns and MVA for the firms that comprise the S&P 500 is over 0.9. Similar results can be found for the major stock market indexes of the United Kingdom and France, although the correlation for Germany is lower (about 0.5). These high correlations suggest that the easily calculated MVA can serve as a useful proxy for the relatively hard-to-calculate excess return. The low correlation in the German market arises mainly because a few companies, most notably Daimler-Chrysler (formerly Daimler Benz) and Siemens, combine hugely positive MVAs with negative excess returns. When these unusual cases are excluded, the correlation between excess returns and MVA is much higher.

Several companies in all four countries combined negative EVAs in 1998 with positive excess returns. Examples include Compaq Computer, MCI Worldcom, Time Warner, Disney, Unilever, Boots, Deutsche Telekom, Veba, Total Fina, and Canal Plus. Even more companies combined positive EVAs in 1998 with negative excess returns. These results are not surprising because EVA is a single-period measure, while our excess return measure captures 10 years of historical performance in addition to market expectations of future performance.

CREATING VALUE

Now that we have seen how to calculate and interpret EVA, MVA, and excess returns, let's discuss what companies must do to increase EVA and thus create shareholder value. As mentioned earlier in the chapter, EVA equals the spread between return on net assets and the cost of capital, multiplied by invested capital:

$$EVA = (RONA - WACC) \text{ invested capital}$$

Looking at this formula, we can see that EVA increases, and value is created, whenever a company can achieve any of the following:

1. *Increased returns on existing capital.* If RONA increases while holding WACC and invested capital constant, EVA increases.
2. *Profitable growth.* When an investment is expected to earn returns greater than the WACC, value is created. Even if a growth strategy is expected to reduce RONA, value is created as long as the *incremental* RONA exceeds the WACC.
3. *Divestment of value-destroying activities.* Invested capital decreases when a business or division is sold or closed down. If the reduction in capital is more than compensated for by the improvement in the spread between RONA and WACC, EVA increases.
4. *Longer periods over which it is expected to earn a RONA greater than WACC.*
5. *Reductions in the cost of capital.*

To illustrate each of these value-creating events, we posit a simple example:

Invested capital	= $15 M
RONA	= 18%
WACC	= 10%

RONA exceeds WACC, and value is created for shareholders, when companies achieve a competitive advantage. In fact, this is precisely why creating and maintaining competitive advantage is so important. It permits companies to generate returns that exceed the cost of capital. An advantage may be in the form of technological or cost leadership, or it may be in the form of brand equity that enables the company to extract premium prices for its products. In competitive markets, however, superior returns attract competition and innovations can be copied. In time, we would expect superior returns to disappear, even for world-class companies.

The question, then, is the sustainability of the high RONAs, which is why we hear so much about "sustaining competitive advantage." To make our example more complete, we need to introduce two more pieces of information. The *competitive advantage period* (CAP) is an estimate of how long a company will be able to enjoy above-normal returns. The *fade rate* describes the mathematical process by which the RONA converges to the WACC.

In this example, the CAP is eight years, which means that the RONA is expected to equal the WACC from year 9 onward; and the fade rate is linear, which means that the positive spread between RONA and WACC will converge to 0 in a straight-line fashion. With this information, we can now estimate future EVAs, the present value of future EVAs, and the value of the firm:

Year	1	2	3	4	5	6	7	8	9
Spread (RONA-WACC)	8%	7%	6%	5%	4%	3%	2%	1%	0
EVA (spread × $15 M, in millions of $)	1.2	1.05	0.9	0.75	0.6	0.45	0.3	0.15	0

Discounting the future EVAs at 10 percent yields a present value of about $4 million. Because the market value (MV) of the firm equals the present value of future EVAs plus invested capital, the market value of this firm is $4 million + $15 million, or $19 million.

Increased Returns on Existing Capital

Now suppose that because of higher profit margins, or improved asset utilization, the company has achieved a RONA of 20 percent, but all other factors are unchanged. The invested capital is still

$15 million, the WACC is still 10 percent, and the spread fades to 0 evenly over the next eight years (at a rate of 1.25 percent per year). What effect does the increased RONA have on value?

Year	1	2	3	4	5	6	7	8	9
Spread (in percent)	10.0	8.75	7.5	6.25	5.0	3.75	2.5	1.25	0
EVA (in millions of $)		1.5	1.3125	1.125	0.9375	0.75	0.5625	0.375	0.1825	0

The present value of future EVAs is now $5 million, while the value of the firm is $20 million ($5 million + the $15 million of invested capital). In this case, the value of the firm has increased by $1 million without any further investment. Therefore, the increase in RONA creates $1 million of value.

Companies improve returns on capital by cutting costs, creating brand equity, and improving asset efficiency. We discuss these issues in more detail in later chapters.

Profitable Growth

Now assume in the base case that the company plans a $5 million investment in a new market, with risk similar to the company's existing product portfolio. This final assumption is important, because otherwise the WACC might change (as the riskiness of a company's activities changes, so too does the cost of capital). The RONA of this investment is expected to be 15 percent for the first four years (a spread of 5 percent), 12.5 percent for the next four years (a spread of 2.5 percentage points), and 10 percent (or the WACC) thereafter. The investment can be valued as follows:

Year	1	2	3	4	5	6	7	8	9
Spread (in percent)	50.0	50.0	50.0	50.0	20.5	20.5	20.5	20.5	0
EVA (in millions of $)	0.25	0.25	0.25	0.25	0.25	0.25	0.25	0.25	0

The present value of future EVAs from this capital project is $1 million, which means that $1 million of value is created for the firm's shareholders. The $5 million investment increases invested capital to $20 million. This investment increases the present value of future EVAs from $4 million to $5 million, and the value of the firm from $19 million to $25 million. Remember that it is not the value of the firm *per se* that we seek. However, holding invested capital constant, the more valuable the firm, the better.

The crucial point in this example is that while the value of the firm increases by $6 million, invested capital increases by only $5 million, which confirms the adage stated often by value champions, from Warren Buffett to Roberto Goizueta, that the key to value creation is to grow the market value faster than you grow the capital.

Divestment of Value-Destroying Activities

This point becomes even clearer when we consider what happens when we get rid of the money-losing operations that are a brake on performance for the entire company. Now assume in the base case that the company has two divisions, one that earns a 22 percent RONA on $12 million of invested capital, and another that earns 2 percent on $3 million of capital, resulting in the companywide RONA of 18 percent [(12/15 $\times$ 22 percent) + (3/15 $\times$ 2 percent)].

If we can sell the underperforming division for its book value, the company's future performance will be

Year	1	2	3	4	5	6	7	8	9
Spread (in percent)	12.00	10.50	9.00	7.50	6.00	4.50	3.00	1.50	0
EVA (in millions of $)	1.44	1.26	1.08	0.90	0.72	0.54	0.36	0.18	0

The present value of future EVAs is now $4.8 million, versus $4 million in the base case. The resulting value of the firm ($4.8 million + invested capital of $12 million, or $16.8 million) is lower than in the original example, but value has been created nonetheless. While value declines by $2.2 million (from the original $19 million to $16.8 million), invested capital declines by even more, $3 million. The result is $800,000 of value creation.

Remember that the goal is to maximize value *added*, not market value. Whether we increase market value faster than we increase invested capital, or decrease invested capital faster than market value, the effect is the same: more wealth for the shareholders.

Even if the present value of future EVAs for a particular division is positive, and therefore it is a value creator, the business may be worth more to other firms than it is to ours. In such cases, firms can create value by selling businesses for a price that is higher than the sum of invested capital and the present value of EVAs.

Longer Competitive Advantage Period

Given the base case, now assume that the CAP is 10 years, instead of 8, with a linear fade rate as before. We can recalculate the EVAs as follows:

Year	1	2	3	4	5	6	7	8	9	10	11
Spread (in percent)	8.0	7.20	6.40	5.60	4.80	4.00	3.20	2.40	1.60	0.80	0
EVA (in millions of $)	1.2	1.08	0.96	0.84	0.72	0.60	0.48	0.36	0.24	0.12	0

The present value of future EVAs now equals $4.625 million, a $625,000 increase over the original example. Market value increases by the same amount, while invested capital is unchanged. In other words, extending the CAP by two years adds $625,000 of value. This example confirms the value of sustaining competitive advantage. The longer a company is able to sustain a competitive advantage, the longer it will be able to earn returns greater than its cost of capital.

Reductions in the Cost of Capital

If we assume that the cost of capital is reduced by 2 percentage points, from 10 to 8 percent, holding all else constant (invested capital, RONA, CAP, and fade rate), the value of the firm would be identical to the scenario in which RONA is increased by 2 percentage points and the WACC is held constant. In either case, the spread increases from 8 to 10 percent in the first year, creating $1 million of value. In other words, decreasing the WACC has the same effect on value creation, for a given percentage change, as does increasing the RONA. Any action or strategy that causes the spread to increase will deliver value to shareholders.

This example demonstrates another important lesson: Finance *can* create value, and it can destroy it too. As we discuss in the next chapter, one of the most important tasks of a company's chief financial officer is to select that capital structure that minimizes the firm's cost of capital and thus maximizes the value of the firm, given the cashflow-generating ability of its assets.

A FINAL NOTE

It is now widely recognized that value depends on capital market perceptions of a company's ability to deliver cashflows to its capital providers, with expected future cashflows discounted at a rate of interest that reflects what investors would expect to get if they put their money in companies of similar risk. Most large, publicly traded companies already incorporate this logic in the way they evaluate capital investments. The discounted cashflow techniques of net present value and internal rate of return are based on it. But, unfortunately, too many companies stop here in their value-based orientation to managerial decision-making. In other words, value may govern whether capital investment proposals are accepted or rejected, but value-based thinking often ignores the other tasks that managers are responsible for, such as the day-to-day running of the business *after* investments have already been made.

Remember that valuation is a forward-looking exercise. The value of a business, capital project, or any proposed investment is a function of the amount, timing, and uncertainty of future cashflows. But managers do not just invest; they also manage. To carry out their responsibilities, senior managers evaluate the performance of subordinates, consistent with whatever corporate goals or strategies have been set forth to create shareholder wealth. In other words, companies need performance measurement systems that senior managers can use to ensure that the company is on track in delivering value to its shareholders. These systems can then be used to reward good performance (through bonuses, promotions, and recognition) and can also serve as a basis for corrective action if performance is substandard.

However, as we discussed, performance measurement, by definition, is historical. We measure, evaluate, and compensate managers on what they have recently achieved, not on what they will achieve in the future. How can we ensure that the performance measurement systems used in our companies are consistent with the principles that govern the creation of value? How can we ensure that there is no disconnect between the *historical* evaluation of performance and the *future*-oriented valuation of our companies by the capital markets? In other words, how do we ensure that our performance measurement systems match the way that investors value companies? And how do we ensure that managers are properly motivated to create shareholder value by actively seeking out value-creating investments, avoiding value-destroying ones, and managing existing assets as efficiently as possible?

This is where value-based management and economic value added come into play. As we show in Figure 2–4, not only can EVA be used for forward-looking valuations, but it can also be readily adapted to performance measurement and, by extension, to management compensation. One of EVA's great strengths is that it provides a link between performance measurement and capital market valuation, helping to ensure that managerial performance

F I G U R E   2–4

EVA: Bridging the Gap between Valuation and
Performance Measurement

The past	The future
Performance measurement Evaluating performance Rewarding performance	Strategic planning Capital budgets Operating budgets

—————————————— EVA ——————————————→

Time ——————————————————————————————→

is evaluated and rewarded in a manner that is consistent with sound corporate finance theory.

To better understand the potential contribution of EVA, think about the process of appraising capital investment opportunities. The process consists of five basic steps. In Step 1, potential value-creating ideas, strategies, product innovations, or promotional campaigns must be identified. The aim of all capital investment should be to create value, which inevitably means creating or sustaining some form of competitive advantage. This advantage can be in the form of process innovation, product innovation, brand equity, or any other way that enables companies to generate supernormal returns in competitive markets.

Once potential value-creating investments have been identified, Step 2 is implemented. Streams of expected free cashflows must be estimated and converted into their present value equivalents using a discount rate that reflects what the company's capital providers could expect to receive investing in other company or capital projects of similar risk.

In Step 3, the decision is made: invest or don't invest. If we have confidence in our analysis in Step 2, the decision is straightforward: Invest in all projects where the present value of the future free cashflows is positive. In other words, invest in all positive NPV projects.

If we give the proposed investment the green light, Step 4 is to implement the investment. Finally, once the project has been implemented, Step 5 occurs: Follow-up, project reviews, and audits are required to confirm whether the project has delivered value as promised and to hold decision makers accountable for committing investor capital to the project.

What does EVA have to offer in this context? The process for value-creating investment is clear enough, as are the quantitative tools for identifying value creation. Asserting value creation as the corporate goal and educating managers on the use of discounted cashflow techniques, however, are merely necessary conditions for success. They are far from sufficient.

Consider Step 1 in the capital allocation process: identifying potentially positive NPV investments. It is not enough just to tell managers that this is their primary mission. They must also be motivated to seek out such investments. Perhaps in a more perfect world, managers would do the right thing for their shareholders without having to be paid for it. But managers have their own agendas, which often conflict with those of the shareholders. One of the great challenges of corporate governance is to devise management contracts and compensation systems that bring both agendas into closer alignment. By linking a portion of managerial pay to EVA, we can provide that added bit of incentive that can spell the difference between adequate performers and managers who are bound and determined to seek out every possible opportunity for achieving wealth creation.

EVA (especially when linked to compensation) not only contributes to value-creating behavior at the beginning of the capital allocation process but also promotes value creation in the implementation and follow-up phases. When companies value future cashflows from projects, often much of the value comes from the first years of a project's life. Given the principles of discounting, such a result is hardly surprising. However, while a project appears to be value-creating, the value creation depends on the ability of management to deliver positive cashflows on time. Delays in project implementation caused by logistical, technical, or personnel problems can lead to delays in the receipt of future cashflows by several months or more. Even if all the cashflows materialize as anticipated, if they arrive later than originally expected, the present value of the cashflows declines. Sometimes, such delays are all that it takes to transform what would otherwise be a positive NPV project into a value destroyer.

This is why some companies are paying extra attention to rapid implementation, time to market, and other factors critical in ensuring that cashflows come on stream sooner rather than later. One advantage of EVA is that linking it to management bonuses provides the added sense of urgency that managers may need to implement projects quickly enough for the company to realize the value promised by those projects.

Finally, once implementation has occurred and the assets are in place, managers need incentives to use those assets as efficiently as possible. Because EVA imposes capital charges on assets, regardless of how the company chooses to finance them, managers whose bonuses are based on EVA have a powerful motivation to squeeze whatever profits and cashflow are possible from those assets.

CONCLUSION

In this chapter we've learned the basics about EVA and key valuation principles such as discounted cashflow and internal rate of return. We also examined the limitations market value added can pose and discussed a possible solution in the form of excess return. We then took an in-depth look at how to calculate and interpret EVA.

Now that we have the fundamentals of EVA under our belts, we can look at how to actually implement it. In Chapter 3, we'll take an overview of the EVA implementation process, including some potential pitfalls and their solutions.

CHAPTER 3

Implementing EVA

The widespread adoption of EVA began in the early 1990s, enough experience to tell us not only what it has done for companies, but also the challenges and pitfalls to look out for. We begin this chapter with a case study of SPX, a large auto parts and industrial products company, and how EVA contributed to an eightfold increase in its share price within four years of adoption.

We will then draw more general lessons on how EVA affects managerial behavior and improves corporate performance, citing examples from several EVA users. Next, we will discuss the major steps involved in a successful EVA implementation, while also contrasting the characteristics of firms with successful EVA programs from those with less positive experiences.

Finally, we will show that while the basic ideas behind it have been known for a long time, EVA *is* a major step forward because it promotes management practices that can deliver superior financial results.

AN EVA SUCCESS STORY: THE CASE OF SPX

SPX was a chronic underperformer in the early 1990s, with low profits and a languishing share price. After John Blystone was hired as CEO in 1995, the company ushered in a series of actions designed to reverse its poor performance. The 1995 annual report proclaimed, "One of the most important of these actions has been the decision to move ahead as quickly as possible to implement EVA."

Formal adoption took place at the end of 1995, and by the end of the following year, a dramatic improvement in performance was already evident. EVA increased by nearly $27 million from the previous year. In the 1996 annual report, the company stated that "EVA, or economic value added, is the gauge of our success. It has helped us improve both our operating performance and the use of capital. More importantly, it has been a catalyst in producing a quick financial turnaround and is driving cultural change."

Improvements continued, and in the following year, the company confidently announced in its 1997 annual report that "EVA continues to be a catalyst for our success. The transformation of this company began in 1995, when SPX had negative EVA of $50 million. Today, nearly 80 percent of SPX associates participate in EVA incentive compensation plans, directly aligning their interests with those of our shareholders. After two years of significant EVA improvement, we are well on our way to making SPX an EVA-positive company in 1998."

In fact, SPX's cumulative EVA improvement reached $60 million in 1998 and $130 million in 1999. By the end of the 1990s, this chronic underperformer had been transformed into a powerful value creator. What did SPX do to achieve this remarkable turnaround, and how was it able to sustain the initial momentum to continue delivering sizable year-on-year improvements after adopting EVA?

What makes this company's experience so instructive is that it was able to create a business culture that put value creation at the center of all key management processes and systems. As the company explained in its 1998 annual report, "EVA is the foundation of everything we do. . . . It is a common language, a mindset, and the way we do business." But while EVA and value-based thinking was infused in all of the company's major business practices, the most important contribution of EVA to the turnaround was its central role in management compensation. The specific actions taken by SPX to deliver such dramatic performance improvement were neither unusual nor particularly innovative. Any competent executive should be familiar with them. The key lesson of the SPX experience, however, is not whether managers are capable of delivering superior performance, but whether they are motivated to do so.

SPX achieved this crucial change in management outlook by making EVA the centerpiece of a broad value creation process. According to the 1999 annual report, one element of this process was to "drive the results expected by shareholders." As we showed in Chapter 2, the key to wealth creation is to exceed the expectations of EVA improvement reflected in a company's share price. SPX motivated managers to do this by tying bonuses to fixed EVA improvement targets, which in turn were derived from the company's share price. Although we will wait until Chapter 8 before showing you how to derive these targets, the important point here is that management had an incentive to achieve, and even exceed, the EVA improvements that SPX shareholders had already paid for. This practice goes to the very heart of value-driven compensation, because it strongly aligns the incentives of managers with those of shareholders. SPX further strengthened these incentives through the use of stock options. As we will see in Chapter 4, stock options play a vital role in value-driven compensation plans because they create strong, value-oriented wealth incentives for managers and provide long-term incentives for value creation, in contrast to EVA bonus plans, which focus mainly on short- and medium-term incentives.

As many EVA companies have done, SPX began with only its most senior managers on the EVA bonus plan, but it quickly expanded participation to a much broader group. In January 1996, 185 managers were put on the EVA bonus plan, increasing to 1000 six months later and 4700 managers by January 1997. In 1997, outside directors were also given target bonuses tied to EVA.

As a result of these strong incentives, SPX engaged in a broad range of actions, all with one purpose: creating shareholder value. For example:

1. *SPX focused its operating units on quality and operating excellence.* One such unit began a next-day delivery policy that helped it to achieve market leadership in North America. Operating efficiencies and sourcing initiatives drove a 12.5 percent improvement in operating profit in 1997.

2. *SPX redefined its core businesses.* In 1996, the company identified specialty service tools as its core business. But two years later, SPX acquired General Signal, a large manufacturer of industrial valves, power transformers, data networking equipment, and a variety of other products. SPX now defines its core businesses as Service Solutions, Technical Products and Systems, Industrial Products, and Vehicle Components.

3. *SPX made a series of acquisitions, mostly small, to advance its value creation strategy.* For example, it acquired Barley Fire Protection in 1999 to provide its life-safety systems business with additional products for growth in the Canadian market. The acquisition of Advanced Performance Technology in that same year expanded SPX's traditional focus on automatic transmission filters to other filtration applications.

4. *SPX consolidated divisions for greater operating efficiency.* For example, in 1996 three divisions were combined into a single tool and equipment division to serve auto manufacturers, while three other tool and equipment divisions were combined to serve the aftermarket. This effort resulted in the closing of two manufacturing facilities, a distribution facility, and the consolidation of sales, marketing, engineering, and administrative functions. The overall cost was about $18 million, but by 1998 annual savings of $23 million were expected.

5. *SPX divested businesses that were apparently worth more to other companies.* For example, as the company explained in its 1999 annual report, "While Best Power had been part of SPX for only a year, we substantially enhanced its performance during that time, as measured by an operating margin improvement from 5 to 13 percent. Best Power's business focus, market share, and relative size made it more valuable to others, so we decided to sell it."

6. *SPX undertook many finance-based initiatives to create shareholder value.* For example, it eliminated its quarterly dividend in 1997 in favor of stock repurchases, a more tax-efficient way of returning cash to shareholders.

What effect did these reactions have on shareholder wealth? When EVA was implemented at the end of 1995, SPX's share price was under $16. By summer 2000, it was selling for nearly $120.

WHAT DO MANAGERS DO IN EVA COMPANIES?

The SPX example shows how the adoption of EVA-linked incentives can lead to a dramatic improvement in a company's financial performance and a sharp increase in its share price. What conclusions can be drawn then about how the adoption of EVA affects managerial behavior?

In Chapter 2, we showed that

$$EVA = (RONA - WACC) \text{ invested capital}$$

This means, holding other variables constant, that EVA increases, and shareholder value is created, when RONA increases, WACC decreases, invested capital increases (assuming new investments earn a RONA greater than the WACC), or invested capital decreases (assuming that the improvement in the spread between RONA and WACC caused by divesting chronic money-losing assets more than offsets the reduction of capital). As the evidence from scores of EVA adopters shows, managers achieve these improvements by

1. *Increasing asset turnover.* For example, Herman Miller, an office furniture company, managed to cut inventories by 24 percent in a two-year period while sales increased by 38 percent. It also cut its days of receivables from 45 in 1992 to 30 in 1997. The cut in receivables is especially interesting because the impetus for this improvement came from the company's operating managers, not the accountants. As Al Ehrbar explains in *EVA: The Real Key to Creating Wealth,* "When they went on EVA and began focusing on capital costs like receivables, Miller employees in the divisions attacked the late payment problem on their own and discovered that the cause of overdue receivables was incomplete orders. When an order arrived missing a piece or two, the customer would withhold all payments until the last items arrived. So the Millerites got receivables down by speeding up production of those missing items and making sure shipments were complete as

well as on time. The result: improvements in both EVA and customer satisfaction."[1] SPX too witnessed dramatic improvement in
asset efficiency. In the first year after adoption of EVA, inventories
were cut by 15 percent, despite higher sales than in the previous
year.

2. *Disposing of unprofitable businesses.* For example, Armstrong, a plastics and floor products company, sold one of its largest divisions when it concluded that the company was incapable
of producing a cost-of-capital return on the $338 million selling
price.[2] In the case of SPX, several divested businesses were profitable, but strategic reviews revealed that the businesses were
worth more to others, and therefore should be sold.

3. *Repairing assets, when possible, instead of replacing them.*
Many companies discover that when managers are placed on EVA
incentive plans, there is a far greater desire to refurbish existing
assets, instead of requesting a capital budget to buy new ones.
Also, when additional capacity is required, managers are more
likely to acquire used assets. This practice has proven especially
popular with trucks, forklifts, and a wide range of factory assets.
The rapid growth of Internet-based secondary markets in capital
goods has made this easier than ever.

4. *Structuring deals that require less capital.* Before it adopted
EVA, Armstrong insisted on having a controlling stake in any acquisition. After adoption, the company began to define the minimum amount of capital that it could put into a deal and still get
what it wanted out of it.[3] Paper and paper products manufacturer
Boise Cascade had a similar goal in mind when it changed the
way it sources raw materials. Before EVA, the company relied
mainly on contracts in which it made an up-front payment for the
right to cut timber over a preset period, usually one to three years.
The practice, known as "timber under contracts," or TUCs, protected the company from swings in the price of logs, but because
of the up-front payment, it also tied up capital. The capital charge
imposed by EVA showed that the price protection offered by the
TUCs was far more expensive than previously thought. As a re-

1. Al Ehrbar, *EVA: The Real Key to Creating Wealth*, New York: John Wiley & Sons, 1998,
      pp. 20–21.
2. Ehrbar, p. 59.
3. Ehrbar, p. 60.

sult, managers began negotiating harder with landowners and entered into fewer TUCs.[4]

5. *Increasing leverage.* As we will discuss in Chapter 5, the natural proclivity of most managers is to underlever their businesses, which means that they rely too much on equity finance and not enough on debt. EVA changes all that, because when managers are charged for capital at the WACC, they have powerful incentives to design capital structures that minimize the WACC. For the underlevered firm, this means taking on more debt, which is precisely what many companies have done after adopting EVA. Engine and turbine producer Briggs & Stratton and credit reporting company Equifax are just two examples among many.

What these examples show is that when managers are evaluated and paid on the basis of EVA, they are more likely than their counterparts in other companies to make the sort of operating, investing, and financing decisions that deliver superior value to shareholders.

EVA AND CULTURE CHANGE

EVA is much more than a measurement system. It's also an instrument for changing managerial behavior. It is about changing mind-sets, getting managers to think differently about their work. Implementing value-based principles requires acceptance and understanding among all managers, who not only must appreciate why value creation is so important but also must grasp the fundamental concepts underlying value creation, such as net present value. In short, one of the cornerstones of value-based management is to make finance accessible to all managers, not just the specialists. If managers are to be expected to create value, they must first understand what value means and how capital markets determine it. One of the great virtues of EVA is that it makes sound finance theory accessible, so that operating managers, including those with no background or experience in accounting or finance, can incorporate insights from these disciplines into the way they run their businesses.

---

4. Ehrbar, p. 64.

Finance professionals too must change their thinking. Traditionally, finance departments have been viewed as guardians of the company's scarce capital, and enforcers who control operations and ensure compliance with the company's reporting policies. Value-based management requires a profound change in the finance professional's mind-set. No longer are they just capital allocators or enforcers, although they continue to bear important control responsibilities. Instead, they must become partners with their operating colleagues, helping them to use the insights and technologies that finance has to offer to identify where value is created in a company and where it is destroyed, which projects to invest in and which to avoid.

Changing attitudes among operating managers requires transparency in the finance and accounting functions, which means not only communicating clear financial goals to employees but also achieving "buy-in." Managers and employees must understand what the company's financial goals are, why those goals were chosen, and what they can do to achieve them. Buy-in, or acceptance of the value-creating imperative, is impossible without such understanding. A growing number of CFOs are learning this lesson.

Remember all the fuss about quality in the 1980s and the resulting growth of total quality management programs? We learned that quality is everyone's responsibility. Value creation, too, is the responsibility of every employee, not just top managers and finance specialists. Finance and accounting professionals lay the groundwork through proper measuring and reporting of results. Finance also contributes in designing appropriate capital structures that minimize the company's cost of capital. But the real value creation rests with operating managers and their employees. These are the people who produce and sell the company's products and services, work closely with customers and suppliers, and create the organizational competencies that make serious value creation possible.

THE EVA IMPLEMENTATION PROCESS

Thousands of companies around the world have at least some experience with EVA and value-based management. Their experiences teach us a lot about what works and what doesn't, and how companies should go about the process of gaining acceptance of EVA among their employees. The first lesson of implementing EVA is that while others have much to teach us, the process is intensely company-specific. Each system must be tailor-made for the company that will use it.

Box 3–1 shows the major steps we advise companies to take in implementing EVA. Because EVA and value-based management are really about changing behavior and attitudes, acceptance must begin at the very top. Although the idea of using EVA is often first proposed by the CFO or the corporate controller, the implementation process must begin with the board and the CEO. The profound attitude shifts that are required to adopt meaningful value-based management practices require commitment at the very highest levels of the firm. Why should employees accept EVA and all that goes with it if the CEO does not appear totally committed to the concept? If company employees see anything less than total commitment, EVA will come to be viewed as just another management fad, "the flavor of the month," and not the powerful change agent that it can be.

In fact, for implementation to work, CEOs must be positively messianic in their zeal, disseminating the EVA message in major communications with staff, in whatever intracompany media there are, and in talks with the analyst community and portfolio managers. Basic buy-in from the CEO and other top managers must happen before the message can be effectively communicated to, and accepted by, divisional managers.

Too often, senior executives mouth empty expressions of support for their shareholders, while their understanding of value creation is superficial and their commitment is only half-hearted. Take, for example, a statement from the declaration of management and leadership principles published by one of Europe's most famous companies:

> [The company] is committed to create value for its shareholders. However, [the company] does not favor short-term profit and shareholder value maximization at the expense of long-term successful business development.[5]

Statements like this, and they are common, reflect a fundamental misunderstanding of value, how capital markets determine it and how companies create it. It is based on the false premise

---

5. S. Barr, "Misreporting Results," *CFO Magazine*, December 1998.

B O X   3—1

A CHECKLIST FOR IMPLEMENTING EVA

Step 1: Establish buy-in at the board and top management levels.
Step 2: Make the major strategic decisions on the EVA program (subject to board approval).

How will EVA measurement centers be defined?
How will EVA be calculated?

   ◆ What adjustments will be made?
   ◆ Divisional versus corporate cost of capital
   ◆ Are changes needed to the company's accounting system?
   ◆ How often will EVA be calculated?

Management compensation

   ◆ Who will be covered initially, and will there be a gradual expansion of participation in EVA-based incentives?
   ◆ Sensitivity of bonuses to EVA performance
   ◆ Will there be a deferred component, and if so, for which managers?
   ◆ The role of stock options in the compensation program
   ◆ Mix of divisional versus company-wide or group EVA bonuses
   ◆ Relation to nonfinancial measures

Step 3: Develop an implementation plan.
Step 4: Set up a training program:

Who will need the training?
How will the training needs be executed?

   ◆ Number of training sessions per employee
   ◆ How will the concept be explained?
   ◆ Ongoing training, after initial implementation

that actions that sacrifice "long-term successful business development" can actually create shareholder value because profits are
boosted in the short term. While many actions companies take can
increase short-term profits (such as cutting back on advertising
and research), if such actions erode the long-term competitiveness
of the company and compromise its ability to generate free cashflows in the future, value will be destroyed. And the destruction
of value will be felt now (or at least when the capital markets
conclude that long-term competitiveness has truly been eroded),
not years in the future. Executives and consultants tasked with
implementing value-based management systems in companies
must take it upon themselves to convince top management that
there are no inconsistencies between value and long-term business
development. Quite the contrary. Value creation is not possible
without it.

Convincing the board and senior managers to think properly
about value is only the start. As shown in Box 3–1, after the board,
the CEO, and other top managers have accepted value-based management and the use of EVA, key strategic decisions must be made
regarding program design.

For example, how will the company define EVA centers? Or
to put it another way, how far down in the organizational hierarchy will EVA be calculated. A logical starting point is to define
EVA centers on the basis of existing profit centers. This approach
offers two key advantages. First, it limits EVA calculation to business units with significant income statement and balance sheet
responsibilities. In units where managers do not have such responsibilities, EVA components (or what are commonly known as
value drivers) are more useful measures of performance than EVA
itself. A second advantage of this approach is that the required
financial reporting machinery is already in place. The only major
difference is that EVA measurement requires estimates of the
WACC in order to calculate capital charges. Although some EVA
consultants have expended considerable efforts in trying to bring
EVA calculations deeper into organizations, our experience tells
us that such efforts rarely succeed. Later in this chapter, we will
discuss why.

A decision must also be made as to how EVA will be calculated. The most critical question here is whether any adjustments
will be made for perceived biases or distortions in the company's

accounting policies. In the calculation template we presented in the Chapter 2, numbers are taken from a company's financial reports without deviation from standard accounting rules, or generally accepted accounting principles. But as we will see later in this chapter, and in still greater detail in Chapter 6, EVA users can choose from a broad range of potential adjustments which, if used properly, can produce a "better" EVA number—one that is more solidly grounded in economic reality. The problem, however, is that adjustments add to the complexity of the measurement system and thus make it harder for operating managers to understand. An additional concern for decision makers is whether there is sufficient information technology (IT) support for the EVA reporting system. They must also decide, based partly on IT constraints, how frequently EVA will be calculated and reported, and whether the WACCs used for calculating divisional EVAs will be based on a single corporate rate or customized for each division.

While the definition of EVA centers and the determination of how EVA will be calculated are important issues, by far the most crucial of all strategic decisions centers on incentive compensation. Two keys lessons should be stated immediately. First, EVA implementation is largely pointless unless management pay is tied to it in a systematic way. This practice goes to the very heart of value-based management. Second, policy decisions on compensation are so delicate that they cannot be delegated. The CEO and other top managers must be involved every step of the way in deciding what the EVA bonus plan is going to look like.

For example, which managers will have bonuses linked to EVA, and what proportion of target, or expected, compensation is covered by the EVA bonus plan? This decision requires both a short-term perspective (who will go on the EVA plan immediately) and a longer-term perspective (who will go on the EVA plan at a later date). A popular approach, described briefly in the SPX example, is to include only senior managers at first, gradually expanding participation to a broader group of employees. Decisions must also be made on how sensitive the EVA bonus will be to under- or overperformance relative to targets, whether there will be a deferred component to compensation, the use of stock options, and the role, if any, of non-EVA measures (such as nonfinancial value drivers) in the compensation plan.

Once these strategic decisions are made, emphasis shifts to developing an implementation plan. Many companies carry out this step by appointing a full-time EVA coordinator, supported by a working committee. This committee works out technical details, such as IT support, and ensures that the compensation elements of the program take proper account of local labor and tax laws. For example, will the bonus plan deliver pay in a tax-efficient manner?

One of the most critical tasks in EVA implementation is designing a training program that draws genuine commitment to value creation from the company's employees. In large companies, the scale of such training can be immense. For example, JCPenney, the large American retailer, trains 20,000 employees each year on EVA.

For most EVA users, the training task is undertaken in stages. Preliminary sessions, sometimes lasting no more than 30 to 45 minutes, introduce employees to the concept. The major aim is to explain the basic ideas behind EVA and why top management has chosen it. Emphasis is placed on the link between EVA and the need for the company to ensure that it earns a competitive return on capital.

Subsequent sessions explore EVA in more detail, likely lasting at least two hours and maybe half a day. Topics include the calculation of EVA, how to interpret the numbers, and ideas on the steps employees can take to boost EVA in their divisions or departments. Short case studies from the company's own experience, or from the experiences of other companies, are especially helpful for this purpose. Employees may also be introduced to the EVA-linked compensation plan, although the sensitivity of any topic having to do with pay may require a separate, dedicated session. In any event, we generally recommend the introduction to EVA and a detailed discussion of how the metric will be linked to bonuses be covered at separate meetings.

From our experience, expecting employees to digest everything in one sitting is not reasonable. EVA is really about culture change, and such change requires reflection. Often, companies will schedule the introductory session and more detailed workshops at least several weeks apart.

A PROFILE OF SUCCESSFUL AND UNSUCCESSFUL USERS

We are often asked if EVA works in all companies. While it is certainly true that all companies can benefit from the shareholder value perspective offered by EVA, on a practical level some companies are far more likely to benefit from it than others. We summarize these differences in Table 3–1.

An important part of the EVA story is that it can provide value creation incentives for divisional managers, not just for top corporate-level executives. This suggests that companies with several largely autonomous business units benefit more from EVA than companies that operate like one large business unit. We have also found that matrix organizations tend to derive fewer benefits from EVA because of the difficulty of establishing accountability for compensation purposes. In addition, companies with substantial shared resources are less likely to benefit from EVA. For example, if common manufacturing facilities or sales staff serve multiple business units, and if these units are not forced to "buy" this manufacturing or selling capacity, investment accountability, EVA measurement, and management incentives can be undermined.

Another critical difference between successful and unsuccessful users is that the former rely on strong managerial wealth incentives tied to business unit performance. The latter tend to place a far heavier emphasis on stock options. Successful EVA companies also rely on stock options (creating the proper long-term incentives are nearly impossible without them), but recognize that the strongest incentives for divisional managers come from line-of-sight measures, not corporate measures such as stock

T A B L E   3–1

A Profile of Successful and Unsuccessful Users of EVA

Successful Users	Unsuccessful Users
Autonomous business units	One large business unit
	Matrix organization
	Substantial shared resources
Strong managerial wealth incentives tied to business unit performance	Excessive emphasis on stock options
	Discretionary approach to compensation
CEO is an enthusiastic advocate	CEO doesn't realize what he/she signed up for
Business unit heads stay put	Short job tenure for business unit heads

price. Unsuccessful users are also more inclined to exercise considerable discretion in paying managers. In other words, such companies frequently override the EVA bonus plan, probably because of low tolerance for large differences in business unit compensation.

In successful EVA users, the CEO is an enthusiastic advocate, constantly reinforcing EVA in speeches and written communication. In unsuccessful users, the CEO may not have realized what he or she signed up for. Maybe EVA was adopted because the CEO thought that's what the markets wanted to hear. Or perhaps there was a failure to appreciate just how much effort was required of a full-scale implementation. As a result, implementation is spotty and erratic.

Another distinguishing feature of successful users is that they try to establish and maintain accountability for business unit heads. This, in turn, requires that these managers stay put for extended periods. In unsuccessful adopters, job tenure for business unit managers is short, and transfers are frequent. This difference is crucial because if managers move around a lot, there is no long-term accountability. And without such accountability, deferred compensation is not possible. As we will see in Chapter 4, deferred compensation, in the form of bonus banks, plays a critical role in ensuring that the EVA bonus plan forces managers to think beyond current year performance to consider what they must do to enhance EVA in future years.

COMMON PROBLEMS IN IMPLEMENTING EVA

In this chapter, we have hinted at a number of potential problems and pitfalls faced by EVA users. But in our experience, two concerns seem to emerge in just about every company, regardless of size or industry. First, executives worry that EVA, and the capital charge it imposes on all assets, discourages managers from investing, because the increased capital charges depress EVA, at least in the short term, and reduce their bonuses. A second concern relates to the measurement of EVA at divisional, and subdivisional, levels.

For the value-creating proposition of a multidivisional company to work, the company must achieve synergy, perhaps in the form of shared services or assets (for example, levering off a common brand name or distribution system), or perhaps in the form of vertical integration strategies that enable the company to capture more control over its value chain. Synergy implies interaction among divisions and between divisions and the corporate center. The problem for the implementation of EVA is that such interactions require overhead allocations and transfer prices. And as anyone who's had experience with either will testify, there is an arbitrary aspect to just about any allocation or transfer price. Unfortunately, the calculation of EVA at a divisional level in synergistic, multidivisional firms is not possible without them.

Ideally, we would like an EVA system that captures synergies in the measurement of divisional results. Otherwise, managers may be discouraged from cooperating with each other, impairing the company's ability to realize the synergies, and destroying value in the process. However, capturing these synergies in the EVA measurement system is sometimes complicated, and often frustrating, so much so that many companies are discouraged from creating EVA centers below the level of large divisions.

The Underinvestment Problem

One common fear of EVA is that it can lead managers to underinvest, both in physical assets and in assets of a less tangible nature, such as R&D and brand equity. This fear stems from the capital charges imposed by EVA and from the belief that managers will try to boost their EVA, and their EVA-linked bonuses, by milking assets: limiting investment in anything not expected to offer an immediate payoff. Although the concern is valid, if implemented properly EVA is unlikely to reduce incentives for undertaking value-creating investments; indeed, it should actually increase them.

First, as we will discuss in detail in Chapter 4, EVA bonuses for senior managers can be paid into bonus banks, where some of the EVA bonuses earned in previous years are held, pending future performance. To access these bonuses, and to earn additional bonuses in the future, managers realize that EVA figures must improve over the long term. It is not sufficient to achieve high EVAs and maintain them. Instead, EVA is expected to increase continuously, especially if the value of the firm includes a sizable future growth value component. Cost-cutting and the milking of existing assets can squeeze out additional EVA in the short term, but managers soon learn that improving efficiency can take them only so far. At some point, working capital is cut to the bone and the asset base is as tenuous as operations will allow. Any further improvement in EVA must come from growth and additional investment. In short, by emphasizing change, instead of levels, in EVA bonus plans, top management can partially neutralize potential underinvestment problems.

The underinvestment problem can be alleviated further through the use of nonfinancial value drivers. For example, if product innovation is viewed as an important indicator of long-term value creation, managerial bonuses can be based on measures of product innovation, in addition to EVA, to help ensure that adequate attention and investment are devoted to innovation.

An alternative solution is to place large investments "off-book" in suspense accounts. The amounts are then brought gradually into invested capital, instead of being charged in full from the moment the investment is made. For example, if a division makes a $20 million investment that will temporarily, and significantly, depress EVA in the short term, thereby reducing the incentive to make the investment, the division's invested capital for EVA measurement purposes can be increased over, say, an estimated payback period. If the payback period is expected to be four years, $5 million is added to invested capital in the current year ($20 million ÷ 4 years), with the remaining $15 million placed in a suspense account. Then gradually, over the ensuing three years, $15 million (plus interest at the cost of capital) is taken out of the suspense account and added to invested capital. In this way, the division does not have to bear a full charge for the capital investment until the benefits are expected to be fully on stream.

Finally, stock options reduce the underinvestment problem because they provide long-term incentives for value creation. Although stock options provide only weak line of sight for divisional managers, they do offer strong wealth creation incentives for corporate executives. Stock options also provide managers with payoffs from investments that might depress EVA in the short term but increase it in the long term. The fact is that EVA adopters have been no less eager to grow their businesses than competitors who use more conventional metrics in their bonus plans. A casual perusal of the *Wall Street Journal* or the *Financial Times* over a period of several weeks will reveal several pronouncements of major capital spending plans by well-known EVA firms, which suggests that the use of EVA has not deterred managers in these companies from investing aggressively when profitable opportunities arise.

To summarize, the underinvestment problems can be at least partly neutralized through the use of

+ Deferred compensation
+ Value drivers that are related to *future* EVAs
+ Suspense accounts
+ Stock options

The Synergy Problem

"Take EVA to the factory floor," some EVA proponents are fond of saying, and it's not hard to see why. Any unit in any company with operating profits and assets also has an EVA. If pay is tied to unit EVAs, or so the theory goes, we can harness the value-creating potential of *all* employees, not just top managers.

Yet resistance to using EVA below the strategic business unit level is strong, even in the most enthusiastic EVA companies. Sometimes management's reluctance is caused by its desire to avoid radical and potentially demoralizing changes, choosing instead to implement value-based management ideas in a gradual fashion. Ideas such as EVA-linked bonuses are tried first at senior management levels and then, if they are deemed a success, can be taken to lower-level employees as well.

In other cases, this reluctance is the result of legitimate concerns over the utility of metrics like EVA below divisional level. To provide more insight into the nature of these concerns, we discuss several conceptual issues in divisional performance measurement.

When we calculate EVA for divisions, we implicitly assume that these units are independent, in much the same way as they would be if their managers took them private in a management buyout. In short, we assume no synergies among the divisions or between the divisions and higher levels of the company. But, in fact, synergies usually do exist.

One common source of synergy is share facilities. By combining two or more entities under the same corporate umbrella, duplication of effort can be eliminated, realizing savings in a broad range of corporate services, including R&D, information technology, human resource management, product design, and marketing. Share facilities require cost allocations to ensure that business unit decisions are based on full, not partial, costs. But bad cost allocations can lead to bad decisions. For example, if an expense, such as R&D, is allocated on the basis of revenue (a common approach) when revenue does not cause the expense to increase, incremental sales that increase shareholder wealth may be rejected because they do not appear profitable.

A second common source of synergy is vertical integration, which provides the company with more control over its value chain, because units in the company sell services or intermediate products to other units in the same company. Vertical integration requires transfer prices to establish business unit revenue and/or expense, and bad transfer prices can lead to bad decisions. If its raw material is overpriced, a business unit may reduce production of a product because it appears to be EVA negative when, in fact, if the supply division's EVA were taken into account, the sales would be EVA positive.

EVA implementation is unlikely to have a big impact on company performance when shared facilities represent a large percentage of business unit assets (e.g., consumer and business customer units sharing the basic network in a telephone company) or intercompany transactions account for a large part of cost of goods sold or sales (e.g., refining and marketing in an integrated oil company). In these cases, a large percentage of employees often end up in one large business unit where their individual actions have little impact on business unit performance. In this situation, EVA incentives have little impact on company performance.

When shared facilities are a small part of total assets or intercompany transactions are few, cost allocation or transfer pricing issues rarely present a major obstacle to successful EVA implementation. In between, however, are the many cases where cost allocation and/or transfer pricing issues can require significant problem solving for EVA implementation to work. Later in this chapter, we'll discuss some alternative approaches that companies use to make EVA implementation successful.

Controllability: A Closer Look

All companies engage in operating, investing, and financing activities. Operating activities are the day-to-day tasks of converting materials, labor, and overhead into products that are then sold and converted into cashflows when receivables owed by customers are paid. These activities include the manufacturing process, inventory management, sales and marketing, the management of customer accounts, and any other function required to get a company's operating cycle to turn. Investing activities consist of buying and selling long-term assets, including land, buildings, machinery, and equipment, and financial securities such as government bonds or shares in other companies. Financing activities concern capital structure events, such as borrowing funds, issuing shares, paying dividends, and buying back shares.

The responsibility that a unit manager has over each of these activities indicates how decentralized that unit is. Some divisions function as stand-alone units with wide discretion over operations and investing, although major financing choices are nearly always made at the corporate level. In such cases, divisional reporting and financial metrics will differ little from those used at the companywide level. But when significant decision-making power over a unit rests with the unit manager's superiors, different sorts of performance reports and measures are needed.

These differences are most commonly expressed in the language of responsibility accounting and responsibility centers. A responsibility center is a decentralized unit within a larger entity that is headed by a responsible manager. The term *responsibility* implies that the unit manager has significant decision-making authority over some aspects of the unit's activities. Otherwise, the manager cannot be held responsible for the performance of the unit.

Most companies with decentralized organizational structures have three types of responsibility centers: cost centers, profit centers, and investment centers. In a *cost center*, inputs, or expenses, are measured in monetary terms, but output is not. Managers of such units are typically evaluated by means of productivity measures that relate the quantity of inputs used to generate the required outputs. Because these managers are not held responsible for selling the company's final products or services, they are not judged on revenues (i.e., monetary outputs) or profits.

In *profit centers*, both inputs and outputs are measured in monetary terms. Managers of these units are typically evaluated on measures that relate expenses (monetary inputs) to revenues (monetary outputs), such as operating profit or gross margin.

An *investment center* is a special type of profit center whose unit manager has not only profit responsibility but also some influence over capital expenditures. Managers are accountable both for operating profit and for the capital used to generate those profits. In other words, they have both income statement and balance sheet responsibility. Measures such as RONA were developed for this purpose. It is also important to note that EVA is an investment center measure of performance, as our discussion will show.

Thus far, we have defined EVA as after-tax operating profit (or NOPAT), net of capital charges. Let's examine these elements in greater detail, beginning with gross margin:

$$\text{Revenues} - \text{cost of goods sold} = \text{gross margin}$$

where cost of goods sold includes all manufacturing costs and overhead for units of product sold during the year (in the case of a manufacturing firm) or the cost of the merchandise inventory sold during the year (for retailers and distributors). Subtracting R&D and selling, general, and administrative (SG&A) expenses from gross margin yields the operating profit:

$$\text{Gross margin} - \text{R\&D} - \text{SG\&A expenses} = \text{operating profit}$$

where SG&A is a catchall category that includes all operating expenses, apart from R&D and cost of goods sold. Operating profit is a pretax measure and represents the *NOP* portion of NOPAT. We then subtract tax to arrive at NOPAT.

Now consider the capital charges. Invested capital is the sum of debt and shareholders' equity. At divisional levels, however, capital is usually measured from an operating, or asset, perspective, instead of from the financing view discussed in Chapter 2. In other words, invested capital is defined as net assets, which is the sum of the working capital requirement, fixed assets, and cash (although cash is often excluded in divisional performance measurement). The working capital requirement consists of inventories and receivables, net of accounts payable and accrued expenses. Net assets are then multiplied by a divisional cost of capital to calculate capital charges.

Let's recap the financial statement components that go into the calculation of EVA:

Revenue
Cost of goods sold
Research and development
Selling, general, and administrative expenses
Operating profit
Income taxes
Net operating profit after tax
Inventories
Receivables
Accounts payable
Fixed assets
Debt
Shareholders' equity

Quite simply, EVA includes *everything* in the income statement and balance sheet. This attribute is one of its strengths; it is a "total factor" measure of performance, incorporating the cost of labor and other inputs, *and* the cost of capital. Unlike operating profit or gross margin, which ignore the balance sheet entirely, or net income, which considers only the cost of assets financed with debt, EVA includes the full impact of the balance sheet in the measurement of divisional results.

The comprehensiveness of EVA is not just a virtue; it is a potential weakness as well. If the entity or division being measured is a largely independent unit, with nearly full decision-making power granted to the divisional manager—including influence over major investment decisions—EVA can serve as a highly effective performance measure. Indeed, under such circumstances, EVA is arguably the best measure of short-term performance because it incorporates profits *and* the productivity of capital. But, as we noted earlier, two critical assumptions underlie this assertion: Divisional management has broad decision-making power over operating and investing activities (major financing decisions are normally made at the corporate level); and either cost allocations and transfer prices have a minimal impact on business unit EVA or the company has developed credible (and defensible) systems for cost allocation and transfer pricing.

When these assumptions prove less valid, EVA starts to lose power as a measure of a manager's contribution to shareholder value. It therefore loses its effectiveness as a motivating tool. This is not to say that EVA should not be used, but it does mean that EVA figures have to be interpreted with caution, and that other criteria are needed to develop comprehensive and meaningful evaluations of performance.

When a total factor measure such as EVA is inappropriate or unworkable, management must seek out value drivers that are strongly correlated with EVA but easier to measure and more directly controllable by unit managers. Not only must senior managers select the appropriate subset of the financial statement components listed above in designing effective measures of financial performance, but they may also need to identify *non*financial measures that can act as leading indicators of future EVAs.

To put it another way, the total factor nature of EVA makes it a "noisy" measure of performance because important components of the EVA calculation are often beyond the control of the managers being evaluated. Companies must be careful to match performance metrics with managerial roles and authority. For this reason, lower-level line managers and functional specialists (human resources, finance, information technology, etc.) are typically evaluated on the basis of detailed value drivers instead of divisional EVA.

The Synergy and Controllability Problems: Potential Solutions

There is no surefire solution to the measurement and controllability problems that arise in divisional performance measurement. But several practices have merit. Of course, each has its flaws or limitations too. Some approaches are designed to produce "better" transfer prices or overhead allocations, while others aim to reduce the potential for conflict among affected managers.

1. *Value drivers.* The most popular approach to the controllability problem is to select value drivers that can be more easily and directly linked to middle- and lower-level managers than broad measures such as EVA. This approach has the twin virtues of tying measurement more closely to the responsibilities of employees below senior manager ranks and of largely sidestepping transfer pricing and overhead allocation issues. We explore this topic in detail in Chapter 7.

2. *Creating groups of divisions.* If there are significant interdependencies between several operating divisions, one possible solution to allocation or transfer pricing problems is to combine the divisions into a group, and then evaluate performance at the group level. This approach doesn't solve the synergy problem entirely because there may be interdependencies *among* groups. But it does offer the important advantage of giving the head of the group an incentive to capture the synergies among the divisions that make up the group, and to resolve any conflicts within the group over the allocation of costs and revenues. The measurement problem doesn't disappear entirely, because the group head must still evaluate the performance of divisional managers. However, any arbitrary overhead allocation or transfer pricing policies used within the group to measure divisional results will have no effect on the measurement of group performance.

There are potential drawbacks to this approach. Creating groups adds another layer of management, and thus another bureaucratic hurdle for divisional managers who need to respond quickly to changes in product markets. There is also a potential free-rider problem. When divisional managers are evaluated on group performance, they may be inclined to relax and rely on their colleagues for superior performance.

3. *Linking part of the EVA bonus to EVA in other divisions.* If there is significant interaction between two divisions, one way to encourage cooperation and reduce the potential for conflict that sometimes arises because of overhead allocation or transfer pricing is to base part of each manager's EVA bonus on the EVA in the other division. For example, 70 percent of the divisional EVA bonus for a divisional manager is based on own-division EVA, while the other 30 percent is linked to the other division's EVA. One problem with this approach is that it can be costly and complicated to administer, especially when more than two divisions are involved. A second problem is that a manager's share of an incremental dollar of EVA in his or her own division is normally much greater than the manager's share of an incremental dollar of EVA in the other division, so that the manager is still better off increasing his or her own division's EVA at the expense of the other division's EVA.

4. *Cost allocation to encourage cooperation.* Professor Jerold Zimmerman of the University of Rochester proposes that all shared overhead costs be allocated to divisions on the basis of divisional profitability.[6] Although the resulting allocations are obviously distorted from a pure measurement perspective, divisional managers have incentives to increase other divisions' EVAs to reduce their own allocated overhead costs. This may also reduce the tendency for divisional managers to dispute transfer prices in the knowledge that even if the prices they receive are too low or the prices they pay are too high, their allocated overhead will decrease. This policy can then be reinforced by linking a portion of each manager's cash bonus to corporate EVA so that they can share in the gains that come from increased cooperation.

5. *Activity-based costing.* Traditional approaches to overhead cost allocation are based on measures of output or volume. Companies create cost pools that are then allocated to products or business units on a basis such as revenues, number of employees, or labor costs. All the conventional allocation bases have one thing in common: they are all volume related. For example, allocating an element of corporate overhead to divisions on the basis of sales implies that units with higher sales impose greater demands on the resource in question than units with lower sales. But often this is not the case. A high-sales division with steady sales, long production runs, and little product innovation imposes fewer demands on corporate support functions than a division with lower but more erratic sales, unpredictable ordering behavior by customers, short production runs, and a constant need to innovate its product line.

Activity-based costing (ABC) is a popular approach developed over the last 15 years to help companies think more ration-

6. J. L. Zimmerman, "EVA and Divisional Performance Measurement: Capturing Synergies and Other Issues," *Journal of Applied Corporate Finance,* Summer 1997, pp. 98–109.

ally about the forces that drive the consumption of overhead resources. Nonvolume allocation bases known as *cost drivers* are
identified to better reflect the cause-and-effect relationship between corporate activities and overhead costs. When they do this,
managers gain a better understanding of the forces that drive
overhead costs in their divisions.

In addition to improving the allocation of overhead costs,
ABC can also be used to assign shared assets to individual operating units, thus enhancing the accuracy of the invested capital
measure used to calculate a division's capital costs. Improving the
process of allocating overhead costs and assets to divisions enhances the quality of divisional financial reports and may produce
more reliable estimates of EVA.

6. *Innovative approaches to transfer pricing.* To promote the use
of EVA in the operating units of their clients, some consultants
have developed highly sophisticated approaches to transfer pricing. The idea is to more accurately capture the prices that the units
would observe if they were truly independent entities. One such
scheme is based on an internal auction that gives a provider of
goods or services the right to refuse the transfer price being proposed by the purchaser, or a buyer the right to refuse a good or
service for which it would be charged.[7] If the right of refusal is
not feasible, marketlike discipline can be achieved with the threat
of arbitration between the buyer and the seller. The mere
threat of either refusal or arbitration is alleged to be enough to get
all parties to arrive at a mutually acceptable transfer price.

The costs of administering such an approach are not trivial,
however. Also, senior managers normally balk at highly complicated transfer pricing schemes, despite their intellectual appeal.

ISN'T EVA JUST GOOD MANAGEMENT? WHAT'S SO NEW ABOUT IT?

It's true that the ideas behind EVA have been around a long time.
In the 1920s, Alfred Sloan implemented an EVA-like system for
General Motors' operating divisions. The Japanese company Mat-

---

7. M. Hodak, "The End of Cost Allocations as We Know Them," *Journal of Applied Corporate Finance,* Fall 1997, pp. 117–124.

sushita established a similar system in the 1930s, as did General Electric in the 1950s. In those days, most people called it something else, such as *residual income* or *economic profit*; the term *EVA* had not yet been coined. In 1965 Wharton Professor David Solomons devoted a large portion of his influential work on divisional performance measurement to residual income, helping to fuel an interest in the topic among finance and accounting academics in the 1960s and 1970s.

But until recently, companies rarely implemented residual income for performance measurement purposes. Few corporate executives really understood it or felt that they needed to, and even those who did could not figure out how to estimate the "interest" on the equity portion of a company's capital base. As residual income came to be resurrected and repackaged as EVA, three distinctive features began to emerge:

1. EVA draws on advances in capital market theory unavailable to the early users of residual income, to derive credible estimates for the cost of equity. Although the model most widely used to estimate the cost of capital for EVA purposes has been widely taught in business schools for a generation, until the 1990s it was used almost exclusively for business and project valuation. EVA extends the cost-of-capital concept to historical performance measurement. By reclaiming the residual income concept as their own, and by tying it to performance measurement, EVA's early proponents focused an unprecedented degree of attention on the cost of capital, especially in companies that link managerial pay to EVA.

2. Conventional measures of residual income accept operating profit as given. Some EVA proponents argue that any profit number based entirely on generally accepted accounting principles (GAAP), including residual income, is likely to give a seriously misleading impression of corporate performance. In a sense, residual income, in the form of EVA, has been "liberated" from GAAP. Perceived biases or distortions inherent in GAAP are corrected, providing presumably more credible measures of performance than unadjusted residual income.

3. EVA advocates go much further than earlier proponents of residual income in linking performance to management compensation. EVA is seen as a way of offering divisional management value-creating incentives similar to the stock options and other equity-based schemes set aside for top management. Of course, this argument assumes a close link between EVA and share price. The case for EVA-linked compensation is based on the assertion that as EVA grows, so too does shareholder wealth. If this is true, increases in management pay can be self-financing. In other words, managers get more pay, but in the process create more wealth for nonmanagement shareholders.

Each of these issues is so fundamental to understanding how EVA works that we discuss them in detail in later chapters. But a few introductory comments will help to put these issues in their proper context.

The Cost of Capital

EVA is based on the idea of economic profit, namely, that earning profits from an economic as opposed to an accounting perspective requires that a company cover not only all its operating expenses but also all its capital costs. These capital costs include not just the most obvious elements, such as interest payments to bankers and bondholders, but also the opportunity cost of the capital invested by the company's shareholders. EVA measurement requires companies to estimate this component of capital cost as well.

The implementation of EVA has forced companies to focus unprecedented attention on the cost of capital: how it is calculated; whether different costs of capital should be used for different divisions (and, if so, how these differences should be determined); and perhaps most important of all, how the cost of capital is to be communicated to operating managers. In our experience, one of the greatest challenges faced by implementers of EVA is convincing nonfinancial executives, such as senior line managers, that their company's cost of capital is not the interest paid to bankers. Instead, it is a function of both the cost of debt finance and the cost of equity finance, weighted for their relative proportions in the company's capital structure. Although this concept is almost universally accepted by finance professionals, it is far from obvious to most nonfinancial managers. Communicating the cost of capital to operating managers is especially critical to the success of EVA implementation, because one of the aims of an EVA program should be to get managers to consider the cost of capital when they make key operating and investing decisions. They will have to consider the cost of capital because it is a component of the EVA calculation for their divisions and will therefore affect their performance reviews and ultimately their pay. But for EVA to have the desired effect on behavior, the measurement system must be transparent and understood by all, not just by the company's finance professionals. In other words, the EVA calculations cannot be treated as a "black box."

A cornerstone of any successful EVA program is transparency and trust. This means that managers must understand how their EVA numbers are calculated, including the cost-of-capital component. We will address this topic in detail in Chapter 5.

Accounting Adjustments

Disparaging accountants and financial statements is popular among finance professionals and corporate executives. And with scores of financial reporting scandals in recent years, there is always fodder for critics of accounting. Taking advantage of skepticism about corporate financial reporting, its earliest advocates promoted EVA as a way to overcome the deceptions of accounting and produce a "true" or "economic" measure of performance.

Although EVA is still a profit measure, it is not bound by accounting conventions. If generally accepted accounting principles distort the measurement of invested capital or operating profit, users can make whatever adjustments are necessary to improve the precision of EVA as a measure of value creation. In fact, much of the selling proposition behind EVA, in contrast to the residual income measure that came before it, is the notion that adjustments are required if any short-term measure of profit, including EVA, is to achieve high correlations with share prices. (Whether these adjustments really do improve correlations will be explored in Chapter 6.) So, what is wrong with accounting? In a speech at New York University, Securities and Exchange Commission Chairman Arthur Levitt condemned what he called the "game of nods and winks" in which accounting rules are routinely bent, stretched, and manipulated. He went on to say

> I fear we are witnessing an erosion in the quality of earnings, and therefore, the quality of financial reporting. Managing may be giving way to manipulation; integrity may be losing out to illusion.[8]

---

8. S. Barr, "Misreporting Results," *CFO Magazine*, December 1998.

Whether financial reporting practices have worsened in recent years is a matter for debate. Critics have leveled similar charges against corporate accounting for many years. But Levitt's comments do express a widely held belief that accounting has somehow failed investors—and with the rapid growth in equity markets, the stakes are higher than ever. Undeniably, some recent financial reporting scandals have been truly spectacular.

Some of the dissatisfaction with financial accounting stems from the discretion managers have under GAAP. Lease financing, for example, can easily be constructed in such a way as to keep the asset and its related debt off of the balance sheet. Managers are fond of off-balance-sheet finance because they think it makes their companies look safer, and if bankers and other capital providers fail to scrutinize company finances closely enough, the managers are right.

Much of the power to manipulate financial statements comes from the application of accrual accounting. All but the very smallest businesses are required to use it. Accrual accounting came into existence because its alternative, the cash basis of accounting (in which revenues are recognized only when cash is received and expenses only when cash is paid out), leads to unquestionably misleading results. Unfortunately, accrual accounting has its own problems.

The accrual method tells companies to recognize revenue when they earn it, not necessarily when they get the cash. Sometimes companies get cash *before* the revenue is earned (when customers make advance payments), and sometimes revenue is earned *as* the cash is received (in a supermarket, for example). But in most companies, most of the time, cash is received *after* the revenue has been earned (i.e., after the sale has taken place). This is why we have accounts receivable. Without accrual accounting, there would be no receivables.

Despite the compelling logic of accruals—and the recognizing of revenue when it is earned, not necessarily when cash is received—managers have been granted considerable latitude to determine just when revenues will actually be recognized in their businesses. In other words, they get to determine what economic event triggers the recognition of revenue on the company's income statement.

For most companies, the revenue recognition decision appears straightforward: Revenue is earned when a good or service is sold. The problem is that determining the precise moment of the sale is *not* always so obvious. For example, when should a travel agent recognize revenue? Several options are available: when the customer makes a reservation, when the customer makes a down payment, when the customer pays for the ticket or holiday in full, or when the customer returns from the trip. The fact that customers might cancel reservations or seek refunds after they have already paid creates some uncertainty as to exactly what must happen (or not happen) for the travel agent to say that the revenue has been well and truly earned.

Similar issues arise in many other industries. Revenue recognition has been at the heart of several financial reporting controversies in e-commerce. For example, if a Web-based business acts as an intermediary for buyers and sellers, should its revenue be based on the gross price paid by the buyer or should it be based only on the intermediary's commission? And anyone in the construction business knows about the controversy over the accounting for long-term construction contracts. Should we use the completed contract method (in which all revenues and expenses are recognized when the project is over) or the percentage-of-completion method (in which the revenues and expenses are recognized gradually over the life of the project)? If the latter method is chosen, how do we determine the percentage completed?

The point is that while accrual accounting is, in theory, a superior way to account for a business's revenues and expenses, its application requires huge amounts of judgment and estimation. Even if managers' intentions are entirely honorable, a manager can make a poor judgment. The result will be misleading financial reports, however inadvertent the misstatements may be. And managers' intentions are not always so honorable. Sometimes they exploit the latitude given to them under GAAP and intend to mislead the capital markets. Anytime there is scope for judgment and estimation, there is also the chance of manipulation.

Applying the accrual method to expenses is just as troublesome. One of the key issues that prompted Arthur Levitt's complaint is the widespread abuse of "big bath" accounting, in which companies take so-called nonrecurring charges year after year to bury current operating expenses or to create hidden reserves that can be used to boost profits in future years. Distortions can also arise inadvertently through the treatment of goodwill, the use of LIFO (last in, first out) inventory accounting, and deferred taxes.

Another problem with contemporary accounting practice is that it is, in some respects, out-of-date. Traditionally, when companies make investments, they buy physical assets such as buildings, machines, and vehicles. These investments would appear on company balance sheets, while nearly all other expenditures—including those for research, training, and advertising—are treated as operating expenses and sent directly to the income statement. This model works fine in an economic environment dominated by smokestack industry. But with the growing dominance of the service sector and e-commerce, along with the increased resources devoted in most industries to product and process innovation, know-how, and brand equity, many companies now spend less on physical capital and more on intellectual and human capital.

Looking at this trend from an economic perspective should lead us to conclude that investment is investment, whether in the form of physical assets or assets of a less tangible nature. Accountants have struggled to keep pace with this thinking, preferring instead to treat investments in physical capital as assets while expensing investments in intangible assets. As companies devote ever-increasing resources to developing employee competence, building brand awareness, and achieving continuous innovation, the conventional accounting model becomes increasingly obsolete. In short, say critics, we need a financial reporting model that treats all investments as investments.

Capitalizing expenditures on intellectual and human capital (i.e., treating them as assets) is a troubling notion to accountants, not because the mechanics are complicated, but because the resulting assets—know-how, brands—are far more difficult than physical assets to observe, measure, and audit. To their credit, many accounting standards-setters recognize this problem and are doing their best to resolve it. But a comprehensive solution is years away, assuming it ever comes.

To correct for the deficiencies of standard financial reporting practice, some users of EVA adjust GAAP-based profits in the hope that the adjustments will produce more reliable EVA figures. Investment in R&D, for example, may be capitalized, in contrast to the standard practice of writing it off. Also, operating leases may be capitalized, putting a popular form of off-balance sheet financing into invested capital. In all, consultants have already identified over 150 potential adjustments. Many of these adjustments can improve the accuracy of accounting measurement, but they do so at a cost. They can be complex and difficult for operating managers to understand. Adjustments can also require assumptions about future performance that investors or directors may not agree with. As we will explain in Chapter 6, these trade-offs need to be evaluated to determine an appropriate set of accounting adjustments. But it is important for implementers to know that explicit policies must be adopted in their companies on how, precisely, EVA is to be calculated. In the interests of transparency, if adjustments are to be made, they must be communicated clearly to managers, especially anyone whose bonus will be tied to EVA.

Management Compensation

EVA practitioners may argue about a lot of things, but on one point they all agree: EVA implementation is a largely pointless exercise unless the company intends, at least eventually, to tie EVA to management compensation in some way. In fact, this topic is so central to our conception of how to make EVA work in companies that we devote two entire chapters to it. Chapter 4 addresses the basic concepts of EVA-linked compensation, along with the major policy issues that companies should consider in designing compensation programs. More technical issues in management compensation are covered in Chapter 8.

Compensation may be a sensitive subject, but top management and board members must come to terms with it if they are to promote a strong value-oriented culture in their companies. The simple fact is that declaring value creation to be the company's top priority is never enough. In our experience, there is no substitute for managerial incentives, and no incentive is more powerful than pay.

Value-based compensation is based on a simple idea. To get managers to focus their efforts on creating shareholder value, they must be given the proper incentives. In short, they must be paid in such a way that the amount of their pay varies, at least to some extent, with their success in creating wealth. The more wealth they create for shareholders, the higher their compensation. To put it another way, managers will not run their companies with the aim of delivering as much wealth as possible to their shareholders unless they start thinking and acting more like owners and less like employees. But it is unrealistic to expect such a profound change in their perspective unless they are provided the right incentives. And the right incentive in this case means bonus programs that tie directly to wealth creation.

CONCLUSION

Once the commitment to EVA has been made, and the scope and nature of the implementation have been determined and agreed upon, creating a management compensation plan is the next step. We've seen that the success of EVA is inextricably linked to creating and managing effective value-based compensation. In the next chapter, strategies for creating such incentives will be explained.

CHAPTER 4

Management Compensation

A few large companies are still run by founders with substantial ownership stakes. But in the typical public company, the CEO owns less than 1 percent of company shares. Directors of these companies must struggle with the question "How can we create strong incentives to increase shareholder value when our managers do not have large equity stakes?" Some corporate governance experts despair of ever finding a solution to this problem, believing that managers will always find it easier to exploit the company's absentee owners through excessive compensation and perquisites (i.e., "perks") than to build their wealth instead by increasing shareholder value for all the company's owners.

We believe that corporate directors can control excessive compensation and perquisites and create strong incentives to increase shareholder value. At the CEO level, large stock option grants can create strong wealth-creating incentives. At the business unit level, however, such grants usually do not create strong incentives because business unit performance usually has only a modest impact on corporate performance. Strong business unit incentives are the only way to create strong shareholder value incentives throughout the organization. As we will show in this chapter, EVA is the best way to create such incentives for most business enterprises.

THE BASIC OBJECTIVES OF MANAGEMENT COMPENSATION

Strong incentives are not the only issue that directors need to worry about. Avoiding a misalignment of management and shareholder interests is important too. A poorly designed bonus plan, even one based on EVA, can create an incentive to maximize current returns without regard to the future. Future EVA, and therefore shareholder value, may even be sacrificed to report higher EVA in the short term. In other words, even when managers are paid on the basis of EVA, alignment between management and shareholders is far from guaranteed.

Shareholder cost is another important concern. Companies can easily create strong incentives with large stock and option grants at the corporate level and large interests in EVA or EVA improvement at the business unit level. But the directors' goal is to maximize the wealth of current shareholders, not to maximize the combined wealth of employees and shareholders. To control costs, directors strive to limit guaranteed compensation and incentive opportunities to the levels that are necessary to attract and retain qualified managers. Controlling shareholder cost leads to granting options instead of stock, setting option exercise prices above the current market price instead of at the current market price (so that the stock price has to increase if the options are to have any value when they expire), giving management a share of EVA improvement instead of a share of EVA, and setting EVA improvement targets that must be met before managers can earn large bonuses. One problem, however, is that while these techniques help to contain shareholder cost, they also increase the risk that poor performance will leave managers with little prospective payoff, and more important, little reason to stay with the company.

What this discussion suggests is that corporate directors have a delicate balancing act to perform in designing appropriate compensation structures for management. To perform it well, each of four fundamental objectives must be considered:

- *Alignment* Giving management an incentive to choose strategies and investments that maximize shareholder value

- *Wealth leverage*   Giving management sufficient incentives to work long hours, to take risks and make unpleasant decisions, and to maximize shareholder value
- *Retention*   Giving managers sufficient total compensation to retain them, particularly during periods of poor performance caused by market or industry factors
- *Shareholder cost*   Limiting the cost of management compensation to levels that will maximize the wealth of current shareholders

ALIGNING MANAGEMENT AND SHAREHOLDER INTERESTS

The alignment of management and shareholder interests has been a major public policy concern ever since business ownership in the United States began to separate from business management in the middle of the nineteenth century. The separation of ownership and control began with the railroads, which had vast capital requirements that far exceeded the resources of any small owner-management group. By 1853, the New York Central Railroad had 2445 shareholders, none of whom held a controlling interest. By the early part of the twentieth century, share ownership was highly fragmented in many sectors of the American economy. In 1929, AT&T's largest shareholder owned 0.70 percent of the company, and its 20 largest shareholders combined owned only 4.0 percent. At U.S. Steel, the largest shareholder owned 0.90 percent and the top 20 just 5.1 percent. A famous corporate governance study published in 1932, *The Modern Corporation and Private Property* by Adolf Berle and Gardiner Means concludes that 44 percent of the 200 largest companies in America were controlled by management, not by their owners.

Berle and Means argue that the self-interest of the managers controlling the corporation no longer ensures that the corporation's assets would be put to their most profitable use. Managers can realize greater personal benefits by taking advantage of the nonmanagement owners than by pursuing their common interest in increasing the value of the business. For example, they could sell property at inflated prices to the corporation or buy property at bargain prices. Berle and Means were also concerned about excessive investment that adds to the stature of the company and its managers but fails to increase the wealth of the company's shareholders, compensation levels higher than necessary to attract and retain qualified management, and expenditures for product quality that aren't justified by consumers' willingness to pay. They saw a growing convergence between public and private enterprise, and an increasing role for government to ensure that corporate managers did not exploit their control to take advantage of either the shareholders or the public. They saw little opportunity for directors to improve management incentives, but almost in passing they suggest that there would be "great social advantage in encouraging the control [i.e., management] to seize for themselves any profits over and above the amount necessary as a satisfactory return to capital."

Since the days of Berle and Means, improved public disclosure and other controls have strongly discouraged the worst managerial abuses such as buying and selling assets at personally advantageous prices. But many of the other problems that concerned them are as important today as they were in 1932 (e.g., the conflict between revenue growth and shareholder value, excessive management compensation, and "too much" quality). Throughout the book, we look at how EVA can help companies solve these problems. We will see that the basic idea of Berle and Means' suggestion—giving management a large interest in an excess profit measure (in effect, excess EVA improvement)—plays a key role in helping companies to align management and shareholder interests in a cost-efficient way.

The public/private enterprise convergence theory remained popular well into the 1960s. In the 1970s, as corporate profitability deteriorated—the average return on capital of American companies declined by 50 percent from 1966 to 1980—concerns about corporate governance reemerged. Entrepreneurs began to see opportunities to enhance corporate value by replacing managers with others who were much more focused on shareholder value. These opportunities, combined with readily available financing, particularly from Michael Milken's junk bond unit at Drexel Burnham Lambert, led to a wave of hostile takeovers in the 1980s. They also enabled a wave of *leveraged buyouts* (LBOs), which peaked in 1988 when the 381 LBOs in that year represented almost

10 percent of total merger and acquisition activity in the United States. Most LBOs were also *management buyouts*, or MBOs, because managers in charge participated in the takeover. In an MBO, management becomes a great deal more focused on shareholder value because the buyout creates a radical change in managerial incentives. To understand the impact of the MBO, and to set the stage for our discussion on EVA-based compensation, we need to introduce the concept of wealth leverage.

WEALTH LEVERAGE: THE KEY MEASURE OF MANAGEMENT INCENTIVES

An entrepreneur who starts a new business has a strong incentive to increase its value because much, if not most, of his or her wealth is tied up in the business. Divisional managers in large companies have a much weaker incentive to increase the value of their businesses. Consider a divisional manager who has an annual salary of $100,000, owns company stock worth $100,000, and owns a home with personal equity of $100,000. The manager's wealth includes the value of his human capital (i.e., the value of the benefit that he can realize from his know-how), which in this case is the present value of future salary and pension. Let's assume that human capital is worth eight times annual salary, or $800,000. This makes his total wealth $1 million.

How much does his wealth change if he doubles the value of his business unit? His salary, and the value of his human capital, do not change at all. The value of his house doesn't change either. The value of his company stock does change, but if his business unit represents only 10 percent of the entire company, a doubling in the value of his business unit will increase the value of the stock by only 10 percent, to $110,000. This means that his wealth increases by $10,000, from $1 million to $1.01 million, an increase of 1 percent. Thus, a 100 percent increase in business unit value produces only a 1 percent increase in the manager's wealth. For the entrepreneur who holds all his wealth in company stock, a 100 percent increase in shareholder wealth produces a 100 percent increase in wealth.

We call the ratio of the percent change in management wealth to the percent change in shareholder wealth the *wealth leverage ratio.* For the division manager in this example, the wealth lever-age ratio is 0.01. For a pure entrepreneur, it is 1.0.

If the division represents 100 percent of the company, a dou-bling in the value of the business unit would increase the value of the manager's stock by 100 percent to $200,000. This would increase the manager's wealth by 10 percent to $1.1 million and raise the wealth leverage ratio to 0.1, but this is still only 10 per-cent of entrepreneurial wealth leverage. It appears from this ex-ample that it is impossible for a corporate executive, much less a business unit manager, to have an incentive as strong as an entre-preneur.

In fact, it *is* possible, but it's not easy. Let's assume that our manager now owns $1 million of stock. This makes his total wealth $1.9 million: $0.8 million of human capital, $1 million of stock, and $0.1 million of home equity. A doubling in shareholder wealth will double the value of his stock and increase his wealth 53 percent to $2.9 million. This makes wealth leverage 0.53, or more than half of entrepreneurial wealth leverage. This shows that more stock ownership increases wealth leverage. The problem with this scenario, however, is that the manager probably does not have an extra $900,000 to buy stock.

Suppose instead that our manager *borrows* $900,000 to pur-chase the $1.0 million of stock. This doesn't require any miracu-lous increase in his net worth. His total wealth is still $1.0 million: $0.8 million of human capital, $0.1 million of net stock ($1 million − $900,000), and $0.1 million of home equity, but his leveraged equity position gives him a much stronger incentive. A doubling in shareholder wealth increases the gross value of his stock by 100 percent from $1 million to $2 million, and the net value of his stock by 1,000 percent from $0.1 million to $1.1 million. This in-creases his wealth by 100 percent from $1.0 million to $2.0 million, resulting in a wealth leverage of 1.00, equal to that of a pure en-trepreneur.

To explore the implications of this example further, we now turn our attention to one of the most important developments in corporate finance over the last two decades—the *management buy-out* (MBO).

CREATING STRONG INCENTIVES:
THE MANAGEMENT BUYOUT

There are two theories of why MBOs have had such a big impact on management behavior and firm performance. One theory is that MBOs give managers a big ownership interest and largely eliminate their incentive to exploit other shareholders through lavish perquisites and the expansion of firm size without regard to profitability. The alternative theory, which we prefer, is that MBOs dramatically increase managers' wealth leverage and, hence, give management a much stronger incentive to maximize shareholder value.

The main problem with the former theory is that most MBOs in the 1980s and 1990s left management with only a modest ownership interest. Kohlberg Kravis Roberts & Co., or KKR as it is often called, was the most prominent LBO firm of the 1980s and 1990s.[1] For example, in KKR's buyout of Beatrice, the large food company, the executive recruited to run it, Don Kelly, was allowed to buy 1 percent of the stock, with an option on another 6.5 percent. The other members of Beatrice's management team bought 5 percent of the stock. This was consistent with KKR's general policy of targeting 5 to 10 percent management ownership in large transactions. In smaller transactions, KKR's management ownership targets ranged up to 25 percent.

In two studies of LBOs, Steve Kaplan of the University of Chicago finds that CEO ownership increased on average from 1.0 percent to 6.4 percent, and total management ownership reached 20 percent.[2] While an increase in ownership from 1 percent to 6 percent appears dramatic, a 6 percent interest does not significantly reduce a CEO's incentive to exploit other shareholders through lavish perquisites or profitless growth. For example, if a 6 percent owner invests in a $100,000 perquisite (for, say, a lavishly appointed office), his own wealth decreases by $6000, but he continues to enjoy the perquisite, which means a net benefit of $94,000. In effect, the manager enjoys a $100,000 asset for a price

---

1. KKR completed 29 LBOs in the 1980s and 14 more between 1990 and 1996 (the last period reported in our data sources).
2. Steven N. Kaplan, "The Effects of Management Buyouts on Operations and Value," *Journal of Financial Economics,* October 1989, pp. 217–254; "The Staying Power of Leveraged Buyouts," *Journal of Financial Economics,* October 1991, pp. 287–314.

of only $6000. It is not difficult to see why the executive continues to make such value-destroying expenditures, despite a higher ownership stake.

The alternative explanation for the impact of the MBO on management behavior and firm performance is that the MBO has dramatically increased management wealth leverage. This was the conclusion of Kraft CEO John Richman when he looked at the post-buyout performance of Kraft's Duracell unit:

> To John Richman, Bob Kidder's longtime boss at Kraft, the emergence of a roaringly successful new Duracell was both jarring and fascinating. For years, Richman thought Kraft was getting the most it could from the Duracell management team. Suddenly, his ex-employees began pounding out quarterly earnings far beyond anything that Richman had ever thought possible. . . . "What's different?" Richman kept asking. "Why are you doing so much better?"
>
> The secret, Richman decided, was big money, and the way it changed people's values. It was as if executives at buyout companies like Duracell played by different rules than the rest of American business. Most executives spend their lives juggling conflicting goals: keeping workers happy, holding to traditions, winning public recognition, and making money for stockholders. In a buyout, only the final priority mattered. Giant financial rewards induced managers to tear through companies in an all-out drive to improve profitability, regardless of the turmoil that such steps might cause.[3]

Richman provides an insightful explanation as to why strong wealth leverage leads to changes in management behavior: Managers become much more focused on a single goal, increasing shareholder value, while previously they had pursued a range of partially conflicting goals. The increased reward for pursuing shareholder value makes managers willing to sacrifice other objectives they had previously pursued. Richman's explanation is confirmed by accounts of key post-buyout decisions made by MBO managers.

Let's look at some of these decisions in companies acquired by KKR (we use companies acquired by KKR because the firm has received far more press coverage and academic scrutiny than any other buyout firm):

---

3. George Anders, *Merchants of Debt: KKR and the Mortgaging of American Business.* New York: Basic Books, 1992, p. 175.

Businesses were forced to make do with less staff and lower budgets.

+ Safeway laid off 8000 headquarters and regional employees.
+ RJR Tobacco laid off 1525 workers and reduced its payroll by 13 percent.
+ Owens-Illinois fired 500 headquarters employees and reduced corporate overhead from $32.4 million to $13 million.
+ Beatrice cut the $975 million marketing budget by 15 percent.
+ Nabisco cut back advertising by 10 percent.

Unprofitable businesses were sold.

+ Safeway raised $1 billion by selling unprofitable divisions in Oklahoma, Arkansas, Texas, Utah, and Kansas. After its divestitures, Safeway had greater profits from 1400 stores than it had from 2200 stores before.
+ Safeway closed its Dallas division and sold the assets as real estate.

Goals and performance measures were changed.

+ Safeway changed its bonus objectives from sales growth to return on market value.
+ RJR Tobacco increased margins by dropping its long-time goal of one-third market share.
+ Fred Meyer measured managers on return on market value, leading managers to cut spending on expansion, close some stores, and focus on improving the profitability of existing stores.

Corporate governance was simplified.

+ Duracell made faster decisions because corporate approval was no longer required for small capital expenditures and for all pay decisions covering the top 30 managers; KKR required approval only for capital expenditures over $5 million and gave Duracell's CEO complete authority over his subordinates' compensation.

Performance differentials were more strongly rewarded or punished.

+ Safeway made bonuses more sensitive to performance, widening the range of payouts from 20 to 30 percent of salary to 0 to 100 percent of salary.
+ The CEO of Owens-Illinois in the late 1980s, Robert Lanigan, described the underlying message from KKR as follows: "If you miss the targets, we don't want to know about the dollar, or the weather, or the economy." In other words, KKR wanted results, not excuses.[4]
+ When Lily-Tulip's CEO failed to sell the corporate airplane, remove redundant relatives from the payroll, or cut overhead costs, KKR fired him.

Growth expenditures were reduced.

+ Safeway cut spending on new stores from $621 million in 1985 to $228 million in 1987 and increased spending on store remodeling.

Perquisites were eliminated.

+ Beatrice CEO Don Kelly terminated Beatrice's race car sponsorship (a favorite of the prior CEO).
+ Owens-Illinois sold two Gulfstream G-1 executive jets.

Why were these decisions not made before the MBO? Greater wealth leverage played a key role. Many of these decisions caused management life to be more difficult or more stressful and would not have been made without large countervailing rewards. Cutting staff and budgets forces managers to work harder, requiring more personal time and effort. Managers have to put in more hours to do work that they could previously delegate. Cutting staff also requires unpleasant personal confrontations that managers are normally eager to avoid. Unpleasant confrontations are also required to enforce more demanding performance standards and punish poor performers by denying bonuses that in the past would have been paid just to keep the peace.

Overcoming resistance to unpleasant tasks was not the only

---

4. Anders, p. 179.

role of greater wealth leverage. For example, with strong incentives in place, KKR was able to unlock value in Duracell by giving its managers more latitude than Kraft headquarters had permitted. Greater wealth leverage also leads to a more single-minded focus on shareholder value. Conflicting goals, such as sales growth, were replaced by a more concentrated focus on paying down debt and increasing profitability, which led to the sale of poorly performing business units.

While increased wealth leverage played a large role in changing management behavior, it was not the only factor. Some key post-buyout decisions reflect differences between KKR governance and typical public company governance. Henry Kravis and George Roberts frequently made an issue of perquisites even though they both had their own private jets. KKR's portfolio companies faced more active and demanding governance than that faced by the typical public company or, indeed, than that faced by the top management of KKR from its limited partners. KKR also played a much more active role than the typical corporate board in encouraging the sale of assets when their value to an outsider exceeded their internal value. In some cases, their concern for the salability of assets led them and their operating managers to reject plans to cut costs by combining operations. For example, the CEO of Beatrice rejected a plan to achieve distribution cost reductions by combining the Tropicana juice business with the processed cheese business because it limited his ability to sell the two business units.

Another major factor that influenced management's post-buyout behavior was the need to pay down debt. A typical KKR acquisition in the 1980s involved 20 percent equity and 80 percent debt (by the 1990s, KKR leverage ratios fell to 60 to 75 percent). Typically, senior bank debt had to be repaid within five years, although repayment periods for subordinated debt were sometimes longer.

THE SHORTCOMINGS OF THE MBO MODEL

While an MBO can provide strong incentives for wealth creation, the resulting debt burden creates a considerable risk of failure. In a study of 124 leveraged buyouts in the 1980s, Kaplan and Stein found that 2 percent of pre-1985 buyouts and 27 percent of post-

1984 buyouts defaulted on their debt, and about a third of the defaulters declared bankruptcy.[5]

The KKR partners were keenly aware of the dangers created by debt and took steps to provide sufficient financial flexibility so that companies could endure an unexpected bout of poor performance. Secured financing was avoided because it gave lenders too much bargaining power. They used strip financing instead, in which lenders also held preferred stock or equity, on the assumption that lenders would be less likely to take actions in default that would reduce the value of their own shares.

There is, however, an even better way to maintain financial flexibility, while at the same time creating the right wealth incentives for managers. EVA, like bank debt, imposes interest and principal payments, but it does so indirectly. The interest payment is in the form of a capital charge, while the principal payment is in the form of a depreciation expense. But the EVA approach is much more flexible than any banker. Depreciation is recovered over the economic life of the asset, while the banker may insist on a short loan term regardless of the asset's economic life. A project that creates positive EVA (on a present-value basis) over the life of the assets acquired increases shareholder value even if it fails to meet the banker's repayment schedule. An EVA company can afford to take on the project, but an MBO company cannot.

In short, EVA can create a highly leveraged compensation plan without forcing the company to take on high levels of debt and risk bankruptcy. Because EVA is more flexible than bank debt, it allows companies to capture value-creating opportunities that its bankers would consider too risky. Even more important, EVA can, unlike an MBO, create strong wealth incentives at the business unit level.

THE MBO AFTERMATH: A DRAMATIC RISE IN STOCK OPTION GRANTS

The popular picture of MBO incentives focuses on leveraged stock *purchases*, but, in fact, stock *options* play a large role too. Don Kelly of Beatrice, as we noted earlier, received an option on 6.5 times as

---

5. Steven Kaplan and Jeremy Stern, "How Risky Is Debt in Highly Leveraged Transactions?" *Journal of Financial Economics*, October 1980, pp. 215–246.

many shares as he purchased. RJR Nabisco executives received four options for every share purchased. In a typical KKR buyout, managers were given five option shares for every share purchased.

Of course, the practice of granting stock options to managers has spread far beyond the world of MBOs and corporate take-overs. Over the past 15 years, the average company has dramatically increased its stock option grants for top management, and many CEOs now have entrepreneurial wealth incentives. In a study of 400 large publicly traded American companies, Brian Hall and Jeffrey Liebman find that the average CEO stock option grant value increased from $155,000 in 1980 to $1,213,000 in 1994, an increase of almost 700 percent.[6] Over the same period, the average salary and bonus increased from $655,000 to $1,292,000, an increase of less than 100 percent. By 1998, half of the 1700 CEOs in the Standard & Poor Execucomp database held options on stock worth 20× base salary or more, and 30 percent held options on stock worth 39× base salary or more. In addition, the stock option movement has spread more recently to Europe, where hundreds of companies now offer options to senior managers.

The main virtue of stock options is that they can, if used properly, create entrepreneurial wealth incentives. Suppose that a manager receives an option to purchase $2 million of stock at an exercise price of $0.9 million. The manager's total wealth is now $2.0 million: $0.8 million of human capital, $1.1 million of option value, and $0.1 million of home equity. A doubling in shareholder wealth increases the value of his option by 182 percent, from $1.1 million to $3.1 million, and increases his wealth by 100 percent, from $2.0 million to $4.0 million. This makes his wealth leverage 1.00, exactly equal to that of a pure entrepreneur.

This example is somewhat unrealistic, however, because we assume that the company is willing to grant a deep-in-the-money option. To be more realistic, suppose the company grants a 10-year at-the-money option on $3.5 million of stock. In other words, if the options are exercised, the manager would pay $3.5 million to buy shares that are now worth $3.5 million. Let's also assume that the value of that option, according to the popular Black-

6. Brian J. Hall and Jeffrey B. Liebman, "Are CEOs Really Paid Like Bureaucrats?" *The Quarterly Journal of Economics,* August 1998.

Scholes option pricing model,[7] is $2.2 million. This makes our manager's total wealth $3.1 million: $0.8 million of human capital, $2.2 million of option value, and $0.1 million of home equity. A doubling in shareholder wealth increases the value of the option from $2.2 million to $5.4 million, and increases wealth by 103 percent, from $3.1 million to $6.3 million. In other words, wealth leverage is 1.03, slightly greater than entrepreneurial wealth leverage. In short, large at-the-money option grants can provide entrepreneurial wealth incentives for corporate managers.

RETENTION RISK AND THE COMPETITIVE PAY MODEL

So far, we have seen three ways to create entrepreneurial wealth leverage: (1) an MBO, in which the manager borrows $0.9 to purchase $1 million of stock; (2) an option grant (without an MBO), in which the manager receives an option on $2 million of stock exercisable at $0.9 million; and (3) an alternative option grant (also without an MBO), in which the manager receives an at-the-money option on $3.5 million of stock. In all three cases, a doubling in shareholder wealth produces a doubling in the manager's wealth, meaning that the wealth leverage ratio is 1.0.

While these examples show three different ways in which a manager with a salary can have entrepreneurial wealth leverage, only the third example is widely followed. The problem in the MBO scenario is that the manager has too much risk. If the stock price drops by 10 percent, the net value of the manager's shareholdings is zero. In the real world, this means that the shares would have to be sold to cover the debt, so there is no upside opportunity to induce him to stay with the company.

The problem with the first option grant example is unfavorable accounting and tax treatment. The option discount at the time of grant, $1.1 million, must be recognized as an accounting expense. The option discount also disqualifies the option from the

7. The Black-Scholes option pricing model was developed by Fischer Black and Myron Scholes and first published in 1973.

"performance-based compensation" exemption from the $1 million cap imposed by U.S. tax law.

While very few executives purchase stock worth 10× salary with 10:1 leverage, and very few companies grant deep in-the-money options on stock worth 20× salary, many companies, at least in the United States, do grant at-the-money options on stock worth 35× salary, or even more. In the Execucomp database of U.S. senior executives, 19 percent of CEOs have been granted options on stock worth at least 35× salary, and as of the end of 1998, 32 percent held options on stock worth at least that much. This means that close to a third of CEOs have entrepreneurial wealth leverage.

Unfortunately, these powerful incentives do not go very deep in the organization, partly because stock-based incentives do not provide good line of sight below top management levels. Only 15 percent of the fifth-highest-paid executives in the Execucomp database hold options on stock worth 35× base salary, and only 5 percent were granted options on stock worth 35× salary. This means that 95 percent of the companies in the Execucomp database are not willing to grant their fifth-highest-paid executives sufficient options for entrepreneurial wealth leverage. While there is no database on wealth leverage at the business unit level, we would guess that no more than 10 to 15 percent of business unit managers of large multidivisional U.S. companies have entrepreneurial wealth leverage. Outside the United States, the percentages are almost certainly close to zero.

Many of the companies that fail to provide entrepreneurial wealth leverage believe that they nevertheless offer strong incentives because their executives have a substantial proportion of their pay at risk each year. Suppose in our example that the manager, who has a base salary of $100,000, receives a target annual bonus equal to 100 percent of salary and an option each year on stock worth 3× salary, or $300,000. We will assume that the expected value of the option is about 60 percent of the stock value. This is a typical Black-Scholes value for a company with no dividend and average stock price volatility. This makes the expected value of the option $180,000 ($300,000 × 60 percent) and gives our manager a target annual compensation of $380,000 (the sum of base salary, $100,000, the target bonus, $100,000, and the option grant value, $180,000). These targets would normally be determined on the basis of compensation survey data to provide competitive compensation. (Chapter 8 includes an extended discussion of competitive compensation analysis.)

Because 74 percent of the target total compensation is tied to performance ($280,000 ÷ $380,000), many companies (and most compensation consultants) are quick to conclude that the manager has a strong incentive to maximize shareholder value. Often, they assume that 74 percent variable compensation is analogous to holding 74 percent equity and 26 percent debt and, hence, provides nearly three-quarters of entrepreneurial wealth leverage. But, in fact, our manager's wealth leverage is far lower than 0.74.

To estimate wealth leverage, we need to calculate the manager's wealth and then estimate the sensitivity of changes in his wealth to changes in shareholder wealth. Raising the manager's expected annual compensation to $380,000 increases the value of his human capital to $3,040,000 (assuming, as we did before, that human capital equals 8× annual compensation). Total wealth is now $3,240,000, including the value of stock ($100,000) and net home equity ($100,000). Let's now consider the impact of a doubling in shareholder wealth. The value of the stock increases $100,000 to $200,000, an increase of $100,000. The value of the manager's current option grant increases by $276,000 from $180,000 to $456,000 (according to the Black-Scholes model), an increase of 153 percent. We will also assume, for simplicity, that his bonus beats the target by the same percentage, giving him a current bonus of $253,000. The increases in the value of his stock, stock options, and bonus make the manager richer by $529,000 ($100,000 + $276,000 + $153,000), a 16 percent increase in wealth. This means that wealth leverage is only 16 percent of entrepreneurial wealth leverage, despite 74 percent of annual compensation at risk.

The reason that the manager's wealth leverage is so low is because current year performance has no impact on *future* compensation. Let's assume that the stock price is originally $100 per share, so that an option on $300,000 worth of stock (3× salary) is 3000 shares. If the stock price doubles to $200 per share, the value of the current-year option increases from $60 per share to $152 per share (using the Black-Scholes model). But what about next year's option?

The value of next year's option doesn't change at all because the number of shares is reduced to offset the increase in the stock price. Instead of 3000 option shares exercisable at $100, the manager receives 1500 shares exercisable at $200. The expected value of the second-year option is still $180,000 (60 percent of the value of the stock), just as before. The expected value of the annual bonus also remains the same, $100,000, because the operating performance target is adjusted to reflect changes in expected performance. For example, if operating profit doubles in year 1 from $5 million to $10 million, the operating profit target for year 2 will not be $5.5 million, but $11 million. A compensation program that annually adjusts option shares and operating performance targets to maintain competitive compensation levels is a *competitive pay model*. It remains the predominant approach to executive compensation in the United States and Europe.

A famous example of the consequences of the competitive pay model is the case of former IBM CEO John Akers. In his first year as CEO, 1986, Akers received an option on 19,000 shares exercisable at $145. In each subsequent year, the stock price dropped and he received an option on more shares exercisable at a lower price. In 1990, he received an option on 96,000 shares exercisable at $97. When he was forced out at the end of 1992, with the stock below $50, his option grants had put him in a position where he would have earned more than $17 million just for getting the stock price back to where he started!

Users of the competitive pay model believe that it achieves the four objectives of executive compensation:

- It provides alignment because incentive compensation is based on stock price and on operating performance measures that are thought to be closely related to shareholder value.
- It provides substantial wealth leverage because a large percentage of compensation is tied to company performance.
- It reduces retention risk because stock option shares and bonus performance targets are adjusted each year to ensure competitive compensation.
- It provides reasonable shareholder cost because stock option shares and bonus performance targets are

adjusted each year to limit compensation to competitive levels.

However, there are three serious flaws in this model. First, the performance measures used in the bonus plan may have only a weak link to shareholder value. Second, current performance has little or no impact on compensation in future periods. While a large percentage of *current* compensation is at risk, wealth leverage is low because future compensation is not at risk. Finally, this approach does a poor job of helping corporate boards and top management to understand the nature of the trade-offs available to them in designing compensation plans. As a result, a company is less likely to promote value-creating behavior in a cost-effective manner.

One way to improve the wealth leverage of a competitive pay policy is to use "front-loaded" or "fixed-share" option grants, although the additional leverage comes at a cost. Grants are front-loaded when several years' worth of options are given all at once. For example, suppose five years' worth of option grants are front-loaded for the manager in our example. Instead of five annual option grants equal to 3× salary, he receives one option grant worth 15× salary. Total wealth remains $3,240,000, but it now includes stock options worth $900,000 (5 × $180,000), human capital of $2,140,000, stock worth $100,000, and a home with net equity of $100,000. A doubling in shareholder value increases his stock by $100,000, his options by $1,380,000, and his current-year bonus by $153,000. This gives a total wealth increase of $1,633,000, or 50 percent. In short, front-loading five years of option grants increases the manager's wealth leverage from 16 to 50 percent of entrepreneurial wealth leverage.

Annual fixed-share grants have a similar effect. Fixed-share grants mean that, in this case, the manager's annual option grant remains at 3000 shares regardless of the change in the stock price. A doubling in the stock price means that the expected value of the future annual grant doubles from $180,000 to $360,000. This increases the present value of our manager's future compensation by $1,440,000 [8 × ($360,000 − $180,000)], and the manager's total wealth by $1,969,000 ($1,440,000 + $529,000), or 61 percent. Thus, switching from competitive to fixed-share grant guidelines raises the manager's wealth leverage from 16 to 61 percent of entrepreneurial wealth leverage.

The problem with front-loaded and fixed-share option grants is that they increase retention risk. If 3000 options are required to provide competitive compensation when the stock price is $100, 6000 options are required when the stock price drops to $50. If we stick to 3000 options when the stock price falls to $50, the expected value of annual total compensation drops from $380,000 to $290,000, a decline of 24 percent. If the previous total compensation of $380,000 was just average, the decline in the stock price means that current total compensation is 24 percent below average. Few directors are willing to take the risk of paying 24 percent below average. This means that they have to face a tough choice. Do they provide fixed-share grants and raise annual total compensation to $500,000, so they can endure a 24 percent decline in total compensation, but still provide average pay? Or do they adopt competitive grant guidelines and accept a weak incentive? These questions are fundamental to understanding the dilemmas often encountered by directors in designing pay programs for their companies' senior managers.

Front-loaded and fixed-share grants are unquestionably powerful tools for increasing wealth leverage at the corporate level, helping to overcome the primary weakness of the typical competitive pay policy. They have little impact on wealth leverage for business unit managers, however, because an increase in business unit value usually has little influence on the corporate stock price. In short, we have a line-of-sight problem. EVA is tremendously important in such cases because EVA, unlike stock options, can provide strong incentives at the business unit level.

BONUS PLAN DESIGN IN THE COMPETITIVE PAY MODEL

The typical, non-EVA bonus plan has three key features: (1) a target bonus paid for achieving target financial performance, typically budgeted operating profit; (2) a threshold level of performance that must be attained before any bonus is earned; and (3) a cap on the bonus payout. This approach is dominant among publicly traded companies in the United States, and is highly popular in Europe as well. Figure 4-1 illustrates how this bonus plan works.

F I G U R E   4–1

A Typical Non-EVA Bonus Plan.

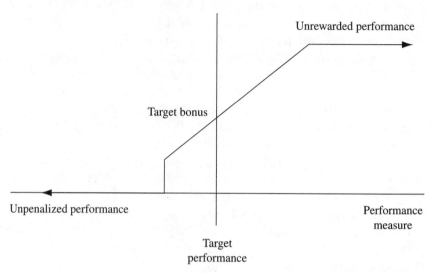

Many bonus plans set the performance threshold at 80 percent of target performance, below which no bonus is earned, and the maximum payout is at 120 percent of target. A typical "80-120" plan pays 50 percent of the target bonus for hitting the threshold and 150 percent of the target bonus for hitting the maximum performance level. The key objectives are to limit retention risk and shareholder cost. Basing financial performance targets on budgets ensures that the expected bonus payout is equal to the target bonus, which helps limit retention risk. The payout cap limits shareholder cost.

There are several major shortcomings to this approach. First, the performance measure, usually operating profit but sometimes a return on capital measure, is not systematically linked to shareholder value, or at least not as convincingly as EVA. Second, the threshold and cap create performance zones in which there is an incentive to *minimize* the performance measure by shifting revenue or expenses to later periods. For example, if the maximum bonus will apparently be earned as early as the ninth or tenth month of the year, a manager might "game" the bonus system by delaying the recognition of revenue, or may even encourage customers to delay their orders until the start of the following year. In this way, profits are stored for future periods when the manager might need them.

A third problem is that annual resets of performance targets undermine leverage and weaken alignment. Leverage is undermined because the new targets normally reflect a "performance penalty," in which superior performance results in higher targets (and a lower percentage interest in profit for the manager), while poor performance results in lower targets (and a higher percentage interest). Alignment is undermined because the prospective of a diminishing percentage interest in above-target profits discourages managers from making profitable long-term investments.

A manager's bonus may be tied to business unit results, but the bonus won't provide an entrepreneurial incentive for two reasons. First, the bonus is normally based on meeting performance targets that are adjusted annually. This means that the manager needs to consider the impact of this year's performance on next year's targets. If the target is beaten this year, the manager will be "punished" with a higher target next year. If results fall short of target this year, the manager will be "rewarded" with a lower target next year. Over a multiyear period, a cautious program of managing and meeting corporate expectations usually has a greater personal payoff than trying to maximize the value of the business unit.

Second, the bonus is often a modest percentage of salary, and an even smaller percentage of total compensation. When the divisional managers think about their net worth in five years, including the value of the bonuses that can be earned over the next five years, it quickly becomes apparent that the value of the business unit in five years has little impact on this net worth.

EVA: A BETTER WAY TO PAY MANAGERS

EVA is a powerful tool for creating strong, sustainable, and cost-efficient incentives at the business unit level. But EVA by itself does not achieve any of the four fundamental objectives of management compensation. It provides closer alignment with shareholder value than operating profit because it recognizes the cost of capital, but its use does not ensure complete alignment because current EVA can be maximized at the expense of future EVA and shareholder value. Over the years, the design of EVA bonus plans has evolved to include a collection of tools that, joined with the EVA metric, provide business unit incentives that achieve the basic objectives of management compensation far more effectively than any known alternative.

Closer manager-shareholder alignment is achieved through the use of

- Fixed percentage interests that make the manager's trade-off between current and future bonus consistent with the shareholder's trade-off between current and future EVA.
- Deferred compensation, in the form of "bonus banks," that discourages managers who might leave the firm from maximizing current EVA at the expense of future EVA.

Stronger wealth leverage is achieved through the use of

- Fixed percentage interests that are not reduced when performance exceeds expectations or increased when performance is below expectations.
- Formula targets that are not lowered when performance is below expectations or raised when performance exceeds expectations.

Tolerable retention risk is achieved through

- Careful analysis of competitive compensation levels.
- Careful risk modeling to ensure that the target bonus is large enough, or the leverage small enough, to limit retention risk.

Reasonable shareholder cost is achieved by

- Setting performance targets (for expected EVA improvement) that are consistent with a cost-of-capital return on the market value of the shareholders' investment.
- Limiting guaranteed compensation to competitive levels.
- Sharing the cost of strong incentives between shareholders, who invest in higher incentive

opportunities, and managers, who accept greater compensation risk.

Let's look at the history of EVA bonus design and how some of these tools developed before we present what we call the *modern EVA bonus plan*.

The Original EVA Bonus Plans

Figure 4–2 illustrates the structure of the "original" EVA bonus plans.

These early plans simply gave management a fixed percentage of EVA. For example, in 1922, General Motors adopted a bonus plan that provided for a bonus pool equal to 10 percent of profit in excess of a 7 percent return on capital. From a contemporary perspective, this bonus plan is remarkable in several respects. The bonus formula was maintained without change (in either the sharing percentage or the capital charge) for 25 years; it covered all bonus-eligible employees at General Motors; and it defined all incentive compensation including stock compensation (which was paid out of the pool). It is a simple, and rather elegant, management/shareholder bargain: management got 10 percent

F I G U R E   4–2

The Original EVA Bonus Plans.

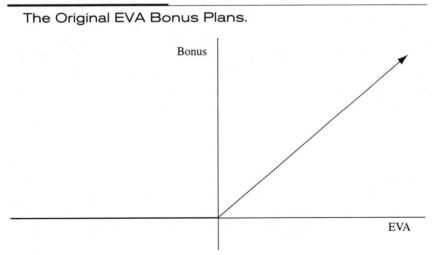

and shareholders 90 percent of the profit after deducting a salary for management and a minimum return for the shareholders.

The downfall of the formula as a comprehensive management/shareholder bargain was the introduction of stock options. While grants of shares could easily be charged against the bonus pool depending on the market value of the shares, options are far more difficult to value and, hence, were very difficult to integrate into the plan. Once options were granted outside the plan, the formula ceased to be the comprehensive bargain between management and shareholders and lost much of its significance.

By providing an uncapped fixed percentage interest, the original EVA plans provided substantial leverage, eliminated one of the negative incentive zones, and for a positive-EVA company, aligned management and shareholder interests in trade-offs between current and future EVA (because both manager and shareholder held a fixed percentage interest).

Yet three major problems exist with the original EVA formulas. First, for the marginal and poor-performing company, a percentage of EVA is, in effect, an option on the good years. This encourages management to shift revenue and expense across years to maximize incentive payouts, making management's effective share of cumulative EVA far greater than its nominal share.

A second problem is that giving management a share of EVA from the first dollar leads to very inefficient trade-offs between the strength of the incentive and the shareholder cost of the incentive. For example, if we apply Walt Disney CEO Michael Eisner's formula of 2 percent of EVA to a company like Wal-Mart, with $1 billion in EVA, the result is a $20 million bonus, which shareholders will rightly feel is far more than necessary to attract highly qualified managerial talent. The seemingly simple solution to this problem is to move the decimal point to the left—that is, give an interest of 0.2 percent of EVA instead of 2.0 percent. But this really isn't a good answer. When we cut management's share of EVA from 2.0 to 0.2 percent, we reduce the incentive at the margin by a factor of 10. The more efficient solution is to give management a share of EVA improvement.

The third problem is that the formulas make no provision for expected EVA improvement and thus can provide substantial payouts even when shareholders lose. The recent history of Wal-Mart provides an example of such a situation. In 1992, Wal-Mart had $957 million of EVA and a future growth value of $55 billion (or $30 billion more than its current operations value of $25 billion). This future growth value implied investor expectations of substantial EVA improvement. When Wal-Mart's EVA went sideways over the next two years ($1,056 million in 1993 and $917 million in 1994), its future growth value dropped by $25 billion, and its stock price declined from $32.00 to $21.25. In this situation, a fixed percentage of EVA would provide substantial bonuses even though the shareholders were losing money.

The next step in the evolution of EVA bonus plans was to make the bonus formula equal to a percentage of EVA plus a (different and normally higher) percentage of EVA improvement:

$$\text{Bonus} = (x\% \times \text{EVA}) + (y\% \times \Delta\text{EVA})$$

This design, popularly known as the XY plan, was used by several early EVA adopters in the United States, and it continues to be used by some companies in the United States and in Europe. For example, Cilcorp, an electric utility that implemented EVA in 1988, and Crane, a manufacturer and distributor of industrial products that implemented EVA in 1990, adopted this plan design.

The XY plan is a more efficient bonus plan design than the original EVA bonus plan (a pure X plan) for both positive- and negative-EVA companies. For positive-EVA companies, the y can be used to provide a stronger incentive, while the x can be used to provide a competitive level of pay. Suppose a company anticipates EVA increasing from $8 million in year 1 to $10 million in year 2 and $12 million in year 3. A bonus formula of (2 percent $\times$ EVA) provides a cumulative bonus of $0.6 million. A bonus formula of (1 percent $\times$ EVA) + (8 percent $\times$ ΔEVA) provides about the same cumulative bonus ($0.62 million) but makes the incentive at the margin four times greater (8 percent versus 2 percent). For negative-EVA companies, the Y can still be used to provide a strong incentive (since x percent of negative EVA is no incentive at all), but the x can't be used to provide a competitive level of pay. If a company anticipates EVA increasing from $-$12 million in year 1 to $-$10 million in year 2 to $-$8 million in year 3, 15 percent of ΔEVA is needed to provide a cumulative bonus of $0.6 million. This provides a strong incentive, but it leads to much higher management compensation costs when improved performance is the result of market or industry factors outside management's control.

The Modern EVA Bonus Plan

The modern version of the EVA bonus plan, and the one we promote most enthusiastically, makes two important modifications to the XY plan. A target bonus is substituted for x percent of EVA, and an expected EVA improvement ("EI") is subtracted from ΔEVA, instead of relying on ΔEVA alone:

$$\text{Bonus} = \text{target bonus} + y\% \, (\Delta\text{EVA} - \text{EI})$$

In this plan, the performance measure is "excess EVA improvement." There are three reasons for this. First, an interest in EVA improvement provides more efficient incentive/cost trade-offs than an interest in EVA. Second, EVA improvement is a measure that applies to all companies, not just companies with positive EVA. Third, EVA improvement provides a more direct link to excess returns, the ultimate measure of shareholder wealth creation, than EVA itself. Whenever a company's market value includes a future growth value (and not just current operations value), EVA improvement is necessary for the company's investors to earn a cost-of-capital return. Figure 4–3 shows the modern EVA bonus plan design.

The bonus earned is the sum of a target bonus plus a fixed percentage of excess EVA improvement (which can be positive or negative). The target bonus is the bonus earned for achieving expected EVA improvement (which makes excess EVA improvement zero). A target bonus is necessary to make the bonus plan consistent with the labor market practice of paying a substantial bonus for normal or expected performance. The bonus earned can be negative and is uncapped on both the upside and the downside.

In addition, the bonus earned is credited to a bonus bank, and the bonus bank balance, rather than the current year bonus earned, determines the bonus paid. Typically, the payout rule for the bonus bank is 100 percent of the bonus bank balance (if positive), up to the amount of the target bonus, plus one-third of the

F I G U R E   4–3

The Modern EVA Bonus Plan.

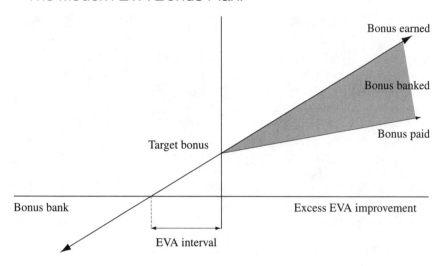

bank balance in excess of the target bonus. When the bonus bank is negative, no bonus is paid.

Table 4–1 illustrates the operation of the modern EVA bonus plan (in thousands of dollars, except where noted). The bonus formula is as follows:

$$\text{Bonus} = \text{target bonus} + y\% \, (\Delta\text{EVA} - \text{EI})$$

$$\text{Bonus} = \$100,000 + 2\% \, (\Delta\text{EVA} - \$5 \text{ M})$$

In year 1, EVA improves from −\$30 million to −\$15 million, which means that ΔEVA equals \$15 million. Subtracting the expected EVA improvement of \$5 million gives an excess EVA improvement of \$10 million. The bonus earned is as follows:

$$\$100,000 + 2\% \, (\$15,000,000 - \$5,000,000)$$

or \$300,000. The bonus earned is first credited to the bonus bank. Under the normal payout rule, we pay out the bonus bank balance up to the amount of the target bonus, plus one-third of the excess. This makes the bonus payout \$167,000 and leaves a bonus bank balance of \$133,000 at the end of year 1.

T A B L E   4–1

The Modern EVA Bonus Plan

	Year 1	Year 2	Year 3
EVA (year 0 = −$30,000)	−15,000	−20,000	−5,000
EVA improvement	15,000	−5,000	15,000
Expected EVA improvement	5,000	5,000	5,000
Excess EVA improvement	10,000	−10,000	10,000
Target bonus	100	100	100
Share of excess EVA improvement	2%	2%	2%
Bonus earned	300	−100	300
Bonus earned + bank	300	33	300
Bonus paid	167	33	167
Ending bank	133	0	133

In year 2, EVA declines from −$15 million to −$20 million, so ΔEVA = −$5 million. Subtracting the expected EVA improvement of $5 million gives an excess EVA improvement of −$10 million, or −$5 million − $5 million. The bonus earned is −$100,000:

Bonus = $100,000 + 2% (−$5,000,000 − $5,000,000) = −$100,000

The bonus earned is credited to the bonus bank and reduces the bonus bank balance from $133,000 to $33,000. Since the bonus bank balance is less than the amount of the target bonus, the entire bank balance of $33,000 is paid out in year 2.

In year 3, EVA improves from −$20 million to −$5 million, so ΔEVA = $15 million. Subtracting the expected EVA improvement of $5 million gives an excess EVA improvement of $10 million. The bonus earned is $300,000:

Bonus = $100,000 + 2% ($15,000,000 − $5,000,000) = $300,000

The bonus earned is credited to the bonus bank and gives an initial bonus bank balance of $300,000. Under the normal payout rule, we pay out the bonus bank balance, up to the amount of the target bonus, plus one-third of the excess. This makes the bonus payout $167,000 and leaves a bonus bank balance of $133,000 at the end of year 3.

The ending bonus bank plus the cumulative bonus paid is exactly equal to three years' target bonus plus 2 percent of the cumulative EVA improvement in excess of the expected EVA improvement. The cumulative target bonus is $300,000. The cumulative EVA improvement is $25 million, or $-$5 million $-$ ($-$30 million), which makes the cumulative excess EVA improvement $10 million, or $25 million $-$ $5 million $-$ $5 million $-$ $5 million. The cumulative bonus earned is $500,000:

$$\$300,000 + 2\% \ (\$25,000,000 - \$15,000,000) = \$500,000$$

The $500,000 is the sum of the cumulative bonus paid, $367,000, plus the ending bonus bank, $133,000. This demonstrates that the modern EVA bonus provides a firm link between cumulative pay and cumulative performance.

The modern EVA bonus plan also addresses the way EVA targets are reset each year, a process known as *bonus plan calibration*. This calibration is based on three key parameters: the target bonus, the expected EVA improvement, and the EVA interval. The target bonus is based on competitive compensation analysis, which helps ensure that expected pay is in line with that of managers with similar responsibilities in comparable companies. Managers earn the target bonus if they achieve the level of EVA improvement that provides the company's shareholders with a cost-of-capital return on the market value of their investment. If they outperform these expectations, the bonus exceeds the target, while underperformance results in a below-target bonus.

The EVA interval represents the level of underperformance (of EVA shortfall) that results in a zero bonus, and the level of overperformance that doubles the bonus award. In short, the interval determines the sensitivity of the EVA bonus to excess EVA improvement (whether positive or negative). The higher (lower) the EVA interval, the lower (higher) the sensitivity of the bonus to over- or underperformance. A logical starting point for determining the EVA interval is to calculate the EVA shortfall that is expected to provide a zero return to shareholders, on the assumption that if shareholders receive zero return on their investment, managers should suffer a similar fate in the form of a zero bonus.

These guiding concepts provide only an initial calibration. They do not ensure that the calibration provides the right balance among the competing objectives of executive compensation. Ultimately, a final calibration requires a careful simulation of the parameters' implications in terms of alignment, leverage, retention risk, and shareholder cost. This issue is addressed in more detail in Chapter 8.

THE LIMITATIONS OF EVA-BASED COMPENSATION

Our experience has taught us that EVA can improve decision making and enhance shareholder wealth in a broad range of corporate settings. The EVA model has succeeded in many different industries and sectors, and in many countries as well. But despite our obvious enthusiasm for EVA-based compensation, we admit that there are at least three major limitations to the model. First, some corporate and national cultures are uncomfortable with strong wealth incentives. In such cases, an EVA bonus plan can backfire by leading to resignations rather than improved performance. Second, in some highly cyclical industries, it can be impossible to achieve strong wealth leverage without either excessive retention risk or very high shareholder cost. Third, EVA (under normal accounting practices) is not the best measure of performance for startups or for operations in some emerging markets.

Different Risk Preferences

Managers and shareholders have different risk preferences. Executives have large, undiversified human capital investments in the companies they manage. For this reason, they tend to be more risk-averse than the companies' shareholders. Their high personal (financial) wealth combined with stock options and other equity participation plans produces some convergence of their risk preferences with those of shareholders. Subordinate managers are typically more risk-averse than their bosses, in large part because they are less wealthy. Most EVA companies find it prudent to give lower-level managers smaller target bonuses (as a percentage of salary) and weaker wealth incentives than their bosses.

In some companies, such as software start-ups, however,

CEOs want employees with the same attitude toward risk that they have. But in larger companies, especially those that operate on a global scale or that employ people with a wide range of ages, education, and experience, differences in people's willingness to bear risk are understandable. Another problem, even for entrepreneurially oriented managers, is that risk preferences change over time. Ownership-like incentives may be fine, indeed even highly desirable, for young managers. But for older managers approaching retirement, caution is more likely. When a person nears the end of a career, it is only natural to try to guarantee a comfortable retirement by hedging the wealth already accumulated. In such cases, the value-creating and wealth leverage incentives offered by EVA may be neutralized by older managers selling company shares to reduce their wealth at risk. If there are too many older managers, the EVA bonus plan may be self-defeating.

Cyclical Industries

Some industries are highly cyclical, often as a result of fluctuations in commodity prices. For example, EVA performance in the paper industry has been volatile as a result of changes in the price of paper. It is difficult to calibrate the modern EVA bonus plan when EVA performance varies dramatically from one year to the next. If the EVA interval is set to provide strong wealth leverage, a down cycle will produce a huge negative bonus bank and lead to serious retention problems unless salaries are set to be competitive with peer companies' salaries and bonuses. But if salaries are set to be competitive with peer companies' salaries and bonuses, and target bonuses are set to provide strong wealth leverage, total compensation levels will be far above competitive levels, and the shareholder cost of EVA compensation will be difficult to justify.

Start-Up Ventures and Emerging Markets

In the early 1990s, the board of Swiss food giant Nestlé embarked on an ambitious plan for the Russian market. Convinced of the country's long-term value potential, Nestlé made a series of investments to build the infrastructure needed to support market growth. Although Nestlé uses a version of EVA for performance measurement at the country level, and EVA is calculated for the

Russian market, senior managers admit to ignoring the metric in evaluating performance. Growth and building market share are considered more important indicators of long-term value, and these factors are receiving far more attention from senior management than financial performance.

The point here is that achieving long-term profitability in developing markets such as Russia may at first require large investments in the sort of market infrastructure that already exists in the advanced market economies. The result is a high level of invested capital in the early years of operations relative to sales and operating profits.

EVA advocates may respond by saying that even if large upfront investments result in negative EVAs in the early years, the important issue is that EVAs are expected to become positive in the future (otherwise, the investment is value-destroying). Managers must be motivated to improve EVA from one year to the next, even if at first this just means making negative EVA figures less negative.

The problem with this logic is that investments in highly risky markets are often made in stages. In markets like Russia, companies are naturally reluctant to commit all required infrastructure and market development investments up front, preferring instead to wait for achievement of specific sales and profit goals before investing still more capital. Recent events in Russia bear out the wisdom of this approach. In such cases, EVA might improve one year but deteriorate the next as additional investments come on line. Companies may prefer to wait until expected investments, especially those related to establishing a market infrastructure, are largely in place before adopting EVA to evaluate managerial performance.

Money Isn't Everything

People want more out of their jobs than money. Many surveys have shown that money usually is not the most important factor when people choose a job or remain in one. Employees value an enjoyable work environment, with comfortable working conditions, good colleagues, opportunities to work with the latest technologies in their fields, and a host of other perks that don't result in more pay but make work more fun. Southwestern Airlines has become famous not only for its superior profitability but also for the emphasis its culture places on fun. Many Southwestern employees, including senior managers, have said that they have passed up opportunities for higher salaries at competing companies because they find working at Southwestern so enjoyable.

However, while money isn't everything, it's still important. Even if other facets of employment motivate people more than money, the question is whether monetary rewards are more likely than other rewards to influence managerial behavior for the better. When we are presented with the "money isn't everything" argument by our clients, we offer a simple response. If money has no influence on particular employees, perhaps these people are not suited for senior management. They may still be highly valued members of our corporate family, but their contributions lie elsewhere. As shareholders, we would like managers to think and act in ways that promote our interests. We find it difficult to imagine managers becoming obsessed with shareholder value creation on the basis of nonmonetary rewards alone.

Cultural Differences

Compensation practices vary widely across the world, not only because of varying levels of acceptance of the importance of creating value for shareholders but also because of national culture. National culture refers to the values, beliefs, and assumptions that differentiate one group of people from another. A national culture tends to be relatively stable, deeply embedded in everyday life, and fairly resistant to change. As R. S. Schuler and N. Rogovsky argue, global companies that ignore these cross-cultural differences in human resources and compensation practices do so at their peril.[8] They note that Lincoln Electric, a success story in the United States, was unable to duplicate that success internationally partly because it failed to understand the differing expectations regarding compensation policies and practices in other countries.

In their empirical work on the influence of national culture on compensation practices, Schuler and Rogovsky draw heavily

---

8. R .S. Schuler and N. Rogovsky, "Understanding Compensation Practice Variations Across Firms: The Impact of National Culture," *Journal of International Business Studies*, 1st quarter, 1998, pp. 159–177.

on the work of sociologist Geert Hofstede, whose work has led to a widely accepted framework based on four fundamental dimensions that characterize national value systems:

+ Power distance
+ Uncertainty avoidance
+ Individualism versus collectivism
+ Masculinity versus femininity

Power distance indicates the extent to which the unequal distribution of power is accepted by those who have it and those who don't. In cultures with low power distance, inequalities (whether in a company or in society) are minimized. Hence, management practices in low power distance countries like the United States emphasize employee participation, while those in the high power distance countries of Southeast Asia and Latin America are more likely to be authoritarian. Accepting sharp inequalities in the distribution of power, a hallmark of countries with high power distance, also implies tolerance for greater discrepancies between the rewards of top management and those of workers.

This is exactly what compensation consultants Towers Perrin discovered in its global survey of chief executive compensation as a multiple of the pay received by manufacturing employees.[9] Among the 23 countries surveyed, the seven highest scores are all in either Southeast Asia or Latin America ($\times$ denotes times):

Venezuela	84$\times$
Brazil	48$\times$
Hong Kong	43$\times$
Mexico	43$\times$
Malaysia	42$\times$
Singapore	35$\times$
Argentina	30$\times$

Uncertainty avoidance represents the degree to which uncertainty and unpredictability are tolerated in a culture. In countries with higher uncertainty avoidance, people are loath to take risks,

---

9. Tony Jackson, "The Fat Cats Keep Getting Fatter," *Financial Times*, August 1–2, 1998, p. 7.

preferring predictability and structure. In lower uncertainty avoidance countries like the United States, people are more willing to take risks and actually welcome the opportunity that comes with ambiguity.

Individualism is the degree to which people are inclined to put their own interests and those of their immediate family above those of others. High individualism is common among the English-speaking countries, including the United States. In collectivist societies, such as Korea or Taiwan, first loyalties are to one's in-groups, which may be defined as clan, work team, company, community, or country. In exchange, individuals expect the group to look after them in case of need. In such societies, responsibilities tend to be group-based and not individual-based as they are in more individualistic societies.

Masculinity is defined as assertiveness and acquisitiveness (i.e., coveting money and material goods). *Femininity*, on the other hand, places a high value on caring for others. The United States and Japan are said to be "masculine" societies, while the Scandinavian countries are "feminine."

As Schuler and Rogovsky demonstrate, these cultural traits have profound implications for the design of corporate compensation programs. They begin by identifying four distinct compensation types:

+ Compensation practices based on status
+ Compensation practices based on individual performance
+ Social benefits and programs
+ Employee ownership programs

The results of their study confirm, for example, that we are more likely to observe compensation practices based on seniority in countries with high levels of uncertainty avoidance. Pay-for-performance, focus on individual (as opposed to group) performance, and individual bonus practices are more likely in countries with high levels of individualism. At the same time, pay-for-performance is less common in countries with high levels of uncertainty avoidance. Social benefits play a more active role in total compensation in countries exhibiting low degrees of masculinity (or high degrees of femininity) and in countries with high levels of uncertainty avoidance. And, finally, employee ownership plans are less prevalent in countries with high levels of power distance and in countries with low levels of individualism.

These findings are a convincing demonstration that differences in compensation practices across companies and across countries are not accidental, nor do they result solely from differing attitudes about the importance of value creation (although it certainly plays a part). But they do tell us that culture matters. In countries exhibiting high levels of power distance, high levels of uncertainty avoidance, low levels of individualism, and low degrees of masculinity, implementation of value-based compensation schemes like the kind we are describing will be considerably more difficult than in countries exhibiting the opposite characteristics.

Managers must be especially vigilant not to draw inferences about the attitudes of employees in one country based on attitudes of employees in another seemingly similar country. For example, because both Singapore and Taiwan are Southeast Asian tigers, both have weathered the region's economic chaos in the late 1990s far better than their neighbors, and both have mainly ethnic Chinese populations, we might suppose that their cultural attitudes are nearly identical. The reality is quite different. Singapore's development model is largely top-down—efficient, highly ordered, and to a large extent government-directed. Taiwan's model is far less controlled, more democratic, and, as an article in the *Far Eastern Economic Review* says, promotes a strong "cult of entrepreneurship."[10]

While Singapore steers its best and brightest into government service, offering civil service salaries that are among the highest in the world, Taiwan is far more likely to find its best and brightest in start-up ventures. This entrepreneurial drive, combined with the Taiwanese government's reluctance to use industrial policy (as in Singapore) to pick winners, has led to a vibrant capital market where funds are available for promising businesses. The result is that Singapore has been hugely successful in attracting foreign investment, but Taiwan has proven more successful in growing its own world-class companies, such as Acer Computer and Taiwan Semiconductor.

Our intent here is not to pass judgment on the relative merits

---

10. Ben Dolven, "Taiwan's Trump," *Far Eastern Economic Review,* August 6, 1998, p. 113.

of these two development models, but to show that attitudes toward risk-taking and entrepreneurship can vary significantly even between two countries with such obvious similarities as Singapore and Taiwan. Such divergence in attitudes has important implications for managers trying to implement EVA bonus plans on an international scale. Many EVA companies recognize national differences by using lower target bonuses (and, hence, lower wealth leverage) in countries where risk taking and entrepreneurship have less appeal.

ALTERNATIVES TO EVA

EVA is not the only way for companies to create entrepreneurial, or MBO-like, wealth leverage for managers. Spin-offs are a popular approach to providing direct equity incentives for managers of the spun-off unit. Another motive for spin-offs is to rid the corporate group of divisions for which there are no apparent synergistic benefits (with other divisions or with the corporate center).

But what if there are potential synergies that make the corporate group worth more than the combined value of the parent and a division, assuming the division is spun off? One advantage of EVA-based compensation over spin-offs, and over MBOs too, is that EVA permits the corporate group to capture these synergies while creating strong, equitylike incentives.

There are alternatives to EVA that not only provide strong wealth-creation incentives but also permit companies to retain control over a business unit. One such alternative is the *equity carve-out*, a type of public offering in which a majority stake in the unit is retained by the parent. Another alternative, especially popular in e-commerce, is *tracking stock*, in which a public offering is made, but the shares in the business unit carry ownership rights only to the dividends paid by that unit. Ownership of the assets rests entirely with the shareholders of the parent.

Equity Carve-Outs

Since the early 1980s, there have been hundreds of initial public offerings (IPOs) by wholly owned units of American corporations. These subsidiary IPOs are known as *equity carve-outs*, and today they account for about a tenth of all IPOs in the United States.

What distinguishes these transactions from corporate spin-offs is that the parent companies receive cash in exchange for any shares sold in the stock market, and they often retain a majority owner-ship stake in the now publicly traded entities. Two of America's best-known corporations, Lucent Technologies and Allstate, are results of carve-outs, although their parent companies (AT&T and Sears, Roebuck and Co., respectively) later spun off their majority interests. The funds that are raised from carve-outs are either transferred to the parent or retained by the subsidiary. In either case, the funds are normally used for investment or to retire debt.

The equity carve-out phenomenon is especially relevant to the subject of incentive compensation because it can restore the line of sight at divisional level for corporate performance indica-tors such as stock price, without completely spinning off the entity. This allows the parent to capture any potential synergies from keeping the division within its corporate family. In other words, an equity carve-out can substitute for an EVA compensation plan. It not only provides equity-based rewards, but it can also provide line of sight, because stock price is now observable at the divi-sional level.

Although the parent retains a majority stake, a carve-out tends to result in significant increases in managerial autonomy, in part because the post-IPO entity has its own board of directors. When combined with stock options that are linked to the stock price performance of the subsidiary's new publicly traded equity, carve-outs can provide both the means (through increased auton-omy) and the incentives (through line-of-sight equity participation and increased wealth leverage) to promote substantial value cre-ation while at the same time allowing the parent to retain any perceived synergies between the carved-out unit and other units in the corporate group.

Jeffrey Allen documents these advantages in his research on Thermo Electron, a Massachusetts-based manufacturer of analyt-ical, biomedical, recycling, and environmental monitoring equip-ment.[11] Between 1983 and 1996, the company completed 19 carve-outs. While many American carve-outs have ultimately resulted

11. J. Allen, "Capital Markets and Corporate Structure: The Equity Carve-Outs of Thermo Electron," *Journal of Financial Economics*, 1998.

in full-fledged spin-offs, Thermo Electron came to view the carve-out as a sustainable organizational form. According to Allen, the carve-outs allow the company to exploit the benefits of small entrepreneurial organizations without sacrificing the advantages enjoyed by larger firms. The centerpiece of this structure is an incentive compensation plan that ties the pay of the subsidiary's management to the equity performance of both the subsidiary *and* the parent. Division managers are granted a high degree of autonomy in strategic decisions and capital investments.

Granting such autonomy offers two important advantages. First, managers have more latitude in undertaking value-creating actions on behalf of the parent. Second, they can respond quickly and decisively to changing market conditions. The stock options granted to the heads of the carved-out units help the company to attract, retain, and motivate talented entrepreneurs while at the same time reassuring investors because of the continued involvement of a well-known and highly respected parent.

The units are, nevertheless, subject to extensive scrutiny from the parent. Representatives of the parent are on every board (which is only logical, given that the parent is the majority shareholder). Also, various reporting, administrative, financial, and legal services are centralized, an important source of synergy for the corporate group. The strategy worked wonders for Thermo Electron's stock, at least until 1998. In the 15 years following the first carve-out, the total returns to company shareholders were almost four times higher than a portfolio of industry firms and more than five times higher than returns on the S&P 500.

The experiences of many other companies also attest to the benefits of carve-outs. Hulburt, Miles, and Woolridge examine 83 carve-outs effected between 1981 and 1990 and find that the carved-out companies had significantly higher profits, revenue and asset growth, and capital spending than their industry averages in the three years after the carve-out.[12] These achievements occurred because 80 percent of the deals tied management compensation to the share price of the carved-out company after it went public. Parent companies benefited too, achieving higher returns on assets in the year following the carve-out.

---

12. H. Hurlburt, J. Miles, and R. Woolridge, "Value Creation from Equity Carve-Outs," working paper, Penn State University, 1998.

Further support for the benefits of carve-outs is provided by
Anand Vijh.[13] He investigates the aftermarket performance (i.e.,
after the shares started trading) of 628 carve-outs in the United
States from 1981 to 1995, comparing carve-outs with other types
of IPOs and with secondary equity offerings (SEOs). It is widely
known that the risk-adjusted returns of IPOs and SEOs in the aftermarket tend to be negative. Vijh finds that, unlike IPOs and
SEOs, carve-out stocks do not underperform the market during
the three-year period following the initial stock issue. On average,
the carve-outs earned annual returns of 14.3 percent, far in excess
of the average returns earned on IPOs and SEOs.

Like all financial innovations, the equity carve-out movement
began in the United States and has gradually spread to other
countries. The phenomenon is becoming especially popular in Europe, and some deals reach into the billions of dollars. The carve-
out of Alstom from Alcatel Alsthom and GEC in 1998 raised over
$3.7 billion. The two parents retained 48 percent of the company,
after publicly listing the other 52 percent. In that same year,
Rhône-Poulenc raised over $1.3 billion from the carve-out of Rho-
dia, while retaining 70 percent of the company's equity. Other no-
table European carve-outs in recent years include Scania (from
Investor), Orange (from Hutchison Whampoa and British Aero-
space), and New Holland (from Fiat).

Despite the obvious appeal of equity carve-outs, they have
their drawbacks. Parent company management must be willing to
give up hands-on control of the unit and play more of an advisory
role. As Allen points out, this does have the benefit of giving unit
managers a valuable opportunity to prove their skills and gain
valuable experience. In some parts of Europe and in most Asian
countries, however, a relative lack of managerial talent makes corporate management reluctant to extend such autonomy to divisional managers, even if they can overcome the historical aversion
in these countries to decentralizing corporate decision making.
Even in the United States, the issue of management talent can be
troublesome, as Thermo Electron's management conceded in attempting to explain its poor share price performance in 1998 (the
company's share price plummeted by more than 50 percent in the

13. Anand M. Vijh, "Long-Term Returns from Equity Carve-outs," *Journal of Financial Economics*, February 1999, pp. 273–308.

first six months of the year, giving back many of its gains from previous years and only partly recovering by the middle of 1999). Thermo Electron's chairman admits, "We got carried away with our own success. We spun out businesses that weren't solid and did not meet our criteria for growth potential and management depth."[14] The company put the Thermo prefix on the names of all its subsidiaries to provide instant credibility, but the tactic backfired when problems in some carved-out units reflected badly on the entire group.

Another concern is that equity carve-outs require public disclosure of financial and operating details that parent companies may not be accustomed to providing. Of course, from the perspective of shareholders, including those who own shares in the parent, the more information, the better. The problem is that the detailed disclosures of the subsidiaries may provide valuable information to competitors. In addition, the sheer volume of financial reporting can be daunting. By the middle of 1999, Thermo Electron had 23 public subsidiaries, each requiring its own annual report and quarterly earnings statements. That means 23 annual reports and 92 quarterly statements, not to mention the endless interactions with analysts.[15]

A further limitation is that the benefits of carve-outs are available only to divisions large enough to have an active secondary market after the IPO. Allen's research shows that the average amount of capital raised in an equity carve-out is more than $80 million. Given that the parent retains a majority stake in the unit, this implies an average market capitalization for the post-IPO firm of at least $160 million, and in many cases far higher. In 1998, the 14 largest carve-outs in the United Stated netted proceeds of $11.5 billion. DuPont, for example, raised $4.4 billion when it sold 30 percent of its oil subsidiary, Conoco. Rupert Murdoch's News Corp took in $2.8 billion with its 18.6 percent carve-out of Fox Entertainment.

Although most carve-outs are far smaller than these examples, there are important limits as to how small a division can be and still rate as a good candidate for a carve-out. Small divisions

---

14. Quoted in Claudia H. Deutsch, "A Lesson in Hatching Businesses," *International Herald Tribune*, June 8, 1999, p. 16.
15. In response to market pressure, Thermo Electron later sold off or consolidated several of these companies.

may not be good candidates because they are unlikely to trade with sufficient frequency or liquidity to generate meaningful share prices. In all but a few countries, securities markets tend to be thin and undercapitalized. Carving out slices of a company for public trading is not a realistic prospect when the parent company itself has not yet achieved desirable levels of liquidity. In such cases, parent company management must fall back on EVA or similar metrics to create the proper incentives for its divisional managers.

One variant of the equity carve-out avoids some of these drawbacks, although it does not involve a *public* offering of shares. Marsh & McLennan, the large American insurance company, created shares in its nontraded subsidiary, Putnam Investments, for sale or grant to key Putnam employees, but none of the shares were sold to the general investing public. As a result, the subsidiary avoids having to make extensive public disclosures because it is not publicly traded. Also, this form of carve-out is not dependent on firm size. The fact that the division remains privately held means that the parent does not have to worry about meeting a certain threshold in market capitalization to ensure adequate market liquidity. The obvious drawback, and it's a big one, is that the shares cannot be sold (or valued) as easily as in a more conventional carve-out in which the shares are floated on a public stock exchange. Still, the employees do become owners, even if they cannot value their stakes with any precision.

EVA still has a crucial role to play here. First, most business divisions, even in large companies, simply lack the size or value potential for a public offering to be viable. In such cases, companies can fall back on EVA to evaluate and pay divisional managers. Even in a carved-out business, however, EVA can sharpen value-creating incentives for managers one or two levels below the top managers (and new shareholders) of the business. In a sense, a carve-out, in much the same way as a spin-off or an MBO, pushes the line-of-sight problem down one level. Previous division managers are now top managers and shareholders. But divisions that are large enough to be spun off, bought out, or carved out are often themselves multidivisional. Now, the emphasis shifts to creating the right incentives for the divisional managers of these new public entities, a task greatly facilitated by the use of EVA.

Tracking Stock

In some cases, a parent company may not want to dilute its ownership interest in a subsidiary or operating division, as it must in an equity carve-out, but it would like to create division-specific equity incentives for its managers. Tracking stock carries dividend rights tied to the performance of a targeted division without transferring ownership or control over divisional assets. In contrast to a spin-off or an equity carve-out, the parent retains full control, allowing it to enjoy any operating synergies, or economies of scale in administration or finance. Another key benefit is that the creation of tracking stock is a nontaxable event.

General Motors (GM) pioneered the concept as a form of reorganization after it acquired EDS from Ross Perot. In the resulting deal, Perot insisted on receiving shares of a stock that would track the success of his former business rather than to GM's entire business. Hence, EDS tracking stock was born, although the company was later spun off. An important innovation occurred in 1991 when USX became the first company to use tracking stock as a vehicle for separating businesses when it created separate classes of stock for its steel and energy operations. But the phenomenon really began to take off in the late 1990s.

The catalyst for the enormous growth of such issues, so far confined mainly to the United States, is the booming Internet sector and, to a lesser extent, telecommunications. A typical candidate is the online business of a large company that needs to provide equity incentives for key employees or risk losing them to competing Internet start-ups. But because of the division's high growth potential, corporate management is unwilling to accept the dilution effect that comes from a carve-out. Increasingly, tracking stock is viewed as the answer.

Recent examples of tracking stock issues include the Internet-related assets of publisher Ziff-Davis, the life sciences business of DuPont, and the online brokerage firm of investment bankers Donaldson, Lufkin & Jenrette. AT&T's Liberty Media, Sprint PCS, and Network Associates' McAfee.com are other examples.

A key advantage of tracking stock is that it offers divisional managers a degree of decision-making authority that might otherwise be unattainable, given top management's reluctance to dilute its control over the division's assets. The practical effect should be to enhance job satisfaction for divisional managers, thus reducing retention risk while also increasing the company's responsiveness to changing market conditions. Also, investors have more direct access to the specific businesses of the parent, which can be highly useful in the case of a diversified company. Another possible reason for the growing popularity of trackers, although one generally left unstated by corporate managers, is that trackers allow mainstream companies to exploit the dual stock-market pricing that seemed to emerge in the late 1990s between conventional bricks-and-mortar businesses and high-tech or Internet pure plays. By creating tracked business units, conventional businesses too can benefit from the pricing frenzy in e-commerce stocks.

Despite these perceived advantages, we are highly skeptical of tracking stock. Shareholders have limited voting rights, if any; and they cannot elect their own boards. In other words, tracking stocks are downright unattractive from a corporate governance point of view. Moreover, if the parent company falls on hard times, conflict could develop between the shareholders of a tracked division, especially if it continues to do well, and the shareholders of the parent. The potential for such conflict could penalize the performance of the tracking stock. Such conflicts can only be aggravated by the possibility of an online business competing with other divisions of its parent.

Also, the alleged advantage of providing the capital markets with more information about the target business is largely illusory. If companies truly seek to help investors better understand these businesses, they need only expand disclosure and provide more detailed information.

Another important drawback with tracking stock is that it can dramatically increase the potential for conflict and litigation over accounting policy. Because the owners of the tracking stock have rights only over dividends, and because dividend payouts will be driven by the recognition of divisional profits, arguments over profit recognition are almost sure to arise whenever tracking stock investors are disappointed in their returns. They will surely be tempted to accuse corporate management of adopting policies that deliberately understate profits.

Because the tracking stock phenomenon is a recent one, such issues are likely to end up in (costly) litigation. In the coming years, a body of case law will develop, possibly augmented by legislation, to mediate some of the controversies. But in the meantime, the legal and economic consequences of tracking stock will be highly uncertain. As one observer writes, "trackers involve an elaborate and complex corporate structure only a lawyer could love."[16]

How well do tracking stocks perform? Again, the experience is very recent, but so far many have done well. A study by investment bankers Lehman Brothers finds that in a sample of 35 tracking stocks, the combined stock price performance of the parent stock and the tracking stock in the six months after the tracking stock was issued exceeded that of peer group companies in 28 of the cases. But this superior performance may simply reflect the boom in telecoms and Internet issues. Companies that invest more aggressively in the Internet than their competitors may exhibit superior stock price performance for this reason in particular, and not because they create tracked business units. In short, more time and experience is needed to draw any firm conclusions about the performance of tracking stock. Meanwhile, we remain skeptical.

CONCLUSION

In this chapter, we've looked at the challenges of promoting the maximization of shareholder value through the use of EVA-driven management compensation. We stressed that an important weakness in the competitive pay model widely used by American and European companies is that it makes future pay practically insensitive to current performance. Managers can underperform without adversely affecting expected pay in future years, because performance targets are adjusted downward. Such plans are a logical consequence of an almost paralyzing fear that corporate leaders have of losing good managers. In short, conventional pay programs elevate the minimization of retention risk to priority number 1, sacrificing alignment and wealth leverage in the process.

---

16. Burton G. Malkiel, "Tracking Stocks Are Likely to Derail," *The Wall Street Journal Europe*, February 15, 2000.

In addition, we noted that while the MBO model can create strong wealth-creating incentives, it also increases the risk of failure due to an increased burden of debt. Also, the huge debt burden reduces managerial flexibility, sometimes causing companies to pass on positive NPV (i.e., value-creating) investments with long-term payoffs, because the economic benefits won't be realized quickly enough to satisfy the demands of lenders. In contrast, a well-designed EVA bonus plan can offer strong alignment and wealth leverage incentives, but in a more flexible manner than MBOs and in a way that can motivate value-creating behavior from divisional managers.

PART TWO

Making It Work

The Technical Side of EVA

CHAPTER 5

The Cost of Capital

Companies create value for their shareholders by earning returns on invested capital that exceed the cost of that capital. But how do managers know their cost of capital? Certainly, they know how much they pay their bankers or bondholders for debt finance; however, the cost of equity finance is elusive. Many managers around the world act as if it is free, which it most definitely is not.

In fact, because equity investment is riskier to an investor than lending money to the same company, the cost of equity must include a risk premium over the rate that a company pays its lenders. How high should this premium be? Therein lies the major problem with identifying a company's cost of capital.

A further complicating factor is that even if a credible estimate for the cost of equity is possible, how do managers know what level of equity capital, or debt finance for that matter, is appropriate for their companies? In short, how do they know which mix of debt and equity will minimize the cost of capital and maximize EVA?

In this chapter, we show how the cost of capital is estimated according to established "best practice." We then discuss the factors that corporate finance managers should consider in designing appropriate capital structures for their firms.

WHAT IS THE COST OF CAPITAL?

The cost of capital for any investment, whether in a project, a business division, or an entire company, is the rate of return a capital provider would expect to receive if the capital were invested elsewhere, in a project, asset, or company of comparable risk. In other words, the cost of capital is an *opportunity* cost. The cost of capital for, say, project A is the benefit we forgo by not investing in other opportunities of similar risk because we invested in A. Why invest in A? Because we expect the return on that investment to be higher than what we would have expected if we invested in the next best alternative. If this weren't true, we would not commit our capital to project A.

Without going into the technical details of how to calculate the cost of capital, we have already learned two important lessons about it:

♦ The cost of capital is based on *expected* returns, not historical returns.
♦ The cost of capital is an opportunity cost that reflects the returns investors expect from other investments of similar risk.

The risk element is crucial to understanding the cost of capital and how it is calculated. All investors are risk-averse, preferring less risk to more. Of course, this does not mean that investors won't bear risk. It only means that they don't like risk, and they must be paid to bear it. How are they paid to bear risk? In the form of higher returns; it is as simple as that. What is not so simple, and requires some technical knowledge of how capital markets work, is just how much more investors must expect to get before they feel adequately compensated for risk. Later in this chapter we explore the issue in some detail.

Calculating WACC

Because different forms of financing carry different risks for investors, they must also carry different costs for the issuing company. As we have already learned, investors require higher returns for buying shares in a given company than they do when they lend, because the former is riskier. Therefore, a company's cost of capital depends not only on the cost of debt and equity financing but also on how much of each it has in its capital structure. This relationship is incorporated in the company's *weighted-average cost of capital*, popularly known as WACC, first introduced in Chapter 2. WACC is calculated as follows:

WACC = debt/total financing (cost of debt) $(1 - T)$
$\qquad\qquad$ + equity/total financing (cost of equity)

where total financing is the sum of the market value of debt and equity finance, and T is the company's tax rate.

To illustrate this, let's assume the following:

Market value of debt	= $30 M
Market value of equity	= $50 M
Cost of debt	= 9%
Tax rate	= 40%
Cost of equity	= 15%

The WACC equals $[30 \div (30 + 50)]$ (9 percent) $(1 - 40$ percent) + $[50 \div (30 + 50)]$ (15 percent), or 11.4 percent.

As the example shows, calculating a company's WACC requires that we know the following:

- The amount of debt in the capital structure, at market value
- The amount of equity in the capital structure, at market value
- The cost of debt
- The tax rate
- The cost of equity

The weightings for debt and equity are based on market values, not accounting book values, because we want to know how much it will cost the company to raise capital today, and that cost arises from market values, not book values. Some companies ignore both market-based and accounting-based weightings, using target weightings instead. The logic of this approach is that even if the company's current capital structure deviates from the target, which it nearly always does (at least to some extent), future financing decisions will bring the capital structure closer to the target. For example, if a company is underlevered relative to its target capital structure, investments in the near future might be financed largely with debt. Because the cost of capital is forward-looking, it makes sense to base the weightings on what they are likely to be in the (not-too-distant) future.

The *cost of debt* is the pretax rate that the company pays to its lenders. If the company has several sources of debt finance, each at different rates, the cost of debt used in the WACC formula is itself a weighted average. The corporate tax rate is important for WACC purposes because interest payments are tax-deductible. For example, if a company pays $20 million each year to its bankers in interest at an interest rate of 10 percent, and its tax rate is 40 percent, its *after-tax* cost of debt is only $12 million, or 6 percent. The deductibility of the interest shields $20 million of the company's revenues from income tax, providing the company with a net benefit of $8 million ($20 million × 40 percent). As we will see later, this tax shield is important not only for calculating a company's cost of capital but also for understanding the debt-equity choice faced by chief financial officers.

The first four elements required to calculate the WACC are thus either directly observable or nearly so. The only major question—and it is a big one—relates to the cost of equity. At its simplest level, the cost of equity is the return that investors require to make an equity investment in the firm. The problem is that we cannot directly observe this return requirement. In the case of debt finance, a contract stipulates repayment terms, including the rate of interest. But there is no such analogue for equity finance.

At this point, you may wonder why we don't just ask equity investors how much of a return they want. Unfortunately, it is not that easy, mainly because in all but the smallest firms there are usually a lot of them. The largest publicly traded companies have hundreds of thousands of shareholders, maybe more. Moreover, even if we could ask them all, they might not be able to express a concrete return requirement in the same way that our bankers can. When asked, shareholders might simply say, "I want a return as high as possible," which obviously would not provide any concrete guidance for estimating the cost of equity. The only option left to managers is to try to deduce investor requirements by observing capital market behavior. This effort requires a model of how risky assets, such as shares in a business firm, are priced by capital markets. The most popular model for this purpose is called the *capital asset pricing model* (CAPM).

The CAPM

The CAPM was developed independently by Professors William Sharpe of Stanford University and John Lintner of Harvard University, drawing on previous contributions to finance theory by James Tobin and Harry Markowitz. Although the model has been the subject of book-length treatments, its basic intuition can be summarized as follows:

$$E(R) = R_f + \text{beta } [E(R_m) - R_f]$$

where $E(R)$ is the expected return on any risky asset, R_f is the return on a risk-free asset (such as a government bond), beta is a measure of risk, and $E(R_m)$ is the expected return on the stock market (usually as measured by the S&P 500, FT-100, or some other market index).

If the formula seems daunting at first, the logic behind it is really quite simple: The expected return on a risky asset, such as an equity investment, equals the return on a riskless asset plus a risk premium. That risk premium equals a *market risk premium*, which reflects the price paid by the stock market to all equity investors, adjusted for beta, a company risk factor. And that's it.

If it is that simple, why is estimating the cost of equity so controversial? The CAPM is an expectational model. That's what the "E" in the term $E(R)$ stands for. The model is based on what investors expect to happen, not on what has already happened. Unfortunately, we cannot observe expectations; we can only estimate or deduce them from the way stock market investors behave. Moreover, determining the appropriate risk-free asset, the market risk premium, and the calculation of company betas requires judgments and interpretations that can lead to differing conclusions.

The latest thinking is that best practice should get us within 3 percentage points of the true cost of equity. If our company is financed one-third with debt and two-thirds with equity (a common proportion), this means that the statistical error estimate of the WACC could be as much as 2 percentage points. This uncertainty has several important implications.

- The cost of equity is clearly greater than zero, and EVA with a best estimate of WACC is a far better measure of performance than earnings with no charge for equity capital,
- Our best estimate of WACC should be changed sparingly and only when the evidence indicates a substantial change, e.g., 1 percentage point or more,
- The true impact of strategies based on changes in the cost of capital, e.g., capital structure changes, cannot be predicted with great accuracy, and hence, companies should be cautious in gambling on such strategies.

On the basis of the CAPM, and a market risk premium of 5 percent, the WACC for most publicly traded companies in the United States is between 8 and 11 percent. For particularly high-risk sectors, such as Internet stocks, WACCs can be far higher than 11 percent because of high operating risk, high market risk (these stocks tend to be volatile), and the near total reliance on expensive equity to finance assets. WACCs in other developed markets, such as Canada, are similar to those of the United States, although finance specialists tend to assign slightly lower WACCs to German companies and slightly higher ones to British companies. These differences are caused mainly by differences in government bond rates. Returns on German government bonds in recent years have been lower than those of U.S. Treasury bonds, while the returns of U.K. gilts have been higher. Logically, as government bond rates differ, so do WACCs.

WHAT IS BETA?

The CAPM makes several assumptions about investor behavior. Among the most important of these are (1) that investors are risk-averse and (2) that risk-averse investors choose to be diversified. Although share prices for all companies traded on a stock exchange tend to move up and down together, there are also stock price movements for individual shares that seem to have no relation to macroeconomic or marketwide factors. Instead, these price movements are driven by events or circumstances unique to a particular company or its industry. This insight implies that stock price movements, and therefore the risk of investing in the equity of a company, can be summarized as follows:

Total risk = market risk + company-specific risk

The important point to grasp about company-specific risk is that investors can effectively eliminate it just by diversifying into other companies. In fact, most of that risk is neutralized in portfolios with as few as a dozen stocks, diversified geographically and by industry. For the average stock, about 70 percent of total volatility is company-specific, which means that only 30 percent is the result of market risk. Of course, the relative influence of market and company-specific risk varies widely from company to company.

Beta, on the other hand, measures the volatility of a company's stock price with respect to the overall stock market. It reflects *market* risk, as opposed to *company-specific* risk and cannot be diversified away. While we can hedge market risk with derivative instruments such as options and futures, we cannot eliminate it simply by investing in more companies.

The CAPM assumes that because company-specific risk can be eliminated through diversification, we shouldn't expect capital markets to reward investors for bearing that type of risk. Market risk, however, is different, for it is not diversifiable. We cannot avoid market risk, or even expect to reduce it, simply by expanding our portfolios. Because this risk is not diversifiable, capital markets must compensate investors for bearing it. We can eliminate this risk completely by using derivatives, but in such cases we cease to be stock market investors and instead become *de facto* investors in government bonds.

In the parlance of the CAPM, market risk is called *systematic risk*, and company-specific risk is called *unsystematic risk*. We can now expand our definition of risk:

Total risk = market risk + company-specific risk
           = nondiversifiable risk + diversifiable risk
           = systematic risk + unsystematic risk

The market is assumed to reward investors in proportion to the amount of systematic risk they are willing to bear. In other words, the greater the systematic risk, the greater the expected return. Beta is a measure of systematic risk. Unsystematic risk, on the other hand, carries no reward. We can bear as much of it as we like, but the market pays us nothing for it. At least that is what the CAPM tells us.

By definition, the average beta in a given market is 1.0; risky companies have betas higher than 1.0, and less risky companies have betas lower than 1.0. Therefore, while the same *market* risk premium applies to all companies, the *company* risk premium used to calculate a WACC depends also on that company's beta. The higher the beta, the higher the company risk premium. And the higher the risk premium, the greater the cost of equity. For example, if the market risk premium is 5 percent, and the company beta is 1.5, the company's risk premium is 7.5 percent (5 percent $\times$ 1.5). A beta higher than 1.0 simply means that the share price of that particular company tends to be more volatile than the stock market as a whole. The reverse is true for companies with betas lower than 1.0.

Calculating Beta for a Publicly Traded Company

So how then is beta calculated, and where does it come from?

Consider the case of Sun Microsystems. Imagine buying shares in Sun at the beginning of December 1997 and then selling the shares at the end of the month. The return on your investment equals the price appreciation or depreciation on Sun's shares plus any dividends paid by Sun in that month (although, in reality, Sun does not pay dividends). Now imagine doing the same for the stock market (which is defined here as the S&P 500 market index). Repeating this exercise for the 59 previous months, we obtain 60 months of paired returns for Sun Microsystems and for the S&P 500, which are shown in Table 5–1. In other words, we calculate total shareholder return for Sun and the S&P 500 over each of the 60 months between January 1993 and December 1997.

We can then graph these 60 data points, with returns for Sun on the y axis and returns for the S&P 500 on the x axis. Regressing Sun Microsystems' returns on the S&P 500's returns yields a trend line, shown in Figure 5–1. This regression reflects the equation, $y = a + bx$, where y is the dependent variable (in this case, returns on Sun Microsystems), x is the independent variable (returns on the S&P 500), a is the y intercept, and b is the slope coefficient that defines the relationship between the x and y variables. The widely

T A B L E   5–1

Monthly Returns for Sun Microsystems and the S&P 500, January 1993–December 1997

	Sun Microsystems	S&P 500		Sun Microsystems	S&P 500
January 1993	0.1599	0.0070	January 1996	0.0082	0.0326
February 1993	−0.0994	0.0105	February 1996	0.1413	0.0069
March 1993	−0.1459	0.0187	March 1996	−0.1667	0.0079
April 1993	−0.1000	−0.0254	April 1996	0.2400	0.0134
May 1993	0.1111	0.0227	May 1996	0.1544	0.0229
June 1993	−0.0125	0.0008	June 1996	−0.0599	0.0023
July 1993	0.0043	−0.0053	July 1996	−0.0722	−0.0457
August 1993	−0.1176	0.0344	August 1996	−0.0046	0.0188
September 1993	−0.0858	−0.0100	September 1996	0.1425	0.0542
October 1993	0.0625	0.0194	October 1996	−0.0181	0.0261
November 1993	0.0441	−0.0129	November 1996	−0.0451	0.0734
December 1993	0.0939	0.0101	December 1996	−0.1180	−0.0215
January 1994	−0.0901	0.0325	January 1997	0.2360	0.0613
February 1994	0.0235	−0.0300	February 1997	−0.0276	0.0059
March 1994	0.0093	−0.0457	March 1997	−0.0648	−0.0426
April 1994	−0.1826	0.0115	April 1997	−0.0021	0.0584
May 1994	−0.0670	0.0124	May 1997	0.1193	0.0586
June 1994	−0.0121	−0.0268	June 1997	0.1541	0.0435

accepted convention is to convert the coefficients a and b into their Greek counterparts, α and β, which is why we use the term *beta*.

The slope of the trend line when we regress the returns for Sun Microsystems on the returns for the S&P 500—1.19—is the beta for Sun Microsystems, which can be interpreted to mean that monthly returns on Sun were approximately 20 percent more volatile than the stock market as a whole. If we assume a market risk premium of 5 percent, the risk premium for Sun's equity would be about 6 percent.

WHY IS BETA CONTROVERSIAL?

The Sun Microsystems example seems simple enough. But several critical assumptions are required to derive a beta for the company,

T A B L E   5–1

Continued

	Sun Microsystems	S&P 500		Sun Microsystems	S&P 500
July 1994	0.0789	0.0315	July 1997	0.2275	0.0781
August 1994	0.1909	0.0376	August 1997	0.0506	−0.0575
September 1994	0.1085	−0.0269	September 1997	−0.0247	0.0532
October 1994	0.1149	0.0208	October 1997	−0.2684	−0.0345
November 1994	0.0228	−0.0395	November 1997	0.0511	0.0446
December 1994	0.0597	0.0123	December 1997	0.1076	0.0157
January 1995	−0.0774	0.0243			
February 1995	−0.0230	0.0361			
March 1995	0.0860	0.0273			
April 1995	0.1474	0.0280			
May 1995	0.1285	0.0363			
June 1995	0.0778	0.0213			
July 1995	−0.0078	0.0318			
August 1995	0.2026	−0.0003			
September 1995	0.0885	0.0401			
October 1995	0.2381	−0.0050			
November 1995	0.0785	0.0410			
December 1995	0.0847	0.0174			

and all these assumptions can be questioned. Let's consider each of them:

+ We chose a return interval of one month. Yet, the CAPM does not specify a particular period for measuring historical returns. (In fact, the CAPM is really based on expectations of future returns, but because such returns are unobservable, historical returns are used instead.) One month is chosen for the sake of convenience, and this is what Standard & Poor's uses for its beta calculations, but some estimates of beta, like those of Bloomberg and Value Line, are based on weekly returns. Indeed, some academic research uses betas from daily returns, although finance specialists reject this approach

F I G U R E   5—1

Scatter plot and trend line; Sun Microsystems and the S&P 500. Based on monthly returns, January 1993 to December 1997.

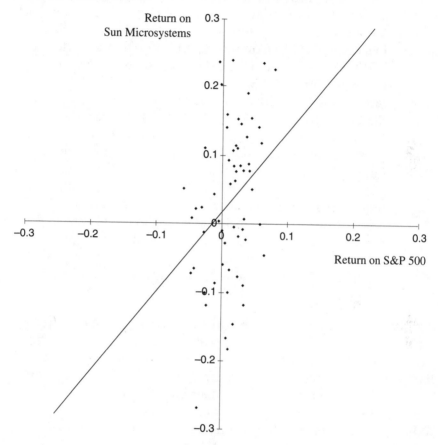

for corporate use because daily share price movements tend to be dominated by noise.

- The beta in our example is based on five years of returns. Again, the CAPM tells us nothing about the appropriate time period required for estimation. Value Line and Standard & Poor's also use five years, but Bloomberg uses only two years.
- The S&P 500 is chosen as our definition of the market. But the "market" referred to in the CAPM formula is the

"market portfolio," which consists of every risky asset in the universe, including human capital. This theoretical construct is, of course, unobservable, which is why we use market proxies such as the S&P 500, which is the choice of both Bloomberg and, not surprisingly, Standard & Poor. Value Line, however, uses the New York Stock Exchange (NYSE) Composite, an index that includes all NYSE stocks. In the UK, betas are usually based on the Financial Times All-Shares index, or the FT-100. In France, the CAC 40 is the standard market index, while the Germans use the DAX and the Italians use the MIBTEL. Furthermore, as capital markets become increasingly global, should one not use a global market index? The decision of which index to use is crucial because different definitions of "market" yield different market risk premiums. For example, the average annual return from 1991 to 1995 in the U.S. markets was 13.7 percent, 14.2 percent, or 19.6 percent, depending on whether the market is defined as the NYSE Composite, the S&P 500, or the Value Line index. Different indexes also yield different betas.

When the market is defined as the S&P 500, the beta for Sun Microsystems is 1.19. But as the scatter plot in Figure 5–1 shows, the relationship between returns on Sun and returns on the S&P 500 is weak. In fact, the R^2 of the regression that yields the trend line is only 10 percent, which means that 90 percent of the variation in returns on Sun Microsystems' stock is caused by factors other than market risk. Sun is one of the constituent stocks of the S&P 500, but it is also part of the NASDAQ 100, an index of America's largest over-the-counter stocks, which includes many of the major players in the computer industry, including Microsoft and Cisco Systems.

Figure 5–2 shows the scatter plot and trend line for Sun Microsystems when the NASDAQ 100 becomes the market proxy. As we can see from the graph, the dispersion around the trend line is less in this case than when we defined the market as the S&P 500, reflecting a much higher R^2 for the NASDAQ than the S&P regression (0.25 versus 0.10). The higher R^2 is to be expected

F I G U R E   5–2

Scatter plot and trend line; Sun Microsystems and the NASDAQ 100. Based on monthly returns, January 1993 to December 1997.

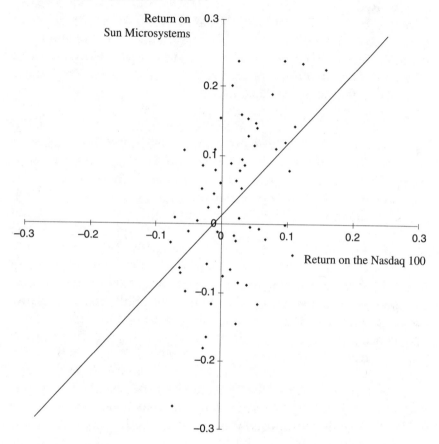

given the greater weighting of computer stocks in the NASDAQ. The slope of the trend line changes, however, and so does the beta. Sun's beta is now 1.06, instead of 1.19. The lower beta does not necessarily imply a lower cost of equity, because the market risk premium is likely to be higher for the NASDAQ 100 than for the S&P 500. Although Sun Microsystems is part of both indexes, the S&P 500 is the more conservative of the two, with more blue-chip stocks.

THE MARKET RISK PREMIUM DEBATE

Much of the current debate over estimating the cost of equity centers on the market risk premium (MRP). Although 5 percent is widely used, plus or minus a percentage point, there are many market professionals, and more than a few prominent financial economists, who believe that the risk premium is substantially lower. A seemingly endless bull market, in progress since the early 1980s, has forced observers to question previously held convictions about financial markets, among them that stock market investors require large return premiums over bonds; otherwise, they will not buy stocks. The problem with a large MRP is that the future earnings or EVAs already impounded in the share prices of many blue-chip companies, assuming an MRP of 5 percent, will require many years of growth rates similar to those observed in booming emerging markets (6 percent, 8 percent, or even higher). When future earnings or EVAs are imputed from lower MRPs, the required growth rates are much lower. This type of analysis has led some financial experts to conclude that the MRP is probably only 2 or 3 percent. Of course, there is a self-serving element to all of this, as investment houses struggle to defend buy recommendations to clients in high-priced markets. Still, there is a growing sense that the MRP is lower than previously thought.

James Glassman and Kevin Hassett of the American Enterprise Institute, a Washington, D.C.-based think tank, have even gone on record as saying that risk premiums are probably zero, or at least are moving in that direction. On this basis, they argue, a level for the Dow Jones Industrials of 36,000 can be easily defended. When they proposed this argument early in 1999, the Dow had just broken 10,000 for the first time.[1]

Glassman and Hassett draw on the research of Jeremy Siegel, a Wharton School professor, who has examined nearly 200 years of stock market returns. His work shows that, over the long run, stocks have always beaten inflation over 20-year holding periods, while bonds often have not. This finding holds even through

---

1. James K. Glassman and Kevin A. Hassett, "Stock Prices Are Still Far Too Low," *Wall Street Journal Europe*, March 18, 1999, p. 12.

world wars, panics, and depressions. In brief, stocks have actually been *safer* than bonds as a long-term investment.

Of course, that stocks have had superior returns over the generations is precisely what led financial economists to conclude that investors expect a substantial risk premium from stocks, or they will put their money elsewhere. But if stocks really are safer than bonds, at least in the long term, this demand for extra return is irrational. Investors fear the volatility of stocks but shouldn't. Will this "irrationality" continue? Glassman and Hassett think not, suggesting that since the start of the great bull market in 1982, investors have become calmer and smarter. They argue that the risk premium today is probably around 3 percent, and it is heading still lower toward its "proper" level of zero. If they are right, the expected EVAs of publicly traded companies will be discounted by the capital markets at much lower interest rates, resulting in huge gains in stock prices.

Why is the risk premium dropping? Glassman and Hassett offer several reasons:

- Investors have become better educated about stocks, in part because of mutual funds and increased media coverage of financial markets.
- The growth of tax-deferred savings, such as individual retirement accounts in the United States, force long-term holdings, and the longer the holding period, the safer stocks become as an investment.
- Thanks to shareholder pressure and global competition, businesses have restructured, becoming more efficient and thus less likely to suffer devastating reversals in a recession.
- Monetary and fiscal management by the U.S. government has greatly improved.
- The regulatory and tax environment, at least in the United States, is more benign than it used to be.
- Foreign threats, such as Cold War rivalries, have diminished (recent wars in the former Yugoslavia notwithstanding).

If these observers are right about the market risk premium, the upside potential for equities is staggering.

Still, there is a compelling reason to believe that the market risk premium is higher than the Glassman and Hassett thesis suggests. Many investors have far shorter horizons than those required for a zero, or near-zero risk premium, and for perfectly sound and rational reasons. For example, middle-aged investors, a group that has been among the most aggressive buyers of equities in recent years, are far from indifferent to stock returns in the short or medium term because many rely on their stock portfolios to support their retirement years. A 50-year-old investor who hopes to retire in five years may not have the time to wait for a market recovery if a bear market occurs. Even younger investors may rationally adopt relatively short investment horizons if their savings are targeted to financing the purchase of a home or a child's education.

In short, we disagree with Glassman and Hassett when they allege that equities are no riskier than bonds because rational investors, such as the pension funds that are playing an increasingly important role in the world's capital markets, will adopt a suitably long investment horizon. Because many investors rationally choose shorter horizons, and as horizons shrink, equities become riskier. It is perfectly logical to expect that the market risk premium is still substantially greater than zero. Although we reject the 7 to 8 percent premiums that are used by some finance specialists, we equally reject the 0 to 3 percent premiums used in some investment circles. In our work, we assume a 5 percent risk premium, and we use this assumption throughout the book.

ESTIMATING BETAS FOR PRIVATE FIRMS AND DIVISIONS

Estimating company betas normally requires stock market returns. But what if a company is not publicly traded, or if we want to calculate WACCs for *divisions* of public companies? Publicly traded firms may have observable returns data, but operating divisions within these firms are essentially privately held companies. Without the opportunity to observe stock market returns, how can we estimate beta?

The approach for estimating betas of operating divisions depends largely on whether the divisions are organized by product line or geography.

Organized Geographically

If divisions are organized geographically, the standard procedure for estimating the cost of equity is to ignore beta. Instead, a company or product line risk premium is added to the rate of return on local government bonds, assuming the division is largely funded in the home currency. If, on the other hand, financing comes mainly from the parent (i.e., the division is not self-financing), the risk premium is added to the government bond rate in the parent company's home currency, but with an additional premium if the division is located outside the developed market economies. For example, if an American company has operations in Poland, but investments in the division are funded mainly in dollars, the cost of capital for the Polish division can be estimated by adding the difference between returns on dollar-denominated Polish government debt and U.S. Treasury bonds. If the difference is, say, 250 basis points, 2.5 percentage points would be added to the corporate cost of equity to arrive at the divisional cost of equity.[2] A target capital structure can then be used to derive a divisional WACC.

Organized by Product Line

If divisions are based on product lines, betas can be estimated from comparable firms in the same or similar industries that are traded on a public stock exchange. To illustrate, suppose we identify five public companies that appear broadly similar to our division in terms of their product offerings. Published sources (such as Bloomberg's or Value Line) reveal betas as follows:

Company A	1.35
Company B	1.10
Company C	1.43
Company D	1.23
Company E	1.24

---

2. Companies will sometimes adjust the risk premium downward to account for expected diversification from investing in emerging markets.

The simplest approach is to take the average of these five betas, or 1.27, and assume that this is our division's beta. There is, however, an important drawback to this approach. Capital structure is known to influence beta. As firms become more highly levered, betas increase. Greater debt increases fixed interest payments, which in turn increases the volatility of earnings, cashflows, and stock returns. To see the impact of debt, assume that the average ratio of debt to equity (at market value) for companies A to E is 0.45, but the target capital structure for our division is 0.25. In other words, the comparables have riskier capital structures than we consider appropriate for our division. If so, the beta based on a simple average of the observed betas for the comparables—1.27—is overstated. In this case, or when our target leverage is higher than the comparables, the average beta for the comparables should be "unlevered," which means that we estimate what the betas of these companies would be if they had no debt in their capital structure. The unlevered beta is then "relevered" with our target capital structure.

We unlever betas using the following formula:

Unlevered beta (β_U)

$$= \frac{\text{Observed, or levered, beta } (\beta_L)}{1 + (1 - \text{corporate tax rate}) \,(\text{debt/equity})}$$

In our example, $\beta_L = 1.27$ and the debt/equity ratio $= 0.45$. Assuming an average corporate tax rate for the comparables of 40 percent, the unlevered beta can now be estimated:

$$\beta_U = \frac{1.27}{1 + [(1 - 0.40)\,(0.45)]}$$

which equals 1.00. This means that while the average observed beta for the five comparables is 1.27, if they had been all-equity firms, with no debt, their average beta would be 1.00.

To derive the beta for our division, we take the unlevered beta of 1.00 and lever it back up again, but this time at our target capital structure:

$$\beta_L = \beta_U \times [1 + (1 - \text{corporate tax rate})\,(\text{debt/equity})]$$

In our example, the target debt/equity ratio is 0.25, which yields the following relevered beta:

$$\beta_L = 1.00 \times [1 + (1 - 0.40)\,(0.25)]$$

which equals 1.15. Therefore, we assign a beta of 1.15 to our division. The same procedure would be followed for estimating betas in privately held firms.

This practice of levering and unlevering betas has its uses even when you are estimating betas for publicly traded entities. Confidence in beta estimation can be increased by using the above procedure to estimate an unlevered industry beta. This beta can then be levered up based on the subject company's capital structure. If the relevered industry beta is close to the company beta (say, within one standard error), no adjustment is required. But if there is a large discrepancy between the company beta and the industry beta, even after controlling for leverage, a revision of the company beta in the direction of the industry beta may be called for.

LIMITATIONS OF THE CAPM

Empirical tests of the CAPM have been conducted since the early 1970s. The early results were encouraging, showing that the average return on a portfolio of stocks was positively related to the beta of the portfolio. This is exactly what the CAPM predicts. The higher the beta, the higher the returns. Not all results were consistent with these findings, but by the late 1970s the CAPM was embraced by financial economists and by their students who later went on to careers in corporate finance. The first serious chink in the CAPM's armor appeared in 1977 with an article by UCLA Professor Richard Roll. Now known as Roll's Critique, it argues that the CAPM is empirically untestable (and therefore we can never really know whether it is true or not) because the "market portfolio" actually includes every risky asset in the universe. Thus, any test using proxies for the market portfolio, such as the S&P 500, is in fact a joint test of two hypotheses: whether the CAPM is correct and whether the chosen proxy is efficient. Efficiency means that the proxy in question produces risk-adjusted returns at least as high as any subset of stocks from the proxy.

In other words, we could form any number of portfolios of stocks that are part of the market proxy, and these portfolios would not outperform the entire proxy on a risk-adjusted basis. If this weren't true, it would suggest that company-specific (i.e., unsystematic) risk is priced by the market and that beta alone does not explain stock returns. In such a case, we might say that the CAPM is wrong; yet perhaps we simply chose the wrong proxy. The point of Roll's Critique is that no empirical test of the CAPM can isolate the jointly tested hypotheses: Is the market portfolio efficient, and did we choose the right proxy for the market? In short, we can never really know whether the CAPM is right or wrong.

Roll's Critique and other developments in capital market theory at the time led to articles proclaiming "beta is dead" as early as 1980. But the CAPM has proven remarkably resilient. Throughout the 1980s, a growing number of companies around the world began using it to estimate their cost of capital. By the end of the decade, the CAPM was widely accepted as best practice. The model received a further boost in 1990 when one of its originators, William Sharpe, received the Nobel Prize for sharing in its development.

But two important articles in the early 1990s by Professors Eugene Fama and Kenneth French raised troubling doubts about the CAPM.[3] Professor Fama's contribution is particularly ironic because he is a coauthor of one of the early articles supporting the model. Fama and French report two major findings. First, they show that the relationship between average stock returns and beta was weak over the 1941 to 1990 period and virtually nonexistent from 1963 through 1990. Second, they argue that stock returns are related to price/earnings ratios and market value-to-book value ratios.

One limitation of these findings is that financial economists have yet to develop a convincing theory that explains why investors demand premiums for investing in low price/earnings and low market-to-book stocks. We also lack a methodology for converting these insights into estimates of risk premiums. Because there is a plausible theory in support of beta, we will continue to use it until a clearly superior alternative emerges.

---

3. E. F. Fama and K. R. French, "The Cross-section of Expected Stock Returns," *Journal of Finance*, 1992, pp. 427–466; and "Common Risk Factors in the Returns on Stocks and Bonds," *Journal of Financial Economics*, 1993, pp. 3–56.

THE ARBITRAGE PRICING
MODEL ALTERNATIVE

The Fama and French findings, along with numerous other critiques of the CAPM that have emerged over the past 20 years, have led to the search for something better. The best-known challenger to the CAPM is the arbitrage pricing model (APM). Although working versions of the APM have been around since the early 1980s, it has yet to catch on with anything even approaching the popularity of the CAPM. Still, the number of APM adherents has been slowly growing.

The logic behind the APM is very similar to that underlying the CAPM. Investors are rewarded only for taking on systematic, or nondiversifiable, risk. The main difference is that the APM allows for *multiple* systematic risk factors, while the CAPM allows for only one, sensitivity to the market portfolio. The term *arbitrage* is used here because investors are assumed to exploit arbitrage opportunities. Arbitrage is based on the "law of one price," which says that two identical assets should sell for the same price. If they sell for different prices, traders can capture riskless profits merely by simultaneously selling the higher-priced asset while buying the lower-priced one. For example, if two portfolios of stocks have the same risk exposure but offer different returns, investors will buy the portfolio that has the higher expected returns while selling the portfolio with the lower expected returns. In this way, prices adjust, bringing expected returns back to equilibrium.

One problem with the APM is that its underlying theory says nothing about what the multiple risk factors might be. In fact, it doesn't even tell us how many factors there are. In response to this problem, users of the APM resort to empirical tests of historical returns to reveal the number and identity of the factors.

The APM assumes that the returns on any asset, including shares in a company, can be deconstructed into an expected, or predictable, return component and an unanticipated, or surprise, component. Because the predictable component of returns should already be impounded in share price, only the surprise component causes share price to change. Therefore, the unanticipated part of the return is the true risk of any investment. We know that this must be true because if we get what was expected, there can be no risk or uncertainty. We can express this insight as follows:

$$R = E(R) + U$$

where R is return, $E(R)$ is expected return, and U is unanticipated return.

As in the CAPM, unsystematic, or company-specific, risk is assumed to be diversifiable and therefore is not rewarded. For example, company news about the impending retirement of its CEO may move the company's share price, but because the impact is limited mainly to just that company, the share price movements caused by such events are likely to wash out in diversified portfolios. In other words, company-specific news may move stock price, but portfolio returns should be unaffected, since the unsystematic price movements of the various stocks that make up a portfolio largely cancel each other out. Surprises in gross domestic product (GDP), inflation, and interest rates, on the other hand, affect nearly all companies to some degree. Thus, unanticipated changes in any of these macroeconomic indicators are potential systematic risk factors. Note that the measures themselves are not risk factors; only *unanticipated changes* are.

If we believe that these three factors are sufficient to describe the systematic risks that influence stock returns, we can restate the relationship between risk and return in this way:

$$R = E(R) + \beta_{\text{GDP}}\, F_{\text{GDP}} + \beta_{\text{INF}}\, F_{\text{INF}} + \beta_{i\text{RATE}}\, F_{i\text{RATE}} + \varepsilon$$

Notice that we now have three betas instead of one as in the CAPM, because we now have three systematic risk factors. Each factor has its own beta and is priced separately by the capital markets. The Greek letter ε measures the unsystematic portion of stock returns, which is simply any return that cannot be explained by the systematic risk factors.

It is not enough that we know, or think we know, the identity of the risk factors. Deriving a cost of equity for the firm requires that we also price each of the factors. For example, how much will the market pay investors to bear the risk of unanticipated inflation? In the case of the CAPM, which has just one risk factor, the answer is straightforward. The market risk premium is the "price" that companies must pay to compensate investors for bearing systematic risk, modified for each company's beta. Thus, when we say that the market risk premium is 5 percent, we are really saying that 5 percent is the price the stock market pays investors who buy shares in companies of average risk. For a macroeconomic factor such as unanticipated inflation to be truly systematic, it too must be "priced." But how would we know that, and how can we estimate it? Although there is a lot of debate these days over the magnitude of the market risk premium under the CAPM, at least we know what we are supposed to be measuring. With the APM, the process of deriving prices for the factors is much more complicated.

First, we need a time series of monthly realizations for each of the systematic risk factors: unanticipated changes in GDP, unanticipated inflation, and unanticipated changes in interest rates, which can be derived from models that compare, for example, *actual* inflation with *expected* inflation. Estimates for expectations are usually based on published consensus forecasts of inflation for a given month made by a sample of macroeconomists. Similar procedures would be followed for GDP and interest rates. To illustrate how we might derive betas from these observations, let's assume that we have 60 months of realizations for each factor covering the period January 1994 through December 1998.

The next step is to estimate the betas (i.e., factor sensitivities) for each of the risk factors based on time series regressions. Unfortunately, if we are estimating the model ourselves, it is not sufficient that we estimate the betas for the firm in question. As we will see shortly, we must also estimate them for a large cross section of other companies traded in the same stock market (let's say 500 of them). Our estimate of the betas is based on the equation:

$$R_{it} = \alpha + \beta_{GDP}\, F_{GDP} + \beta_{INF}\, F_{INF} + \beta_{iRATE}\, F_{iRATE} + \varepsilon$$

where R_{it} is the return in month t (60 months in all) for company i, α is a regression constant, and ε is the unsystematic portion of returns. In the language of econometrics, we would say that stock market returns for our sample of companies (including our own) in each of the 60 months between January 1994 and December 1998 are regressed on the realizations of the three systematic risk factors (the Fs in the equation) over the same 60-month period. Therefore, we will have three betas for each of the 500 companies in our sample.

We need betas for a large number of companies, because without them we cannot estimate the price for each of the risk factors. These prices are estimated with a series of cross-sectional regressions—that is, monthly returns for each of the 500 companies in, say, January 1999 are regressed against the betas we calculate from the time series regressions. The coefficients that emerge from these regressions, which are usually represented by the Greek letter gamma (γ), represent the prices of the systematic risk factors:

$$R_i = R_f + \gamma_{\text{GDP}}\, \beta_{i\text{GDP}} + \gamma_{\text{INF}}\, \beta_{i\text{INF}} + \gamma_{i\text{RATE}}\, \beta_{ii\text{RATE}} + \varepsilon$$

where R_f is the risk-free rate (i.e., the return on government bonds), γ_{GDP} is the price paid by the market for bearing exposure to unanticipated changes in GDP, γ_{INF} is the price paid for bearing exposure to unanticipated inflation, $\gamma_{i\text{RATE}}$ is the price paid for bearing exposure to unanticipated changes in interest rates, and ε is an error term.

We would repeat this regression for each of the remaining months in 1999, and then average the gammas over the 12-month period. We can then estimate our own company's cost of equity using the equation:

$$E(R_{\text{equity}}) = R_f + \beta_{\text{GDP}}\, \gamma_{\text{GDP}} + \beta_{\text{INF}}\, \gamma_{\text{INF}} + \beta_{i\text{RATE}}\, \gamma_{i\text{RATE}}$$

where $E(R_{\text{equity}})$ is the expected return on the company's shares, the betas are the company's own sensitivities to each of the risk factors, and the gammas are the average gammas calculated over 1999. As in the CAPM, the APM assumes that investors in equities expect to earn the risk-free rate plus a risk premium. In this case, however, there are three risk premiums, not just one.

If it's so complicated, why bother? Despite the obvious difficulties in deriving a cost of equity using the APM, the model does offer advantages over the CAPM. First, because it allows for multiple risk factors, the APM can explain a larger portion of stock returns than the CAPM, resulting in the likelihood of more reliable estimates for the cost of equity. The Alcar Group claims that its version of the APM, which is based on five macroeconomic variables, explains on average 37 percent of stock price movements, versus only 22 percent for the CAPM. Other users of the APM claim similar improvements in explanatory power.

The APM offers the further advantage of helping corporate managers to understand their risk exposures better. Instead of a market beta, the APM reveals sensitivities to a series of macroeconomic variables, thus affording a certain intuitive appeal that the CAPM lacks. We know that elements of business risk, such as operating leverage (the proportion of fixed costs in a company's cost structure) influence CAPM betas, but we cannot know by how much. Yet when we have variables linked to observable macroeconomic phenomena such as economic growth, inflation, interest rates, oil prices, housing starts, and so on, we can measure the contribution that each factor makes to systematic risk.

These insights help companies to better understand the forces that buffet their share prices and can also offer important advantages to investment managers. For example, if a portfolio manager believes that inflation will be lower than the consensus forecast, a portfolio can be constructed with stocks having high inflation betas. If the manager's forecast is correct, this portfolio will outperform other portfolios having the same CAPM beta. In other words, investment strategies can be fine-tuned to exploit or avoid specific macroeconomic risks. Such fine-tuning is not possible with the CAPM.

Despite the APM's intellectual appeal, and its potential as a more accurate and powerful tool for measuring company exposure to market risk, we continue to rely on the CAPM. As we note above, the theory behind APM tells us nothing about the identity of the risk factors or how many factors there are. In addition, the risk premium puzzle that besets the CAPM creates even more problems for the user of the APM. We have described a well-accepted procedure for estimating the price of each risk factor. However, because the resulting risk premiums are measured with error, and because historical results may not apply to the future, we have the same problem that we had previously in determining the proper market risk premium under the CAPM, only now the problem is compounded by the multiple risk factors of the APM.

Finally, the APM is far more difficult to apply in practice than the CAPM. Some corporate users believe that the benefits more than compensate for the costs, but we are not yet convinced. Until we are, or until a better model that is both conceptually sound and practical comes along, we will continue to use the CAPM to estimate cost of equity as part of the weighted-average cost of capital.

FINANCIAL STRATEGY AND VALUE CREATION

The cost of capital is more than just one element in the calculation of EVA. It is a cost of doing business, and like any other cost, management should aim to minimize it, without sacrificing the firm's primary business mission.

As the EVA calculations make clear, managers can boost EVA, and promote value creation, by using assets more efficiently. Fewer assets mean less capital, lower capital charges, and higher EVA. Generating as much revenue and profit as possible from a company's assets is a critical component of operating efficiency, and we address this in greater detail later in the book. Of course, capital charges can also be reduced, and EVA increased, by reducing the firm's cost of capital.

The essence of corporate financial strategy is to seek financing alternatives that minimize the cost of capital, thereby maximizing EVA. Yet, as this discussion shows, it's not possible for finance directors to know their companies' costs of capital with precision. And if we do not know something precisely, it is hardly possible to minimize it. Although there are several factors that finance professionals consider in devising optimal capital structures for their companies, no credible model exists that can reveal, with precision, the appropriate levels of debt and equity, and long-term and short-term finance. In other words, there is no substitute for judgment, experience, and an intimate knowledge of capital markets and investor expectations.

In designing a capital structure, corporate finance specialists choose from a broad array of financing alternatives:

* Short-term debt (bank loans or money market instruments)
* Long-term debt (fixed- or floating-rate bonds or bank loans)
* Retained earnings
* New equity issues (public or private placement)
* Convertibles
* Preferred shares
* Warrants

Managers can choose from straight debt, straight equity (in the form of retained earnings or new equity issues), and hybrid instruments that combine elements of debt and equity (such as preferred shares and convertibles). At its most basic, however, the capital structure question centers on how much debt and how much equity a firm should use to finance its assets. Once that decision is made, the firm can then determine which instruments are most appropriate for achieving the target capital structure. The two most important factors to consider in the debt-equity choice are as follows:

+ The tax shield from interest payments
+ The costs of financial distress that can arise with too much debt

Two other factors also play a role in capital structure decisions:

+ The agency costs caused by the separation of ownership and control
+ Asymmetric information

Tax Shields

Nobel laureates Franco Modigliani and Merton Miller prove that in a world without taxes and bankruptcy costs, asset financing doesn't matter. Any increase in leverage, in which expensive equity is replaced with cheaper debt, also raises the cost of the equity that remains in the capital structure. The net result is that the cost of capital does not change. Changes in the value of the firm depend entirely on changes in the present value of the cashflows produced by its assets; no one capital structure is better than any other.

It is tempting to think that because debt finance is cheaper than equity finance for any level of leverage, we need only increase leverage to reduce the WACC and increase the value of the firm. Reality is more complicated, however. Debt may be cheaper than equity, but the key issue is whether using debt finance increases the value of the firm. In the restrictive Modigliani and

Miller world, it does not. This insight is one of the cornerstones of modern corporate finance theory.

In the real world, of course, there are taxes, and this simple fact changes everything. Interest on debt is tax-deductible, but the cost of equity is not. Therein lies the principal benefit of injecting debt into a company's capital structure. It pays to borrow as long as a company has sufficient taxable income and, as we will see later, as long as the debt does not seriously imperil the survivability of the firm.

Consider the example in Table 5–2. Two firms are identical in every respect but one. The first of the firms is all-equity, which means that all of its assets are financed with shareholder funds. The second firm finances $100 of its assets with debt at an interest rate of 10 percent. Earnings before interest and tax (EBIT) are $20 for both firms, and the corporate tax rate is 40 percent.

Notice that the $10 interest payment shields $10 of EBIT from taxes, because the interest payment is tax-deductible. This shield saves the company $4 in tax, which provides $4 of additional cash-flow to the company's capital providers. Even though the two firms have the same asset configuration and the same operating profit, the second firm is worth more than the first, assuming the different capital structures persist in future periods. The difference between the value of these firms equals the present value of the future tax shields expected by the levered company.

T A B L E   5–2

	All-Equity Firm	Firm with $100 of Debt, at 10%
EBIT	$20	$20
Interest	0	10
Earnings before tax	20	10
Tax @ 40%	8	4
Net income	12	6
Interest	0	10
Payments to capital providers	$12	$16

Figure 5–3 represents the value implications of debt. V_U is the value of an all-equity firm, V_L is the value of the same firm with leverage. The difference between the value of the levered firm and its unlevered counterpart is equal to the present value of the tax shields enjoyed by the former but not by the latter. Does this mean the more debt, the better? Not exactly.

So far, we have focused entirely on corporate taxes, while ignoring personal taxes. Interest payments have tax consequences for investors, just as they do for companies, because interest payments can result in taxable income to the holders of the debt. Unless they are tax-advantaged in some way (like a tax-exempt pension fund), the recipients of the interest payments will pay taxes according to their marginal tax rates. If, on the other hand, the company continues to rely on equity finance, the resulting capital gains expected by investors can be tax-deferred for as long as investors wish (they can choose not to sell and thus defer their gains). When taxes on capital gains are finally paid, the rates are usually lower than the rates paid on income. The correspondingly higher yields that bond investors must be offered to compensate for the additional taxes they have to pay on interest income will

F I G U R E   5–3

The Value of Leverage.

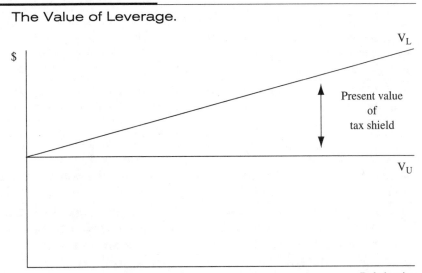

partly offset the tax benefits of debt finance. In short, if a company's marginal tax rate is 35 percent, the net tax advantage of debt is certainly not 35 cents for every dollar of interest paid (although it is still substantially greater than 0).

There is a further complication in the notion that the more debt a company has the better. In the real world, we have not only taxes but also financial distress and bankruptcy costs. These costs impose constraints on the amount of debt that is optimal for a given firm. It's the presence of such costs and the uncertainty about the true tax benefit that stops companies from levering up to the hilt.

The Costs of Financial Distress

Many firms encounter financial distress, or even bankruptcy. Outside the artificial Modigliani and Miller world, financial distress is costly, and its risk therefore can dramatically reduce the value of a firm. Among the costs of financial distress are direct out-of-pocket expenses paid to lawyers, accountants, and investment bankers to reorganize a firm, renegotiate its debts, or undertake other activities to fend off bankruptcy. Even more significant are the indirect costs of financial distress, costs that cannot be directly observed but that have profound value implications. For example, in industries in which after-sales service and warranty protection are critical product attributes, customers may be reluctant to buy from companies that are thought to be in financial difficulty. It is not that the products are inferior, but rather that customers fear that the company will not be around in the future to provide needed service or to satisfy warranty claims. In such cases, financial distress causes lost sales as customers flee to stronger competitors.

Baan NV, a large Dutch software company, faced this problem when it reported large losses in the fourth quarter of 1999. Once one of Europe's high-tech success stories, the company suffered through declining sales, departing executives (including its CEO), and accounting scandals. The result: a loss of confidence in it by large corporate customers. Without such confidence, how are customers to know that the company will be around to maintain and upgrade the software? As one equity analyst explained, "Just imagine that you are going to tell the chief executive that you plan to spend about $30 million for a whole new system from a company called Baan, and that he has been reading all the bad articles about Baan. You don't put your job on the line for a purchase."[4] Even if Baan's product is as good or superior to that of its rivals, a company in search of software to run its computer networks would logically turn to Oracle or SAP.

Suppliers, too, are reluctant to deal with companies in financial distress. This attitude is understandable, given that one of the first levers managers of troubled companies pull is to extend payment periods for suppliers. Disruptions in the supply chain are the likely result. Another important cost is the time and energy that management has to devote to sheer survival. While competitors focus on markets and innovation, managers of a troubled firm concentrate on keeping the company afloat, with the result that the company falls still further behind its competitors. And even if positive NPV projects emerge, the firm may be unable to raise the necessary capital. Employee morale and productivity suffer as well, as people fear job losses.

In addition, value-destroying conflicts of interest between shareholders and creditors can arise in overlevered companies. For instance, imagine a troubled firm with two investment possibilities: a low-risk project and a high-risk project. Also, assume two possible economic states in the next period, recession or boom; the probability of either is 50 percent. Finally, assume the company's outstanding debt is $50 million. For the low-risk project, the worst-case scenario (recession) results in a value for the firm in the next period of $50 million, which is just enough to cover the amount owed to the company's bankers. The bankers lose nothing, while the shareholders' interest is worthless because all of the firm's value is captured by the bankers. If the economy booms, however, the firm will be worth $100 million, leaving $50 million for the shareholders.

Now consider the high-risk project. The higher risk affords the prospect of greater gains in the event of an economic boom,

4. Edmund L. Andrews, "Baan's Chief Executive Quits Amid Big Losses," *International Herald Tribune*, January 5, 2000, p. 4.

but also heavier losses if a recession hits. Assume that in a recession, the firm would be worth only $25 million. Shareholders' interests are still worthless, just as they would be if a recession hits and the company had invested in the low-risk project. But now the bankers lose. While before they could recover their $50 million investment, even in a recession, they now lose half of what is owed to them. If the economy booms, however, the value of the firm rises to $125 million.

If you were a shareholder, which investment would you choose? The high-risk project, of course. If the economy goes into a recession, your equity stake is worthless in either case. But if the economy booms, the value of your equity stake is $75 million, the value of the firm less the outstanding debt ($125 million − $50 million). Notice that if the economy booms but the company invests in the low-risk project, your stake is worth only $50 million, the $100 million value less the outstanding debt. In this case, the incentives are clear. Investment in the high-risk project makes all the benefits accrue to the shareholders, because the bankers are entitled only to the $50 million of outstanding debt and they bear all of the cost (i.e., the risk). If a recession hits, the shareholders' stakes are worthless regardless of which project is chosen. The bankers recover only half of their investment in a recession if the high-risk project is chosen.

This example shows one of the conflicts that can arise between shareholders and creditors in troubled companies. This phenomenon is similar to that of heavily indebted gamblers who stake everything on one last roll of the dice in the hope that they can recover their losses. The problem is that any further losses are borne by the bankers. In effect, the shareholders have bought a lottery ticket, and the company's creditors have paid for it.

The potential for such conflicts does not necessarily disadvantage bankers and bondholders, because they can impound the added risk in any lending contracts they have with the company. In other words, lenders can call on defensive mechanisms before they even agree to extend credit, including higher interest rates and restrictive covenants that limit management's flexibility and impose additional monitoring of company performance. The important point here is that these defensive mechanisms can increase the company's cost of capital and thereby reduce its value.

F I G U R E   5–4

The Impact of Financial Distress Costs on Value.

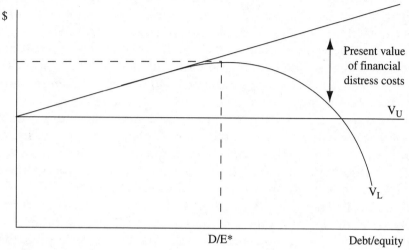

D/E* = value-maximizing debt/equity ratio

What does all this mean for capital structure design? The presence of financial distress costs results in a more complicated picture than that in our previous graph. Note in Figure 5–4 that while the present value of the tax shield increases company value, the present value of financial distress costs takes it away. In light of these costs, we can now state the major task of capital structure design: Choose the combination of debt and equity that balances the benefits of the tax shield with the costs of financial distress and therefore minimizes the cost of capital. Conditional on the cashflows generated from the company's assets, this capital structure maximizes the value of the firm.

More easily said than done, however. As we noted earlier, the presence of personal taxes complicates the valuation of corporate tax shields. As difficult as it may be to value tax shields, quantifying the costs of financial distress is even harder. The uncertainty over estimating these costs has led to a controversy among financial economists over just how important these costs really are. Professors Gregor Andrade and Steven Kaplan of the University of Chicago argue that these costs tend to be seriously overstated by chief financial officers, as well as in previous studies by other financial economists, because of their failure to distinguish between *financial* distress and *economic* distress.[5] Financial distress is related to an excessive debt burden; economic distress is caused by operating inefficiencies or strategic failures.

Andrade and Kaplan looked at 136 highly leveraged transactions (such as management buyouts, financed mainly with debt) in the United States during the 1980 to 1989 period; of these transactions (hereafter, "HLTs"), 31 eventually encountered financial distress, either defaulting on debt payments, restructuring debt, or filing for bankruptcy. Andrade and Kaplan measure the change in the value of the HLTs from the time just prior to the transaction to the resolution of the distress, and they find that the value of these firms actually *increased* over the observation period. If the value of distressed HLTs did not decline, even after considering the costs of distress, imagine the value creation possibilities for HLTs that do not become distressed. This evidence implies that the benefits from leverage for HLTs (namely, the tax deductibility of interest) largely outweigh the costs of distress.

Andrade and Kaplan go on to estimate the costs of distress, based on the declines in operating and net cashflow margins from the year before distress to the year after resolution. These costs are highly significant, ranging from about 10 to 20 percent of firm value, depending on how they are measured. But when the authors attempt to isolate distressed firms that experienced economic shocks (unrelated to excessive financial leverage) from those that didn't, they find that financial distress costs for the latter group were close to zero. In other words, the significant costs associated with distressed firms are the result of economic factors not related to debt. Firms with high levels of debt appear to suffer no reductions in operating or cashflow margins, as long as they do not suffer from adverse economic shocks. One interpretation of this finding is that lost sales, disruptions in supply, and the other potentially negative effects of high leverage on operating margins may be relatively inconsequential, or at least substantially overestimated by corporate executives.

---

5. G. Andrade and S. N. Kaplan, "How Costly Is Financial (Not Economic) Distress? Evidence from Highly Leveraged Transactions That Became Distressed," *Journal of Finance*, October 1998.

The authors admit that financial distress might amplify the poor operating performance of firms that are subjected to economic shocks. Also, as most corporate finance directors would no doubt respond, it's precisely the possibility of such shocks that makes debt risky. Still, these findings suggest that the costs of *pure* financial distress are lower than managers think, especially for large firms in mature industries that are not R&D-intensive (and, therefore, relatively stable). If Andrade and Kaplan are right, many such firms are seriously underlevered, failing to properly exploit valuable tax shields.

OTHER INFLUENCES ON CAPITAL STRUCTURE

Although the trade-off between tax shields and financial distress costs dominates the debate over capital structure, other factors can influence the debt-equity choice, including agency costs and asymmetric information.

Agency Costs

Shareholders have their particular agendas, and so do managers. These agendas often conflict. While shareholders obviously desire ever-increasing wealth for themselves, managers may want things that conflict with shareholder value creation, such as excessively high compensation, job protection, and the trappings of executive power (lavish entertainment, plush offices, and so forth). Any divergence between what business owners want and what managers want gives rise to agency cost, a term based on the idea that corporate managers are "agents" and shareholders are "principals." Agents are supposed to act in the best interests of the principals, but incentives might compel them to act in ways that are actually detrimental to principals.

This shareholder-manager conflict influences capital structure decisions. It shouldn't, but it does. Unless they are motivated to do otherwise, managers tend to underlever their companies. The capital market theory we have discussed in this chapter helps to explain why. Corporate executives invest in the companies they manage, just as shareholders do, but with one crucial difference. For most managers, their investment is primarily in the form of human capital, or the value of their relevant knowledge, experience, and expertise; however, human capital investment is not diversifiable in the way that financial investments are.

When companies suffer losses or go bankrupt, shareholders lose a portion of their wealth. For shareholders, this need not be devastating if they have been rational and chosen to be diversified. For managers, the consequences of corporate failure are far more serious, because much of their human capital and, often, most of their holdings in stocks and options are specific to the companies they work for. If they lose their jobs because of corporate bankruptcy, a significant portion, maybe even most, of their personal wealth is extinguished. Because managers hold only one job, their wealth portfolio, dominated by human capital, is not well diversified. For this reason, managers and shareholders have very different risk preferences. In short, managers are more conservative (i.e., less risk-taking) than shareholders would like them to be.

Managers in general try to make their firms safer, both in terms of the investments that they undertake and in terms of capital structure. What propelled the drive toward diversification among American companies in the 1960s and 1970s, and among European and Asian companies through the 1980s, was the desire of managers to limit their own risk, not the shareholders' risk. Investors can diversify more efficiently than individual companies ever can simply by acquiring shares in several companies in several industries. Although managers may cite shareholder interests to justify diversification strategies, the motivation is much more likely to be managers' eagerness to protect *themselves* against the vagaries of business cycles. This is a classic agency conflict.

There are similar problems in manager decisions on the proper mix of debt and equity for their firms. As we have seen, debt provides companies with valuable tax shields. (The great paradox of debt is that the companies that need it the least—those with enough internally generated cashflow to finance all positive NPV projects—are the very ones that need it the most, because they have a lot of taxable profits.) Regardless of the obvious benefits of debt, managers have little motivation to use it. The reason is that all the gains from a tax shield go to shareholders, while the costs (in the form of higher risk) are borne almost entirely by managers. As companies lever up, they become riskier, which also imperils managers' human capital. Betas do increase with leverage, but as the CAPM tells us, shareholders are rewarded for this risk. To protect their human capital, managers have reason to underlever.

Any managerial action or strategy that drives a wedge between potential value and actual value creates agency costs. The central issue in corporate governance these days is to devise monitoring and contractual arrangements that minimize these costs. Railing against managers for their behavior is pointless; shareholders would behave the same way if faced with the same risks and incentives.

Asymmetric Information

Managers know more about their companies than the markets do. Stock market investors understand this, and they react to signals sent to them by managers about corporate profitability and value. In other words, although corporate managers possess private information—a phenomenon described as "asymmetric information"—there are many ways, and indeed incentives, for them to reveal this information to the investing community. As the markets learn of these beliefs, or deduce them from managerial actions, share prices adjust accordingly.

When a company announces it intends to buy back shares, for example, stock market investors interpret this action to mean that managers believe the company's shares to be undervalued. Not surprisingly, the markets usually react positively to this news, as several studies of buybacks have shown. This reaction would not occur if managers were not thought to have private information. Another example is that share price reaction is usually negative when companies announce new equity issues. In this case, investors apparently interpret share issuance to mean that managers believe the company to be *over*valued.

As these examples show, the existence of asymmetric information influences the debt-equity choice. Management's first obligation is to its current shareholders, not prospective shareholders, which is why markets react negatively to new equity issues. If the company's shares are *under*priced, a new equity issue would constitute a gift to new shareholders at the expense of current shareholders. Markets logically assume that managers have no intention of giving new investors such a windfall. Quite simply, if managers, with their private information, believe their shares to be overvalued, they should be more inclined to finance additional capital requirements with equity. When shares are undervalued, however, companies should lever up. The manner in which they lever up depends on whether they have surplus cash or are unable to finance their capital needs from internal cashflows. If surplus cash exists, the company should buy back shares. If access to external capital is required, the company should issue bonds or increase bank debt.

One important virtue of debt is that it provides companies with a credible signal to the capital markets that management expects future cashflows to grow. Additional debt, that is, obligates the firm to make a fixed set of cash payments over the life of the loan. When they commit the firm to make such payments, managers signal their confidence that the company will generate sufficient cashflows to meet its new obligations. This argument reinforces the idea that if managers consider their shares to be undervalued, future growth opportunities should be financed with debt.

THE PECKING ORDER THEORY

Our discussion of capital structure has thus far assumed that there is a target capital structure that minimizes a company's WACC, thereby maximizing EVA, excess return, and the value of the company. Considerable empirical evidence in the academic finance literature supports the idea that companies act as if there is an optimal capital structure, and that firms take appropriate action when they deviate from it. For example, when debt ratios are high relative to historical averages, companies tend to issue equity. When the reverse is true, they issue debt. This evidence suggests that corporate CFOs have an ideal capital structure in mind. The evidence also shows that taxes influence corporate financing decisions in much the way we have described. For example, companies with high marginal tax rates are more likely to issue new debt than companies with low marginal tax rates.

Some finance specialists, however, support a very different theory of corporate financing. The pecking order theory posits that capital needs are met first with internally generated cashflows. If external capital is required because internal funds are not sufficient to finance all investment opportunities, debt is the financing vehicle of choice. According to this theory, additional equity issues are the financing of last resort.

The pecking order theory turns the optimal capital structure theory we have been discussing on its head. For example, while we would expect firms with high operating cashflows (and therefore high profits) to take on more debt than other firms (because they have more profits to shield from tax), the pecking order theory suggests otherwise. Because such firms generate so much capital internally, they do not need to resort to external financing. Therefore, their debt levels will be low.

The pecking order theory has been around a long time, and it has strong intuitive appeal to nonfinance managers. The empirical evidence on this question is mixed, but the durability of the theory suggests that financial economists have yet to develop a convincing, unified theory of capital structure that can serve as a definitive guide for corporate managers. It is hard not to argue that taxes and bankruptcy costs are logical places to start in thinking about the debt-equity choice, though.

ACHIEVING CAPITAL STRUCTURE TARGETS

Achieving and maintaining an appropriate capital structure is an ongoing process. Market conditions change, and so do tax laws and competitive forces. Even if a company has achieved what its CFO believes to be the right mix of debt and equity, changing business circumstances can quickly render any capital structure obsolete. For example, it is easy for highly profitable companies to become underlevered, unless managers take action to maintain leverage, either through borrowing or buying back shares.

When the CFO believes the company to be over- or underlevered, an important question emerges: Should the company's leverage converge to the target capital structure quickly or in some gradual fashion? Generally, companies prefer a more gradual approach because abrupt capital structure changes tend to be costly.

Figure 5–5 summarizes the issues that any CFO should consider in deciding on a strategy for reaching the target.

If the company is thought to be overlevered, the CFO must determine if the company faces imminent threat of bankruptcy or serious financial distress. If so, debt must be reduced immediately, and in large amounts. Otherwise, the company faces extinction. Assets can be sold off, with proceeds used to pay off debts. Negotiations with creditors can alter payment terms to improve chances of repayment or can focus on trying to convince creditors to swap the outstanding debt for shares.

All these actions are drastic and expensive, and companies that do not have to lever down quickly will avoid them. Less dramatic and more gradual approaches are called for in this case. The method of reducing leverage depends on whether the company is thought to have positive NPV projects. If so, leverage should be reduced by funding projects as they come along with equity, either in the form of operating cashflows (i.e., retained earnings) or new equity issues. If not, debt can be gradually repaid with retained earnings or by cutting dividends. Alternatively, new equity can be issued, with the proceeds used to pay off outstanding debt. In this case, it is crucial that management communicate its intention of using the proceeds to pay off debt and not for investment. Otherwise, investors may infer that the company intends to invest in value-destroying projects and will penalize the company's share price accordingly.

Incremental or gradual options are not practical if the company is threatened by bankruptcy. Relying on operating cashflows or dividend cuts does not help a company needing to pay down debt in a hurry. Nor are share issues possible; why would investors be interested in companies on the verge of failure?

If the company is underlevered, the decision to lever up quickly or gradually depends mainly on whether there may be a takeover threat. Of course, one reason why companies become targets is because they are underlevered. Buyers can use the target's unused debt capacity to finance the acquisition. When the threat of hostile takeover is imminent, a large and rapid increase in leverage is often the most effective defense. This increase can be easily affected by a leveraged recapitalization (leveraged recap, for short). When companies want to increase leverage, it is logical

F I G U R E   5–5

A Framework for Capital Structure Decisions.

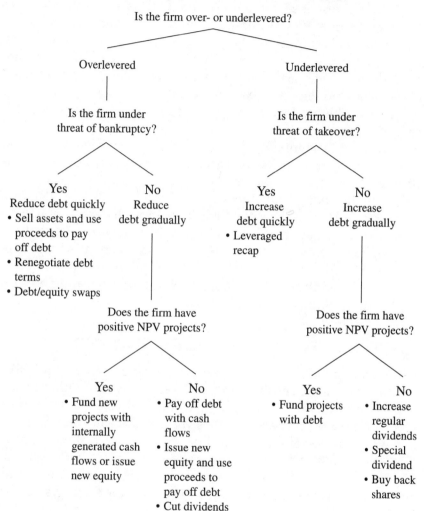

Is the firm over- or underlevered?

Overlevered

Underlevered

Is the firm under
threat of bankruptcy?

Is the firm under
threat of takeover?

Yes
Reduce debt quickly
• Sell assets and use
  proceeds to pay
  off debt
• Renegotiate debt
  terms
• Debt/equity swaps

No
Reduce
debt gradually

Yes
Increase
debt quickly
• Leveraged
  recap

No
Increase
debt gradually

Does the firm have
positive NPV projects?

Does the firm have
positive NPV projects?

Yes
• Fund new
  projects with
  internally
  generated cash
  flows or issue
  new equity

No
• Pay off debt
  with cash
  flows
• Issue new
  equity and use
  proceeds to
  pay off debt
• Cut dividends

Yes
• Fund projects
  with debt

No
• Increase
  regular
  dividends
• Special
  dividend
• Buy back
  shares

Source: Adapted from Damodaran (1997).

for them to borrow. But what should the company do with the borrowed funds? Investment in profitable capital projects is the appropriate response for underlevered firms that can afford to lever up gradually. A far more immediate, dramatic, and effective action is to distribute the borrowed funds to the shareholders, either in a share buyback or as a special dividend. In short, not only does a leveraged recap increase borrowing, but it also reduces shareholders' equity. The result is a very different, and much more highly levered, capital structure than before the leveraged recap.

When the company does not face an imminent takeover threat, leverage is usually increased more gradually. As in the case of overlevered firms, the means of converging to the optimal structure depends on whether the company has positive NPV projects. If it does, managers can finance them with debt. If not, managers can lever up the firm indirectly by increasing payouts to shareholders, either through dividends or share buybacks. Increased borrowing is probably not appropriate in these circumstances because the company does not have value creating projects to absorb the funds.

CAPITAL STRUCTURE DOES MATTER

Forty years ago Franco Modigliani and Merton Miller (MM) told us that financing doesn't matter, at least in a world without taxes or bankruptcy costs. Of course, the world we live in has both. Why then should we still care about MM? Because MM remind us of two valuable lessons that any business manager should know. First, the taxes and bankruptcy costs of the real world give us important indications concerning what managers must think about to design capital structures that work for their businesses. Capital structure *does* matter precisely because companies pay taxes and bear costs related to financial distress. This simple insight provides a logical starting point for thinking about capital structure and the debt-equity choice.

The second reason MM are important has to do with finance. The MM assertion that company value is driven by the asset-generated cashflows and not by how the assets were financed is a powerful reminder that finance should not be more than a second-order priority for the value-creating firm. In other words, it's the left-hand side of the balance sheet that drives value, not the right-hand side. This idea is reinforced by the continuing debate among financial economists over corporate financing policy. Does an optimal capital structure even exist? Most finance experts say "yes," but not all.

In short, the ultimate driver of value is a sound corporate vision that identifies a distinct competitive advantage for the firm and enables returns to exceed the cost of capital, regardless of where that capital comes from. Not only must this competitive advantage be identified, but strategies, systems, and processes must also be put into place to create and sustain it. It is from this effort that real value creation emerges.

CONCLUSION

In this chapter, we've shown how the weighted-average cost of capital can be calculated for both publicly traded and privately held companies. We've also discussed how to calculate the cost of equity, contrasting the CAPM and APM approaches. In addition, we discussed the factors that should guide the corporate finance manager in designing a capital structure in order to minimize the company's cost of capital and maximize EVA. In the next chapter, we'll take an in-depth look at the pros and cons of using accounting adjustments when calculating EVA.

CHAPTER 6

EVA

The Accounting Adjustments

To correct for the perceived inadequacies of standard financial reporting practice, some users of economic value added adjust profits prepared under generally accepted accounting principles (GAAP) in the hope that the adjustments will produce more reliable EVA figures. The general aim is to correct for perceived biases or distortions that arise either because of the tendency of managers to "game" accounting numbers or because of deficiencies in the GAAP model, such as a failure to properly account for investments in intellectual capital.

In this chapter, we will thoroughly explore the benefits and drawbacks of EVA accounting adjustments. There is no accepted canon of these adjustments, because they are directed at a variety of accounting, performance measurement, and incentive issues. Not only is there disagreement over the importance of each issue, but in some cases EVA proponents disagree on the correct way to address it. With this in mind, let's look at the possible adjustments and how they impact EVA.

EVA accounting adjustments are designed primarily to

- Reverse the conservative bias in GAAP that requires
  "Successful efforts" accounting
  Expensing R&D costs
- Make the accounting return on capital a better proxy for the economic, or internal, rate of return by

Substituting "sinking-fund" and economic depreciation for amortization and depreciation by the straight-line method
Recognizing future period cash costs on a present-value basis (e.g., deferred tax expense, bad debt expense, and warranty expense)
♦ Increase accountability for shareholder funds by Eliminating pooling of interest accounting
Recognizing off-balance-sheet debt
Recognizing stock options as a business expense
♦ Limit management's ability to "manage" earnings by Eliminating accruals for
Bad debts
Warranties
♦ Eliminate noncash charges such as
Goodwill amortization
Deferred tax expense
♦ Make current EVA a better measure of market value by Capitalizing restructuring and other special charges
Excluding nonoperating income and assets
Capitalizing part of the capital charge

No EVA proponent advocates all of these adjustments. Some are inconsistent with others. For example, improving the accounting return on capital by recognizing warranty expense on a present-value basis is inconsistent with limiting management's ability to manage earnings by eliminating accruals for warranty expense. Similarly, recognizing deferred tax expense on a present-value basis is inconsistent with eliminating it as a noncash charge.

THE MAJOR ACCOUNTING ADJUSTMENTS

In the discussion that follows, we highlight the most important of these adjustments. For several cases, we show how the adjustment is made by using financial statement disclosures from a sample of American and European companies.

Successful Efforts Accounting

Successful efforts accounting is based on the idea that balance sheets should include only those investments that succeed. Unsuccessful efforts should be written off. The logic of this approach is that assets should be of future value to the firm. If an asset's value is significantly impaired, and so too is the company's ability to extract economic benefits from it, the asset should be written down or, if worthless, disappear entirely from the balance sheet. Its best-known application is in the oil exploration business, although the successful efforts approach is applied to a broad range of industries.

See Table 6–1 for an illustration of how the successful efforts approach works. Let's assume that a company, after performing geological surveys, invests $5 million in five oil wells, each costing $1 million. The company expects at least one of the wells to hit the subterranean pool of oil and anticipates that the pool will provide $2 million of annual oil revenue for five years. This makes the project an attractive one, with an internal rate of return of 29 percent.

To simplify the discussion, we assume that no taxes are paid. Later in the chapter, we return to this example and include taxes. If, as expected, four of the five wells prove to be "dry holes," a common failure rate in the industry, how should we account for the exploration costs? Big petroleum companies use "successful efforts" accounting, by which only the costs of successful wells (those with significant quantities of oil) are capitalized and placed on the balance sheet. These costs are then written off to future periods as the oil is taken out of the ground. In our example, only

T A B L E   6–1

Successful Efforts Approach for an Oil Exploration Company*

	Year					
	0	1	2	3	4	5
Exploration costs	−5					
Oil revenue		2	2	2	2	2
Income taxes paid		0	0	0	0	0
Cashflow	−5	2	2	2	2	2
Internal rate of return	29%					

* In millions of dollars.

$1 million of the initial investment would appear on the balance sheet; the remaining $4 million will be written off to earnings in the current year.

Most accountants support this approach on the grounds that balance sheets should report only those assets with future service potential. If an oil well is a dry hole, and no future cashflow from it is possible, we shouldn't call it an asset. Small exploration companies take a different approach, arguing that you cannot get the one well with oil in it unless you dig the other four. It is in the nature of the business. Obviously if we knew which wells have significant quantities of oil, we would dig only those and ignore the rest. But we do not know. If we therefore have to invest in five wells just to get one that works, shouldn't we capitalize the cost of our entire exploration effort, not just the portion that pays off?

Think of the consequences of writing off the unsuccessful oil wells. Write-offs mean costs are charged against earnings, which in turn means that those costs disappear from the balance sheet. Once 80 percent of the exploration costs are written off, the project appears to be extremely profitable, much more profitable than it really is, as is shown in Table 6–2.

The accounting return on beginning invested capital is 180 percent in the first year and reaches 900 percent in the fifth year,

T A B L E   6–2

Writing Off Unsuccessful Oil Wells*

		Year				
	0	1	2	3	4	5
Oil revenue		2.0	2.0	2.0	2.0	2.0
Exploration expense	4.0	0.2	0.2	0.2	0.2	0.2
Income tax expense		0	0	0	0	0
NOPAT	−4.0	1.8	1.8	1.8	1.8	1.8
Invested capital	1.0	0.8	0.6	0.4	0.2	0
Return on invested capital		180%	225%	300%	450%	900%

* In millions of dollars.

even though the true economic return is only 29 percent. Successful efforts accounting does not give us a meaningful picture of period performance.

The obvious solution to this problem is to abandon successful efforts accounting. The implications of such a policy are profound. Although most accountants associate the term "successful efforts" with the oil and gas industry, it has a much broader application in the world of EVA, where it may be used to describe any asset write-offs or nonoperating losses. For example, impairment losses recognized under the FASB's Financial Accounting Standard No. 121 are applications of successful efforts accounting. When companies make large restructuring provisions for underperforming assets, they too are applying successful efforts accounting. Their managers and accountants don't call it that, but the practical effect of writing off unproductive investments while leaving more promising ones on the balance sheet is the same as for the oil company that charges the costs of its dry holes to earnings.

If we capitalize the cost of the dry holes and amortize them over the five-year life of the oil reserve, we get a better picture of the economic performance of the project (see Table 6–3).

Capitalizing the dry-hole costs makes the project's accounting return on capital much closer to its economic return. Still, it is far from perfect. Three of the five years have accounting returns on

T A B L E   6–3

Capitalizing Dry-Hole Costs*

		Year				
	0	**1**	**2**	**3**	**4**	**5**
Oil revenue		2	2	2	2	2
Exploration expense		1	1	1	1	1
Income tax expense		0	0	0	0	0
NOPAT	0	1	1	1	1	1
Invested capital	5	4	3	2	1	0
Return on invested capital		20%	25%	33%	50%	100%

* In millions of dollars.

invested capital that exceed the economic return (and by quite a lot in years 4 and 5). The project also shows a steady improvement in performance even though the same $2 million of oil is being lifted each year with no reduction in any cash operating cost. The problem is straight-line amortization. If we use sinking-fund depreciation (see Table 6–4; depreciation method is explained later in this chapter), the project's accounting return does match its economic return.

Our drilling cost example shows that expenditures that are an essential part of an investment project must be capitalized and amortized over the project's life to give us a meaningful measure of period performance. If we can reasonably project the project's future cashflows, we can use sinking-fund depreciation to make the project's accounting return equal to its economic return. In many cases, however, the project's future cashflows are uncertain, and we face difficult decisions about the best method of depreciation.

Research and Development (R&D)

As we noted earlier, much is said these days about the importance of intellectual capital. Although it's not always easy to define just exactly what *intellectual capital* means, there is a growing sense in some companies that this sort of investment is becoming more

T A B L E   6–4

Sinking Fund Depreciation*

		Year				
	0	1	2	3	4	5
Oil revenue		2.000	2.000	2.000	2.000	2.000
Exploration expense		0.568	0.730	0.939	1.208	1.555
Income tax expense		0	0	0	0	0
NOPAT	0	1.432	1.270	1.061	0.792	0.445
Invested capital	5.000	4.432	3.702	2.763	1.555	0
Return on invested capital		29%	29%	29%	29%	29%

*In millions of dollars.

important than investments in physical assets such as buildings and machines. The problem is that accountants struggle with investments in anything other than what they can see and touch. If they can't kick it, accountants are loath to put it on the balance sheet. Investments in skill building, new technologies, brand names, and customer loyalty may create genuine economic assets, but traditionally accountants have taken the easy route, expensing costs incurred for such items as they are incurred. In other words, while operating managers may look on these costs as investments, accountants usually treat them as operating expenses.

There is already some recognition of the problem among accounting authorities. The International Accounting Standards Committee (IASC), based in London and responsible for promulgating international GAAP, introduced a rule in 1998 that will require companies to start accounting for investments in brands, software, patents, and even customer loyalty as assets. These intangibles will start appearing on the balance sheets of companies in the more than 100 countries that adhere to IASC standards in some form, with companies required to amortize the costs of the investments over their estimated "useful lives." Frequent revaluation, to confirm that the assets still have value, will also be required. The IASC acknowledges that requiring estimates of fair market value for such assets is a step too far; companies will base initial valuations on cost. Nevertheless, the move does show that accounting regulators are beginning to recognize some of the problems that EVA adjustments are designed to address.

The difficulty of accounting for intangible assets is widely acknowledged in the United States. However, for the moment, U.S. GAAP has changed little to adapt to the new economic realities. Consider R&D, for example. In the United States, as in most countries, companies expense R&D costs as incurred. The logic behind this policy is that the relation between current R&D expenditures and future benefits is often so uncertain that writing off the expenditures is the only prudent course of action. In a sense, writing off R&D is an extreme application of successful efforts accounting, except that none of the efforts are deemed successful. But the reality of R&D is that it is an investment. Sometimes that investment pays off, sometimes it doesn't; in either case, it is still an investment.

For this reason, many EVA proponents advocate the capital-ization of R&D. This argument extends to investments in other intangibles, including brand names. The basic principle of the ad-justment is to capitalize any operating expense that is not intended to create income in the current period but is designed to create income in future periods. Another argument for capitalizing R&D is that managers might otherwise be tempted to underinvest in R&D, because short-term profits will be adversely affected by the expenditures, while the benefits will not be realized until future periods.

If R&D is written off, an adjustment is made by adding back R&D costs to NOPAT. The capitalized costs are then written off gradually, with an amortization period equal to the number of years expected to benefit from whatever products or services are developed from the R&D. Of course, an obvious problem is choos-ing the appropriate amortization period. One promising approach is to base the amortization period on the average length of time that a company chooses to defend its patents from infringement. An approximation like this provides at least some connection with the average economic (as opposed to legal) life of the products that emerge from the R&D process. The amortization period can then be based on the sum of the average economic life of the products and the average length of time needed to transform R&D projects into serviceable patents.

Unamortized R&D is added to invested capital, thereby re-sulting in a treatment of R&D costs that is consistent with the way that companies account for investments in tangible assets. All R&D adjustments are made gross, not net, of tax because the full tax benefit is received as R&D costs are incurred, not when they are amortized. An example is shown in Box 6–1.

To illustrate the potential advantages of capitalizing R&D, assume a company is in steady state earning a 15 percent return on invested capital, with a NOPAT of $12 million and capital of $80 million each year (see Table 6–5). The company then invests $15 million in R&D, with expected incremental cashflows of $6 million for each of the next five years. We assume, again for sim-plicity, that the tax rate is 0 percent. The economic, or internal, rate of return on this investment is 28.65 percent.

Since we have been earning 15 percent on $80 million of in-vested capital and are adding a project with a 29 percent return

B O X   6–1

ADJUSTING R&D USING STRAIGHT-LINE AMORTIZATION: PEPSICO

In its 1995 annual report, PepsiCo discloses R&D expenditures of $96 million, $152 million, $113 million, $102 million, $99 million for 1995, 1994, 1993, 1992, and 1991, respectively. All R&D costs were expensed as incurred. To calculate EVA for 1995, the current year's R&D costs, $96 million, are restored to NOPAT. We then estimate what amortization expense would have been if R&D had been capitalized and then amortized on a straight-line basis over, say, a five-year period. To arrive at this figure, we add R&D costs for each of the last five years, 1995's included, and divide by 5. The resulting amortization expense, $112.4 million, is then subtracted from NOPAT. Any unamortized R&D, from 1995 and previous years, is added to invested capital. In this case, the amount equals 0.8 ($96 million) + 0.6 ($152 million) + 0.4 ($113 million) + 0.2 ($102 million), or $233.6 million. By the end of 1995, all of the 1991 R&D costs would have been amortized.

To recap:

NOPAT	Increase by $96 M
	Decrease by $112.4 M
Invested capital	Increase by $233.6 M

T A B L E   6–5

Potential Advantages of Capitalizing R&D*

	Year				
	0	1	2	3	4	5
R&D expenditure	−15					
Incremental NOPAT		6	6	6	6	6
After-tax cashflow	−15	6	6	6	6	6
Internal rate of return	28.65%					

* In millions of dollars.

on a $15 million investment, we would expect an increase in the return on invested capital. The new return should be a weighted average of the original return and the return on the new investment, $[(80/95) \times 15$ percent$] + [(15/95) \times 28.65$ percent$]$, or 17.2 percent. But with conventional R&D accounting, the return drops to -4 percent before recovering to 23 percent (see Table 6–6). The -4 percent return in year 0 assumes that the R&D expenditure in that year is a total loss, when in fact the investment yields substantial returns in future years. But the 23 percent in years 1 through 5 is also wrong. We would need to invest $113 million at 28.65 percent to bring our average return up to 23 percent,[1] but we know that only $15 million has been invested.

Capitalizing the R&D expenditure and amortizing it on a straight-line basis over five years gives us a more accurate picture of business performance (see Table 6–7). The project has no effect on year 0 NOPAT and increases NOPAT in years 1 through 5 by $3 million each year.

In contrast with conventional accounting, which drops the return on invested capital to -4 percent, then sharply increases it to 23 percent, capitalizing R&D with straight-line amortization leads to a small, steady increase in the return on invested capital from 15 percent in year 0 to 18.1 percent in year 5 (see Table 6–8).

T A B L E   6–6

Return on Invested Capital under Conventional R&D Accounting*

	Year					
	0	1	2	3	4	5
Steady-state NOPAT	12	12	12	12	12	12
Year 0 R&D project	−15	6	6	6	6	6
Adjusted NOPAT	−3	18	18	18	18	18
Invested capital	80	80	80	80	80	80
Return on invested capital	−4%	23%	23%	23%	23%	23%

*In millions of dollars.

---

1. $[(80/193) \times 15\%] + [(113/193) \times 28.65\%] = 23\%$

T A B L E   6-7

Capitalizing the R&D Expenditure and Amortizing It on a Straight-Line Basis*

	Year				
	0	**1**	**2**	**3**	**4**	**5**
Incremental operating margin		6	6	6	6	6
Capitalized R&D amortization		−3	−3	−3	−3	−3
Incremental NOPAT		3	3	3	3	3

* In millions of dollars.

T A B L E   6-8

Capitalizing R&D with Straight-Line Amoritization*

	Year				
	0	**1**	**2**	**3**	**4**	**5**
Steady-state NOPAT	12	12	12	12	12	12
Year 0 R&D project		3	3	3	3	3
Adjusted NOPAT	12	15	15	15	15	15
R&D capital	15	12	9	6	3	
Invested capital	95	92	89	86	83	80
Return on invested capital		15.8%	16.3%	16.9%	17.4%	18.1%

* In millions of dollars.

While capitalizing R&D with straight-line amortization is a big improvement over conventional R&D accounting, it is not perfect. The steady increase in the return on capital is not a true sign of improving performance, but a distortion caused by straight-line amortization, a problem just like the one we encountered with full-cost accounting. And the distortion is much greater when we look at the return on the R&D investment alone. The return on R&D capital increases from 20 percent ($3 million divided by beginning the R&D investment of $15 million) in year 1 to 100 percent in year 5. The return on invested capital (i.e., the accounting rate of return) never matches the economic return of 28.65 percent. In years 1 and 2, the accounting return is below the economic return, and in years 3 through 5, the accounting return is greater than the economic return.

We get a better picture of performance if we use sinking-fund amortization (see Table 6–9). Sinking-fund amortization shows that the return on capital jumps from 15 to 17.2 percent in year 1 and then declines each year thereafter. This pattern makes sense from an economic point of view. In the first year, we add $15 million in capital, earning 28.65 percent, to our original capital of $80 million earning 15 percent. Our first-year return of 17.2 percent is a weighted average of these two returns: [(15/95) × 28.65 percent] + [(80/95) × 15 percent], or 17.2 percent. In year 2, the return on invested capital declines because we recover some of our investment in the more profitable R&D project and do not reinvest it in a new R&D project. Our first-year amortization of $1.703 million reduces invested capital at the end of year 1 to $13.297 million, reducing our weighted average return on capital to 16.9 percent even though the return on our R&D investment remains at 28.65 percent. By year 5, the return on invested capital falls to 15.8 percent, or 2.3 percent lower than the inflated return produced by straight-line amortization.

If we start a new R&D project each year, the difference between straight-line and sinking-fund amortization gets smaller. With a new $15 million R&D project each year, the return on invested capital with straight-line amortization rises to a constant 21.6 percent in year 5 and thereafter (see Table 6–10).

T A B L E   6–9

Sinking-Fund Amortization*

		Year				
	0	1	2	3	4	5
Steady-state NOPAT	12	12.000	12.000	12.000	12.000	12.000
Year 0 R&D project		4.297	3.810	3.182	2.375	1.336
Adjusted NOPAT	12	16.297	15.810	15.182	14.375	13.336
R&D capital	15	13.297	11.107	8.289	4.664	0
Invested capital	95	93.297	91.107	88.289	84.664	80.000
Return on invested capital		17.2%	16.9%	16.7%	16.3%	15.8%

*In millions of dollars.

T A B L E   6–10

Return on Invested Capital with Straight-Line Amortization

	Year					
	0	**1**	**2**	**3**	**4**	**5**
Steady-state NOPAT	12	12	12	12	12	12
Year 0 R&D project		3	3	3	3	3
Year 1 R&D project			3	3	3	3
Year 2 R&D project				3	3	3
Year 3 R&D project					3	3
Year 4 R&D project						3
Adjusted NOPAT	12	15	18	21	24	27
Year 0 R&D capital	15	12	9	6	3	
Year 1 R&D capital		15	12	9	6	3
Year 2 R&D capital			15	12	9	6
Year 3 R&D capital				15	12	9
Year 4 R&D capital					15	12
Year 5 R&D capital						15
Invested capital	95	107	116	122	125	125
Return on invested capital		15.8%	16.8%	18.1%	19.7%	21.6%

With sinking-fund amortization, the return rises to a constant 20.4 percent in year 5, and thereafter (see Table 6–11). By year 5 (the end of the R&D project's useful life), NOPAT is the same whether we use straight-line amortization or sinking-fund amortization, $27,000. This figure is $15,000 higher than our base case NOPAT of $12,000 and represents $30,000 of incremental operating margin less $15,000 of annual R&D amortization. Why is the invested capital (and, hence, the return on invested capital) different for sinking-fund amortization? With straight-line depreciation, R&D capital by year 5 is $45,000, which is exactly half of the $90,000 R&D investment made over the five years. That may seem like the correct result, but it's not. The R&D capital with sinking-fund depreciation is $52,357 in year 5, and thereafter. This figure is the correct one because it makes our accounting return on R&D capital exactly equal to the economic return on R&D investment, 28.65 percent.

T A B L E   6–11

Return on Invested Capital with
Sinking-Fund Amortization

		Year				
	0	1	2	3	4	5
Steady-state NOPAT	12	12.000	12.000	12.000	12.000	12.000
Year 0 R&D project		4.297	3.810	3.182	2.375	1.336
Year 1 R&D project			4.297	3.810	3.182	2.375
Year 2 R&D project				4.297	3.810	3.182
Year 3 R&D project					4.297	3.810
Year 4 R&D project						4.297
Adjusted NOPAT	12	16.297	20.107	23.289	25.664	27.000
Year 0 R&D capital	15	13.297	11.107	8.289	4.664	0
Year 1 R&D capital		15.000	13.297	11.107	8.289	4.664
Year 2 R&D capital			15.000	13.297	11.107	8.289
Year 3 R&D capital				15.000	13.297	11.107
Year 4 R&D capital					15.000	13.297
Year 5 R&D capital						15.000
Invested capital	95	108.297	119.404	127.693	132.357	132.357
Return on invested capital		17.2%	18.6%	19.5%	20.1%	20.4%

Deferred Tax

Deferred tax arises from timing differences between taxable income and the book income recognized under GAAP. The greatest
source of deferred tax in most companies is depreciation, at least
in the Anglophone countries, but any temporary difference in tax
and book income can give rise to deferred tax.

To illustrate, most companies in the United States use
straight-line depreciation for book income but more accelerated
write-offs for tax purposes. Total depreciation over an asset's life
is the same in either case, but timing differences in the recognition
of depreciation expense will arise. Normally, this timing difference
results in more book income than tax income and a deferred tax
liability. Deferred tax *assets* occur when companies make provisions for future costs that reduce current book income—to cover

warranties, restructuring, environmental cleanup, and so on—but are not tax-deductible until the company actually spends the cash in a later accounting period.

Some EVA proponents argue that deferred tax expense should be ignored because it is not a cash cost. They eliminate the impact of deferred taxes by adding the change in the net deferred tax liability for the year to NOPAT; that is, an increase is added and a decrease is subtracted. If the company has deferred tax assets that are not netted against deferred tax liabilities, an increase in the deferred tax assets for the year is subtracted from NOPAT and a decrease is added. The deferred tax account balance is included in (subtracted from) invested capital if the balance is a liability (asset). The NOPAT adjustment removes the influence of GAAP on income tax expense, which yields a tax expense for EVA purposes that is closer to what the company actually owes to the tax authorities that year. See Box 6–2 for an example.

Although the deferred tax expense is not a current cash cost, it can reflect a significant economic cost. Consider the following example. A company invests $5 million in a five-year project in which it expects to earn an annual pretax profit of $2 million and recover its initial investment in full at the end of the fifth year. The company pays income tax but operates in a jurisdiction with an unusual tax rule: taxable income is reported currently, but taxes are not payable for five years. The company's cashflows are as follows (dollar amounts in thousands):

Years	Description	Annual Cashflow
0	Capital investment	−$5000
1–5	Operating profit	2000
5	Capital recovery	5000
6–10	Income tax	−800

The economic, or internal, rate of return for these cashflows is 36.6 percent. While none of the taxes are due in the project's operating years, they do have a clear economic cost. Without any tax liability, the project's economic return would increase to 40.0

B O X   6–2

ADJUSTING DEFERRED TAXES: QUAKER OATS

In its 1995 annual report, Quaker Oats, an American cereal and beverages company, reported year-end deferred taxes of $82.2 million and $233.3 million for 1994 and 1995, respectively. The deferred tax assets were not netted against the deferred tax liabilities. Instead, deferred tax assets were included in current assets and, therefore, under the shortcut approach to calculating EVA discussed in Chapter 2, were also included in the working capital requirement and invested capital. The amount of deferred tax assets included in current assets was $91 million and $128.4 million for year-end 1994 and 1995, respectively. The $151.1 million increase in the deferred tax liabilities is added to NOPAT; the $37.4 million increase in deferred tax assets is subtracted from NOPAT as indicated previously. If deferred tax liabilities are already part of invested capital, as recommended in the shortcut approach, no further adjustment is required for the liabilities. The balance in deferred tax assets, $128.4 million, however, should be subtracted from invested capital. The net effect is that our estimate of invested capital is the same as it would have been had the deferred tax assets been netted against the liabilities.

To recap:

NOPAT	Increase by $151.1 M
	Decrease by $37.4 M
Invested capital	Decrease by $128.4 M

percent. Therefore, ignoring deferred tax liabilities, as we do in the Quaker Oats example, can overstate company performance.

The more sophisticated argument for ignoring deferred taxes is that these amounts often arise, at least in the United States, because of timing differences in book and tax depreciation. Because the company will continue to invest, as earlier timing differences are reversed, new timing differences emerge, and the deferred tax liability remains on the balance sheet. In other words, the liability is never really paid off, which implies that the deferred tax is more like equity than debt. Therefore, any charges to profit during the year as a result of deferred taxes should be restored to NOPAT. The logic in this adjustment is that if the liability will not be paid, the related expense should not be recognized.

A major problem with this logic is that it assumes that deferred taxes are driven by depreciation. Although depreciation is often the major component of deferred taxes in the United States, the United Kingdom, and other Anglophone countries, *any* temporary difference between book income and tax income gives rise to deferred tax. For companies in continental Europe, factors other than depreciation, such as provisions, may play a more important role in the determination of deferred tax. In such cases, the timing differences are more likely to reverse, resulting in future tax savings for deferred tax assets and additional tax payments for deferred tax liabilities.

Another problem with this logic is that many companies do experience reductions in their deferred tax liability. To illustrate, 37 percent of the companies in the S&P 500 with a positive deferred tax liability in 1997 had a lower deferred tax liability in 1998.

If deferred taxes do have to be paid, how should we account for them? The GAAP approach is to charge the future tax expense against current income without any adjustment for the time value of money, as we see in Table 6–12, drawn from our earlier example. To limit our analysis to five years, we assume that the company, at the end of year 5, uses $1.725 million (the future tax liability discounted at the project's economic return) to pay off the tax liability. Any remaining cash is distributed to shareholders (which implies a $2.275 million gain on the elimination of debt in year 5).

There are two problems with the GAAP accounting: It makes the return on invested capital (i.e., the accounting rate of return) a poor proxy for the economic return, and it gives an incorrect value for free cashflow (which means that it can't be used to value the business). The accounting return on capital is constant at 24 percent, but far below the project's economic return (36.6 percent). The free cashflow is understated because the deferred tax liability is not recognized on a present value basis. For example, in year 1, $2.0 million is paid to equity holders and a liability to pay the government $0.8 million in year 6 is incurred. The correct free

T A B L E   6–12

Using the GAAP Approach*

		Year				
	0	1	2	3	4	5
Capital investment	−5					3.725
Operating profit		2.0	2.0	2.0	2.0	2.0
Income tax expense		0.8	0.8	0.8	0.8	0.8
NOPAT		1.2	1.2	1.2	1.2	1.2
Invested capital	5.0	5.0	5.0	5.0	5.0	0
Return on invested capital		24%	24%	24%	24%	24%
Free cashflow	−5	1.2	1.2	1.2	1.2	8.475
IRR	29.1%					
Net income		1.200	1.200	1.200	1.200	3.475
Equity capital	5	4.200	3.400	2.600	1.800	0
Deferred tax liability		0.800	1.600	2.400	3.200	0
Invested capital	5	5.000	5.000	5.000	5.000	0

*In millions of dollars.

cashflow is $2.0 million − $0.8 million / 1.36^5$), or $1.832 million, but GAAP accounting gives $1.2 million because the tax liability is not recognized on a present value basis. Free cashflow in year 5 is $8.475 million, or the $5.275 million distributed to equity holders − $0.800 million of additional debt incurred + $4.0 million of repaid debt. The GAAP accounting free cashflow gives an economic return of 29.1 percent, well below the actual economic return of 36.6 percent.

To make the accounting return on capital equal to the project's economic return and get the correct free cashflow, we need to recognize deferred tax expense on a present-value basis (see Table 6–13). The income tax expense in year 1 is the present value, discounted at the internal rate of return, of the $0.8 million income tax payable in year 6 (which equals $0.8 million$/(1 + IRR)^5$, or $0.168 million. Because we are not paying the tax in year 1, we must recognize a deferred tax liability of $0.168 million on the balance sheet. Free cashflow in year 5 is $6.832 million, or the $5.275 million distributed to equity holders − $0.168 million of additional debt incurred + $1.725 million of repaid debt.

T A B L E   6–13

Deferred Tax Expense on a Present-Value Basis*

			Year			
	0	1	2	3	4	5
Capital investment	−5					3.725
Operating profit		2.000	2.000	2.000	2.000	2.000
Income tax expense		0.168	0.168	0.168	0.168	0.168
Tax expense interest			0.062	0.146	0.261	0.418
NOPAT		1.832	1.771	1.686	1.572	1.415
Equity capital		4.832	4.603	4.289	3.860	0
Deferred tax liability		0.168	0.397	0.711	1.140	1.725
Total invested capital	5	5.000	5.000	5.000	5.000	0
Return on invested capital		37%	37%	37%	37%	37%
Free cashflow	−5	1.832	1.832	1.832	1.832	6.832
IRR	36.6%					
Net income		1.832	1.771	1.686	1.572	1.415
Equity capital	5	4.832	4.603	4.289	3.860	0

*In millions of dollars.

Provisions for Warranties and Bad Debts

The accrual method of accounting requires companies to make provisions for costs that are expected in the future as a result of events or decisions that have already occurred. Bad debts, restructuring, and warranties are among the most common items companies make provisions for. Some EVA proponents argue that the recognition of provisions takes accounting profits farther from cashflow and what's more, provisions are popular vehicles for manipulative financial reporting behavior such as income smoothing. "Cash is king," they say, and only actual cashflows for such items should enter into the calculation of NOPAT. As we noted previously in our discussion of deferred taxes, this is not a very thoughtful argument, since the absence of current cash warranty expense does not imply that there is no economic tax expense.

Consider the following example, which is similar to the one we used with deferred taxes. A company invests $5 million in a five-year project that is expected to earn an annual after-tax profit of $1.2 million before warranty expense and to recover its initial

investment in full at the end of the fifth year. The company expects
warranty costs to be $0.4 million a year for five years beginning
in year 6. The company's cashflows are as follows:

Years	Description	Annual Cashflow
0	Capital investment	−$5000
1–5	After-tax profit	2000
5	Capital recovery	5000
6–10	Warranty costs	−400
6–10	Income tax expense	−160

The economic, or internal, rate of return for these cashflows
is 22.2 percent. While none of the warranty costs are paid in the
project's operating years, they do have a clear economic cost.
Without warranty costs, the project's economic return would increase to 24.0 percent.

A more sophisticated argument for recognizing warranty expense on a cash basis is that reserves are subjective and will be
exploited by managers to obscure their true performance results.
(The manipulation of such provisions is one of the two most common ways that managers manipulate profits; the other being revenue recognition.) If we accept this argument, we can convert to
cash accounting for warranty expense by

♦ Adding back to NOPAT, on an after-tax basis, any
  increase in the warranty provision and subtracting from
  NOPAT, on an after-tax basis, any decrease in the
  warranty provision
♦ Adding the warranty provision back to invested capital

If the "shortcut" approach to calculating EVA (described in
Chapter 2) is used, long-term provisions are already included in
the invested capital figure, although short-term provisions and the
allowance for doubtful accounts are not (in the latter's case, because it is normally treated as a contra-asset and does not appear
in the provisions account). Therefore, the only adjustments required to invested capital would be short-term provisions and the

allowance for doubtful accounts. Of course, if the shortcut approach is not followed, *all* provisions should be added to invested capital.

The examples in Boxes 6–3 and 6–4 assume that the shortcut approach has been followed.

Our adjustment to NOPAT is done on an after-tax basis because we need to reverse the impact of the warranty expense accrual on the deferred tax liability. If, for example, we accrue $0.4 million of warranty expense, this accrual reduces book taxable income by $0.4 million. This, in turn, reduces the income tax provision by $0.160 million, assuming a 40 percent tax rate, and creates a deferred tax asset in the same amount (representing future deductibility of the warranty expense when the cash is actually paid out). If the deferred tax liability is reported net of deferred tax assets, the warranty expense accrual decreases the liability by $0.160 million. To reverse the warranty expense accrual, we need to add $0.4 million to NOPAT. However, to restore the income tax provision to what it would have been in the absence of the warranty expense, we must add $0.160 million to income tax expense.

B O X   6–3

ADJUSTING FOR PROVISIONS: AB VOLVO

In the notes to its 1995 annual report, AB Volvo, the Swedish automobile manufacturer, reported allowances for doubtful accounts of 929 million kroner and 1034 million kroner for year-end 1994 and 1995, respectively. To make this adjustment, the increase in the provision, 105 million kroner, is added to NOPAT, net of Volvo's 28 percent tax rate, for a net adjustment of 75.6 million kroner. The year-end 1995 balance in the allowance account is added to invested capital, because this provision is treated as a contra-account to receivables and not as a provision (i.e., other long-term liabilities). Therefore, under the shortcut approach, it is not automatically included in invested capital.

To recap:

NOPAT	Increase by 75.6 million kroner
Invested capital	Increase by 1034 million kroner

B O X   6–4

ADJUSTING FOR PROVISIONS: FIAT

Fiat, the Italian automobile maker, reported warranty provisions of 1259 billion lire and 1390 billion lire at year-end 1994 and 1995, respectively. To use our adjustment, the increase in the provision, 131 billion lire, net of Fiat's 41 percent corporate tax rate, or 77 billion lire, is added to NOPAT. Fiat's effective tax rate in 1995 was only 24 percent, because of tax loss carryforwards. But the notes to Fiat's financial statements reveal that these losses, which reduced the effective tax rate by 17 percent, will no longer be available when Fiat incurs the costs of servicing the warranties. In other words, the tax rate in effect when Fiat actually disburses the cash related to the provisions is likely to be about 41 percent. No further adjustment is required for invested capital, because the warranty provision should already be included under the shortcut approach.

To recap:

NOPAT	Increase by 77.3 billion lire
Invested capital	No adjustment required

The net adjustment is the after-tax warranty expense, $0.4 \times (1 - 40$ percent$)$. To reverse the effect of the warranty expense accrual on the balance sheet (and on invested capital), we must add the warranty provision, net of tax, to invested capital.

To account for warranties in a way that makes the accounting return on capital equal to the project's economic return, we need to recognize warranty expense on a present-value basis, just as we did previously with deferred tax (see Table 6–14). We assume, as before, that the company pays off the warranty liability at its present value, $0.684, at the end of year 5.

LIFO Reserves

In some countries, companies can use last-in, first-out (LIFO) for inventory costing. This treatment method offers important tax advantages over other approaches in periods of rising prices, and it also produces cost-of-sales figures that more closely approximate

T A B L E   6–14

Accounting Return on Capital*

	0	1	2	3	4	5
				Year		
Capital investment	−5					4.316
Operating profit		2.000	2.000	2.000	2.000	2.000
Warranty expense		0.147	0.147	0.147	0.147	0.147
Warranty expense interest			0.033	0.072	0.121	0.181
Warranty income tax expense		−0.059	−0.059	−0.059	−0.059	−0.059
Income tax expense interest			−0.013	−0.029	−0.048	−0.072
Cash income tax expense		0.800	0.800	0.800	0.800	0.800
NOPAT		1.112	1.112	1.112	1.112	1.112
Warranty liability		0.147	0.326	0.545	0.812	1.140
Deferred tax liability		−0.059	−0.130	−0.218	−0.325	−0.456
Equity capital	5.000	4.912	4.805	4.673	4.513	0
Total invested capital	5.000	5.000	5.000	5.000	5.000	0
Return on invested capital		22.2%	22.2%	22.2%	22.2%	22.2%

*In millions of dollars.

the replacement cost of inventory, resulting in a better matching of revenues and expenses. LIFO does have one serious drawback, however. When inventory increases in any year, a "LIFO layer" of old product costs is left behind. Old LIFO layers create two problems for EVA. First, inventory can be seriously understated, which in turn understates net assets and invested capital. Second, when old LIFO layers are liquidated, which happens whenever inventory decreases from one year to the next, both operating income and EVA are overstated. This overstatement is caused by matching old product costs against current revenues.

Companies that use LIFO normally report a LIFO reserve in the notes to their financial statements, which is the difference between the carrying value of the inventory and its current cost (see Box 6–5). The reserve is added to invested capital, and the year-on-year increase (decrease) in the LIFO reserve is added back to (subtracted from) NOPAT.

B O X   6-5

ADJUSTING LIFO:
CAMPBELL SOUP COMPANY

In its 1996 annual report, Campbell Soup Company, a large American food processing company, reports inventory figures as follows (in millions of dollars):

	1996	1995
Raw materials	323	317
Finished products	461	505
	784	822
−Adjustments of inventory to LIFO basis	45	67
	739	755

Inventories under LIFO are lower because of low-cost layers of inventory left over from earlier years when the prices of Campbell Soup's production inputs were lower. For EVA calculations, the 1996 LIFO reserve, $45 million, is added to the year-end 1996 invested capital. In short, if Campbell Soup had not used LIFO, the inventory balance (and invested capital) would be $45 million higher. Also, NOPAT in 1996 would be lower by an amount equal to the reduction in the LIFO.[2] A reduction in the reserve indicates that old low-cost layers of inventory had been liquidated, resulting in the matching of low costs of goods sold against the current year's revenues. The effect is an overstatement of income. This adjustment requires a decrease in NOPAT of $22 million decrease in the LIFO reserve ($67 million − $45 million).

To recap:

> NOPAT   Decrease by $22 M
> Invested capital   Increase by $45 M

---

2. No tax adjustment is required, because the company has already benefited from the LIFO tax break. The logic here is similar to that of the R&D adjustment, which is also made on a pretax basis.

Depreciation

In our discussions of successful efforts and R&D accounting, we showed that sinking-fund depreciation makes the return on invested capital constant and equal to the economic, or internal, rate of return, while straight-line depreciation shows a rising return on capital that starts below the economic return and ends up above the economic return. Our examples were based on the assumption that the project's cash operating margin was constant from one year to the next. If this assumption is not true, and the project's cash operating margin is declining from one year to the next, we can make a stronger case for straight-line depreciation.

Table 6–15 illustrates this case. Suppose we invest $5 million in a piece of equipment that provides a declining cash operating margin over its five-year life. The operating margin is $2 million in year 1, but it declines steadily to $1.2 million in year 5. With a cost of capital of 10 percent, the machine is a good investment, providing a 20 percent return (for simplicity, we again assume that taxes are zero). In this situation, straight-line depreciation makes the accounting return on capital constant and equal to the economic return (see Table 6–16).

While making the accounting return on capital equal to the economic return is a desirable objective, we cannot determine the depreciation or amortization schedule needed to do so unless we know the future cash operating margin provided by the asset. Suppose, in our example, that the cash operating margin stays

T A B L E   6–15

The Internal Rate of Return for a Capital Investment*

		Year				
	0	1	2	3	4	5
Equipment purchase	−5.0					
Cash operating margin		2.0	1.8	1.6	1.4	1.2
Income taxes paid		0	0	0	0	0
Cashflow	−5.0	2.0	1.8	1.6	1.4	1.2
Internal rate of return	20%					

*In millions of dollars.

T A B L E   6–16

The Investment's Accounting Rate of Return*

		Year				
	0	1	2	3	4	5
Cash operating margin		2.0	1.8	1.6	1.4	1.2
Depreciation expense		1.0	1.0	1.0	1.0	1.0
Income tax expense		0	0	0	0	0
NOPAT	0	1.0	0.8	0.6	0.4	0.2
Invested capital	5.0	4.0	3.0	2.0	1.0	0
Return on invested capital		20%	20%	20%	20%	20%

* In millions of dollars.

constant at $2 million each year (see Table 6–17). This raises the project's economic return to 29 percent. In this case, we need sinking-fund depreciation to make the return on invested capital equal to the economic return, as shown in Table 6–18.

The sinking-fund depreciation expense is equal to the cash operating margin minus the economic return on capital:

Year 1　　$568 = $2000 − (28.65% × $5000)

Year 2　　$730 = $2000 − (28.65% × $4432)

In effect, the depreciation or asset recovery charge is what's

T A B L E   6–17

Showing the Cash Operating Margin Constant at $2 Million Each Year*

		Year				
	0	1	2	3	4	5
Equipment purchase	−5					
Cash operating margin		2	2	2	2	2
Income taxes paid		0	0	0	0	0
Cashflow	−5	2	2	2	2	2
Internal rate of return	29%					

* In millions of dollars.

T A B L E   6–18

Sinking-Fund Depreciation Makes Return on Invested
Capital Equal to Economic Return*

	Year					
	0	**1**	**2**	**3**	**4**	**5**
Cash operating margin		2.000	2.000	2.000	2.000	2.000
Depreciation expense		0.568	0.730	0.939	1.208	1.555
Income tax expense		0	0	0	0	0
NOPAT	0	1.432	1.270	1.061	0.792	0.445
Invested capital	5.000	4.432	3.702	2.763	1.555	0
Return on invested capital		29%	29%	29%	29%	29%

*In millions of dollars.

left over after we provide the economic return on the investment. It works just like a home mortgage. The amount of the
payment in excess of interest on the loan goes to reduce the principal balance.

This general approach also works when the cash operating
margin is not constant. In this case, however, the depreciation is
generally described as "economic depreciation," rather than sinking-fund depreciation, because we no longer have a level annual
payment like a home mortgage.

The illustration in Table 6–19 supposes that the cash operating margin increases by 10 percent each year. This increases the
economic return to 36.311 percent.

Depreciation expense for years 1 and 2 is now:

$$\$184 = \$2000 - (36.311\% \times \$5000)$$

$$\$451 = \$2200 - (36.311\% \times \$4816)$$

Table 6–20 shows depreciation expense for all five years.

If the increase in cash operating margin is rapid enough, we
get an odd result: the depreciation expense is negative in the early
years. For example, suppose that the cash operating margin increases by 25 percent a year. This increases the economic return
to 47.538 percent, as is shown in Table 6–21. But a 47.538 percent

T A B L E   6–19

Supposing a 10 Percent Increase Each Year in the
Cash Operating Margin*

	Year					
	0	1	2	3	4	5
Equipment purchase	−5.000					
Cash operating margin		2.000	2.200	2.420	2.662	2.928
Income taxes paid		0	0	0	0	0
Cashflow	−5.000	2.000	2.200	2.420	2.662	2.928
Internal rate of return	36.311%					

*In millions of dollars.

T A B L E   6–20

Depreciation Expense for Years 1 through 5*

	Year					
	0	1	2	3	4	5
Cash operating margin		2.000	2.200	2.420	2.662	2.928
Depreciation expense		0.184	0.451	0.835	1.381	2.148
Income tax expense		0	0	0	0	0
NOPAT	0	1.816	1.749	1.585	1.281	0.780
Invested capital	5.000	4.816	4.364	3.529	2.148	0
Return on invested capital		36%	36%	36%	36%	36%

*In millions of dollars.

return on our investment of $5000, or $2377, is more than our first-
year cashflow of $2000. This means that depreciation is negative:

$$-\$377 = \$2000 - (47.538\% \times \$5000)$$

Negative depreciation means that our asset is increasing in value,
not decreasing. Table 6–22 shows that the present value of the
future cashflows from the machine increases from $5000 at the end
of year 0 to $5377 at the end of year 1. The "decline" in the value

T A B L E   6–21

Showing an Increase in Cash Operating Margin by 25
Percent a Year*

	Year					
	0	1	2	3	4	5
Equipment purchase	−5.000					
Cash operating margin		2.000	2.500	3.125	3.906	4.883
Income taxes paid		0	0	0	0	0
Cashflow	−5.000	2.000	2.500	3.125	3.906	4.883
Internal rate of return	47.538%					

*In millions of dollars.

T A B L E   6–22

Negative Depreciation*

	Year					
	0	1	2	3	4	5
Cash operating margin		2.000	2.500	3.125	3.906	4.883
Depreciation expense		−0.377	−0.056	0.542	1.581	3.310
Income tax expense		0	0	0	0	0
NOPAT	0	2.377	2.556	2.583	2.325	1.573
Invested capital	5.000	5.377	5.433	4.891	3.310	0
Return on invested capital		48%	48%	48%	48%	48%

*In millions of dollars.

of the machine, −$377, is the depreciation for that year. When tax and accounting treatments differ, economic depreciation is needed to make the after-tax return on invested capital equal to the after-tax economic return. Let's return to the example at the beginning of this chapter. In this example (on successful efforts accounting), we ignored taxes. If full-cost accounting is used for EVA calculations (i.e., we abandon successful efforts by capitalizing all costs of exploration, even for dry holes), but successful efforts is used for tax purposes, we do not pay income taxes until the final three years of the five-year project, as shown in Table 6–23.[3] In this case, we need an unusual "up-down-up" pattern of amortization to make the return on invested capital, or the accounting rate of return, equal to the project's economic return (see Table 6–24).

T A B L E   6–23

Using Full-Cost Accounting for EVA and Successful Efforts Accounting for Tax Purposes*

	Year					
	0	1	2	3	4	5
Exploration costs	−5.000					
Oil revenue		2.000	2.000	2.000	2.000	2.000
Income taxes paid		0	0	0.560	0.720	0.720
Cashflow	−5.000	2.000	2.000	1.440	1.280	1.280
Internal rate of return	20%					

* In millions of dollars.

T A B L E   6–24

"Up-Down-Up" Pattern of Amortization*

	Year					
	0	1	2	3	4	5
Oil revenue		2.000	2.000	2.000	2.000	2.000
Exploration expense		0.990	1.190	0.870	0.886	1.065
Income tax expense		0	0	0.560	0.720	0.720
NOPAT	0	1.010	0.810	0.570	0.394	0.215
Invested capital	5.000	4.010	2.821	1.951	1.065	0
Return on invested capital		20%	20%	20%	20%	20%

* In millions of dollars.

3. This occurs because the exploration costs written off under successful efforts offset any oil revenues from years 1 and 2. As a result, no taxes are paid until year 3.

Our examples show that straight-line depreciation does not make the accounting return on capital equal to the economic return unless future cashflows are declining. We also know from our consulting experience that few companies anticipate declining cashflows from their assets. Nonetheless, almost all EVA companies rely exclusively on straight-line depreciation. What accounts for this paradox?

To our knowledge there has not been any systematic study of the reasons why almost all EVA companies rely on straight-line depreciation. We speculate that the two main reasons companies don't use sinking-fund depreciation are that it is harder to explain to managers with EVA-linked bonuses, and it makes EVA improvement on the current invested capital base harder to achieve. (Remember that returns on invested capital tend to increase over time under straight-line; therefore, abandoning straight-line in favor of sinking-fund depreciation reduces the chances of EVA increasing over time simply because of a depreciating asset base.)

Sinking-fund depreciation makes EVA improvement on the current capital base harder to achieve because sinking-fund depreciation charges are increasing each year and, hence, require NOPAT improvements just to maintain current EVA. Sinking-fund depreciation does make it easier in the early years to gain EVA improvement from new assets, but for most if not all EVA companies, the penalty from rising depreciation on the old asset base would more than offset the gain from lower depreciation on new assets.

If a company decides to use sinking-fund depreciation, it must first develop a forecast of future cashflows. A conservative approach is to assume that future cashflows are constant and have a present value equal to the acquisition cost of the asset. This implies that the economic return on the investment is equal to the cost of capital.

For example, suppose that a $5 million asset has an expected economic life of five years. If the cost of capital is 10 percent, an annual cashflow of $1.319 million is required to make the present value of the future cashflows $5 million. To calculate the annual cashflow, we divide the purchase price by the valuation multiple for a constant annuity:

$$[1 - (1/(1+\text{WACC}))^{\text{Life}}]/\text{WACC}$$

which equals 3.791. This cashflow must cover a cost-of-capital return on investment, income tax expense, and depreciation. If

straight-line is the most favorable depreciation treatment allowed
for tax purposes, taxable income each year equals $1.319 million
minus depreciation of $1.0 million, or $0.319. With a 40 percent
tax rate, income tax expense is 40 percent × $0.319 million, or
$0.128. This implies that the annual cashflow of $1.319 million will
leave $0.691 million for depreciation in year 1 after providing a
10 percent return on investment ($0.5 million) and paying $0.128
in income tax. Table 6–25 shows the depreciation for the remaining years and demonstrates that the depreciation under the
sinking-fund approach results in a constant 10 percent return on
invested capital and zero EVA, assuming annual cashflows of
$1.319 million.

Goodwill

Goodwill arises whenever companies acquire other companies for
a price exceeding the fair market value of all identifiable assets,
net of liabilities. The accounting treatment of goodwill varies from
country to country; some countries permit the immediate write-
off of goodwill to reserves. Most countries, including the United
States, require capitalization and subsequent amortization.

T A B L E   6–25

Depreciation under the Sinking-Fund Approach*

	Year				
	0	**1**	**2**	**3**	**4**	**5**
Cash operating margin		1.319	1.319	1.319	1.319	1.319
Depreciation		0.691	0.761	0.837	0.920	1.012
Income tax expense		0.128	0.128	0.128	0.128	0.128
NOPAT	0	0.500	0.431	0.355	0.271	0.179
Invested capital	5.000	4.309	3.548	2.711	1.791	0.779
Return on invested capital		10%	10%	10%	10%	10%
Capital charges		0.500	0.431	0.355	0.271	0.179
EVA	0	0	0	0	0	0

*In millions of dollars.

Most EVA proponents believe that both of these approaches are wrong. The immediate write-off of goodwill to reserves by-passes the income statement and undermines the linkage between operating free cashflow and financing free cashflow that is the foundation of shareholder value analysis. In short, the present value of future free cashflows from an operating perspective (i.e., operating cashflows net of investment or, alternatively, NOPAT − Δ Invested capital) must equal the present value of future free cashflows from a financing perspective (i.e., interest and principal paid to providers of debt finance plus dividends and share buy-backs for shareholders).

Consider the operating performance forecast and valuation analysis in Table 6–26. Our forecast shows an initial investment of $10 million in a business that grows by 15 percent each year

T A B L E   6–26

Operating Performance Forecast and Valuation Analysis*

		Year				
	0	1	2	3	4	5
Operating forecast						
Capital growth rate		15%	15%	15%	15%	15%
Invested capital	10.000	11.500	13.225	15.209	17.490	20.114
Return on invested capital		20%	20%	20%	20%	20%
NOPAT		2.000	2.300	2.645	3.042	3.498
Valuation						
Change in invested capital	10.000	1.500	1.725	1.984	2.281	2.624
Free cashflow		0.500	0.575	0.661	0.760	0.875
Present value of free cash-flow		0.455	0.475	0.497	0.519	0.543
Cumulative present value of free cashflows	2.489					
Terminal value	44.600					
PV of terminal value	27.693					
Market value	30.182					
Cost of capital	10%					

* In millions of dollars.

and earns a 20 percent return on capital. The terminal value estimate is based on the assumption that the value of the business at
the end of year 5 is equal to 12 times year 5 NOPAT plus the new
capital invested in year 5. This results in a value for the business
at the end of year 5 of ($3.498 million × 12) + $2.624 million, or
$44.6 million.

   If we buy the business for its market value at the end of year
0, we recognize the difference between the purchase price ($30.182
million) and book (i.e., invested) capital ($10 million) as goodwill,
or $20.182 million. For simplicity, we assume that goodwill is not
tax deductible. If we write off the goodwill in year 1 by a direct
charge to equity that does not go through the income statement,
the operating calculation of free cashflow, NOPAT − Δ Invested
capital, no longer provides the correct value for the business (see
Table 6–27). If we do write off goodwill in year 1 against NOPAT
(see Table 6–28), we get the correct calculation of free cashflow
and the right value for the business, but the result is a poor measure of annual performance.

   If we do not permit direct charges to equity, the change in
equity is equal to net income plus the net equity contribution from
shareholders (i.e., new equity contributions minus dividends
and share repurchases). Financial reporting under these ground
rules is called *clean surplus accounting*. The write-off of goodwill
with clean surplus accounting does not change our valuation analysis, but it does imply, incorrectly, that year 1 is a horrible-
performance year. We could just as easily write off the goodwill
in year 2 and make that the horrible-performance year. In either
case, the apparently poor results have nothing to do with current
operating performance.

   U.S. GAAP requires the straight-line amortization of goodwill over a period not to exceed 40 years. We can easily see (Table
6–29) that this accounting treatment does not reflect economic reality if we compute post-acquisition EVA. We acquired the company for fair value, i.e., the present value of future free cashflow,
but EVA drops precipitously, from $0.870 million pre-acquisition
to −$1.523 million post-acquisition, a decline of $2.393 million. The
decline in EVA says that the acquisition destroys shareholder
wealth, but we know that that is not true because we paid no
more than the fair value of the target company, based on the forecast of free cashflows. When we buy at the fair value implied by

T A B L E   6–27

Writing Off Goodwill against Equity*

	0	1	2	3	4	5
			Year			
Operating forecast						
Capital growth rate		15%	15%	15%	15%	15%
Operating capital	10.000	11.500	13.225	15.209	17.490	20.114
Goodwill	20.182	0				
Total invested capital	30.182	11.500	13.225	15.209	17.490	20.114
Return on operating capital		20%	20%	20%	20%	20%
NOPAT		2.000	2.300	2.645	3.042	3.498
Valuation						
Change in invested capital	30.182	−18.682	1.725	1.984	2.281	2.624
Operating free cashflow		20.682	0.575	0.661	0.760	0.875
PV of free cashflow		18.802	0.475	0.497	0.519	0.543
Cumulative present value of free cashflows	20.836					
Terminal value	44.600					
PV of terminal value	27.693					
Market value	48.529					
Cost of capital	10%					

* In millions of dollars.

a forecast, and then realize the forecast, we should have zero EVA each year because no excess returns, positive or negative, have been achieved.

Some EVA practitioners argue that the problem is that goodwill amortization is not a cash cost, and they advocate adding goodwill amortization back to invested capital. This is not a convincing argument, however. Goodwill amortization is not a cash cost, but the same could be said for depreciation of tangible assets and the amortization of R&D or oil exploration costs. The issue is whether goodwill is (1) a wasting asset that needs to be recovered through positive amortization charges, (2) a nonwasting, but nonappreciating, asset that needs no amortization charges at all, or (3) an appreciating asset that needs to be recognized with negative amortization charges.

T A B L E   6–28

Writing Off Goodwilll against NOPAT*

	Year					
	0	1	2	3	4	5
Operating forecast						
Capital growth rate		15%	15%	15%	15%	15%
Operating capital	10.000	11.500	13.225	15.209	17.490	20.114
Goodwill	20.182	0				
Total invested capital	30.182	11.500	13.225	15.209	17.490	20.114
Return on operating capital		20%	20%	20%	20%	20%
NOPAT		−18.182	2.300	2.645	3.042	3.498
Valuation						
Change in invested capital	30.182	−18.682	1.725	1.984	2.281	2.624
Free cashflow		0.500	0.575	0.661	0.760	0.875
PV of free cashflow		0.455	0.475	0.497	0.519	0.543
Cumulative present value of free cashflows	2.489					
Terminal value	44.600					
Present value of terminal value	27.693					
Market value	30.182					
Cost of capital	10%					

*In millions of dollars.

If we accept the second assumption (i.e., goodwill is a non-wasting, but nonappreciating asset), good amortization is added back to NOPAT and is restored to invested capital. An example of this treatment is shown in Box 6–6. We still have a performance measurement problem (see Table 6–30); the acquisition leads to negative EVA just as it does when straight-line amortization is used. Although EVA is obviously less negative when amortization of goodwill is avoided, it is still negative. Again, the EVA figures seem to be telling us, contrary to fact, that the acquisition destroys value.

EVA is negative even though investors are earning a cost-of-capital return on market value each year (see Table 6–31). The conflict with conventional EVA accounting arises because investors are receiving part of their return in appreciation that is not

T A B L E   6–29

Computing Post-Acquisition EVA with Straight-Line Amortization of Goodwill*

Operating Forecast	Year					
	0	1	2	3	4	5
Capital growth rate		15%	15%	15%	15%	15%
Operating capital	10.000	11.500	13.225	15.209	17.490	20.114
Goodwill	20.182	19.677	19.173	18.668	18.164	17.659
Total invested capital	30.182	31.177	32.398	33.877	35.654	37.773
Return on operating capital		20%	20%	20%	20%	20%
NOPAT		1.495	1.795	2.140	2.537	2.993
Capital charges		3.018	3.118	3.240	3.388	3.565
EVA	0.870	−1.523	−1.322	−1.099	−0.851	−0.572
Cost of capital	10%					

* In millions of dollars.

B O X   6–6

ADJUSTING GOODWILL: GEORGIA-PACIFIC

Georgia-Pacific is one of the world's largest manufacturers and distributors of building products, pulp, and paper. In 1995, the company recognized $59 million of goodwill amortization. Accumulated amortization by the end of 1995 was $366 million. For EVA calculations, the $59 million amortization expense is added to NOPAT. The accumulated goodwill amortization of $366 million is added to invested capital.

To recap:

NOPAT	Increase by $59 M
Invested capital	Increase by $366 M

T A B L E   6–30

Adding Back Goodwill Amortization*

Operating Forecast	0	Year 1	2	3	4	5
Capital growth rate		15%	15%	15%	15%	15%
Operating capital	10.000	11.500	13.225	15.209	17.490	20.114
Goodwill	20.182	20.182	20.182	20.182	20.182	20.182
Total invested capital	30.182	31.682	33.407	35.391	37.672	40.296
Return on operating capital		20%	20%	20%	20%	20%
NOPAT		2.000	2.300	2.645	3.042	3.498
Capital charges		3.018	3.168	3.341	3.539	3.767
EVA	0.870	−1.018	−0.868	−0.696	−0.497	−0.269
Cost of capital	10%					

*In millions of dollars.

T A B L E   6–31

Negative EVA Even Though Investors Earn a Cost-of-Capital Return on Market Value*

	0	Year 1	2	3	4	5
Market value	30.182	32.700	35.395	38.273	41.340	44.600
Free cashflow		0.500	0.575	0.661	0.760	0.875
Year-end investor wealth		33.200	35.970	38.935	42.101	45.474
Return on beginning market value		10.0%	10.0%	10.0%	10.0%	10.0%

*In millions of dollars.

recognized as income in conventional EVA accounting. Year 1 NOPAT is $2.0 million, which provides only a 6.6 percent return on beginning market value, or 3.4 percent less than the cost of capital. A quarter of NOPAT, or $0.5 million, is distributed as free cashflow, while the remaining three-quarters, $1.5 million, is reinvested in the business. The market value of the business at the end of year 1, the present value of its future free cashflow, is $32.7 million, an increase of $2.518 million over year 0. Reinvested NOPAT causes $1.5 million of this increase, but that leaves an additional increase of $1.018 million. This increase is the appreciation in the value of the business in excess of additional capital invested—that is, additional goodwill. If we recognize this *negative* economic depreciation, we get the correct economic result (shown in Table 6–32), zero EVA for every year of the forecast horizon.

While negative economic depreciation is a perfectly correct solution to the acquisition problem, EVA companies are reluctant to use it because the concept of negative depreciation is so novel. More commonly, EVA companies use a pro forma base year to avoid discouraging value-creating acquisitions. The acquisition

T A B L E   6–32

Recognizing Negative Economic Depreciation*

	Year				
	0	1	2	3	4	5
Decline in market value		−2.518	−2.695	−2.878	−3.067	−3.260
Add back new investment		1.500	1.725	1.984	2.281	2.624
Economic depreciation		−1.018	−0.970	−0.895	−0.786	−0.636
Adjusted acquisition book capital		32.700	35.395	38.273	41.340	44.600
Adjusted NOPAT		3.018	3.270	3.540	3.827	4.134
Adjusted capital charges		3.018	3.270	3.540	3.827	4.134
EVA		0	0	0	0	0

* In millions of dollars.

goodwill is included, on a pro forma basis, in prior year invested capital. See Table 6–33.

With the use of a pro forma base year, a zero NPV acquisition does not cause a reduction in EVA. Although the resulting EVAs are still negative (when they should be zero), this approach eliminates the incentive plan bias against acquisitions because EVA bonus plans are normally based on EVA improvement. But it also creates a windfall gain because a zero NPV acquisition leads to a steady increase in EVA. To eliminate these windfall gains, EVA companies need to increase their expected EVA improvement targets when they use this method.

In some countries, notably the United Kingdom and the Netherlands, goodwill can be written off directly against equity on the date of acquisition. In such cases, goodwill never appears on the balance sheet, and, therefore, there is no goodwill to amortize. The effect, especially in companies that are active in the takeover market, is to dramatically understate invested capital. Box 6–7 shows how to correct for this problem, although the illustration ignores the negative goodwill issue.

For similar reasons pooling-of-interests (i.e., merger) accounting should be reversed. The problem with merger accounting is that it assumes neither company has bought the other, and, accordingly, there can be no goodwill. *For EVA purchases all corporate*

T A B L E   6–33

Using a Pro Forma Base Year*

Pro Forma Base Year	Year					
	0	1	2	3	4	5
Capital growth rate		15%	15%	15%	15%	15%
Invested capital	10.000	11.500	13.225	15.209	17.490	20.114
Goodwill	20.182	20.182	20.182	20.182	20.182	20.182
Total invested capital	30.182	31.682	33.407	35.391	37.672	40.296
Return on invested capital		20%	20%	20%	20%	20%
NOPAT		2.000	2.300	2.645	3.042	3.498
Capital charge		3.018	3.168	3.341	3.539	3.767
EVA	−1.149	−1.018	−0.868	−0.696	−0.497	−0.269

* In millions of dollars.

B O X   6–7

ADJUSTING GOODWILL: ICI

At ICI, goodwill is written off directly to reserves (i.e., shareholders' equity) at the time of acquisition. Therefore, it never appears on the balance sheet. The notes to ICI's 1995 annual report revealed that reserves at the end of the year had been reduced by £823 million for direct write-offs of goodwill, including £178 million from 1995. An adjustment to 1995 NOPAT is not required for EVA calculations because the goodwill was not amortized. Instead, invested capital is increased by the cumulative goodwill write-off of £823 million.

To recap:

NOPAT	No adjustment required
Invested capital	Increase by £823 M

acquisitions should be accounted for using the purchase method. For analysts relying mainly on external accounts, it may be impossible to make such an adjustment; normally companies that use merger accounting do not provide sufficient disclosures to help outside readers determine what the accounts might have looked like if purchase accounting had been used instead. Thankfully, merger accounting is not often used, especially outside the United States, although it has made something of a comeback in the late 1990s as high share prices have led to a sharp increase in the number of all-stock corporate control transactions. Although poolings are likely to disappear within the next few years—the Financial Accounting Standards Board has already proposed eliminating the practice—the sheer size of recent poolings makes this a difficult topic to ignore. In the United States, four of the five biggest deals in 1998 used pooling-of-interests accounting—Exxon and Mobil, Citicorp and Travellers Group, SBC Communications and Ameritech, and Bell Atlantic and GTE.

To see how EVA can be adjusted for poolings, consider the illustration in Box 6–8.

Using the same logic, companies should also increase invested capital for "in-process R&D" that is written off at the moment of an acquisition. In 1986, the SEC began pushing companies to equalize the treatment of internal R&D, which is expensed by American companies, and externally acquired R&D, which is

B O X   6–8

ADJUSTING FOR POOLING-OF-INTERESTS: SMITHKLINE BEECHAM

In July 1989, SmithKline Beckman, an American health care company, merged with Beecham Group, a British company, and became SmithKline Beecham. The transaction was accounted for under merger accounting rules, but because of differences in U.K. and U.S. GAAP, the transaction would not have qualified for pooling-of-interests in the United States. The reason is that the conditions under which a company can use pooling-of-interests accounting are stricter in the United States than in the United Kingdom. In this case, if the transaction had been accounted for under U.S. rules, the purchase method would have been required, resulting in the recognition of goodwill. Because SmithKline Beecham shares are traded in the United States, the company files Form 20-F with the U.S. Securities and Exchange Commission. Form 20-F reconciles net income and shareholders' equity figures prepared under home country GAAP with U.S. GAAP.

The SmithKline Beecham example provides a rare opportunity to illustrate how to adjust invested capital for goodwill that is excluded from the balance sheet because pooling-of-interests accounting is used. The merged company's 1989 20-F filing reveals that goodwill from the acquisition—which would have been included under U.S. GAAP but was excluded from the balance sheet because the principal financial statements were prepared under U.K. GAAP—was £2665 million. Remember that for EVA purposes, there is no pooling-of-interests accounting. Therefore, we should add the excluded goodwill to invested capital. Because no goodwill was recognized, and there was no goodwill amortization, no adjustment is required for NOPAT.

To recap:

NOPAT	No adjustment required
Invested capital	Increase by £2665 M

sometimes capitalized. Companies were urged to determine the portion of a target company's purchase price that is intended for R&D efforts already in process. To ensure that this R&D would be treated identically to internal R&D expenditures, the acquiring company would then write off the full amount of the in-process R&D on the date of the acquisition.

The write-off of in-process R&D by American companies is similar to the Anglo-Dutch practice of immediate goodwill write-offs, but with one important difference. In-process R&D write-offs must go through the income statement, while the immediate write-off of goodwill bypasses the income statement forever. In effect, companies that recognize in-process R&D elect to take the loss all at once, thus saving future years from goodwill amortization. As a result, companies report higher profits in the years after the acquisition than would have been the case if the in-process R&D had been included in goodwill and then amortized.

The amounts involved can be enormous. On average, in-process R&D write-offs since 1980 have equaled nearly three-quarters of the purchase price. As a result, the SEC has back-tracked and is now repudiating the same policy that it had urged companies to adopt in the 1980s. The SEC's recent scrutiny of the practice has reduced the size of the write-offs. Before its current campaign, write-offs of greater than 80 percent were common. More recently, 40 to 50 percent write-offs have become the norm, but the numbers involved are still huge.

For EVA purposes, and assuming that goodwill is a non-wasting asset, in-process R&D should be added to invested capital. Any write-offs in the current year should be added to NOPAT.

Operating Leases

An *operating lease* is a form of secured borrowing, but for accounting purposes, the lease payments are treated as a rental expense, while the related asset and debt do not appear on the balance sheet. This treatment understates invested capital, because the lease is really a debt. NOPAT is also understated, because a portion of the lease payments includes the implied interest costs of the lease, which should be classified as interest expense and not included in operating profit.

An adjustment is made by adding to invested capital the present value of future lease payments as of the balance sheet date, discounted at the company's borrowing rate. The EVA adjustment for interest expense is calculated by multiplying the capitalized value of the leases by the borrowing rate. This amount is added to NOPAT. The tax shield on this interest must then be subtracted from NOPAT. The basic principle of the adjustment is to capitalize any operating expenses that are really financial costs in disguise. An example is shown in Box 6–9.

But while the magnitude of operating leases is substantial in many companies, the impact on EVA measurement is surprisingly small. To illustrate why, consider these figures for a hypothetical company:

Market value and book value of equity	= $80 M
Market value and book value of debt	= $60 M
Pretax cost of debt	= 8%
Corporate tax rate	= 40%
Cost of equity	= 12%
NOPAT, unadjusted	= $20 M

Because market value of the firm equals its book value (i.e., invested capital), the market value added (market value of the firm – invested capital) of the company is 0. The WACC is thus calculated as follows:

$$\text{WACC} = [(60 \div 140)\,(8\%)(1 - 40\%)] + [(80 \div 140)\,(12\%)]$$
$$= 8.914\%$$

where 60/140 and 80/140 represent the weightings in the capital structure for debt and equity.

We can now calculate EVA (all dollar amounts in millions):

NOPAT	$20.00
Capital charges ($140 × 8.914%)	12.48
EVA	$ 7.52

Now assume that our hypothetical company has operating leases with a present value of $30 million and an implied interest

ADJUSTING FOR OPERATING LEASES: RHÔNE-POULENC

Rhône-Poulenc's 1995 annual report reveals this information about operating leases:

Minimum noncancelable operating lease payments as of December 31, 1995 (in millions of French francs, FF):

1996	747
1997	671
1998	436
1999	395
2000	260
Thereafter	3087

For EVA purposes, invested capital is increased by the present value of future lease payments. To calculate this present value, we need to make an assumption about the timing of the lease payments (either beginning of the year, end of the year, or during the year) and the applicable interest rate. For our adjustment, we will assume that payments are made at the beginning of the year. Rhône-Poulenc does not report an interest rate for its operating leases. In such cases, we can use the pretax borrowing cost of the company's other debts, which the company reports to be 6.8 percent. The present value of the lease payments as of the end of 1995 is FF 2281 million, discounting the operating lease payments in 1996 through 2000 at 6.8 percent, and ignoring all payments beyond 2000 (because the exact timing is unknown). This amount is added to 1995 year-end invested capital.

To calculate the effect on NOPAT, we must also know the present value of future lease payments as of the end of the previous year (revealed in the 1995 annual report). The 1994 year-end present value is FF 1384 million, based on payments of FF 399 million, FF 340 million, FF 349 million, FF 243 million, and FF 215 million over the ensuing five years. The interest portion of 1995 leases payments is assumed to equal the product of the average value of operating leases during the year [(FF 2281 million + FF 1384 million) ÷ 2] and the pretax cost of borrowing (6.8 percent), or FF 1832.5 million × 0.068, which equals FF 124.6 million. This amount is added to NOPAT. The final adjustment is for the tax shield on the interest, which equals the company's 33 percent tax rate times the interest portion of lease payments (FF 124.6 million), or FF 41.1 million. This amount is subtracted from NOPAT.

To recap:

NOPAT	Increase by FF 124.6 M
	Decrease by FF 41.1 M
Invested capital	Increase by FF 2281 M

rate of 8 percent, the same rate that the company pays for its other debts. Lease payments are accounted for as rental expenses, with the entire amount subtracted from sales in calculating the firm's NOPAT.

Three types of adjustments are required to convert the accounting for these leases into that of a capital lease. First, the implied interest portion of the lease payments made during the year is added back to NOPAT. If we assume that the present value of the leases remains constant at $30 million throughout the year (as the present value of some leases declines, other leased assets are acquired), the interest portion of the lease payments equals $30 million (the present value of the leases) × 8 percent (the pretax cost of debt), or $2.4 million. Because interest expense is tax-deductible, we must also subtract from NOPAT the value of the tax shield that the company would have received from the interest payments to completely convert the accounting for these leases to that of capital leases.

To recap:

Unadjusted NOPAT	20.00
+ Interest portion of lease payments ($30 × 8%)	2.40
− Tax shield on interest expense ($2.40 × 40%)	0.96
Adjusted NOPAT	$21.44

Meanwhile, invested capital increases by $30 million to $170 million. But WACC changes too. The cost of debt and the cost of equity are not affected by the adjustment, but if the leases are now considered debt, the weightings for debt and equity must change. And when the weightings change, the WACC changes:

$$\text{WACC} = [(90 \div 170)\ (8\%)(1 - 40\%)] + [(80 \div 170\ (12\%)]$$
$$= 8.188\%$$

Previously, debt accounted for less than 43 percent of total financing (60 ÷ 140); it now accounts for nearly 53 percent of the total. Given the fact that the cost of debt is lower than the cost of equity, the effect of capitalizing the lease is to reduce our estimate of WACC from 8.914 to 8.188 percent. With new estimates of NOPAT, invested capital, and WACC, we can recalculate EVA as follows:

Adjusted NOPAT	$21.44
Capital charges ($170 × 8.188%)	13.92
EVA	$ 7.52

Notice that adjusted EVA is exactly the same as the unadjusted EVA. This result will always hold as long as the market value added of the company is 0. The operating lease adjustment will have an impact on EVA, though, if MVA is positive or negative. The greater the absolute value of MVA, the greater the impact of the adjustment on EVA. MVA and the present value of the leases would both have to be huge for the effect to be significant, however.

To illustrate, consider the same example, except that now the invested capital is $90 million instead of $140 million. In other words, market value is unchanged, but now MVA equals $50 million. For positive-MVA firms, the effect of the adjustment is to decrease EVA. First, the unadjusted calculations:

Unadjusted NOPAT	$20.00
Capital charges ($90 × 8.914%)	8.02
EVA	$11.98

If we adjust NOPAT to $21.44 million, just as in the previous example, and invested capital increases by $30 million if the leases are capitalized, this yields an adjusted invested capital of $120 million ($90 million + $30 million). We can now recalculate EVA as follows:

Adjusted NOPAT	$21.44
Capital charges ($120 × 8.188%)	9.83
EVA	$11.61

In this case, EVA declines by a modest $0.37 million. This result holds whenever MVA is positive (i.e., the market value of the firm is greater than invested capital). Even in a more extreme case where, say, invested capital before capitalization of the leases is only $10 million (and MVA is $130 million instead of $50 million), the effect of the lease adjustment on EVA is still less than $1 million (about 5 percent of the unadjusted EVA).

The opposite effect occurs in firms with a negative MVA. To illustrate, assume all facts are the same as in the original case, except that invested capital is now $160 million instead of $140 million, resulting in an MVA of −$20 million:

Unadjusted NOPAT	$20.00
Capital charges ($160 × 8.914%)	14.26
EVA	$ 5.74

When the operating leases are capitalized, invested capital becomes $190 million:

Adjusted NOPAT	$21.44
Capital charges ($190 × 8.188%)	15.56
EVA	$ 5.88

In this case, EVA increases by $0.14 million. Still, the effect on EVA of the lease adjustment is modest. Only in companies with very high positive or negative MVAs and large amounts of operating leases is it possible for the adjustment to have any significant impact on the EVA figures.

This is not to say that the operating lease adjustment is wrong. The logic behind it is unassailable. The issue for corporate managers is whether the adjustment produces significantly different results and therefore leads to significantly different behavior or interpretations of corporate performance. For most companies, the answer is no. There is still a case for capitalizing operating leases, because it provides a more accurate picture of a company's true indebtedness. However, for most companies EVA numbers will not be significantly affected.

Restructuring Charges

Some EVA proponents argue that restructuring and other special charges should be capitalized. The argument is that the restructuring charge is a necessary investment in the future success of the business. Suppose, for example, that the restructuring charge represents the costs of shutting down a plant. The charge is not capitalized under GAAP because the shutdown costs are not considered an asset—that is, an expected future benefit. EVA proponents argue for a broader construction of "asset," taking the position that the restructuring charge is part of the cost of maintaining the business.

Generally, EVA proponents who capitalize restructuring charges do not amortize the charge into expense over a subsequent period. While this is usually justified on the grounds of simplicity, a good case can be made for subsequent amortization of the capitalized restructuring charge. When a plant is shut down and the difference between the carrying cost and the salvage value is charged against GAAP earnings, the capitalized restructuring charge represents costs that would have been charged to depreciation over the remaining life of the plant if the restructuring charge had been amortized over the remaining life of the plant at the time of the shutdown (see Box 6–10). To our mind, there is no reason why shutting down a plant should extend its life.

Accounting for the Capital Charge

An important, but neglected, area for research is the accounting for the capital charge. Many studies of EVA and MVA have shown that far more companies have a positive MVA than a positive EVA. In our analysis of the nonfinancial companies in the S&P 500, 99 percent had a positive MVA at the end of 1998, but only 61 percent had a positive EVA for the year 1998. Two explanations have commonly been offered for this discrepancy. One is that GAAP depreciation schedules (generally, straight-line or accelerated) lead to a systematic understatement of capital, and hence, to an overstatement of MVA. The second is that the cost of equity used in the WACC calculation is too high and leads to a systematic overstatement of the capital charge, and hence, to an understatement of EVA. We would like to offer a third possible explanation.

The fundamental relationship that the market value of a company is equal to the present value of its future free cashflows discounted at the WACC is true only if WACC is a market-weighted average of the cost of equity and the cost of debt. This is why finance theory tells us to weight the debt and equity portions of the WACC on the basis of market values. However, an unfortunate

B O X   6—10

ADJUSTING FOR NONRECURRING GAINS AND LOSSES: ICI

In its 1995 annual report, Imperial Chemical Industries (ICI), a large British paint and acrylics firm, disclosed that £94 million of restructuring and litigation costs were included in trading (i.e., operating) profit. Exceptional gains of £71 million on the sale of operations were also reported, but these gains were not included in operating profit. We make the EVA adjustment as follows: NOPAT is increased by £63 million (the £94 million of restructuring and litigation costs included in operating profit, net of the 33 percent corporate tax rate), and invested capital is increased by the same amount. A NOPAT adjustment is not required for the £71 million gain because it is excluded from NOPAT, but invested capital is decreased by the gain, net of tax, or £44.6 million (£71 million × 0.67).

To recap:

NOPAT	Increase by £63 M
Invested capital	Increase by £63 M
	Decrease by £44.6 M

implication of market weighting is that a higher market value (which results in a higher MVA) leads to a higher WACC and, hence, a lower EVA. Table 6–34, which is loosely modeled on General Electric, shows that an increase in the equity market-to-book ratio (that is, the market value of equity divided by the book value of equity) from 1.0 to 8.0 increases the capital charge by 50 percent and transforms a positive EVA company into a negative EVA company.

The WACC increases as the equity value rises, because the company's equity holders require a higher dollar return on the larger market equity value. The difficult issue for EVA accounting is whether or not all of this additional return should be considered a current period expense. When the equity market-to-book ratio reaches 8.0, the company's future growth value exceeds its market equity value. Should the capital charge attributable to future

T A B L E   6–34

An Increase in Equity Market-to-Book Ratio Transforms
a Positive EVA Company into a Negative One

Equity market-to-book ratio	1.0	2.0	4.0	8.0
Market equity	100.0	200.0	400.0	800.0
Book equity	100.0	100.0	100.0	100.0
Cost of equity	11.7%	11.7%	11.7%	11.7%
Debt	1000.0	1000.0	1000.0	1000.0
Pretax cost of debt	6.9%	6.9%	6.9%	6.9%
Tax rate	35.0%	35.0%	35.0%	35.0%
After-tax cost of debt	4.5%	4.5%	4.5%	4.5%
Market capitalization	1100.0	1200.0	1400.0	1800.0
Market leverage	90.9%	83.3%	71.4%	55.6%
WACC	5.1%	5.7%	6.5%	7.7%
Operating return on book capital	9.5%	9.5%	9.5%	9.5%
Operating profit	104.5	104.5	104.5	104.5
NOPAT	67.9	67.9	67.9	67.9
Book (equity) capital	1100.0	1100.0	1100.0	1100.0
Capital charge	56.6	62.6	72.0	84.6
EVA	11.4	5.4	−4.1	−16.7
Current operations value	1321.3	1194.3	1037.6	883.1
Future growth value	−221.3	5.7	362.4	916.9

growth value be a current period EVA expense or should it be
capitalized and allocated to the future periods when we expect to
realize the EVA improvements reflected in the future growth
value? The answer to this question can have a profound influence
on EVA calculations, especially in companies with a large future
growth value component.

EVA ACCOUNTING ADJUSTMENT PROCESS

Now that we have discussed various adjustments, we'll take a
look at the combined impact of several such adjustments on EVA.
To do so, we'll use our example from Chapter 2 for Harnischfeger
Corporation. Supplemental information from the company's 1996
annual report includes the following:

♦ A restructuring charge of $43 million, $27.950 million on an after-tax basis (tax rate = 35 percent), was included in 1996 operating income.

♦ In 1995, after-tax, nonoperating and extraordinary losses totaled $34.716 million. These losses are not included in our earlier estimate of NOPAT.

♦ Goodwill amortization was $21.608 million in 1996.[4] Accumulated goodwill amortization was $93.383 million at the end of fiscal year 1996 and $98.200 million at the end of fiscal year 1995.

With this information, we can now reestimate Harnischfeger's EVA for 1996 (see Table 6–35). Adjusted EVA equals $14.909 million if based on average invested capital, or $35.633 million if based on beginning capital.[5] These figures suggest significantly better performance for Harnischfeger than the unadjusted figures we calculated previously.[6] Before adjustments, EVA

T A B L E   6–35

Reestimate of Harnischfeger's EVA for 1996*

	NOPAT	Invested Capital 31/10/96	Invested Capital 31/10/95
Unadjusted	162.857	1662.535	1340.266
Restructuring charge, 1996	27.950	27.950	—
Goodwill amortization	21.608	93.383	98.200
Nonoperating losses, 1995	—	34.716	34.716
	212.415	1818.584	1473.182

*In millions of dollars.

---

4. This information is not revealed directly in Harnischfeger's annual report. The figure is based on an estimate given to the authors by HOLT Value Associates.

5. $212.415 million (NOPAT) − [$1645.883 million (average invested capital) × 12%] = $14.909 million.

   $212.415 million − [$1473.182 million (beginning invested capital) × 12%] = $35.633 million.

6. This is the case even though the addition of the equity equivalents to invested capital results in a smaller MVA (31 / 10 / 96): $2704.984 million (market value) − $1818.584 million, or $886.400 million. Unadjusted MVA was over $1 billion.

is –$17.311 million and $2.025 million, based on average and beginning invested capital, respectively. Of course, EVA would change again if additional adjustments were made.

A second case in point that demonstrates the impact of adjustments can be seen in Table 6–36, which contrasts the EVA figures for Coca-Cola from its 1995 annual report and those calculated by Stern Stewart & Company. In most years the differences are substantial; Coca-Cola's self-reported EVA is sometimes more than twice that calculated by Stern Stewart. The differences exist because of differing opinions over which accounting adjustments to make and which to avoid. Different estimates for the cost of capital also help to explain differences in EVA measurement.

A FRAMEWORK FOR THINKING ABOUT EVA AND ACCOUNTING ADJUSTMENTS

Most EVA advocates argue that companies implementing EVA should be conservative in making accounting adjustments. There are two good reasons for this conservatism. First, adjustments

T A B L E   6–36

EVA for Coca-Cola Company*

	Coca-Cola Self-Reported	Stern Stewart & Company
1995	2172	1976
1994	1881	1469
1993	1488	1090
1992	1300	880
1991	1038	538
1990	918	521
1989	817	981
1988	717	300
1987	490	NR
1986	331	NR
1985	266	NR

*In millions of dollars.

NR = not reported.

Sources: Coca-Cola Company; Stern Stewart & Company.

make EVA more difficult to understand and hence, run the risk of reducing the impact of EVA on management decision-making. Second, adjustments that increase EVA may appear to be self-serving and can undermine the credibility of EVA in the eyes of directors, shareholders, equity analysts, and the media. We believe that accounting adjustments should be evaluated on four criteria:

- Is the adjustment based on sound finance theory?
- Does the adjustment have a significant impact on the EVA measure (for example, EVA improvement) that is used for incentive compensation?
- Does the adjustment significantly improve EVA's ability to explain returns and market values?
- Is the adjustment likely to have a significant impact on managerial decision making?

When a company adopts EVA, it should evaluate the accounting adjustments we've discussed in this chapter by applying these criteria to its own circumstances. In practice, it is difficult for a company without a large staff or consulting budget to satisfy the third criterion. There is a great need for statistical studies to assess the explanatory power of EVA accounting adjustments. The marketing battles of competing value-based consulting practices have generated more heat than light on this issue. Far more research needs to be conducted in this area.

While the accounting adjustments ultimately need to be evaluated in the context of a specific company, we can make some general comments about the adjustments we have discussed in this chapter:

- Adjustments designed to eliminate noncash charges, such as deferred tax expense, goodwill amortization, and bad debt accruals, do not satisfy the first criterion. As we saw earlier in the chapter, it is irrelevant whether or not an expense represents a current cash outlay. The relevant question is whether the expense is the amortization of a prior cash outlay or the present value of a future cash outlay.
- Capitalizing leases has a very minor impact on the EVA measure.

- Very few EVA companies have made any use of sinking-fund depreciation. It is generally viewed as the most complex of all the accounting adjustments, and it is unlikely that it will be more widely used in the absence of compelling statistical evidence that it significantly increases EVA's ability to explain stock returns.

- Many EVA companies have struggled with acquisitions because they often find that a prospective acquisition has a positive NPV in their valuation analysis, but will significantly reduce their EVA. Adding back goodwill amortization is recommended by many EVA consultants, but adding back the amortization expense is rarely sufficient to make the acquisition EVA positive. EVA companies are reluctant to use negative economic depreciation because it is a novel concept that can appear self-serving. The most common approaches employed by EVA users are to establish a suspense account (in which assets from the acquisition are brought into invested capital on a gradual basis) or restate the previous year's EVA (the base year for calculating EVA improvement) for the invested capital and NOPAT of the acquired company.

Taken together, the practical implications of these observations is that the typical corporate EVA user makes only a small number of adjustments (fewer than five in most cases). The challenge, of course, is identifying the appropriate set of adjustments.

That said, the investment analyst's perspective on adjustments should be different from that of the corporate user. Unlike corporate users of EVA, who adopt the measure with the aim of better aligning managerial and shareholder interests, analysts seek accounting numbers, whether EVA or more conventional profit measures, that they can use to help them value companies and make informed investment decisions. In other words, the *quality* of the earnings number is of paramount importance to the analyst. This means that accounting adjustments that offer little in the way of improvement in managerial behavior may still be worth making for an analyst who needs to isolate the transitory components of earnings from those that are more permanent or persistent in nature. Otherwise, earnings figures are of little practical use in forecasting future earnings. When the issue is viewed in this way, we can appreciate, for example, the usefulness of adjusting for provisions and non-recurring items. But then seasoned analysts have long understood this point.

REVA: AN ALTERNATIVE TO ACCOUNTING-BASED EVA

There is an approach to calculating EVA that reduces reliance on accounting conventions. In this version of EVA, invested capital is based on the market value of the firm, instead of the book value of invested capital. Although NOPAT is still based on GAAP under this approach, invested capital is not. In this way, its advocates assert, the relationship between EVA and share price significantly improves.[7]

To understand the nature of this argument, consider an example:

Total market value, beginning of year	$100 M
Invested capital, beginning of year	$ 50 M
Net operating income	$ 8 M
WACC	10%

When conventionally measured, based on beginning invested capital, EVA equals $3 million [$8 million − ($50 million × 10 percent)]. Critics argue, however, that the firm's $100 million market value implies that its capital providers would have expected a $10 million return ($100 million × 10 percent) had they invested their funds elsewhere. Therefore, as the argument goes, if the company is to create value in that year, it must generate a return greater than $10 million. In this case, despite a *positive* EVA of $3 million, net operating income is obviously not sufficient to earn an acceptable return on capital. The problem stems from the measurement of capital, which is based solely on the assets in place

7. J. M. Bacidore, J. A. Boquist, T. T. Milbourn, and A.V. Thakor, "The Search for the Best Financial Performance Measure," *Financial Analysts Journal*, May/June 1997, pp. 11–20.

and ignores the net present value of future investment opportunities (which may be priced by the market but ignored on the balance sheet).

The proposed solution is a modified version of EVA that its creators call *refined EVA* (or REVA). Under REVA, capital charges are based on the *market value* of the firm, and not the adjusted book value approach. In this example, REVA equals a *negative* $2 million [$8 million − ($100 million × 10 percent)], which is allegedly more consistent with the company's performance that year from the shareholders' perspective and more highly correlated with stock market returns than conventional EVA. But because it is measured from market values, and market values are usually available only at the firmwide level, REVA can be used only at the corporate level. EVA would still be needed at lower levels of the organization.

Even at the corporate level, however, REVA's usefulness as a performance measure is suspect. The problem with REVA results from confusing market values (which incorporate expectations of future performance for the long term) with single-period measures of operating performance.

Consider the case of Coca-Cola. Suppose Coca-Cola has a market value of $150 billion at the beginning of the REVA measurement period. If its WACC is 10 percent, capital charges total $15 billion. These days, even outstanding performance by the company in the coming year—say, a NOPAT of $5 billion—will yield a REVA of *negative* $10 billion! Does this mean that the company *destroys* value? Probably not. It is quite possible, indeed even probable, that Coca-Cola can produce NOPAT of $5 billion (and a negative REVA of $10 billion) and still cause its share price to increase because the $5 billion of NOPAT in the current period is higher than what the market expected. The market may then reasonably interpret this performance to indicate that even more EVA will be generated in the future than was expected before Coca-Cola's results were known. In other words, even if REVA is hugely negative, which is always the case for the most successful value creators, the implications of the current year's performance for future EVAs could result in a higher share price. How then do we interpret a negative REVA?

One of REVA's creators has privately conceded this point to us but argues that the measure's real value is detecting mispriced securities and not as a measure of corporate performance. Companies with highly negative REVAs would be viewed as relatively overpriced, while highly positive REVA stocks would be viewed as underpriced. The problem with this logic is that nearly all companies with large EVA growth expectations impounded in their existing share price will have a negative REVA. Are *all*, or even most, such companies overpriced?

As we showed in Chapter 2, the value of a company equals the sum of its current operations value and its future growth value (FGV). The first component reflects the value of the company assuming that its current performance is maintained, while the second component reflects the capitalized value of the market's expectations of future improvement. For a company like Coca-Cola, and indeed for all companies with very high excess returns, most of the company's value is based on market expectations of future growth.

Under the REVA approach, invested capital is measured on the basis of total market value, including the capitalized value of future growth opportunities. Meanwhile, NOPAT is based entirely on current operating performance, ignoring, as does any short-term financial measure, the value-creating effects of investing activities (such as R&D) that may deliver huge amounts of EVA in the future.

If a company is systematically creating future growth value, its capital charges under REVA will increase from one year to the next. For Coca-Cola, the company's huge market value at the beginning of the period ($150 billion) is a result of its success in previous periods of creating FGV. In other words, the company has been highly successful in convincing the capital markets that future EVAs will be much higher than historical EVAs. Perhaps the company has created valuable strategic options that are expected to translate into outstanding financial results in the future. While the value of these options is reflected in market value, it will not, and cannot, be reflected in REVA. In short, REVA will always ignore value-creating activities that are not reflected in the current year's operating results, while charging management for a capital base that includes the capitalized value of such activities from previous years.

Coke's REVA may be −$5 billion, implying massive underperformance, but because it created valuable growth opportunities that year, shareholder value was created, not destroyed. The irony of REVA is that those companies that are most successful in creating future growth opportunities, and therefore the companies with the highest excess returns, will have the lowest (i.e., most negative) REVAs.

EXPLAINING STOCK MARKET RETURNS: IS EVA REALLY BETTER?

EVA's usefulness as a substitute for stock price and excess return is based on the assumption that EVA drives stock prices, especially if the figures are adjusted for GAAP-based distortions. A study by one of the authors of this book shows that EVA (based on the accounting adjustments of consultants Stern Stewart and Company) explains 31 percent of the variation in market value-to-invested capital ratios versus 17 percent for NOPAT.[8] In this analysis, the NOPAT regression was forced through the origin to ensure that the predicted market value depends only on NOPAT, not on NOPAT and invested capital, which would be the result with a nonzero constant term. This study was based on data from 1985 to 1993 for companies in the 1993 Stern Stewart Performance 1000. The study also shows that EVA, with separate coefficients for positive and negative EVA, separate coefficients for each industry, and a size adjustment term, explains 56 percent of the variation in the market value-to-invested capital ratio. While the purpose of this study was to compare the explanatory power of EVA and NOPAT, not to validate the Stern Stewart accounting adjustments (in any case, the NOPATs used in the study also reflected the Stern Stewart accounting adjustments), it has been challenged by Professors G. C. Biddle, R. M. Bowen, and J. S. Wallace, who argue that earnings has more explanatory power than EVA.[9] The Biddle, Bowen, and Wallace study provides evidence on the information content of EVA, residual income (i.e., unadjusted EVA), net income (before extraordinary items), and cashflow from operations. Information content describes the relation between the measure in question and changes in stock prices.

---

8. S. F. O'Byrne, "EVA and Market Value," *Journal of Applied Corporate Finance*, Summer 1996, pp. 115–125.
9. G. C. Biddle, R. M. Bowen, and J. S. Wallace, "Does EVA Beat Earnings? Evidence on Associations with Stock Returns and Firm Values," *Journal of Accounting & Economics*, December 1997, pp. 301–336.

The first question addressed is whether EVA (either in its adjusted or unadjusted form) dominates net income and cashflow from operations in explaining annual stock market returns. When they look at a large sample of firms covering the period 1984 to 1993, the authors find an R^2 for net income of 12.8 percent, versus 7.3 percent for residual income (i.e., unadjusted EVA), 6.5 percent for EVA (the adjusted version), and 2.8 percent for cashflow from operations. In other words, annual accounting earnings had nearly twice the power of EVA in explaining one-year stock returns. The authors then extended the study to include five-year return intervals. Again, accounting earnings did better with an R^2 of 31.2 percent, versus 18.9 percent for cashflow from operations, 14.5 percent for EVA, and 10.9 percent for residual income. The differences in explanatory power between net income and each of the three other performance measures are highly significant for both the one-year and the five-year intervals. The authors even segmented the sample for firms known to have adopted EVA and those that had not, on the assumption that firms may adopt EVA at least in part because their past experience indicates a strong relation between EVA and stock returns. Also, investors may become more attuned to EVA and, therefore, more likely to incorporate it in pricing shares for companies that announce they are adopting it. Alas, EVA still fails to outperform earnings, although earnings no longer dominate EVA.

The study then addresses whether components unique to EVA or residual income help to explain stock returns beyond that explained by net income and cashflow from operations. The logic behind this test can be seen in Figure 6–1. Cashflow from operations is embedded in net income. The difference between the two figures is a function of accrual accounting. Depreciation, deferred taxes, and receivables are examples of items that cause cashflow from operations and net income to diverge. In short, cashflow from operations ± the various elements of accrual accounting equal net income. Adding after-tax interest expense back to net income produces a measure of unlevered profit, or NOPAT. Residual income is calculated by subtracting capital charges from NOPAT. The difference between residual income and EVA is caused by the various adjustments we have discussed earlier in this chapter. These adjustments are added to or subtracted from residual income to produce EVA. The first three elements in the EVA calculation—cashflow from operations, accruals, and interest expense—are already included in the profit numbers that companies are required to disclose in their annual reports. The question the authors seek to answer is whether or not the two elements *not* explicitly included in mandated disclosures—capital charges and accounting adjustments—are significantly related to stock prices. Unhappily, the answer is no. They show that while the cashflow and accrual components are consistently significant, the components unique to EVA are not.

Still, the Biddle, Bowen, and Wallace results are not entirely persuasive. One problem is that their regression analysis seems to show that while investors put great weight on the cost of debt, the cost of equity is apparently ignored.[10] The independent variables in these regressions are current and prior period values for each of the five EVA components shown in Figure 6–1: CFO, accruals, after-tax interest expense, capital charges, and accounting

F I G U R E   6–1

Components of EVA.

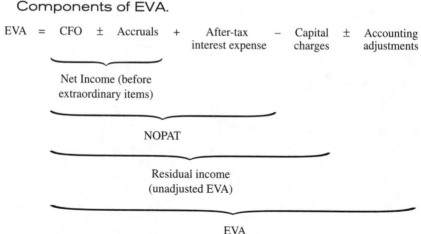

Adapted from Biddle, Bowen, and Wallace (1997).

---

10. For a more extensive critique of the Biddle, Bowen, and Wallace study, see S. F. O'Byrne, "EVA and its Critics," *Journal of Applied Corporate Finance*, Summer 1999.

adjustments.[11] Table 6–37 shows the coefficients for the regression on five-year stock returns, where the independent variables are five-year sums.

The coefficients tell us that an additional dollar of cashflow from operations adds $2.128 to the five-year return, while an additional dollar of capital charge subtracts $0.088. This implies that $24 of capital charge (or $2.128/$0.088) is needed to offset the economic benefit of $1 of cashflow from operations, which suggests that investors are virtually indifferent to capital costs. This is a far cry from EVA, which reminds us of what should be an obvious fact—$1 of capital charge offsets the economic benefit of $1 of earnings.

However, a more careful look at the regression coefficients shows that capital costs matter a good deal more than the capital charge coefficient suggests. The regression obscures the impact of capital costs because it does not fully separate financing and operating performance. Cashflow from operations includes after-tax interest expense. This means that current period after-tax interest

T A B L E   6—37

Coefficients for Regression on Five-Year Stock Returns

Variable	Coefficient	Predicted Sign
Constant	−0.373	
CFO—current	2.128	+
CFO—prior	−0.731	−
Accrual—current	1.659	+
Accrual—prior	−0.072	−
AT interest—current	−0.509	−
AT interest—prior	0.089	+
Capital charge—current	−0.088	−
Capital charge—prior	0.275	+
Acct. adj.—current	0.549	+
Acct. adj.—prior	0.487	−

---

11. The prior period values are used as a proxy for investor expectations so that the combination of the current and the prior period values gives a measure of the unexpected value of the EVA component.

expense appears in the regression three times: as a negative component of cashflow from operations; as a positive component of the capital charge; and as a separate independent variable. This implies that the aggregate coeffecient on current period after-tax interest expense is -2.735 (or $-2.128 + -0.509 + -0.088$). This, in turn, has two very puzzling implications. First, it implies that $1.29 (or $2.735/$2.128) of positive cashflow from operations is needed to offset the economic cost of $1 of after-tax interest expense. Since after-tax interest expense is computed using the statutory corporate tax rate, one explanation for this odd differential is that the effective tax saving is less than the statutory rate. Second, and much more puzzling, it implies that $1 of after-tax interest expense has the same economic cost as $31 (or $2.735/$0.088) of equity capital cost.

This is an odd result, because it suggests that equity capital is basically free. Biddle, Bowen, and Wallace may have overlooked the issues raised by after-tax interest expense because they expected the AT Int variable to have a negative sign. It should have a positive sign in the regression, just as it does in the EVA components equation, since after-tax interest expense is adding back the expense buried in cashflow from operations.

SUMMING UP

More than 150 possible adjustments have been identified by EVA consultants, but even the most ardent EVA advocate would concede that no company should make more than, say, 15 adjustments. Interestingly, the number of recommended adjustments seems to have declined in recent years. At first, consultants argued for 10 to 12 adjustments, with each company choosing an appropriate subset of adjustments, but more recently five or fewer have become the norm. There are two apparent explanations for this trend. First, corporate executives are resistant to the idea of diverging significantly from GAAP-based numbers. Second, many companies have discovered through back-testing and simulation that most of the proposed adjustments have little or no qualitative impact on profits. The result is that most companies adopting EVA or EVA-like metrics limit the number of adjustments to fewer than five, and many make no adjustments at all on the grounds that the system is then easier to administer and comprehend.

Whatever the intellectual case may be for the adjustments is of no consequence to corporate managers trying to implement value-based performance measures in their companies. The goal of corporate performance measurement should never be the most accurate numbers possible, but rather a cost-effective evaluation and compensation system that encourages managers to create value for their company's shareholders.

The problem with the accounting adjustments proposed for the calculation of EVA is not that they are illogical. In our view, of far greater relevance to the corporate user is whether any distortions that arise from GAAP result in suboptimal behavior and whether adjusting the numbers will improve managerial behavior. In other words, would managers act differently and, more important, would they be more inclined to undertake value-creating initiatives and less inclined to engage in value-destroying ones if adjustments are made to GAAP-based numbers? In deciding whether or not to adjust, this question is of paramount importance, at least from the perspective of the corporate user.

In some circumstances, adjustments are necessary. For example, in cases where retail companies lease nearly all their assets and thus keep them off the balance sheet, meaningful EVA figures require that leases be capitalized, even if GAAP says differently. Still, for most companies, the assumption of zero adjustments is a logical starting point in deciding how EVA is to be measured.

CONCLUSION

In this chapter we discussed the advantages and disadvantages of EVA accounting adjustments. We concluded that the number of adjustments should be minimal, and should take into account the cost of deviating from GAAP. We did note, however, that one such adjustment, sinking-fund depreciation, offers the important advantage of bringing the accounting rate of return (i.e., RONA) closer to the economic rate of return. This result holds when depreciating both tangible assets, such as machinery and equipment, and intangible assets, such as capitalized R&D expenditures. But in the absence of evidence that this adjustment increases the statistical association between EVA and stock price, or that it is likely to improve managerial decision making, companies are reluctant to adopt it.

CHAPTER 7

Value Drivers

The goal of the value-oriented firm is to maximize its stream of future EVAs. Nevertheless, even the most ardent user of EVA would admit that other metrics can provide better measures of performance for employees who have little impact on overall business unit performance. While EVA can restore the line of sight that is lost at divisional level when using corporate measures of performance such as excess return or share price, it has its own potential line-of-sight problem, particularly when companies try to bring the metric deeper and deeper into the organizational hierarchy. We introduced this issue in Chapter 3 as the "synergy problem." In this chapter, we will address the linking of financial measures of performance and nonfinancial value drivers to improve future EVA and promote value-creating behavior within organizations.

EVA AND THE SYNERGY PROBLEM

EVA works well in relatively autonomous, stand-alone business units, but as the degree of interaction between EVA centers within the company increases, a logical consequence of efforts to capture potential synergies, the measurement of EVA comes to depend increasingly on transfer prices and overhead allocation. The EVA calculated for a particular unit may therefore be more a function of the company's particular transfer pricing policies than of the unit management's performance. The severity of this problem can be reduced by ensuring that transfer pricing policies are consistent across time, and by emphasizing changes in EVA instead of levels. However, the problem doesn't disappear.

Remember too that EVA is a total factor measure of performance, meaning that all operating costs, including the cost of labor, and all capital costs are included. This attribute is a strength when measuring the performance of senior managers, given their responsibility for all the factors that go into the company's output. However, it may be a serious drawback for subordinate managers because the outcomes of their actions and decisions are concealed by a myriad of factors over which they have no control but that do affect EVA. In other words, EVA becomes too noisy to serve as an effective motivator of performance, creating the same line-of-sight problem that excess return or MVA does for senior divisional managers.

Value Drivers and EVA

However, while EVA may not be of much practical use to lower-level managers, EVA improvement must continue to be the goal of their bosses. In response to this challenge, companies are turning to *drivers* of EVA that can be more accurately measured at the level of a particular unit than EVA itself, and that more closely correspond to the responsibilities of unit managers. One approach to identifying such value drivers is to disaggregate EVA, dissecting it into discrete components that can be more easily measured at lower levels of the company than EVA. For example, the head of a production facility might be evaluated on cycle times in the factory, inventory turns, or some other measure that more directly relates to that manager's responsibilities and to the means available at that level to influence the EVA measured at higher levels of the company. In other words, while the production manager's boss may be evaluated on EVA, the production manager is evaluated on the basis of components or drivers of EVA. Of course, in selecting such measures it is crucial to ensure not only that they relate to the responsibilities of the particular manager, but also that they are linked to EVA. Otherwise, improvements in the measure do not necessarily translate into improvements in EVA.

This approach too has its limitations. Selecting components of EVA may help to restore the line of sight lost by EVA at lower levels of the company, but it neglects another crucial aspect of value-creating behavior. Remember that the ultimate goal of value-oriented companies is the present value of *future* EVAs. This means that managers must not only be encouraged to improve the EVA of their divisions in the current year, but they must also be encouraged to take steps that will improve EVA in future periods. Otherwise, managers will focus only on the short term, neglecting the drivers of long-term performance.

Taking actions that increase future EVA requires both knowledge and motivation. Managers need to know what actions in the current year are likely to increase future EVA and be motivated to take those actions when the present value of the expected increases in EVA exceeds the current-year cost. To help managers understand which current-year actions are likely to increase future EVA, a different set of performance measures are called for. These measures are not components of EVA as such, but rather are *leading indicators of future EVA*. For example, in technology-intensive companies, where a stream of product innovations is required to sustain or grow market share, the current year's EVA may be a much weaker indicator of future EVA than product development measures.

To motivate managers to sacrifice current EVA when an action increases the present value of future EVA by a greater amount, companies can take two approaches. One approach, which is reflected in the modern EVA bonus plan, is to guarantee managers an equal percentage interest in future EVA improvement so that the trade-off they face between their current bonus and the present value of future bonuses mirrors the shareholders' trade-off between current EVA and the present value of future EVAs. This approach is never perfect because the shareholder weighs the present value of all future EVAs while the manager only weighs the present value of future bonuses during his or her expected job tenure. An alternative approach, which some EVA companies use (see Chapter 8), is to tie some current compensation to a leading indicator of future EVA, e.g., market share. For this approach to boost shareholder value, the trade-off the manager faces between the current EVA bonus and the market share (or other leading indicator) bonus must mirror the shareholders' trade-off between current EVA and the present value of future EVAs. This, in turn, requires that the bonus value of the leading indicator reflect the present value of the future EVA associated with the indicator. The major problem here is the difficulty of quantifying the present value of the future EVA associated with the indicator.

Even when companies choose to rely entirely on EVA incentives, without resorting to other metrics, value drivers play a key role in helping managers understand what current actions increase current and future EVA. Broadly speaking, these value drivers fall into two basic categories:

- Components of EVA (financial drivers)
- Leading indicators of EVA (nonfinancial drivers)

Best practice in performance measurement is converging to a balanced set of measures—financial and nonfinancial, leading and lagging—with a value-based metric such as EVA at the center of the performance measurement system. Compensation practices remain divided, however, as some companies rely on long-horizon EVA incentives, while others tie current compensation to EVA *and* leading indicators.

VALUE DRIVERS: THE FINANCIAL PERSPECTIVE

As we showed in Chapter 2,

$$EVA = (RONA - WACC) \text{ invested capital}$$

This simple formula provides us with our first important insight on value drivers. Clearly, as RONA increases, EVA also increases, holding WACC and invested capital constant. Therefore, RONA is a component of EVA. Alternatively, it can be thought of as a value driver. But RONA is a broad-brush measure of performance, much like EVA. A thorough value-based perspective in a company requires a far more detailed and disaggregated approach to understanding the components of EVA. These EVA drivers, RONA included, can solve the line-of-sight problem that arises when companies try to implement EVA below the level of major divisions or business units.

Consider Nucor, a large American producer of steel and steel products. Nucor's 22 most-senior managers are paid bonuses based on return on equity (ROE) in excess of a minimum ROE to ensure that shareholders are adequately compensated before management bonuses are paid.[1] Although the measure is expressed in percentage terms, it is similar to EVA in that the bonus is paid on ROE after subtracting the cost of equity.

The heads of Nucor's major facilities are paid on the basis of RONA, reflecting the popular approach of limiting ROE measurement to the top management level while using operating measures not influenced by capital structure at the division level. The use of RONA in the bonus plan compels division managers to consider both asset productivity and cost control. Bonuses for senior and division managers are paid on an annual basis. Bonuses for division managers can, in exceptional circumstances, exceed 80 percent of base salary.

As we noted in Chapter 2, an important disadvantage of RONA, compared to EVA, is that managers with RONA-linked bonuses might bypass value-creating projects that would lower RONA, assuming division RONA already exceeds the cost of capital. In such cases, the existing RONA becomes the *de facto* WACC. If a manager evaluated on the basis of RONA has achieved a RONA of 20 percent, for example, and the division WACC is 10 percent, the manager might turn down projects that are expected to earn more than 10 percent (and therefore would create shareholder value) but less than 20 percent, because the divisional RONA would be reduced. No such risk exists in the case of the EVA measure, because any project with returns greater than the cost of capital, even if those returns are lower than the existing RONA, will eventually cause EVA to increase. This drawback of RONA, compared to EVA, is far less pronounced for managers with only limited discretion over the level of capital invested in their units. This is why it is common to apply the EVA measure at top management levels and for managers of major divisions, but apply RONA at the next level of the organization.

When we get to Nucor production employees, asset productivity is what matters. In an industry where the ability to squeeze

---

1. Nucor's incentive compensation system is described in S. F. Jablonsky and P. J. Keating, *Changing Roles of Financial Management: Integrating Strategy, Control, and Accountability,* Morristown, NJ: Financial Executives Research Foundation, 1998, pp. 66–78.

as much output as possible from assets is the critical value driver, employees are granted weekly incentive bonuses that can more than double their base wage if productivity targets are reached, while maintaining quality standards. Annual or even quarterly bonuses are not swift enough to provide workers with the immediate feedback they need to guide them in doing what's best for the firm's shareholders. At such levels of the corporate hierarchy, paying bonuses on the basis of EVA or RONA is unlikely to contribute anything to value-creating behavior and may even be counterproductive if it diverts attention from the key value drivers.

DuPont Analysis

Companies produce a vast range of financial data, but how can they use this data to form measures that contribute to the creation of EVA? DuPont analysis, a framework popular with investment professionals for analyzing financial statement ratios, is one particularly appealing approach, for it involves the progressive disaggregation of RONA, providing important insights into the sources of EVA.

Remember that RONA is a measure of operating profitability, because the numerator (NOPAT, or net operating profit after tax) measures what the profits of the company would have been had all of its assets been financed with equity. In this way, NOPAT neutralizes the influence of financing on profit. In short, it measures profitability of the company's net assets independently of how they are financed.

As we see in the following equation, RONA can be disaggregated into two elements, profit margin and total asset turnover:

$$\text{RONA} = \underbrace{\frac{\text{NOPAT}}{\text{sales}}}_{\text{PROFIT MARGIN}} \times \underbrace{\frac{\text{sales}}{\text{average net assets}}}_{\text{TOTAL ASSET TURNOVER}}$$

The virtue of this approach can be seen in the 1995 financial performance figures from Equifax, America's leading provider of consumer credit information (shown in Table 7–1). Equifax is an EVA company, and the company's own EVA calculations are shown in its 1995 annual report.

T A B L E   7-1

Equifax, Inc. Economic Value Added and Financial
Ratio Analysis

	1995	1994	1993
Sales	$1623.0 M	$1422.0 M	$1217.2 M
Net income	$ 147.7 M	$ 120.3 M	$ 63.5 M
NOPAT	$ 176.6 M	$ 143.2 M	$ 110.1 M
Capital charges	$ 162.5 M	$ 121.7 M	$ 121.3 M
Economic Value Added	$ 14.1 M	$ 21.5 M	$- 11.2 M
Weighted-average cost of capital	12.6%	11.2%	12.0%
Average invested capital	$1289.7 M	$1086.6 M	$1010.8 M
RONA	13.7%	13.2%	10.9%
Profit margin	10.9%	10.1%	11.1%
Cost of services (% of sales)	64.0%	63.6%	64.1%
SG&A expenses (% of sales)	19.8%	21.3%	22.1%
Net asset turnover	1.26	1.31	1.19
Market capitalization	$ 3147 M	$ 2002 M	$ 2048 M

Source: Equifax 1995 Annual Report.

Equifax's RONA increased from 10.9 percent in 1993 to 13.2 percent in 1994 and 13.7 percent in 1995. DuPont analysis reveals that profit margin increased from 9.0 percent in 1993 to 10.9 percent in 1995, while asset turnover increased from 1.20 to 1.26. The increase in profit margin explains 75 percent of the improvement in RONA. With no increase in asset turnover, 1995 RONA would have been 13.1 percent, an improvement of 2.1 percentage points, or 75 percent of actual improvement.

Despite the improvement in RONA each year, Equifax's EVA declined from $21.5 million in 1994 to $14.1 million in 1995. The major reason for the decline is the increase in Equifax's cost of capital from 11.2 percent in 1994 to 12.6 percent in the following year. The increase in the cost of capital reduced 1995 EVA by $18.1 million. If Equifax had maintained its 1993 cost of capital of 12 percent, EVA would have increased from -$11.2 million in 1993 to \$12.8 million in 1994 and \$21.8 million in 1995. As we argued in Chapter 5, it is smart to limit changes in the cost of capital because there is a lot of statistical error and changes are often reversed. The wisdom of this policy was confirmed by the stock market. Despite the decline in 1995 EVA (by Equifax's calculation), the company's market capitalization increased by more than 50 percent (from \$2002 million to \$3147 million).

The example shows that linking EVA to DuPont analysis makes it possible to quantify the impact of improvement or deterioration of key ratios on EVA, and ultimately on value. This form of analysis is indispensable to corporate managers seeking to better understand a company's financial performance.

But the disaggregation of EVA and RONA doesn't stop here. Profit margin and asset turnover can also be disaggregated. In the case of profit margin, we can calculate expense components—such as cost of goods sold, selling and administrative expenses, taxes, depreciation, and personnel expenses—as a percentage of sales. Analysis of these ratios over a period of, say, three years can reveal important sources of improvement or deterioration in a company's profit margin:

$$RONA = \underbrace{\frac{NOPAT}{sales}}_{\text{PROFIT MARGIN}} \times \underbrace{\frac{sales}{average\ net\ assets}}_{\text{TOTAL ASSET TURNOVER}}$$

- ◆ Cost-of-sales percentage
- ◆ SG&A percentage
- ◆ Other expense percentages

Total asset turnover can be similarly dissected. *Fixed asset turnover* measures the efficiency of the company's long-term assets in generating sales. The other turnover ratios, normally measured in days, provide a perspective on the management of working capital.

$$RONA = \underbrace{\frac{NOPAT}{sales}}_{\text{PROFIT MARGIN}} \times \underbrace{\frac{sales}{average\ net\ assets}}_{\text{TOTAL ASSET TURNOVER}}$$

- ◆ Fixed asset turnover
- ◆ Working capital efficiency
  - ◆ Inventory period
  - ◆ Receivables period
  - ◆ Payables period
  - ◆ Cash conversion

Most EVA companies make a major effort to improve EVA working capital. The reason for this emphasis is that the management of components of working capital—receivables, inventories, and payables—are the instruments over which operating managers below senior management levels typically have the greatest and most immediate control. In fact, when companies implement EVA and tie bonuses to it, improvement in operating performance is usually noticed first in working capital. Cycle times get shorter, logistics with suppliers improve, and cash is collected more quickly from customers.

A survey of American companies conducted jointly by *CFO Magazine* and the REL Consultancy Group, a London-based firm, reveals that the scope for improvement in working capital management is immense.[2] By focusing on these measures, companies can deliver substantial improvements in EVA, without necessarily focusing on EVA itself.

In the metal products industry, for example, Jefferson Smurfit achieved inventory turns of 13× in 1996, while several of its competitors could manage turns of only 5× or 6×. Similar spreads can be found in other industries and for other components of working capital. Among publishing and printing firms, for example, Media General collected its receivables in 39 days, while E. W. Scripps took almost three weeks longer. As the DuPont framework reminds us, improvement in any of these measures translates into higher RONA—and higher EVA.

The wide divergence in working capital management and the enormous potential for improvement can be seen in the *cash conversion efficiency* (CCE) ratio, which is calculated by dividing sales into cashflow from operations. All else being equal, the more efficiently a company manages its working capital, the higher the CCE ratio. And the higher the ratio, the more successful the company has been at converting its sales into cashflows that can be used for investment or as cash returns to investors. In the building materials sector, for example, the industry average in 1996 was 6.6 percent, but Vulcan Materials achieved a whopping 19.5 percent, while competitors Donnelly and Ply Gem Industries were both under 5 percent.

---

2. S. L. Mintz, "Inside the Corporate Cash Machine," *CFO Magazine,* June 1997.

Dispersion in CCE ratios is equally pronounced in Europe. A 1998 survey of European companies shows that among diversified holding companies, Investor (the main investment vehicle of Sweden's powerful Wallenberg family) achieved over 31 percent, while Germany's Veba and CGIP of France barely reached 10 percent.[3] In the food industry, Nestlé's CCE ratio was 8.6 percent, while its British competitor Cadbury Schweppes achieved 13.1 percent. One of the reasons for Cadbury's superior performance is that its inventory turned over faster than Nestlé's ($5\times$ versus $4\times$).

In short, potentially huge improvements in working capital management can be realized in many companies, resulting in higher EVAs. To motivate such improvements, it is not essential that companies reward middle managers, those employees likely to have the greatest impact on the day-to-day management of working capital, on the basis of EVA. Instead, companies can focus on more detailed measures linked to EVA, but that are more directly related to these managers' responsibilities. See the appendix to this chapter for more financial statement ratios.

VALUE DRIVERS:
THE NONFINANCIAL PERSPECTIVE

While it is true that financial ratios such as profit margins, fixed asset turnover, and inventory periods contribute to our understanding of EVA, all financial indicators are historical in nature. Financial ratios may be value drivers, but they explain performance only after the fact. In other words, they are *lagged* indicators of value creation.

DuPont analysis confirms that if we increase profit margins or asset turnover, RONA and EVA will increase, and so too should excess return. But because RONA and EVA are short-term historical measures, divisional managers can undertake actions that boost these measures in the short run, but destroy value in the long run. For example, managers could cut back on credit terms or cut corners in after-sales service, either of which will increase current EVA but also erode customer satisfaction, thus jeopardizing EVA in future periods. Very simply, evaluating managerial

---

3. J. Kersnar, "Europe's Corporate Cash Machine," *CFO Europe*, June 1998.

performance on the basis of current EVA alone is no guarantee that managers will think and act in the long-run interests of shareholders.

Nowhere is the importance of forward-looking value drivers more critical than in the burgeoning Internet sector. Few of the major players have reported significant profits, and yet all have market capitalizations in the billions of dollars. External analysts have scrambled desperately for performance indicators in an industry where there is no discernible relation between current financial results and share price. Corporate managers too are looking for ways to gauge their companies' progress, recognizing that sizable profits may yet be some years off. The result is an approach to measurement that derives from the unique operating characteristics of the sector, used both by external analysts trying to pick winners and by managers trying to track company performance.

For example, investors in the Internet sector tend to emphasize top-line performance (revenues) instead of the more usual emphasis on bottom-line performance (net income or EVA). Also, great emphasis is placed on gross profits, because they display results before the large marketing and acquisition costs that tend to depress net income. This approach makes sense if such expenses are viewed more as investments than as operating costs.

Most other popular metrics among Internet companies relate either directly or indirectly to revenue and market reach. Examples include the following:

+ *Reach,* or the percentage of Internet users in the country (say, the United States) who visit the site.
+ *Unique visitors,* or the number of unduplicated users who visit the site in a given month. The term *eyeballs* is sometimes used instead.
+ Total number of pages viewed.
+ Number of registered users.
+ Average time spent by users at a company's Web site.
+ *Cost per addition,* or the cost of finding new customers.
+ *Churn rates,* an industry term for customer retention.

If these metrics really are the true long-term drivers of value and future EVAs in the industry, the huge market capitalizations for Amazon.com, Yahoo!, and Lycos are easier to comprehend. For example, Amazon.com had over 10 million unique visitors in

March 1999 alone, while Yahoo! and Lycos both had over 30 million visitors. In that same month, the reach for the latter two was
over 50 percent. In addition, while all the major players reported
losses or, at best, modest profits, gross margin percentages were
far healthier. For example, although globe.com reported net losses
for 1998 even greater than total sales revenue, the gross profit
percentage was a healthy 60 percent, suggesting that each additional customer the company brought in was highly profitable.
Therefore, to an investor trying to value the company's shares, its
ability to grow revenues and market share is a more critical indicator than current profit or current EVA. To put it another way,
the company's ability to bring in additional customers is a more
important factor than its current profits. Much of the market's
confidence in Yahoo! throughout 1998 and the first half of 1999
was caused by gross profit margins of nearly 87 percent. In short,
the market has already recognized that current profit and EVA
performance are not good predictors of future performance. For
that, corporate managers and analysts have to look elsewhere.

The Importance of Nonfinancial Drivers

As we have often stated, the financial goal of the value-based firm
is to create a future stream of ever higher EVAs. But in some companies, in a range of business sectors, the best predictors of future
EVA may be factors other than the *current* year's EVA. For example, customer satisfaction may be a better predictor of a company's ability to deliver high EVA in the future than its EVA in
the most recent year. If so, can subordinate managers be relied on
to do the right thing if judged (and paid) only on the basis of
EVA? If the company is unwilling to take a contractual approach
to compensation and guarantee subordinate managers equal percentage interests in current and future EVA improvement, the answer is no. This is why a growing number of firms, including
some avid EVA adopters, have turned to nonfinancial value drivers to augment financial performance measures.

   Professors C. D. Ittner, D. F. Larcker, and M. V. Rajan confirm
this fact in a study of CEO compensation practices among American companies.[4] Table 7–2 reports the performance measures they

---

4. C. D. Ittner, D. F. Larcker, and M. V. Rajan, "The Choice of Performance Measures in
   Annual Bonus Contracts," *The Accounting Review*, April 1997, pp. 231–255.

T A B L E   7–2

Performance Measures Used in CEO Annual Bonus Contracts

Financial measure	
Earnings per share	28.5
Net income	27.2
Operating income or income before tax	25.3
Return on equity	19.5
Sales	13.7
Cashflow	12.8
Return on assets	9.6
Cost reduction	7.6
Return on invested capital (i.e., RONA)	5.4
Stock price return	4.4
Return on sales	3.8
Unspecified financial measures	3.2
Economic value added	**0.9**
Other miscellaneous measures	12.1
Nonfinancial measures	
Customer satisfaction	36.8
Nonfinancial strategic objectives	28.0
Product or service quailty	21.0
Employee safety	16.6
Unspecified nonfinancial measures	16.6
Efficiency or productivity	14.9
Market share	11.4
Employee satisfaction	8.7
Process improvement and reengineering	8.7
Employee development and training	7.0
New product development	6.1
Leadership	5.2
Workforce diversity	4.3
Innovation	2.6
Other miscellaneous measures	39.4

Source: Ittner et al. (1997)

find in annual bonus contracts. Among 317 firms surveyed, all but five use at least one financial measure (with an average of 1.7 measures per firm), and 114 use nonfinancial measures (with an average of 2.3 measures per firm). Interestingly, RONA is used by barely more than 5 percent of the surveyed firms, while EVA is used by only 1 percent. This study is based on data in 1993 and 1994, just as RONA and EVA were gaining in popularity, however. A later survey of large multinational companies by KPMG shows that 26 percent of the sampled firms used EVA, or something like it, for incentive compensation plans.[5]

Both sets of results, however, confirm that conventional accounting measures continue to dominate bonus contracts. Among the nonfinancial measures, customer satisfaction, meeting strategic objectives, and quality are the most important. Surprisingly, new product development and innovation do not figure prominently, at least not in this sample, despite the role these factors are thought to play in helping companies to sustain and build market share.

An important contribution of the Ittner et al. study is that it compares the characteristics of firms that rely exclusively on financial measures and those that also use one or more nonfinancial measures. A critical assumption in this investigation is that compensation contracts should be closely linked to a company's strategy to ensure that managers' incentives are aligned with the company's goals. In other words, bonus plans should support strategic intent.

Competitive strategy can be thought of as a continuum between differentiation and cost leadership. Differentiators, or prospectors, try to identify new product market opportunities, quickly adapt to changes in the external environment, and come first to market with product or service innovations. At the other end of the spectrum are cost leaders, or defenders. These firms try to provide stable product or service lines to well-defined markets while emphasizing improvement in operating efficiencies to lower costs. Because the primary goal of cost leaders is improving their operating efficiencies, short-term historical performance measures such as operating profit, RONA, or EVA are relatively informative measures.

The problem with short-term financial measures in prospector firms that do not rely on multiyear compensation contracts is that managerial actions that are essential for long-term success

---

5. E. W. Freher, "Designing the Annual Management Incentive Plan," in *Paying for Performance: A Guide to Compensation Management*, P. T. Chingos, ed., New York: John Wiley & Sons, 1997, pp. 161–175.

(such as product development) may take years to be revealed in financial results. As a consequence, short-term financial performance measures, including current EVA, are relatively less informative about managerial effort expended in areas that are most crucial to long-term value creation. Some might argue that stock options and other forms of equity participation help to provide management with the right long-term incentives. While this argument is certainly true, stock price performance as a measure of management's success in undertaking desirable actions (such as bringing new products to market) is limited by the fact that current actions might not be reflected in current stock price, because management holds proprietary information that cannot, and should not, be released to the markets.

For these reasons, we would expect firms that follow a prospector or differentiator strategy to rely more on nonfinancial criteria than firms that follow a cost leadership strategy. Although it is not always obvious how a particular firm should be classified in the strategy spectrum, Ittner et al. offer four alternative measures:

- *The ratio of R&D to sales.* This variable measures a firm's propensity to seek out new products. Prospectors are expected to engage in more R&D than defenders.
- *The market value-to-book value ratio.* This variable is a proxy for a firm's growth and investment opportunities. Prospectors should have more growth potential than defenders.
- *The ratio of employees to sales.* This variable measures a company's ability to produce and distribute its products efficiently. Because their strategies focus on cost efficiency, defenders should have fewer employees per sales dollar.
- *The number of new product or service introductions.* This variable reflects the emphasis a company places on expanding its product offerings; it should be higher for prospectors than for defenders.

These insights are summarized in Figure 7–1. The closer a firm is to the cost leader profile, the more inclined it is to rely on financial measures to evaluate and compensate the performance

FIGURE 7–1

The Strategy Spectrum

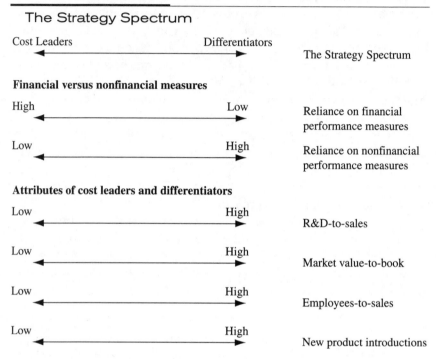

Cost Leaders   Differentiators

The Strategy Spectrum

Financial versus nonfinancial measures

High   Low

Reliance on financial
performance measures

Low   High

Reliance on nonfinancial
performance measures

Attributes of cost leaders and differentiators

Low   High

R&D-to-sales

Low   High

Market value-to-book

Low   High

Employees-to-sales

Low   High

New product introductions

of top managers. The reverse is true for differentiators. Firms at the differentiator end of the spectrum are more likely to use non-financial measures than cost leaders.

Ittner et al. report, as predicted, that the reliance on nonfinancial measures is significantly correlated with each of these four variables. That is, as R&D-to-sales, market value-to-book, employees-to-sales, or number of new product introductions increase, so too does the likelihood that a firm will use nonfinancial measures in CEO bonus contracts.

While the Ittner et al. study documents the determinants that drive the use of nonfinancial measures in CEO compensation, it does not analyze the performance effects of such compensation plans. In other words, do companies that incorporate nonfinancial measures deliver superior financial performance in future periods? Until now, the empirical evidence on this question has been sketchy, but a recent study by Professors R. D. Banker, G. Potter, and D. Srinivasan provides some encouragement.[6] In their study of 18 hotels managed by a hospitality firm, they show that non-financial measures of customer satisfaction are significantly associated with future financial performance, independent of past financial measures. In other words, even after controlling for past financial performance, hotels that achieve higher levels of customer satisfaction tend to deliver superior financial returns. Given the limited scope of their study, it remains an open question whether compensation based on customer satisfaction measures would have the same effect for a company that guarantees managers equal percentage interests in current and future financial performance.

FUTURE GROWTH OPPORTUNITIES AND VALUE DRIVERS

In Chapter 2 we show that the value of a firm can be divided into two components: the current operations value and the future growth value. Among companies with exceptional growth opportunities, it is not uncommon that the future growth component accounts for more than 90 percent of total firm value. This is why it is so important for corporate managers to address the factors that drive future growth in their performance measurement systems. Otherwise, they run the very considerable risk of focusing company attention on activities or measures that won't deliver shareholder value.

The evidence that differentiators are more likely than cost leaders to rely on nonfinancial measures is useful, but it neglects another important factor that should drive corporate reliance on such metrics: The greater the proportion of total value that the future growth component represents, the greater the need for management to seek out measures that relate to the expected behaviors reflected in that component. This is true whether a firm is a cost leader or a differentiator.

---

6. R. D. Banker, G. Potter, and D. Srinivasan, "An Empirical Investigation of an Incentive Plan that Includes Nonfinancial Performance Measures," *The Accounting Review,* January 2000, pp. 65–92.

As the example of Internet companies earlier in the chapter showed, sales growth can be a more important driver of stock price than current profitability. Although the Internet sector may be an extreme case, sales growth is a key determinant of value in many other industries. This helps explain why many companies include sales or sales growth as a factor in determining management bonuses. In theory, pay based on EVA, with bonus banks and stock options to extend management planning horizons, should be sufficient to motivate managers to grow sales. But in companies whose share prices are based on expectations of growth, boards may prefer to measure and reward sales growth directly instead of relying on EVA alone to provide the right incentives.

Of course, sales growth is a financial measure too. But if we extend the logic behind the link between sales growth and future growth value, we can see how the need for nonfinancial metrics arises.

To illustrate, suppose that most of our firm's value is reflected in the future growth value component, and sales growth is a key determinant of this component. We can then ask if some sales are more important than others in helping the company achieve the sales growth impounded in current stock price. For example, we may want to measure new customers as a percent of total sales, on the assumption that new customers will increase their level of purchases in future years. Or, we may determine that new product development is a key value driver. If so, the attempt to capture the degree of success in managing this process should be reflected in the company's performance measurement system. Inevitably, such measures will be nonfinancial in nature.

Successful product design and introduction involves many diverse functions and activities in a company, such as research and development, market analysis, prototype development, testing, material purchases, production planning, and financial planning. A successful effort requires careful control and coordination across several operating units and functional departments. In short, new product development is a process that cuts through a company horizontally. It involves a sequence of activities that must be carefully choreographed to serve the interests of customers while delivering superior returns to shareholders. This means that performance measures must focus on the horizontal work flow and not on organizational boundaries. This perspective is very different from the typical EVA measurement system, which tends to focus on discrete business units within the company, especially those with full balance sheet and income statement responsibilities.

New product development is one example of a "core process" that encompasses all the functions and activities required to implement a particular business strategy and deliver a product or service to the customer. Customer service, supplier management, and order fulfillment are other examples.

To illustrate this concept, consider the order fulfillment process—that is, the system that receives an order for a product or service and delivers it to the customer. Order processing, design, purchasing, production, distribution and shipping, and installation may all be involved in the process. Like all core processes, order fulfillment is really just a network of internal suppliers and customers with one overall goal: to deliver the product to the external customer in a timely fashion and in a way that enhances customer satisfaction and retention, while providing superior returns to shareholders.

The first step in developing a proper performance measurement system for such a core process is to map it, identifying the sequence of activities and the key players. The next step is to determine the areas where performance indicators are critical to the success of the process. Managers can use broad measures of performance, such as cycle times or inventory levels, to gauge whether the company is making progress in improving operating efficiency, but these measures are lagged. By mapping the process and identifying key indicators of performance at various steps along the way, management attention is focused on the concrete actions that can be taken now to deliver better financial performance in the future.

Richard Lynch and Kelvin Cross illustrate how this might work using the order fulfillment process of a computer manufacturer.[7] A "performance pyramid," shown in Figure 7–2, depicts how a corporate vision (i.e., a value-creating proposition for the

7. R. L. Lynch and K. F. Cross, *Measure Up!*, 2d ed., Cambridge, MA: Blackwell Publishers, 1995, p. 47.

F I G U R E   7–2

The Performance Pyramid for a
Computer Manufacturer

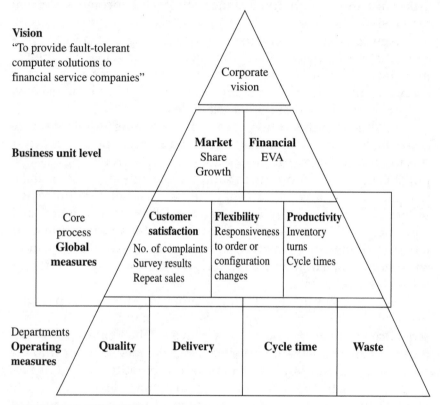

Vision
"To provide fault-tolerant
computer solutions to
financial service companies"

Business unit level

Departments
**Operating
measures**

Adapted from Lynch and Cross (1995)

business) translates into measures at the business unit level. Objectives for each business unit are then defined in market and financial terms, and strategies are formulated describing how these objectives will be achieved. Market measures focus on the external effectiveness of the strategy. For example, are we growing sales or market share? Financial measures by contrast focus on internal efficiency. For example, are we achieving growth in a profitable way? EVA is particularly well suited to answer such a question.

Each business unit is responsible for managing its core processes, including order fulfillment, in support of its business strategy. This requires the setting of concrete operating objectives related to the three critical elements of a core process: customer satisfaction, flexibility, and productivity. *Customer satisfaction* signifies how customer expectations are managed. *Flexibility* refers to how efficiently the process can meet the changing demands of customers. *Productivity* denotes how efficiently financial and human resources are managed to achieve customer satisfaction and flexibility objectives.

For a business unit manager who needs to track progress on customer satisfaction, flexibility, and productivity objectives, measures can be relatively broad. Customer satisfaction, for example, might be measured by retention rate, revenue per customer, or ratings from customer surveys. The managers of departments within a unit, though, need different, more operational measures that relate directly to their responsibilities and that can be monitored on a more frequent basis. This can be seen at the base of the performance pyramid, where objectives are expressed in terms of specific operating measures related to quality, delivery, cycle times, and waste for each discrete department or unit with a key role in the process.

In Figure 7–3, we can see that the materials department contributes to quality and delivery goals (the two major components of customer satisfaction) with high fill rates and accurate counts. The production department contributes by producing on schedule, while the distribution department is expected to achieve problem-free deliveries and installations.

In short, while the business unit manager relies on more global measures that describe performance in relatively broad terms, the department managers need specific work flow measures that they and their employees can control on a day-to-day basis. At such levels of the company, metrics such as EVA are too broad to guide most day-to-day decision making.

THE BALANCED SCORECARD

In this chapter, we've seen that nonfinancial value drivers are important because they may be better predictors of future EVA (and future growth opportunities) than current EVA or the components of current EVA. According to the pioneering work of Robert Kaplan and David Norton, more and more companies are using the

F I G U R E   7–3

The Order Fulfillment Process of a Computer Manufacturer

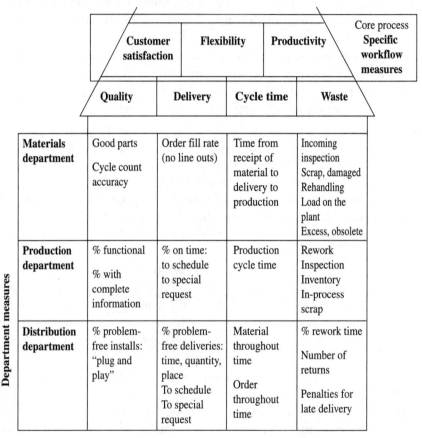

Department measures		Customer satisfaction	Flexibility	Productivity	Core process Specific workflow measures
		Quality	Delivery	Cycle time	Waste
	Materials department	Good parts Cycle count accuracy	Order fill rate (no line outs)	Time from receipt of material to delivery to production	Incoming inspection Scrap, damaged Rehandling Load on the plant Excess, obsolete
	Production department	% functional % with complete information	% on time: to schedule to special request	Production cycle time	Rework Inspection Inventory In-process scrap
	Distribution department	% problem-free installs: "plug and play"	% problem-free deliveries: time, quantity, place To schedule To special request	Material throughout time Order throughout time	% rework time Number of returns Penalties for late delivery

Adapted from Lynch and Cross (1995)

balanced scorecard to identify these key value drivers.[8] Part of its attraction is that the scorecard can summarize, sometimes in just a single page, a set of leading and lagging performance indicators based on different perspectives, both financial and nonfinancial.

---

8. R. Kaplan and D. Norton, "The Balanced Scorecard—Measures that Drive Perform- ance," *Harvard Business Review,* January–February 1992; "Putting the Balanced Scorecard to Work," *Harvard Business Review,* September–October 1993; "Using the Balanced Scorecard as a Strategic Management System, *Harvard Business Review,* January–February 1996; *The Balanced Scorecard: Translating Strategy into Action,* Bos- ton: Harvard Business School Press, 1996.

Although the balanced scorecard was not created with EVA in mind, the framework has proven to be highly complementary to EVA.

For the value-based firm, future EVA growth must still be the paramount goal, but as we have already seen, especially for companies closer to the differentiator end of the strategy spectrum, reliance on a single, short-term financial indicator runs the risk of ignoring other admittedly "softer" indicators, such as customer satisfaction and product innovation, that may be the most important drivers of future EVA. By identifying other nonfinancial indicators of performance, the balanced scorecard becomes not only a performance measurement, evaluation, and compensation tool but also a mechanism for transmitting the strategic vision of top management throughout the organization.

In a sense, the balanced scorecard formalizes the intuition introduced in the first chapter of this book. Although the overarching corporate goal may be the creation of shareholder wealth, shareholders are residual claimants and thus the last of the company's constituencies to get paid. Value creation is made possible only by satisfying all the company's other important constituencies—for example, customers, employees, and suppliers. To gain market share and consistently deliver value to shareholders, companies must also be seen to deliver value to their customers in ways that their competitors cannot. Whether that value is delivered through innovation and product differentiation strategies or cost leadership, or some combination of the two, customers must be convinced to buy from a company because customers always have other options. Convincing customers that their products and services offer superior value to those of competitors requires managers and employees—not just at the top management level, but throughout the organization—who are capable of delivering that value. In addition, companies must provide the internal processes, systems, training, and organizational learning to support its employees in their quest for continuous improvement in the goods and services they offer their customers.

The Kaplan and Norton version of the balanced scorecard is shown in Figure 7–4. Key performance measures are identified from four distinct perspectives: financial, customer, internal business processes, and learning and growth. For example, EVA can be used as a financial measure, customer satisfaction as a customer perspective measure, and so on. Targets are then identified for

F I G U R E   7-4

The Four Perspectives of the Balanced Scorecard

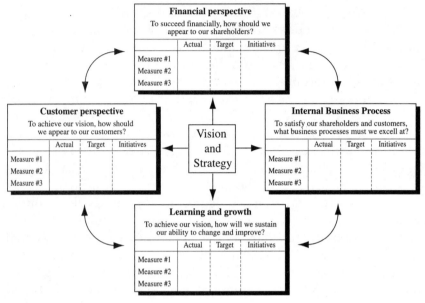

Adapted from "*Linking the Balanced Scorecard to Strategy,*" by Robert S. Kaplan and David P. Norton, California Management Review (July 1996)

each measure, and proposed initiatives for achieving those targets are also identified. Such a document gives management a convenient bird's-eye view of the major tasks that must be accomplished and how they will be measured to realize the vision and strategy that top management has developed to create value for the shareholders.

Managers interested in scorecards should know that there is nothing sacred about the Kaplan and Norton approach. Many successful users define the categories quite differently. For example, Sears, Roebuck and Co., the large American retailer, simplifies the scorecard to what it calls the "three compellings":

$$\underset{\substack{\text{LEADING} \\ \text{INDICATOR}}}{\underset{\text{to shop}}{\text{Compelling place}}} \times \underset{\substack{\text{LEADING} \\ \text{INDICATOR}}}{\underset{\text{to work}}{\text{Compelling place}}} = \underset{\substack{\text{LAGGING} \\ \text{INDICATOR}}}{\underset{\text{to invest}}{\text{Compelling place}}}$$

The company has developed objectives and performance indicators for each of the three categories. For example, the first "compelling" focuses on providing quality merchandise at attractive prices, customer service, and making Sears a fun place to shop. Progress on objectives is measured by a set of performance indicators, including measures of customer satisfaction and retention. The logic of the approach is that if Sears succeeds in becoming both a compelling place to shop and to work, the financial results will follow.

The graphic representation of the balanced scorecard shown in Figure 7–4 is sometimes misinterpreted as implying that the four perspectives are equal. Some critics fear that financial performance will be compromised in the interest of promoting goals from the other three perspectives. If the balanced scorecard is used properly, these fears are unfounded.

Financial performance, whether measured by EVA or some other metric, should always be the end goal, but the balanced scorecard reminds us that financial measures are lagging indicators. They tell us how well the company performed *after the fact*. Delivering ever-increasing amounts of EVA requires that we understand the *leading* indicators of value, the measures that signal value-creating or value-destroying behavior before the results ever show up in EVA. In many companies, last year's EVA is not the best indicator of future EVA.

To better understand the importance of leading indicators and why financial measures are sometimes insufficient to promote value-creating behavior, consider an example described by Marc Epstein and Jean-François Manzoni.[9] A first-level supervisor in the claims processing unit of an insurance company takes it upon himself to change the way work is allocated within the unit he manages. Staff reaction is negative, and the quality of their work suffers as a result. Some claims, for example, are processed more slowly or less accurately, staff are less courteous with customers over the telephone, and so on.

Of the customers who meet with this poorer service, some will complain to the company, some may tell their friends, and some may simply stay quiet but take their business elsewhere. Maybe customers will not desert the company immediately, although some might. However, at some point in the future, the

---

9. M. Epstein and J. F. Manzoni, "Implementing Corporate Strategy: From Tableaux de Bord to Balanced Scorecards," *European Management Journal*, April 1998, pp. 190–203.

company's revenues will begin to suffer. As revenue and profits decline, EVA declines too, but by then it is too late. Nonfinancial measures of customer satisfaction make it more likely that such problems will be detected before they affect the company's financial results, giving management time to correct the problem. It is possible, for instance, for the company to frequently measure the speed and accuracy of processing, telephone courtesy, unit morale, and the level and content of customer complaints to gauge whether customer service and satisfaction are being achieved. If not, the problems can be pinpointed and discussed with the relevant employees, and joint solutions can be developed. This is just one example among many possible scenarios in which nonfinancial indicators capture management performance more quickly than financial measures such as EVA.

As Figure 7–5 shows, the balanced scorecard includes both lagging indicators and leading indicators. In practice, these indicators should be thought of as a continuum. Customer satisfaction is a leading indicator of EVA, but it may also be a lagging indicator of on-time delivery. In other words, better on-time delivery improves customer satisfaction, which leads to higher sales and the speedier collection of receivables, which in turn lead to higher EVA. While on-time delivery is a leading indicator of customer satisfaction, it may also be a lagging indicator of production cycle time and the quality of both the manufacturing process and the products themselves. Process and product quality, rework rates, and cycle times are, in turn, lagging indicators of employee skills and morale. The balanced scorecard focuses management attention on these causal relationships.

One obvious problem with nonfinancial indicators of performance is that they are usually more difficult to measure than financial indicators. And, indeed, much of the effort that companies put into implementing a balanced scorecard focuses not just on identifying the right indicators, but also on ones that can be measured on a regular basis.

Finding the Right Value Drivers

Different models for identifying nonfinancial performance measures can work, and a company must select the approach that is most appropriate for its circumstances. Regardless of how one

Organizing Performance Indicators in a Causal Chain

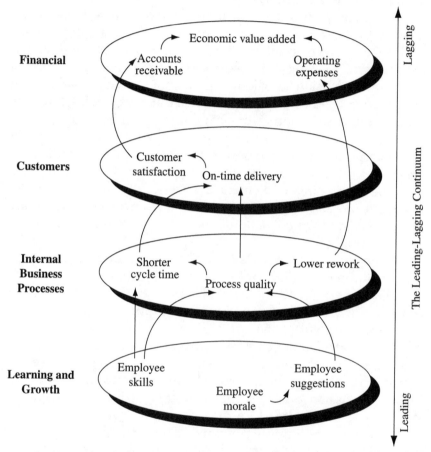

Adapted from Kaplan and Norton (January–February 1996)

goes about it, the two most important success factors in implementing a balanced performance measurement system are
whether top managers have clearly articulated the firm's strategic
vision and whether they have identified the key performance indicators for measuring the success of the strategy. In short, there
must be a clear cause-and-effect relationship between the measures that are chosen and the realization of the company's strategy.
Although the details of implementing a system are sometimes
complicated, and poor planning can doom an effort to failure,

companies that have properly addressed those two success factors have gone much of the way toward developing a workable performance measurement system.

Most companies use a facilitator to coordinate the development of the scorecard. In some companies, the facilitator is a senior-level employee; in others, the facilitator is an external consultant. A logical starting point is to describe the company's mission and strategic vision. It should go without saying that without clearly articulated corporate goals and strategies, the identification of key performance indicators is a largely pointless exercise. Performance measures are intended to be instruments for communicating corporate strategy in terms that make sense to middle managers and other employees; they are ways to measure whether strategies are being implemented successfully. If top managers cannot clearly and convincingly describe what those strategies are, they should not expect subordinates to understand them and to act accordingly.

"Top managers" are defined here as executive board members, including the CEO and CFO, as well as the most senior divisional managers and the head of human resources. Early in the process, a workshop can be organized to introduce these managers to the concept of the balanced scorecard and to solicit their input on strategic objectives and possible performance measures.

Some thought must be given to determining the levels at which scorecards will be developed. We mentioned a similar issue in our discussion on the implementation of EVA in Chapter 3. While we can calculate EVA at a corporate level, how are EVA centers defined within the company? The same question arises in building the balanced scorecard. Although EVA centers and scorecard centers may largely coincide (i.e., we calculate EVA for an entity, and we also prepare a scorecard for that entity), if the scorecard is to focus on work flow measures that are more directly controllable by low-level managers, the scorecard measures must pertain to entities below the lowest level for which EVA is calculated. Indeed, this is one of the major reasons why scorecards are prepared. They facilitate the identification of EVA drivers that unit managers can more readily influence.

As senior managers take a first pass at identifying performance measures, they might ask: If the strategic vision for our company is successful, how will performance differ for shareholders, customers, internal business processes, and development of our own human resources? For example, what does "success" imply for EVA, for customer retention, for cycle times? From the answers, the facilitator can prepare a first draft of the scorecard at the corporate level for circulation to the participants for comment.

A follow-up workshop can then be conducted, where senior managers are joined by some key managers one or two levels lower in the hierarchy. The workshop may be preceded by a training session for participants to whom the balanced scorecard is new. At the second workshop, corporate goals and strategies might be discussed further, although at this stage more clearly articulating these goals and strategies is a better idea. Most companies that try to implement the balanced scorecard already have several change programs under way. The second workshop ought to link ongoing programs to the performance measures in the scorecard. A preliminary implementation plan can be formulated. Finally, stretch targets are identified, at the corporate level, for each measure proposed.

If there is a final consensus among senior managers regarding strategies, goals, and measurements, a detailed implementation plan can be drawn up to address issues such as the communication of the scorecard to employees, the information needs of the scorecard, and the role that scorecard measures will play in management compensation.

Once senior management has finalized the scorecard at the corporate level, a subgroup should develop an implementation plan. This group might include senior operating managers (but below board level), human resource specialists, an information technology expert, and representatives from the CFO's office (for example, the chief accountant). The plan should address training requirements for employees, integration of the scorecard into existing management and planning systems, and the development of information systems to support the scorecard. Targets for each measure must be set, along with tactical plans on how managers responsible for a measure can meet or exceed the targets.

The implementation group should also facilitate the development of measures below the corporate level. The overriding aim is to provide performance indicators that promote value-creating behavior at levels of the company where the use of EVA is not practical. The scorecard is more than an instrument of identifying leading nonfinancial drivers of value. It must be usable at lower levels of the corporate hierarchy, providing measures that are more closely attuned to the actions and responsibilities of lower-level managers.

Once the scorecard is in operation, the metrics should be evaluated every year as a logical extension of the planning, goal setting, and budgeting processes. This is necessary to ensure that the scorecard continues to be a proper reflection of the company's current strategic priorities. Some companies review their score-cards more frequently, perhaps even continually. Markets can change quickly, and companies may conclude that they cannot wait until the next planning cycle to determine whether they need to change tactics.

Value Drivers and Compensation

By identifying key performance indicators and by paying bonuses linked to the outcomes of these indicators, companies can moti-vate managers to focus on the actions that will ultimately increase corporate EVA and thereby deliver wealth to shareholders. In the-ory, bonus plans based on scorecard measures should function in much the same way as bonus plans linked only to EVA. In prac-tice, however, bonuses linked to non-EVA measures are nearly al-ways capped, even in companies that do not impose caps on EVA bonuses.

One potential problem in scorecard-based bonus plans is that if participants are judged on several measures, they can succeed in some measures while failing in others and still receive a big reward. The likely result is that managers focus attention on the indicators (and actions) that will lead to favorable outcomes and big bonuses while neglecting other indicators that may be just as important in creating value but that are harder to achieve. Careful planning and design is needed to neutralize this problem. In some programs, for example, bonuses for a scorecard measure can be negative, just as they can be in EVA plans with bonus banks, off-setting positive bonuses earned from other measures. A more com-mon response is to impose caps, thus reducing the incentive to focus on one measure to the exclusion of other measures. Floors may also be imposed to help ensure that minimum levels of per-formance are achieved along all important dimensions before pay-outs can occur.

Another difficult challenge in tying scorecard measures to bonuses is the inherent subjectivity of any weighting scheme. A common approach is to (1) determine an appropriate set of performance indicators that will be linked to bonuses, (2) establish targets for each indicator in the coming year, and (3) assign a weighting to each measure depending on perceptions of its relative importance.

An example of this approach is used by the European division of Whirlpool, the large American white goods manufacturer. The company rates its managers (approximately 700 out of a total workforce of 12,000) on the basis of three sets of measures: financial, customer-based, and employee-based. Financial measures count for 50 percent of the total bonus weighting, while the other two sets of measures split the remaining 50 percent. Within each category, several metrics are employed; EVA is one of four metrics used in the financial category. In each business unit, targets are set at the beginning of the year for all four of the financial metrics. The business unit then receives a total score for financial performance ranging from 0.5 (worst) to 1.5 (best); 1.0 indicates performance approximately in line with targets. A similar procedure is followed for customer- and employee-based measures.

The score in each category and the assigned weightings produce a total score. As with the ratings assigned to the three categories, the total score can range from 0.5 to 1.5. If financial performance is rated 1.2, while the other two categories are rated 1.0, the overall score is 1.1 (reflecting the double-weighting given to financial measures). The unit would therefore receive a bonus slightly above the target.

This approach is popular. Some companies take it one step further and assign a multiplier for each manager, depending on targets set for that individual. In a business unit with a total score of 1.0, for example, some managers might receive bonuses above the target level set for them at the beginning of the year because of superior individual performance, while some of their colleagues receive below-target bonuses.

In the Whirlpool bonus program, both the weightings assigned to the three sets of measures and the weightings of the metrics within each set are arbitrary. Bonus plans based solely on EVA are not entirely immune to this problem. For example, there is sometimes considerable subjectivity in setting target EVAs and target bonus levels. The multimeasure nature of scorecard-based bonus plans compounds the subjectivity. Still, most companies that link scorecards to management bonuses do not agonize over the problem, because they believe that strategy implementation has been improved and that affected managers better understand what their priorities should be.

Using Value Drivers: Critical Success Factors

Unlike financial measures of performance, nonfinancial value drivers can be defined over a practically limitless range. Metrics such as EVA can be employed in the vast majority of companies; the same cannot be said for specific nonfinancial measures. The reason is that the predictors of future EVA, and therefore the drivers of long-term value, vary from industry to industry. For example, new product development is a key predictor of future financial results in some sectors, but not in others. The same could be said for many other types of nonfinancial drivers.

Successful scorecards have several attributes in common, even if the actual measures employed will differ markedly from one company to the next. Certain factors are shared by nearly all companies that adopt effective performance measurement systems. These companies

- Clearly articulate a strategic vision, consistent with the goal of creating value.
- Select key performance indicators that are linked to that strategic vision.
- Cast a wide net in identifying key performance indicators, seeking input not only from internal sources but also from customers and suppliers.
- Let measures evolve over time, as conditions and strategic priorities change.
- Link key measures to management compensation, not just for senior managers but also for lower-level managers.
- Implement formal communication plans to build support for the measures and to reinforce use of the measures once they have been adopted.
- Cascade measures deep into the organization.

- Ensure that all nonfinancial measures are linked in some way, if only indirectly, to summary measures of financial performance, such as EVA.
- Assign an "owner" to each measure.
- Cap the total number of measures reported to top management at 20, or even fewer.
- Report key measures at least on a quarterly basis, preferably on a monthly basis (and even more frequently if information technology allows).

THE BALANCED SCORECARD: A FINAL WARNING

Many finance professionals are skeptical of the balanced scorecard, not to mention a growing reliance on nonfinancial metrics. We think there is a compelling logic for nonfinancial performance measures (although a much weaker case for their use in compensating business unit heads), and we know they have rapidly come to be viewed as indispensable in a growing number of companies. To some extent, however, the skepticism is valid. The choice of terminology in the "balanced scorecard" is somewhat unfortunate, because it is too often interpreted—mistakenly, we believe—to mean balancing the claims of customers, employees, and other key constituencies against those of the owners, the shareholders. The implication would be that all groups have more or less equal claims. This attitude will lead to disaster more often than not.

The problem, in short, is that some users of the scorecard confuse means and ends. Investment in customers, supplier relations, and employees is not desirable as an end in itself, but rather as a means to deliver value to shareholders. When managers forget this fundamental point, the scorecard can become a pretext for defending the company's failure to produce superior financial results.

CONCLUSION

In this chapter we explained the importance of nonfinancial drivers in creating future EVA and stressed that the financial goal of any value-based firm is to create ever-increasing EVAs. We also determined that many of the drivers generating future EVAs are in many respects intangible and difficult to measure, but they are nevertheless of critical importance. In particular, in high-growth industries such as Internet firms, forward-looking drivers are more important in predicting future EVA than current EVA. As we pointed out earlier in the chapter, last year's EVA may not necessarily be the best indicator of future EVAs. When used and managed wisely, a comprehensive approach to value drivers, incorporating both financial and nonfinancial measures, promote the creation of EVA far more effectively than reliance on EVA alone.

In the next chapter, we'll revisit the issues regarding management compensation that were initially addressed in Chapter 4. This time, however, we'll take a closer look at the calibration of EVA bonus plans and show how actual EVA bonus plans work.

APPENDIX
Key Financial Statement Ratios

$$\text{Profit margin} = \frac{\text{net operating income after tax}}{\text{sales}}$$

$$\text{Return on assets (RONA)} = \frac{\text{net operating profit after tax}}{\text{average net assets}}$$

$$\text{Cost of goods sold percentage} = \frac{\text{cost of goods sold}}{\text{sales}}$$

$$\text{Selling and administrative expense percentage} = \frac{\text{selling and administrative expense}}{\text{sales}}$$

$$\text{Net asset turnover} = \frac{\text{sales}}{\text{average net assets}}$$

$$\text{Accounts receivable turnover} = \frac{\text{sales}}{\text{average accounts receivable}}$$

$$\text{Receivables period} = \frac{365}{\text{accounts receivable turnover}}$$

$$\text{Inventory turnover} = \frac{\text{cost of goods sold}}{\text{average inventories}}$$

$$\text{Inventory period} = \frac{365}{\text{inventory turnover}}$$

$$\text{Accounts payable turnover} = \frac{\text{purchases*}}{\text{average accounts payable}}$$

$$\text{Payable period} = \frac{365}{\text{accounts payable turnover}}$$

$$\text{Fixed asset turnover} = \frac{\text{sales}}{\text{average fixed assets}}$$

---

*Purchases = Cost of goods sold + ending inventories − beginning inventories.

CHAPTER 8

Management Compensation Revisited

Chapter 4 presented the basic objectives of management compensation—alignment, leverage, limited retention risk, and reasonable shareholder cost. We also introduced the important concept of wealth leverage, the design of the modern EVA bonus plan, and the basic concepts of EVA bonus plan calibration. This chapter explores these issues in greater detail. We discuss the calibration of EVA bonus plans, the actual bonus plans of EVA companies, competitive compensation analysis, and the impact of stock-based compensation.

EVA BONUS PLAN CALIBRATION

In the modern EVA bonus plan, the bonus earned by an executive is equal to the sum of a target bonus plus a fixed share of excess EVA improvement, or ΔEVA minus an expected EVA improvement (EI):

$$\text{Bonus} = \text{target bonus} + y\% \, (\Delta\text{EVA} - \text{EI})$$

The bonus can also be expressed as the product of the target bonus and a "bonus multiple":

Bonus = target bonus $\times$ bonus multiple

   = target bonus $\times$ $[1 + ((\Delta EVA - EI)/EVA\ interval)]$

   = target bonus + [target bonus/EVA interval]
        $\times (\Delta EVA - EI)$

With this approach, managers receive a target bonus if they achieve the level of EVA improvement already impounded in their company's share price at the start of the measurement period. To put it another way, their pay is based on the extent to which they deliver the expected EVA improvements that investors have already paid for. If they outperform these expectations, they receive an above-target bonus; if they underperform, their bonus falls below the target. The sharing percentage (i.e., the proportion of excess EVA improvement that belongs to managers), or y percent, equals the ratio of the target bonus to the EVA interval. The EVA interval is simply the shortfall in excess EVA improvement that results in a bonus of zero.

The basic philosophy behind this approach is to provide unlimited upside potential to managers, giving them incentives not only to reach market expectations of improved performance but to exceed them. It also imposes serious penalties for underperformance, on the theory that if managers fail to achieve the necessary EVA improvement, the share price is likely to drop. If shareholders suffer, so too should managers. In short, this type of bonus plan is designed to reward managers for producing excess EVA improvement (because such improvements are an important source of excess returns for shareholders) while penalizing them for failing to deliver on the performance improvements paid for by investors. The effect is to produce a payout pattern for bonuses that more closely corresponds to increases and decreases in shareholder wealth than more conventional approaches to compensation, including older versions of EVA bonus plans. In this way, the modern EVA bonus plan helps companies achieve the twin goals of manager-shareholder alignment and high managerial wealth leverage.

Figure 8–1 highlights the plan's three key parameters: the target bonus, the expected EVA improvement, and the EVA interval. For each of these parameters, we normally start the calibration with these guiding concepts:

The Target Bonus, the Expected EVA Improvement, and the EVA Interval

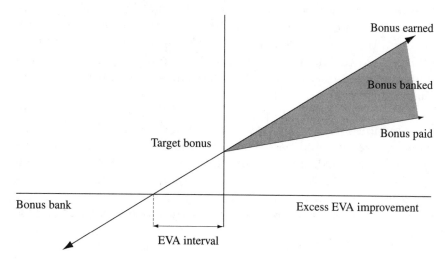

- The target bonus is based on peer company compensation levels.
- Expected EVA improvement targets are chosen that, if met, will provide shareholders with a cost-of-capital return on the market value of their investment.
- An EVA interval is used to define the amount of EVA shortfall that makes the investor return equal to zero and therefore leads to a zero bonus for the manager.

These guiding concepts provide an initial calibration, but they do not ensure that the company has achieved the right balance between the four competing objectives of executive compensation. A bonus plan design based on the preceding approach is usually judged to create too much retention risk (because the probability of a multiyear zero bonus—which would cause managers to quit—is too high). A final calibration is developed by using Monte Carlo to assess the implications of alternative parameters in terms of alignment, leverage, retention risk, and shareholder cost. Remember that the preceding calibration is only a first step.

Adjustment is nearly always required to provide the right sort of incentives without scaring managers into leaving the firm.

In this chapter, we use Hershey Foods to illustrate the calibration of an EVA bonus plan. For our target bonus analysis, we use peer compensation data for 1998, the most recent year available. For our analysis of expected EVA improvement and the EVA interval, we use data from 1992 to 1997 to simulate five years of payouts, thus allowing comparison of the simulated payouts with shareholder returns.

Our competitive compensation analysis is based on U.S. public companies in the food and beverage industry. It shows that the median size-adjusted base salary for the CEOs in Hershey's peer group is $932,000, and the median size-adjusted cash compensation is $1,768,000. To provide competitive target cash compensation, our simulation assumes a base salary for the Hershey CEO of $900,000 and a target bonus equal to 100 percent of base salary.

EXPECTED EVA IMPROVEMENT

The starting point in determining expected EVA improvement is the fundamental EVA valuation equation:

$$\text{Market value} = \text{IC} + \text{PV of future EVAs}$$

where IC equals invested capital. This equation is derived from the definition of market value added, which states that MVA equals market value minus IC. Because MVA equals the present value (PV) of future EVAs, IC plus the present value of future EVAs must equal market value.

In the modern EVA bonus plan, capital market expectations for EVA improvement are the basis for determining management bonuses. Therefore, we must quantify the expected EVA improvement implicit in a company's market value. To do this, we need to isolate the perpetuity value of current EVA (a component of *current operations value*) and the present value of expected EVA improvement (or *future growth value*):

$$\text{Market value} = [\text{IC} + (\text{EVA}_0/\text{WACC})] + \text{PV of annual } \Delta\text{EVAs}$$

$$= \text{current operations value} + \text{future growth value}$$

Current operations value (COV) is the value of the company based on its current invested capital and EVA performance, IC +

(EVA$_0$/WACC). COV is what the market value of the firm would be if the market expected the company to sustain its current level of EVA into perpetuity.

Future growth value (FGV) is simply the present value of future annual EVA improvements:

FGV = [(1+WACC)/WACC] × PV of future annual ΔEVAs

where the ΔEVA in any given year equals EVA in that year minus EVA in the previous year. Hence:

Market value = IC + (EVA$_0$/WACC) + [(1+WACC)/WACC]
× PV of future ΔEVAs

Hershey's invested capital at the end of 1992 was $2.208 billion, its EVA in 1992 was $61.8 million, and the cost of capital was 11.59 percent.[1] This gave Hershey a current operations value of $2.741 billion, or $2.208 billion + ($0.0618 billion/0.1159). Its market value was $5.148 billion, which means that buyers of Hershey's stock at the end of 1992 were willing to pay $2.407 billion for expected growth in EVA ($5.148 billion − $2.741 billion).

Of course, Hershey investors did not purchase this FGV without expectation of a return. We assume that they expect a cost-of-capital return on the total market value of their investment, current operations value *and* future growth value. A cost-of-capital return on market value requires the following:

WACC × market value = (WACC × COV) + (WACC × FGV)
= WACC [IC$_0$ + (EVA$_0$/WACC)]
+ WACC × FGV$_0$
= (WACC × IC$_0$) + EVA$_0$
+ (WACC × FGV$_0$)
= NOPAT + (WACC × FGV$_0$)

The required return on COV, [(WACC × IC$_0$) + EVA$_0$], is actually just NOPAT, assuming no EVA improvement. If ΔEVA = 0, then EVA$_1$ = EVA$_0$, and [(WACC × IC$_0$) + EVA$_0$] equals

---

1. The cost of capital was calculated using the same procedure outlined in Chapter 5. We assume a 5% market risk premium.

$[(WACC \times IC_0) + EVA_1]$, which in turn must equal $NOPAT_1$, because $EVA_1 = [NOPAT_1 - (WACC \times IC_0)]$. This shows that NOPAT, with no EVA improvement, is just enough to provide a cost-of-capital return on current operations value, but it leaves nothing left over to provide a return on future growth value.

If we set the required return equal to the actual return to be received by shareholders (Δmarket value + free cashflow to share-holders),[2] we can show that the required return on future growth value must satisfy the following condition:[3]

$$WACC \times FGV_0 = \Delta EVA_1 + (\Delta EVA_1 / WACC) + \Delta FGV_1$$

where ΔEVA_1 is the change in EVA from the previous year (year 0), $\Delta EVA_1 / WACC$ is the increase in COV from the previous year that results from the increase in EVA, and ΔFGV_1 is the change in the FGV over that same period. If the EVA improvement is distributed as free cashflow, the return on FGV has three components: the contribution of EVA improvement to free cashflow, the contribution of EVA improvement to COV (i.e., $\Delta EVA_1 / WACC$), and the change, if any, in FGV. If the EVA improvement is reinvested (and not distributed to shareholders), the return on FGV has just two components: the contribution of EVA improvement to COV and the change, if any, in FGV. However, in this case, COV increases not just by $\Delta EVA_1 / WACC$, as it does when EVA is paid out as free cashflow, but also by ΔEVA_1 (because IC increases by that amount).

If we ignore ΔFGV, assuming that the change in FGV is expected to be zero, estimating required EVA improvement is a simple task. For Hershey, a cost-of-capital return on FGV equals $2.407 billion (FGV at the end of 1992) times the WACC (11.59 percent), or $279 million. Each dollar of EVA in 1993 above the 1992 level of $61.8 million adds $1 of cashflow to investors (assuming that the increase in EVA is paid out) and $8.63 ($1/0.1159)

---

2. Free cashflow to shareholders is defined here as the sum of dividend payments and share buybacks.
3. A derivation of this formula can be found in M. L. Sirower and S. F. O'Byrne, "The Measurement of Post-Acquisition Performance: Toward a Value-Based Benchmarketing Methodology," *Journal of Applied Corporate Finance*, Summer 1998.

of additional current operations value, or \$9.63 in total.[4] Required EVA improvement is thus \$279 million divided by 9.63, or \$29 million. This level of EVA improvement adds \$29 million to 1993 cashflow and \$250 million to COV (\$29 million/0.1159), for a total return of \$279 million (the required return on FGV). Therefore, the EVA target for 1993 is \$61.8 million (EVA in the previous year) plus \$29 million, or \$90.8 million in total.

However, if we relax the assumption that expected ΔFGV_1 is zero, identifying market expectations of EVA improvement becomes more complicated than the above approach suggests. The \$29 million EVA improvement target for Hershey assumes that investor expectations of future EVA improvement are not affected by current period EVA. But investors might reasonably revise their future growth expectations based on current period performance. If so, EVA targets based on the assumption that $\Delta FGV = 0$ may require performance from management substantially greater or less than that required by the capital markets.

For example, investors may expect FGV to increase in the coming year because the passage of time brings them closer to expected EVA improvements. Even if expectations are unchanged, the present value of EVA improvements will increase. To illustrate this point, assume that investors expect that a company's ΔEVA will be \$1, increasing by 3 percent per year into perpetuity. With a WACC of 10 percent and a 3 percent growth rate in ΔEVA, the present value of annual EVA improvements is \$1/(0.10 − 0.03), or \$14.29. Every dollar of EVA improvement adds \$11 to the value of the firm: \$1 from additional cashflow in the current year and \$10 from additional COV (\$1/0.10). Therefore, FGV equals \$14.29 × 11, or \$157.14. The cost-of-capital return on this value is \$15.71 (10 percent × \$157.14). On this basis, we might conclude that the

---

4. Even if the increase in EVA is not paid out as a cashflow, its impact on the value of the firm is the same as if it were. If the increase is retained in the business, invested capital increases. Because current operations value equals invested capital plus the present value of current-period EVA, current operations value would increase not just by the increase in the continuing value of the EVA improvements (ΔEVA_1 / WACC), but also by the increase in invested capital. In the case of Hershey, this means that current operations value would increase by \$9.63 with a \$1 increase in 1993 EVA, the same as if the \$1 increase would be paid to shareholders as a dividend.

required ΔEVA is \$1.43 (\$15.71/11). But we already know that investors expect an EVA improvement of only \$1. Therefore, the ΔEVA target of \$1.43 must be wrong.

This target is wrong because it ignores a fundamental truth about FGV in cases where ΔEVA is expected to grow (which is common). In our example, even if investor expectations of ΔEVA do not change, the FGV at the end of the following year will increase to \$161.86 [\$1.03/(0.10 − 0.03) × 11], because the ΔEVA in the following year is expected to be \$1.03 instead of \$1. This means that some of the return in the following year is expected to come from an increase in FGV. If so, the company does not need to generate as much ΔEVA in that year as our previous calculation suggests.

To adjust for the expected growth in ΔFGV, we can divide \$1.43 by [WACC/(WACC − g)], where g is the expected growth rate in ΔEVA. This gives us a required EVA improvement of \$1.43 ÷ (0.10/0.07), or \$1, which we know to be the correct answer.[5]

If we use the same growth rate assumption for Hershey (3 percent), expected EVA improvement in 1993 becomes \$21.5 million, \$29 million (the pre-adjustment target) ÷ (0.1159/0.0859). This means that the EVA target is \$83.3 million, instead of \$90.8 million, as calculated previously.

Although this approach provides a sound first approximation, we can fine-tune our estimate of expected EVA improvement even further. For example, our research has shown that the magnitude of a company's FGV, scaled by its market value, can affect expected changes in FGV. When a company's ratio of FGV to market value is high in comparison to other firms, there is a tendency for FGV to decline in future years, perhaps reflecting the common statistical phenomenon known as *mean reversion*. Therefore, if FGV-to-market-value at the beginning of the year is high, investors might expect that value to decrease by the end of the year, at least partly offsetting the effect of expected growth in ΔEVA. In other words, the effect of adjusting for mean reversion in FGV is to *increase* the ΔEVA target.

---

5. If EVA grows at g, $FGV_1 = g \times FVG_0$ and EVA_1 must satisfy (WACC − g) × FGV_0 = $EVA_1 + EVA_1/WACC$.

Other Influences on FGV

Our research has identified other potential influences on FGV, although the impact of these factors varies widely from industry to industry. For many companies, R&D spending and sales growth are associated with significant changes in expected FGV, independent of any effect these variables may have on current ΔEVA. If a company is investing successfully in R&D to develop new products, investors will bid up FGV in the expectation of future EVA growth, but current EVA will not increase because the new products make no contribution to current performance. Even at a latter development stage, the new products may contribute to sales, but not earnings, and hence, sales growth may be a better proxy for FGV than current EVA improvement. Therefore, expected increases in R&D and revenue often lead to higher FGV, and correspondingly lower requirements for ΔEVA one period hence. To put it another way, the increase in FGV expected from R&D and sales growth provides part of the cost-of-capital return on beginning FGV required by investors, thereby reducing the EVA improvement required in that year.

Increases in goodwill can also have a positive effect on ΔFGV, because acquisitions often involve negative economic depreciation (a subject we introduced in Chapter 6), which is not recognized in the calculation of NOPAT. The reduction in NOPAT reduces current operations value, but not market value, thus increasing the size of the FGV component. In other words, if a company increases its investment in goodwill, the market can reasonably expect an increase in the FGV component of total market value. Like sales growth and increases in R&D spending, this too will reduce the ΔEVA required by investors in the coming year.

Another common influence on ΔFGV is the overall return on the market or industry, which is normally defined as a major market index such as the S&P 500 or an industry component such as the S&P food company index. The logic here is that industry and market returns reflect factors that are expected to increase or decrease future EVA for a large number of businesses. Higher industry or market returns translate into higher FGV for most firms, which in turn reduces the requirement for ΔEVA in the short term.

Given the many potential influences over ΔEVA, how can we develop a high-confidence estimate of what the capital markets really demand in terms of EVA improvement? Our approach relies on industry-specific, multifactor models, based on historical five-year changes in FGV. Table 8–1 summarizes the results of our models for 29 industry sectors.

The only sector where there is no apparent mean reversion tendency for beginning FGV is Drugs & Biotechnology. The two sectors where goodwill has a positive effect on FGV are Communications Equipment and Broadcasting. The two sectors where R&D has a negative effect on FGV are Household Furnishings and Aerospace/Defense. In several cases, these variables are insignificant because our samples are small. For 16 of the 29 sectors, our model is based on fewer than 200 cases (with each case defined as a five-year change in FGV for a sample company). When we combine all sectors in a single model, with nearly 6000 cases, all of the above variables are statistically significant, except for goodwill, and all have a positive effect on FGV, except for beginning FGV.

Note that we calibrate EVA expectations over a five-year period. This has important advantages over annual calibration in that it becomes easier for managers to estimate the effects of long-term decisions on their bonuses, and thereby facilitates planning. It also provides higher wealth leverage (as we show later).

T A B L E   8–1

Results of Multifactor Models for 29 Industry Sectors

Variable	Sectors with Negative Effect on ΔFGV	Sectors with No Significant Effect on ΔFGV	Sectors with Positive Effect on ΔFGV
Beginning FGV	19	9	1
S&P 500 return	0	15	14
Sales growth	0	16	13
Capital growth	3	16	8
R&D spending	2	23	4
Goodwill	3	24	2

For a five-year period, a cost-of-capital return on FGV requires the following:

$$FV(\Delta EVA_i) + \Delta EVA_5/WACC + \Delta FGV_5$$
$$= [(1+WACC)^5 - 1] \times FGV_0$$

where $FV(\Delta EVA_i)$ denotes the future value (at the end of year 5) of the annual EVA improvements for years 1 through 5; $\Delta EVA_5/WACC$ is the increase in continuing, or current operations, value over the five-year period; and ΔFGV_5 is the change in the future growth value over that same period.

For Hershey, we developed a multifactor model based on 39 companies in the U.S. food and beverage industry. This model attempts to explain five-year changes in FGV, using data available from 1980 through 1992. We will then see how bonuses would have been earned and paid out in the period 1993 to 1997 if an EVA bonus plan based on this model had been used by Hershey.

The dependent variable is $\Delta FGV_5/Mkt\ Val_0$, the five-year change in FGV, adjusted for market value at the beginning of the period. In all, there are 344 five-year FGV changes in our sample. The resulting model explains 33 percent of the variations in these changes. The coefficients of the model are as follows:

	Coefficient
Constant	0.311
$\Delta EVA^+/WACC$	0.292
$\Delta EVA^-/WACC$	−0.799
FGV_0	−0.671
Food industry return	0.131

where $\Delta EVA^+/WACC$ is the impact of ΔEVA on continuing value when EVA is positive, $\Delta EVA^-/WACC$ is the impact of ΔEVA when EVA is negative, FGV_0 is future growth value at the beginning of the five-year period (to account for the mean reversion effect discussed earlier), and the food industry return is the return on the S&P food company index (to account for the influence of food industry returns on FGV). Although we tested other variables, the above variables are the only ones that proved to be statistically significant for the food and beverage industry.[6]

To scale for differences in size among our sample firms, all variables, except the food industry return, are standardized by Mkt Val$_0$, the value of the firm at the beginning of the measurement period. When we multiply both sides of the regression equation by Mkt Val$_0$, the predicted change in FGV equals the following:

$$0.311 \ (\text{Mkt Val.}_0) + 0.292 \ (\Delta EVA_5{}^+/WACC_5)$$

$$- \ 0.799 \ (\Delta EVA_5{}^-/WACC_5) - 0.671 \ (FGV_0)$$

$$+ \ 0.131 \ (\text{industry wealth ratio} \times \text{Mkt Val}_0)$$

where WACC$_5$ is the WACC five periods hence, which we assume is equal to WACC at the beginning of the measurement period, $\Delta EVA_5{}^+/WACC_5$ is the continuing value effect of ΔEVA in cases where EVA$_5$ is positive, and $\Delta EVA_5{}^-/WACC_5$ is the continuing value effect in cases where EVA$_5$ is negative.

Our objective in using this equation is to express ΔFGV as a function of ΔEVA so that we can solve for the ΔEVA needed to provide a cost-of-capital return on FGV$_0$ (the future growth value at the beginning of the five-year period). Returns on the S&P food industry index are expressed in the form of a wealth ratio, which reflects what \$1 invested in the market is expected to be worth five years later. For example, at the end of 1992, the expected return on the S&P food industry index equals the government bond rate in effect at that time (7.45 percent) plus a market risk premium of 5 percent, or 12.45 percent in total.[7] This expected rate of return implies that the five-year wealth ratio is $(1.1245)^5$, or 1.80. In other words, an investor who puts \$1 in the food companies in the stock market at the end of 1992 would expect to have \$1.80 at the end of 1997.

Of course, this return is an expectation and is therefore unknown at the time of the bonus plan calibration. The same is true

---

6. The variables tested include sales growth, capital growth, the change in goodwill, and the change in capitalized R&D.

7. Our analysis assumes that the beta for the food industry is 1.00. In other words, the volatility of food industry stocks is approximately the same as that of the overall stock market. This means that the industry's risk premium is the same as the market risk premium, which we assume to be 5 percent.

for the future cost of capital. Our model assumes that the WACC five years hence is identical to the WACC at the time the calibration is made. In short, we assume that the cost of capital remains constant over the five years, and that the S&P food industry wealth ratio will reflect the expected return on the S&P food industry index] at the beginning of the period.

The use of expected values for the cost of capital and the S&P food industry wealth ratio pose a basic design issue: Should we recalibrate expected EVA improvement during the five-year period as the cost of capital and S&P return become known? The argument in favor of recalibrating is that it more closely aligns incentive plan payouts with shareholder value and, hence, leads to better investment decisions. However, our experience suggests that the arguments against calibration are more compelling. First, if the plan is not adjusted for subsequent changes in WACC or stock market returns, it becomes easier for managers to project the incentive consequences of investment decisions and therefore increases the likelihood that the incentive plan will influence management behavior. Second, WACC and stock market returns are beyond the control of managers. Adjusting expected EVA improvement for changes in stock market returns is likely to have little effect on management decision making because there is nothing a manager can do to influence returns. Adjusting expected EVA improvement for changes in the cost of capital could influence management behavior because some decisions, such as those on capital structure, do affect the cost of capital. However, few managers make decisions that affect the cost of capital (and, in any event, cost of capital estimates are subject to substantial error). Therefore, no EVA companies that we are aware of change expected EVA improvement targets because of changes in the cost of capital. In short, when we establish five-year targets, we normally do not adjust for subsequent changes in market returns or WACC.

We now return to the estimation of expected EVA improvement using our ΔFGV model. The five-year expected return on future growth value equals $2.407 billion (the FGV at the beginning of the period) times the cumulative cost of capital over the five years, 0.7303 ($1.1159^5 - 1$), or $1.758 billion. This tells us that EVA improvement and ΔFGV need to provide $1.758 billion in value by the end of year 5:

$$FV(\Delta EVA_i) + (\Delta EVA_5/WACC) + \Delta FGV_5 = 1.758 \text{ billion}$$

To solve this equation, we need to express ΔFGV in terms of ΔEVA, which requires that we eliminate the influence of non-ΔEVA factors:

$$\Delta FGV = 0.311 \text{ (Mkt Val}_0) + 0.292 \text{ } (\Delta EVA_5^+/WACC_5)$$
$$- 0.799 \text{ } (\Delta EVA_5^-/WACC_5)$$
$$- 0.671 \text{ (FGV}_0) + 0.131$$
$$\text{(S\&P Food Industry Wealth Ratio} \times \text{Mkt Val}_0)$$

The three non-ΔEVA factors in the model are beginning market value (\$5.148 billion), beginning FGV (\$2.407 billion), and the expected S&P 500 food industry wealth ratio (1.80). When we substitute these values into the ΔFGV equation, we get the following:

$$\Delta FGV = 0.311 \text{ (5.148 billion)} + 0.292 \text{ } (\Delta EVA_5^+/WACC_5)$$
$$- 0.799 \text{ } (\Delta EVA_5^-/WACC_5)$$
$$- 0.671 \text{ (2.407 billion)}$$
$$+ 0.131 \text{ (1.80} \times \text{5.148 billion)}$$

which simplifies to

$$\Delta FGV = 1.199 \text{ billion} + 0.292 \text{ } (\Delta EVA_5^+/WACC_5)$$
$$- 0.799 \text{ } (\Delta EVA_5^-/WACC_5)$$

Because Hershey's current EVA is positive, we can further simplify the expression for FGV to

$$\Delta FGV = 1.199 \text{ billion} + 0.292 \text{ } (\Delta EVA_5^+/WACC_5)$$

We can now substitute this expression for ΔFGV in our required return equation (where \$1.758 billion is the cost-of-capital return on beginning FGV):

$$FV(\Delta EVA_i) + \Delta EVA_5/WACC + \Delta FGV_5 = 1.758 \text{ billion}$$

$$FV(\Delta EVA_i) + \Delta EVA_5/WACC + [1.199 \text{ billion} + 0.292$$
$$\times \Delta EVA_5/WACC_5] = 1.758 \text{ billion}$$

$$FV(\Delta EVA_i) + [(1.292 \times (\Delta EVA_5/WACC_5)]$$
$$+ 1.199 \text{ billion} = 1.758 \text{ billion}$$

$$FV(\Delta EVA_i) + [(1.292 \times (\Delta EVA_5/WACC_5)]$$
$$= 0.559 \text{ billion}$$

If we assume that ΔEVA_i changes at a constant annual rate, a solution to the last equation depends on only one variable, ΔEVA_1. We assume that ΔEVA_i grows at 4.27 percent per year because the required return from EVA improvement represents a compounded annual return of 4.27 percent on the beginning FGV of \$1.758 billion. This assumption implies that ΔEVA_1 equals \$8.282 million.

To verify that our expected EVA improvements are correct, we need to show that they increase the five-year return by \$559 million (the difference between \$1.758 billion and \$1.199 billion). Each \$1 of EVA improvement affects cash, the EVA component of current operations value (EVA/WACC), and future growth value. To calculate the effect of expected EVA improvement on cash, we need to calculate each annual EVA improvement and its future value at the end of year 5:

Year	ΔEVA	Future Value of ΔEVA
1	8.282	12.843
2	8.636	12.000
3	9.004	11.212
4	9.388	10.476
5	9.789	9.789
Total	45.100	56.321

The cumulative future value of the EVA improvements is \$56.321 million at the end of year 5. This is the effect of the EVA improvements on cash. The effect of the EVA improvements on current operations value is $\Delta EVA/WACC$, or \$45.100/0.1159, which equals \$389.129 million. The effect of the EVA improvements on FGV is $0.292 \times \Delta EVA/WACC$, or $0.292 \times (\$45.100/0.1159)$, which equals \$113.626 million. The total return from the EVA improvements is the sum of these three values, \$56.321 million + \$389.129 million + \$113.626 million, or approximately \$559 million.

THE EVA INTERVAL

To calculate the EVA interval (or the shortfall in EVA) that would reduce Hershey's investor return from the cost of capital to zero, we must first calculate the expected return. With a market value of $5148 million in 1992 and a cost of capital of 11.59 percent, Hershey's expected investor return is $597 million (5148 billion × 0.1159). This is a free cashflow return that includes the combined effects of stock price appreciation, dividends, and after-tax interest payments. If Hershey loses $1 of EVA, and investors expect the reduction in EVA to persist in perpetuity, the loss in value to Hershey investors is $1 plus the perpetuity value of $1 forever beginning the following year, or $1/WACC. Thus, the total loss in value from a $1 decline in EVA is $1 + $1/WACC or $1 × (1 + WACC)/ WACC. This means that a decline in EVA of $62 million will wipe out the expected return of $597 million [$62 million × (1.1157 ÷ 0.1157) = $597 million]. Therefore, $62 million is the zero-return EVA interval.

While it is undeniably appealing to reduce management's bonus to zero when investor return is zero, our experience suggests that this approach results in too much retention risk. A popular alternative is to calibrate the bonus plan such that the probability of managers receiving a zero bonus over, say, a three-year period is reduced to a negligible level, normally 5 percent. The calculation of the 5 percent probability interval is based on Hershey's stock price volatility, leverage, cost of capital, and two critical assumptions: (1) investor wealth follows a lognormal distribution, and (2) excess returns are fully reflected in current operating performance. The appendix to this chapter shows how this procedure works for Hershey. The effect is to increase Hershey's EVA interval from $62 million to $91 million. Although the effect of this adjustment on the EVA interval will vary from company to company (because of variations in stock price volatility, leverage, and the cost of capital), the increase in the EVA interval we observe for Hershey (roughly 50 percent) is fairly typical of publicly traded companies in the United States and Western Europe, at least for those outside the highly volatile technology sector.

THE CALIBRATED BONUS FORMULA

Our preliminary calibration has produced a target bonus of $900,000, expected EVA improvement of $8.282 million (which we round to $8.3 million), and an EVA interval of $91 million. Plugging these parameters into the bonus formula gives us the following:

$$\text{Bonus} = \text{target bonus} + [\text{target bonus/EVA interval}]$$
$$\times (\Delta EVA - EI)\ \$900,000 + 0.989\%\ (\Delta EVA - \$8.3\ M)$$

The other key element in the bonus plan is the *bonus bank*. We begin with a balance of $0, and use a payout rule that provides a competitive cash payout for achieving expected EVA improvement. The bonus earned is credited to the bonus bank, and then the bonus paid is determined from the bonus bank balance using the following rule: pay the bonus bank balance, up to the amount of the target bonus, plus one-third of the bonus bank balance in excess of the target bonus. No payout is made when the bonus bank balance is negative.

Table 8–2 shows the implications of our bonus plan parameters for the period 1993 to 1997. Hershey's EVA in 1993 declined by $47.1 million from the previous year, resulting in an excess EVA improvement of −$55.4 million (−$4.1 million − $8.3 million). From the excess EVA improvement, the bonus earned can be calculated either by using the management share of excess EVA improvement or by using the EVA interval to calculate a bonus multiple. The first approach emphasizes the ownership element of the EVA bonus, while the second approach emphasizes a more traditional bonus calculation. Using the first approach, the bonus earned is $900,000 + (0.00989 × −$55.4 million), or $352,000 (rounded). Under the second approach, we first calculate a bonus multiple that is equal to 1 + (excess EVA improvement/EVA interval), or 0.391, given an excess EVA improvement of −$55.4 million and an EVA interval of $91 million. The bonus earned is then equal to the target bonus ($900,000) times the bonus multiple. The bonus earned of $352,000 is credited to the bonus bank to determine the bonus paid. The bonus paid is $352,000 because the bank balance is less than the target bonus.

In 1994, Hershey's EVA improvement is positive, $45.2 million, which makes its excess EVA improvement $36.6 million ($45.2 million − $8.6 million).[8] The bonus earned in 1994 is equal

---

8. Note that the expected EVA in 1994 is $8.6 million.

T A B L E   8–2

EVA Bonus Plan Simulation for Hershey Corp.

	1992	1993	1994	1995	1996	1997
EVA ($mil)	$61.800	$14.700	$59.900	$14.400	$91.600	$151.100
EVA improvement ($mil)		($47.100)	$45.200	($45.500)	$77.200	$59.500
Expected EVA improvement ($mil)		$8.300	$8.600	$9.000	$9.400	$9.800
Excess EVA improvement ($mil)		($55.400)	$36.600	($54.500)	$67.800	$49.700
EVA interval		$ 91.000	$ 91.000	$ 91.000	$ 91.000	$ 91.000
Earned bonus multiple		0.391	1.402	0.401	1.745	1.546
Hershey CEO base salary ($000)		$900.000	$900.000	$900.000	$900.000	$900.000
Target bonus percentage		100%	100%	100%	100%	100%
Target bonus ($000)		$900.000	$900.000	$900.000	$900.000	$900.000
CEO share of excess EVA improvement		0.989%	0.989%	0.989%	0.989%	0.989%
Bonus earned ($000)		$352.000	$1262.000	$361.000	$1571.000	$1392.000
Bonus earned (percent of target)		39%	140%	40%	175%	155%
Cumulative bonus earned (percent of target)		39%	90%	73%	98%	110%
Initial bonus bank ($000)		$352.000	$1262.000	$602.000	$1571.000	$1839.000
Payout percent above target		33.3%	33.3%	33.3%	33.3%	33.3%
Bonus paid ($000)		$352.000	$1021.000	$602.000	$1124.000	$1213.000
Bonus paid (percent of target)		39%	113%	67%	125%	135%
Cumulative bonus paid (percent of target)		39%	76%	73%	86%	96%
Ending bonus bank ($000)		$0	$241.000	$0	$447.000	$626.000

to the target bonus plus 0.989 percent of the excess EVA improvement, or $900,000 + (0.00989 × $36.6 million), which equals $1.262 million. Using the bonus multiple approach, the bonus earned equals the target bonus × [1 + ($36.6 million/$91 million)], which again yields the same answer as the first approach. The bonus earned is credited to the bonus bank, which increases the bank balance from $0 to $1.262 million. The bonus paid is equal to the amount of the bonus bank balance ($1.262 million) up to the amount of the target bonus ($900,000), plus one-third of the bonus bank balance in excess of the target bonus ($362,000). The bonus paid comes to $1.021 million ($900,000 + one-third of $362,000), which leaves a year-end bonus bank balance of $241,000. Continuing the bonus calculations through 1997, we find that the cumulative bonus earned is 110 percent of target and exceeds the cumulative bonus paid by $626,000. This figure then becomes the ending bonus bank balance.

The bonus bank approach ensures that the cumulative bonus earned is always equal to the sum of the cumulative target bonus plus management's share of the cumulative excess EVA improvement. At the end of 1997, the cumulative bonus earned is 110 percent of target, or $4.937 million. The cumulative excess EVA improvement is the 1993 to 1997 EVA improvement of $89.3 million ($151.1 million − $61.8 million) minus the cumulative expected EVA improvement of $45.1, or $44.2 million. The sum of the cumulative target bonus, $4.5 million plus 0.989 percent of the cumulative excess EVA improvement, is $4.937 million. The cumulative bonus earned is equal to the sum of the cumulative bonus paid ($4.311 million) plus the ending bonus bank balance ($626,000). This relationship continues to hold even if the ending bonus bank balance is negative. A negative bank is a telling measure of accountability: It tells us that the cumulative bonus paid exceeds the cumulative bonus earned.

If expected EVA improvement does, in fact, reflect investor expectations, and excess EVA improvements are capitalized at a constant multiple—for example, 1 + (1.292/WACC) based on our ΔFGV model, there is an exact relationship between the excess EVA bonus (i.e., the EVA bonus in excess of the target bonus) and the dollar value of the excess shareholder return. Under these assumptions, the dollar value of the excess shareholder return equals the constant multiple times the future value of excess EVA improvement. This, in turn, implies that the future value of the excess EVA bonus earned will be a fixed percentage of the excess shareholder return. Based on Hershey's 1997 cost of capital of 9.95 percent, a 0.989 percent interest in excess EVA improvement should translate into a 0.071 percent, or [0.989 percent $\times$ WACC/ (1.292 + WACC)], share of excess shareholder return.

Table 8–3 shows, however, that the future value of the cumulative EVA bonus earned was only 0.005 percent of Hershey's 1992 to 1997 excess shareholder return of $4.6 billion. The reason for the discrepancy is that Hershey's excess shareholder return of $4.6 billion was 16.68/WACC times its cumulative excess EVA improvement, while our expected multiple, based on our ΔFGV model, is only 1 + 1.292/WACC. This means that the unexpected future growth value recognized by investors over this period was $154, or [(16.68 − 1.292)/WACC − 1], for every dollar of excess EVA improvement.

This preliminary bonus plan calibration is designed to limit retention risk by reducing the probability of a three-year zero bonus to 5 percent. But does the plan provide enough leverage? To answer this question, we need to estimate cash compensation wealth leverage for Hershey's CEO. We do this by calculating the impact on five-year cash compensation if investor wealth were to double.

With beginning investor wealth of $5.148 billion and a cost of capital of 11.59 percent, expected investor wealth at the end of five years is $8.9 billion ($5.148 billion $\times$ 1.1159^5). Doubling this figure leads to investor wealth five years hence of $17.8 billion, half of which is expected wealth while the other half is excess return. In our calibration, we determined that each dollar of EVA improvement provided $12.4 of five-year return (the five-year required return from EVA improvement ÷ cumulative expected EVA improvement, or $559.1/$45.1). This means that $718 million of additional EVA is needed to provide $8.9 billion of additional return ($8.9 billion ÷ 12.4 = $718 million). This, in turn, implies an additional bonus of $7.1 million because the CEO's share of excess EVA improvement is 0.989 percent. This additional bonus increases the CEO's cash compensation from $9.0 million (five years of $900,000 salary and $900,000 target bonus at expected performance) to $16.1 million, an increase of 79 percent. The wealth leverage of cash compensation is therefore 0.79:

TABLE 8-3

Excess Bonus and Excess Return for Hershey Corp.

	1992	1993	1994	1995	1996	1997
Stock price	$25.69	$22.31	$26.25	$37.94	$54.25	$73.25
Annual dividend		$0.57	$0.63	$0.69	$0.76	$0.84
Cumulative dividend value		$0.57	$1.26	$2.12	$3.13	$4.33
Shareholder wealth		$22.88	$27.51	$40.06	$57.38	$77.58
Cost of equity		11.9%	10.8%	13.1%	12.1%	11.5%
Expected shareholder wealth		$28.75	$31.85	$36.01	$40.38	$45.02
Excess shareholder wealth per share		($5.87)	($4.33)	$4.04	$17.00	$32.56
Actual cumulative return pct of expected return		-92%	30%	139%	216%	268%
Shares outstanding (mil)	180.37	175	173	155	153	143
Dollar excess return ($mil)		($1028)	($752)	$625	$2601	$4654
Excess EVA improvement ($mil)		($55)	$37	($55)	$68	$50
Cumulative excess EVA improvement (w/interest)		($55)	($24)	($81)	($22)	$25
Capitalized cumulative excess EVA improvement		($558)	($274)	($789)	($233)	$279
CEO share of excess EVA improvement		0.99%	0.99%	0.99%	0.99%	0.99%
Cost of capital	11.59%	11.02%	9.69%	11.51%	10.56%	9.95%
Target share of excess return		0.078%	0.069%	0.081%	0.075%	0.071%
Excess EVA bonus earned		($548)	$362	($539)	$671	$492
Cumulative bonus earned (w/interest)		($548)	($239)	($806)	($220)	$250
Actual percent of excess return		0.053%	0.032%	-0.129%	-0.008%	0.005%

325

	Expected Performance	Double Investor Wealth	Percent Change
Investor wealth	$8.9 billion	$17.8 billion	100
Cash compensation	$9.0 million	$16.1 million	79
Wealth leverage			0.79

If we decide that the CEO should have entrepreneurial wealth leverage, we have to face some tough choices. We could increase wealth leverage by reducing the EVA interval, but that will increase the probability of a three-year zero bonus above the 5 percent threshold, likely resulting in too much retention risk. We could increase wealth leverage by cutting base salary and increasing the target bonus, but that too increases retention risk if the base salary then becomes uncompetitive. An alternative approach is to increase the target bonus without reducing the base salary. If we raise the target bonus from 100 percent of salary to 175 percent, entrepreneurial wealth leverage is achieved:

	Expected Performance	Double Investor Wealth	Percent Change
Investor wealth	$8.9 billion	$17.8 billion	100
Cash compensation	$12.4 million	$24.8 million	100
Wealth leverage			1.00

With a target bonus equal to 175 percent of salary, cash compensation for expected performance is $12.4 million (five years with a salary of $900,000 and a target bonus of $1.575 million), but the CEO's share of excess EVA improvement increases from 0.989 percent to 1.731 percent. With this larger share, the $718 million of additional EVA (which causes the doubling of investor wealth) provides $12.4 million of additional bonus. This means that the doubling in investor wealth also doubles the CEO's five-year cash compensation.

If we repeat the leverage calculations using only the EVA bonus, we can see that the leverage of the EVA bonus is 1.57:

	Expected Performance	Double Investor Wealth	Percent Change
Investor wealth	$8.9 billion	$17.8 billion	100
EVA bonus	$7.9 million	$20.3 million	157
Wealth leverage			1.57

Cash compensation leverage is a weighted average of base salary leverage, which is zero, and EVA bonus leverage, 1.57. When the target bonus is 100 percent of salary and the bonus is 50 percent of target cash compensation, leverage is 0.79:

$$(50\% \times 0) + (50\% \times 1.57) = 0.79$$

When the target bonus is increased to 175 percent of salary, the bonus is 64 percent of target cash compensation. Leverage is now 1.00:

$$(36\% \times 0) + (64\% \times 1.57) = 1.00$$

Entrepreneurial wealth leverage has been achieved, but at a cost. Increasing the target bonus achieves such leverage without increasing retention risk, but only because target compensation is 38 percent above market. This example illustrates the fundamental dilemma in incentive plan design: Who pays for a strong incentive? Does management pay by accepting greater compensation risk? Or do the shareholders pay by providing above market compensation?

Another important question in EVA bonus plan design is whether the bonus for division managers should be based entirely on results in their own divisions or also include a component based on corporate performance. The argument in favor of the latter approach is that it presumably encourages cooperation. A common practice is to have, say, 75 percent of the bonus based on business unit performance and 25 percent based on corporate performance. This type of incentive structure is widely believed to give business unit managers an incentive to cooperate when business unit and corporate goals conflict. The reality, however, is that the corporate weighting is rarely large enough to provide an incentive to cooperate.

Consider a multiunit promotional campaign that reduces business unit EVA by $1 million but increases corporate EVA by $1 million. Suppose also that the business unit head's target bonus is $100,000, the business unit's EVA interval is $2 million, and the corporate EVA interval is $8 million (because the company is four times larger than the business unit). If 75 percent of the business unit head's target bonus is allocated on the basis of business unit EVA, the business unit head has a 3.75 percent interest in business unit EVA improvement and a 0.3125 percent interest in corporate EVA improvement. With these percentage interests, the business unit head loses $37,500 in business unit bonus by cooperating and gains only $3125 in corporate bonus. To have a financial incentive to cooperate, the business unit head needs the same percentage interest in corporate EVA that he or she holds in business unit EVA. This requires a bonus weighting of 80 percent corporate and 20 percent business unit. The obvious problem with such a weighting is that it sharply weakens line of sight. Managers are paid largely on the basis of a measure (in this case, corporate EVA) over which they have little control. A more sensible solution to this problem is a transfer payment. The company could pay the business unit enough to offset the impact of the promotional campaign on the business unit's EVA.

Setting EVA Improvement Goals for Divisions

Thus far in this chapter we have shown how to link management bonuses to the capital market expectations of EVA improvement reflected in the market value of the firm. But if the use of EVA is to provide strong value-creating incentives for all managers, not just those at the top, EVA improvement targets must be allocated to divisions. The problem, of course, is that while the EVA targets at corporate level can be derived directly from an observable stock price, the same cannot be said for divisions. So how do we set EVA improvement targets below the CEO level?

We illustrate the process in Table 8–4 using recent data from a NYSE-traded company having five major operating divisions. (To preserve confidentiality, the identity of the company has been withheld.) The easiest and most obvious way to allocate expected EVA improvement to divisions is to use either invested capital or continuing operations value, both of which are readily observable in any business unit for which EVA is calculated. The problem

TABLE 8-4

Allocating Expected EVA Improvement*

	Corporate	Division 1	Division 2	Division 3	Division 4	Division 5
EVA	(43.607)	12.289	17.924	(70.867)	(1.515)	(1.438)
WACC	9.0%	9.0%	9.0%	9.0%	9.0%	9.0%
Capitalized value of current EVA	(484.522)	136.544	199.156	787.411	16.833	15.978
Invested capital (IC)	2,294.550	199.559	219.780	1,535.456	39.215	300.540
Current operations value (COV)	1,810.028	336.103	418.936	748.045	22.382	284.562
Market value	2,282.346					
Future growth value (FGV)	472.318					
Estimated market value	2,294.550	479.375	403.427	1,676.363	84.085	373.639
Estimated FGV		143.272	(15.509)	928.318	61.703	89.077
Greater of COV and IC		336.103	418.936	1,535.456	39.215	300.540
Expected EVA improvement	10.229					
Divisional allocation basis						
Invested capital		0.890	0.980	6.845	0.175	1.340
Current operations value		1.899	2.368	4.228	0.126	1.608
Greater of COV and IC		1.307	1.629	5.971	0.153	1.169
Estimated FGV		1.214	−131	7.868	523	725
Peer model coefficients						
Invested capital		2.042	2.149	1.939	2.867	0.754
Ln (invested capital)		−0.117	−0.105	−0.095	−0.197	0.088
EVA$^+$/WACC		1.432	0.279	0.869	3.780	−0.107
EVA$^-$/WACC		0.274	0.327	0.293	0.000	0.242

* In millions of dollars.

with either approach is that it can create strong biases that unfairly penalize some divisions while favoring others. For example, allocations made on the basis of invested capital tend to penalize underperforming divisions in favor of divisions with the best EVA performance, because invested capital does not include the continuing value of EVA performance. For a division with high EVA, the failure to incorporate the continuing value of current EVA in the allocation process effectively "lowers the bar" for the managers of this division while raising it for negative EVA divisions. In effect, allocating EVA improvement on the basis of invested capital implicitly assumes that all divisions earn an EVA of 0.

The obvious solution may seem to be the use of current operations value (COV). Unfortunately, this approach creates a bias in the opposite direction. Negative EVA divisions tend to be favored, receiving a smaller proportion of the total EVA improvement target, because the continuing value of their negative EVAs causes the COV to fall below invested capital (remembering that COV equals invested capital plus the continuing value of current EVA performance, which in this case is negative). Meanwhile, COV exceeds invested capital for all positive EVA divisions.

We can see the consequences of these two alternatives in Table 8–4. Division 3, the largest of the five divisions in this company, is assigned $6.845 million of the expected EVA improvement ($10.229 million at corporate level) when allocation is based on invested capital, but only $4.228 million when allocation is based on COV. This result occurs because of its negative EVA. By contrast, Divisions 1 and 2, the only positive EVA performers among the five divisions, are allocated twice as much of the improvement under the COV approach than under invested capital.

An improvement over either approach is to value each division according to invested capital or COV, whichever is greater. This means that invested capital will be used for negative EVA divisions, while COV is used for positive EVA divisions. In this way, the continuing value of current EVA performance is captured in the allocation process for positive EVA divisions, but negative EVA divisions do not get a free ride, because for them allocation will be based on invested capital, without a "discount" for the continuing value of negative EVAs that arises when COV is used instead. As expected, the resulting allocations tend to fall between the two extremes of invested capital and COV (with the exception of Division 5, which has a lower allocation than under either of the other two approaches).

Although this approach is clearly better than the first two, an even better solution bases allocations on a divisional future growth value, which in turn is based on an estimated market value. This approach requires an empirical model for each division, based on historical data from publicly traded companies in its sector or industry. The question each model aims to answer is how the market would value a company in a particular industry, with invested capital and EVA performance equal to that of our target division. Subtracting the division's COV from this estimated market value yields an estimate of the future growth value. Expected EVA improvement is then allocated on the basis of the future growth value for each division.

To illustrate, a regression model was developed for Division 1 based on several years of data from publicly traded companies in its industry. The dependent variable in this model is MV/IC, where MV = market value and IC = invested capital. This variable was regressed against the log of invested capital and two variables that represent the continuing value of current EVA—one variable for cases with positive EVA and the other for cases with negative EVA. Because Division 1's current EVA is positive, only the first of these coefficients applies. Each of the independent, or explanatory, variables was scaled by invested capital to ensure that the largest companies in the sample did not unduly influence the results and to improve the statistical accuracy of the estimated coefficients.

Both sides of the regression equation were multiplied by invested capital to then permit each variable to be expressed in dollars. The model coefficients are shown in Table 8–4. Based on this model, estimated market value for Division 1 is calculated as follows:

$$\text{Estimated market value} = [2.042 - 0.117 \, (ln \, 199.559)]$$
$$\times \, 199.559 + 1.432 \, (136.544)$$
$$= 479.375$$

where 199.559 is the invested capital and 136.544 is the continuing value of EVA (both in millions of dollars). The result can be interpreted to mean that based on historical precedent in Division

1's industry, we would expect a company having invested capital of nearly $200 million and a continuing EVA value of about $136 million to have a total market value of $479 million. We can then subtract the COV of $336.103 million to derive the estimated future growth value of $143.272 million. A similar procedure was used for the other four divisions.

The main virtue of this approach is that it makes the assignment of EVA improvement targets at the divisional level consistent with the approach used to derive targets at the corporate level. The empirical model is not particularly complicated, but it does depend on a reasonably large and robust set of data. Also, this approach tends to work only in companies that organize their divisions on the basis of sector, industry, or product line. In cases where divisions are defined geographically, identifying comparable firms so that an empirical model can be estimated is a very difficult, if not impossible, task. But in companies where publicly traded comparables can be observed, this model provides the most theoretically sound approach to allocating EVA improvement targets to divisions.

THE ACTUAL BONUS PLANS OF EVA COMPANIES

In our examination of EVA-linked compensation, we focus on the practices of 54 American companies, all of which are known to use EVA in their bonus plans.[9] We limit our study to companies that file proxy statements (detailing compensation practices) with the U.S. Securities and Exchange Commission (SEC). These companies are listed in Table 8–5, along with their 1997 sales, end-of-

9. The Web site of EVA consultants Stern Stewart & Company (www.sternstewart.com)
     identifies 66 companies that were clients of the firm, and that presumably have
     adopted EVA. Although many other companies have adopted EVA in some
     form—using other consultants or choosing to implement on their own—we think
     this list is as good as any in examining the compensation practices of EVA compa-
     nies. Ten of these companies were deleted because examination of proxy state-
     ments revealed that either they had never used EVA for management compensa-
     tion despite being listed as "EVA companies" (seven cases), or they had used EVA
     for compensation but no longer did as of 1999 (three cases). We exclude two other
     companies from our sample, one of which uses EVA in its long-term bonus plan
     but relies on a subjective appraisal of strategic and operational accomplishments
     for annual bonuses, and another that has not filed a proxy statement with the SEC
     since it began implementing EVA.

TABLE 8-5

A Sample of EVA Companies in Order of Market Capitalization, December 31, 1997*

	Sales	Market Cap	Primary Business
Coca-Cola Co.	18,813	170,339	Beverages
Lilly (Eli) & Co.	9,237	99,810	Pharmaceuticals
Monsanto Co.	8,648	37,220	Chemicals and allied products
Sprint Fon Group	16,017	33,698	Telecommunications
Penney (JC) Co.	31,380	19,730	Department stores
Guidant Corp.	1,897	17,009	Surgical, medical instruments
Tenet Healthcare Corp.	9,895	16,664	Hospitals
Becton Dickinson & Co.	3,117	11,392	Surgical, medical instruments
Hershey Foods Corp.	4,436	10,184	Confectionery
Georgia-Pacific Group	13,223	9,635	Paper and allied products
Quaker Oats Co.	4,843	9,060	Grain mill products
Federal-Mogul Corp.	4,469	8,132	Motor vehicle parts
Donnelley (R. R.) & Sons Co.	5,018	6,944	Commercial printing
Whirlpool Corp.	10,323	6,844	Household appliances
Case Corp.	6,149	6,095	Farm machinery, equipment
Equifax Inc.	1,621	5,705	Credit reporting
Vulcan Materials Co.	1,776	4,496	Mining
Ryder System Inc.	5,189	4,436	Auto rent and leasing
Armstrong World Inds. Inc.	2,746	4,354	Plastics products
Boise Cascade Corp.	6,162	4,129	Paper and paper products
Grainger (W. W.) Inc.	4,341	4,126	Durable goods—wholesale

TABLE 8-5

Continued

	Sales	Market Cap	Primary Business
Rubbermaid Inc.	2,400	4,120	Plastics products
Montana Power Co.	1,254	4,101	Electricity
Centura Banks Inc.	671	3,773	State commercial banks
Webster Finl Corp. Waterbury	666	3,737	Savings institutions
SPX Corp.	1,825	3,531	Fabricated metal products
Safety-Kleen Corp.	1,185	3,311	Hazardous waste management
ADC Telecommunications	1,380	3,306	Telephone, telegraph equipment
Kansas City Power & Light	939	2,996	Electricity
Millennium Chemicals Inc.	1,597	2,635	Inorganic chemicals
Miller (Herman) Inc.	1,719	2,574	Office furniture
Crane Co.	2,269	2,482	Lumber, plywood
Acxiom Corp.	730	2,428	Data processing, preparation
Noble Drilling Corp.	788	2,306	Drilling oil and gas wells
Polaroid Corp.	1,846	1,651	Photography supply
Harnischfeger Industries Inc.	2,054	1,595	Mining machinery, equipment
EG&G Inc.	1,408	1,532	Engineering services
Olin Corp.	1,426	1,531	Metals
Briggs & Stratton	1,328	1,054	Engines and turbines
Manitowoc Co.	695	907	Construction machinery
Wellman Inc.	968	876	Plastics, synthetic materials

	Sales	Market Cap	Primary Business
Columbus Mckinnon Corp.	511	826	Construction, mining equipment
Calmat Co.	470	776	Mining
Intl Multifoods Corp.	2,297	564	Groceries
Standard Motor Prods.	649	474	Electric machinery, equipment
Allied Holdings Inc.	1,027	407	Trucking
Silicon Vy Bancshares	227	391	Banking
Furon Co.	493	384	Gaskets, hoses, plastics
GC Companies Inc.	407	307	Movie theaters
Material Sciences Corp.	469	254	Coating, engraving
Johnson Worldwide	329	203	Misc. durable goods
Knape & Vogt Mfg. Co.	182	143	Partitions, shelving, lockers
Insteel Industries	266	77	Steel
Heist (C. H.) Corp.	136	35	Help supply services

* In millions of dollars.

1997 market capitalization, and primary line of business. We look first at the 22 companies that combine EVA with at least one other measure in their bonus plan before turning to the 32 companies that rely entirely on EVA. We later examine several companies that adopted EVA, only to abandon or curtail the use of it in later years.

Companies Combining EVA with Other Measures

The non-EVA performance measures used by the 22 companies that use both EVA and at least one other performance measure include the following:

Measure	Number of EVA Companies Using Measure
Earnings (EPS, net income, operating income)	18
Revenue	8
Return on investment (RONA, CFROI, ROE)	6
Cashflow	4

Other measures used by these 22 EVA companies include strategic goals, safety, capital expenditures, debt coverage, diversity, shareholder return, customer satisfaction, and employee satisfaction.

While the use of non-EVA measures may sometimes signal a lack of commitment to EVA (we present evidence on this point below), such measures can address important concerns. For example, the use of earnings as a second measure can address the concern that using the cost of capital for internal performance measurement increases underinvestment risk (namely, the tendency for managers to avoid value-creating investments because EVA in the short term may decline). Rather than relying on longer-term incentives alone (such as bonus banks and stock options), companies may prefer to mix EVA with operating profit. The practical effect of this practice is to reduce the capital charges imposed on managers with EVA-linked compensation plans.

To illustrate, consider a bonus plan based on the following formula:

$$\text{Bonus} = (2\% \times \text{NOPAT}) + (2\% \times \text{EVA})$$

This expression is equivalent to the following:

$$2\% \times \text{NOPAT} + 2\% [\text{NOPAT} - (\text{WACC} \times \text{invested capital})]$$
$$= 4\% \times \text{NOPAT} - 2\% (\text{WACC} \times \text{invested capital})$$
$$= 4\% \times [\text{NOPAT} - (\text{WACC}/2) \text{ invested capital}]$$

The last expression shows that the bonus payout is increased by any investment that earns more than WACC/2. An equivalent result could be achieved by reducing the EVA cost of capital from WACC to WACC/2. Of course, this raises the question, why use EVA at all if we don't want managers charged for the company's entire cost of capital? The logic seems to be that by effectively reducing the cost of capital, wrong though it may be, a company can resolve a potential underinvestment problem. In other words, two wrongs make a right.

The use of revenue growth as a second measure can address the common concern that EVA improvement from downsizing or improvements in operating efficiency (i.e., growth in EVA without growth in revenues) is less valuable to investors than EVA improvement from growth.

While there is a legitimate basis for these two concerns about EVA, the inclusion of other measures in the bonus plan will not provide a stronger incentive, or one that is better aligned with shareholder value, unless (1) the plan is structured to allow the plan participants to understand the quantitative trade-off between EVA and the other measure, and (2) the trade-off built into the plan is consistent with market valuation. JCPenney uses EVA, earnings, and revenue in its incentive plans, but EVA is in a separate plan with "predetermined EVA growth targets," while earnings and revenue are in the annual bonus plan and revenue growth is measured against targets set annually. There is no suggestion in the JCPenney proxy statement that the two plans were designed in tandem to reflect specific trade-offs between earnings, sales, and EVA. It seems unlikely that an executive operating under these two plans would be able to quantify, or even understand, the implicit cost of capital reduction or the EVA-sales trade-off.

In short, while the concerns that motivate the use of non-EVA measures in senior management bonus plans are genuine, unless companies exercise special care, few if any benefits will be realized and a heavy cost may be imposed in the form of greater confusion among managers over corporate goals. In addition, while the use of non-EVA measures does not by itself signal a lack of commitment to EVA, there is some evidence that companies add such measures because they have not fully bought into the logic of EVA-based compensation. Based on our sample of firms, EVA companies that use non-EVA measures are less likely to use three key plan design features that significantly increase wealth leverage: multiyear targets (for example, setting ΔEVA goals over a five-year horizon, as we did in the Hershey example), uncapped bonus payouts, and negative bonus banks:

	Companies Using EVA with Other Measures (*N* = 22)	Companies Only Using EVA Measure (*N* = 32)
Multiyear targets	2	14
Uncapped bonuses	2	11
Negative bonus banks	2	16
Any of the three features	3	19

This finding suggests that companies that combine EVA with other measures may be less committed to other critical aspects of EVA-linked compensation.

Companies Using EVA Only

Of the 32 companies using EVA as their only performance measure, 12 use a bonus bank with the typical payout rule of the modern EVA bonus plan: pay 100 percent of the bonus bank balance (if positive), up to the amount of the target bonus, plus one-third of the bank balance in excess of the target bonus. No bonus is paid when the bank balance is negative. Another seven of these 32 companies use similar payout rules. Insteel Industries and Webster have the same payout rule for positive bank balances, but they do not disclose whether negative bank balances are recognized. Knape & Vogt and Manitowoc have the same payout rule for positive bank balances, but a modified payout rule when the bonus

bank balance is negative. In such cases, the companies pay whatever bonus is earned in the year up to one-third of the target
bonus. Briggs & Stratton and Harnischfeger pay 100 percent of
the bonus bank balance (if positive), up to 125 percent of the
target bonus, plus one-third of the bank balance in excess of 125
percent of the target bonus. Briggs & Stratton also has a modified
payout rule for negative bonus banks. When the bonus bank balance is negative, the company pays out any bonus earned in the
year up to 75 percent of the target bonus. Furon pays the bonus
earned, from 0 percent to 100 percent of the target bonus in cash
and from 100 percent to 150 percent of the target bonus in deferred
stock, and they bank any bonus in excess of 150 percent of the
target bonus.

The payout rule modifications of Briggs & Stratton, Furon,
Knape & Vogt, and Manitowoc are designed to mitigate the penalty of poor performance and, hence, reduce retention risk. This
comes at a cost, however. Paying bonuses when the bank balance
is negative reduces the alignment of bonus compensation with
EVA improvement and shareholder wealth. A negative bank implies that the cumulative bonus paid exceeds management's share
of the cumulative excess EVA improvement (plus the cumulative
target bonus). A policy of paying no bonus when the bank balance
is negative provides better alignment unless it leads to a crisis
situation requiring the forgiveness of negative bonus balances. In
1999, Harnischfeger forgave negative bank balances, and International Multifoods announced that any negative bank balance in
the first year of its EVA implementation would be forgiven. A
major challenge of EVA bonus plan calibration is to limit the risk
of plan failure (and the need for bonus bank forgiveness) while
maintaining alignment and substantial leverage.

Early EVA implementers, like Crane and Cilcorp (a company
that has since dropped EVA from its bonus plan), tended to use
the XY plan. This approach requires no explicit concept of target
EVA performance, but it makes retention risk more difficult to
manage because it lacks a concept of target bonus. "Second stage"
implementers, like Furon, which began its implementation in September 1992, use the bonus multiple model expressed in terms of
the difference between actual and target EVA:

$$\text{Bonus} = \text{target bonus} \times [1 + (\text{actual EVA} - \text{target EVA})/\text{EVA interval})]$$

An early approach to setting EVA targets was to make the current-year EVA target the average of the prior-year EVA and the prior-year EVA target. This is equivalent to making the target EVA equal to prior-year EVA plus half of the difference between prior-year actual and prior-year target:

$$\text{Target EVA}_1 = (\text{EVA}_0 + \text{target EVA}_0)/2$$

$$= \text{EVA}_0 + 50\% (\text{target EVA}_0 - \text{EVA}_0)$$

Furon modified this formula to limit the target reduction on the downside to 30 percent of the prior year shortfall:

> Under the formula, the Company's target EVA performance for a fiscal year will be the prior year's target plus 50 percent of the difference between that target and actual EVA performance if the actual EVA performance equals or exceeds the target or, if it does not, it will be the prior year's target less an amount equal to 30 percent of the difference between that target and the actual EVA performance. [1999 proxy]

The Furon approach to target setting was later modified to make target EVA equal to the average of the prior-year EVA and the prior-year EVA target, plus an expected improvement:

$$\text{Target EVA}_1 = (\text{EVA}_0 + \text{target EVA}_0)/2$$

$$+ \text{ expected EVA improvement}$$

Manitowoc, Briggs & Stratton, and C. H. Heist (among others) continue to use this formula. Here is Manitowoc's description of the EVA target:

> To measure the improvement (or deterioration) in EVA, an EVA target is set yearly for each business unit based on the average of the prior fiscal year's target and actual EVA plus the expected improvement in EVA for the current fiscal year. [1999 proxy]

Briggs & Stratton's target calculation drops the expected EVA improvement once the average of prior-year actual and prior-year target exceeds $25 million:

> The Target EVA is the average of the Target EVA and Actual EVA for the prior Plan year plus an Expected Improvement. Expected Improvement for each fiscal year is $4 million. In the event the average of the Target EVA and the Actual EVA for the prior year exceeds $25 million, the Expected Improvement factor will not be added to the target. [1998 proxy]

Averaging prior-year actual and prior-year target was designed to increase bonus plan leverage (relative to using prior-year actual only). When prior-year performance exceeds target, the current-year target is less than the prior-year actual, and when prior-year performance has fallen short of target, the current-year target is greater than the prior year's actual. For example, if prior-year actual EVA is $20 while the prior-year target is $10, the current-year target is $15, or $5 less than the prior-year actual. If prior-year EVA is $0 with the same $10 target, the current-year target will be $5, or $5 more than the prior-year actual. Relative to using prior-year actual only, averaging prior-year actual and prior-year target lowers targets (and increases payouts) for superior performance and raises targets (and reduces payouts) for poor performance.

The main disadvantage of the averaging approach is that it commingles target setting and leverage decisions and, hence, makes the implications of each more difficult to understand. Target setting should focus on determining the expected EVA improvement—that is, the EVA improvement needed for investors to earn a cost-of-capital return on market value. The calculation of expected EVA improvement is much easier when improvement is measured relative to prior-year actual than when it is measured relative to the average of prior-year actual and prior-year expected EVA improvement. Leverage analysis ultimately focuses on the probability of a negative bonus bank. This analysis is also much simpler when EVA improvement is measured relative to the prior-year actual.

More recent EVA implementers have largely abandoned the averaging of prior-year actual and prior-year target in favor of prior-year actual plus expected improvement. Some companies, like Federal Mogul, focus on a bonus multiple:

Specifically, the Bonus Multiple will be calculated under the following formula:

Bonus Multiple = 1 + (EVA Improvement

 − Expected Improvement)/EVA Interval

The EVA Improvement is the actual increase in EVA for the plan year, compared to the prior year. The Expected Improvement is the expected increase in EVA prescribed by the Compensation Committee for the plan year. The EVA Interval is a leveraging factor determined by the Compensation Committee, and represents the amount by which the EVA Improvement must exceed the Expected Improvement for a participant's bonus to be greater than one times his or her target bonus [1999 proxy].

Other companies, like SPX, focus on the share of excess EVA improvement:

The EVA bonus plan is based on three key concepts: (1) a target bonus, (2) a fixed share of EVA improvement in excess of expected EVA improvement ("excess EVA improvement") and (3) a bonus bank. The EVA bonus earned is equal to the sum of the target bonus plus the fixed share of excess EVA improvement (which may be negative) [1997 proxy].

Most companies that use expected EVA improvement have been content, like Federal Mogul, to simply characterize it as a company goal. A few companies have sought to explain the intended linkage between expected EVA improvement and investor returns:

The Expected Improvement is intended to reflect the stock market's expectation of annual EVA® growth, based upon the share price of the Company's common stock [Herman Miller 1998 proxy].

The specific year over year EVA improvement goal, known as "Expected EVA Improvement," was established by the Committee by a quantitative analysis intended to reflect the stock market's expectation of annual EVA growth, based upon the share price of the Company's common stock [Montana Power 1999 proxy].

For hundreds of satisfied users, EVA has energized employees and better aligned managerial and shareholder goals. But not all practitioners have been happy with the results. In some cases, EVA has not fulfilled either management or shareholder expectations. A closer look at these failures provides fresh insight into the dos and don'ts of successful EVA implementation.

WHEN IT ALL GOES WRONG: THE ABANDONERS OF EVA

Several companies, including corporate giants such as AT&T, Georgia-Pacific, and Monsanto, enthusiastically embraced EVA only to later curtail their commitment to it in compensation plans and investor communications. EVA continues to be used in these companies, but far less prominently than in the past.

For example, AT&T implemented EVA in 1992 and 1993, gradually extending the EVA bonus plan to its entire white-collar workforce, over 100,000 people in all. The company also featured EVA in communications with investors and actively promoted the use of the metric among its employees. More recently, however, EVA has been supplanted by earnings per share (EPS) and various expense-to-revenue ratios. In short, productivity of capital has taken a backseat to measures that ignore the balance sheet, focusing entirely on current profit performance. Also, the company stopped using EVA in the documents released by its investor relations unit. Our recent review of over 700 documents on the company's investor relations Web site reveals only two with any mention of EVA, and both were released in 1993.

Even more striking than AT&T's retreat is the case of Georgia-Pacific. EVA featured prominently in its 1995 annual report, in the most extensive and ambitious treatment we have ever seen of the subject in public financial disclosures by an EVA company. For this reason, we quote it at length. As the company proclaims in the first pages of the report:

> Our story is about adding VALUE to every ream of paper, every sheet of structural paneling, every share of stock. It is about a new operating standard that defines our progress in economic terms, synchronizing management's goals with our shareholders' financial objectives. It is called EVA, and it's now in place. Please read on . . . .

The report goes on to say

> EVA . . . gauges an organization's success, not by production levels or assets, but by its capacity to produce real after-tax returns. We have linked this financial metric both to the company's operating goals and to a tiered structure of stock and cash incentives. . . . To heighten our returns, we must intelligently streamline the work process. Precise operating targets and incentives encourage everyone, from individual managers to entire divisions, to work smarter and evaluate with care. In effect, G-P's wide-ranging asset base becomes subject to a single perspective—that of the shareholder. How many steps can be refined? How many minutes saved? Because of EVA, time is now more money to more people. . . . EVA supplies the motivation and momentum to sustain more focused scrutiny of each business expense.

In fact, the entire annual report before the discussion of financial results is devoted to EVA. Yet strangely there is no mention of EVA in the annual reports after 1995. Although Georgia-Pacific continues to use EVA, the metric's importance in the company's executive bonus plan and in its communications with investors has been sharply reduced.

Monsanto also reduced its reliance on EVA for both management bonuses and investor relations, placing increased emphasis on more conventional profit measures such as net income and operating income. As further proof of its retreat from EVA, in early 1999 the position of EVA Director was eliminated, and the manager in question was put in charge of the company's Y2K ("millennium bug") preparations. A similar retrenchment occurred at Quaker Oats, formerly a featured client in the advertisements of EVA consultants, Stern Stewart & Company.

Health care provider Grancare dropped its EVA bonus plan and now uses EPS instead. Donaldson has done likewise. Early in 1997 Cilcorp abandoned its EVA bonus plan for all but its top four managers. Around the same time, sport shoe company L.A. Gear replaced its EVA bonus plan with bonus payments based on accounting profits. Premark made similar changes.

So, why did these companies partially or totally abandon their commitment to EVA? We think that the study of their experiences is highly instructive. First, it reveals the issues that companies can find especially frustrating in trying to get EVA to work. Second, it reveals approaches to EVA implementation that increase the likelihood of failure. The causes of EVA failure vary, but our research suggests that two particular problems were overwhelmingly the most important contributing factors.

Why Did They Leave?

First, several companies encountered difficulties in adjusting for special events such as spin-offs, divestitures, and acquisitions. AT&T, for example, struggled to reset EVA targets after Lucent Technologies and NCR were spun off and AT&T Capital was sold, as did Monsanto after the spin-off of its chemical business. Premark faced a similar problem after a major spin-off and divestiture.

Georgia-Pacific had problems in setting targets, although not because of major restructuring events. In 1995 the company exceeded the level of EVA set by top management for maximizing bonuses, which is probably one reason why EVA featured so prominently in that year's annual report. Unfortunately, EVA fell significantly below the maximum in the following two years. Management struggled to recalibrate bonus plan targets in light of adverse changes in commodity prices. L.A. Gear's problems with target setting were brought on by near bankruptcy after a protracted period of heavy losses. These losses meant no EVA-linked bonuses for three consecutive years.

Second, several companies expressed doubts about the relationship between current EVA and shareholder returns. Grancare's compensation committee declared that "fulfilling EPS expectations is the most essential short-term objective for those having corporate responsibilities. It is also simple for . . . members of the Company's Board of Directors and the investment community to understand and is a prevalent performance measure in the healthcare management industry." Directors at AT&T came to a similar conclusion, noting that despite achieving its 1996 EVA target, the company's stock price in that year declined by 9 percent, whereas the broad market rose by 20 percent.

Those Who Left versus Those Who Stayed

While the experiences of these companies may help to explain their disappointment in EVA, our research has revealed three important differences in the way that the companies implemented EVA compared to companies that have continued, or even strengthened, their commitment to EVA:

1. None of the companies that partially or totally abandoned EVA provided managers with an uncapped interest in EVA or EVA improvement.
2. None of the companies adopted multiyear (i.e., deferred) EVA compensation plans. In all cases, EVA bonuses earned were paid out in full in the year in which they were earned.
3. All the companies relied heavily on compensation committee discretion, even after adoption of the EVA bonus plan.

In short, despite public proclamations of corporate support for shareholder value and EVA, and despite bringing EVA into executive bonus plans, these companies compromised on crucial aspects of EVA implementation. By failing to uncap bonuses and to defer a portion of payouts to future years, and by sacrificing bonus plan objectivity to discretion, these companies signaled, perhaps unwittingly, a lack of trust in and genuine commitment to EVA.

We suspect another factor may help to explain the disappointment that some companies have experienced after implementing EVA. Many companies adopt EVA because of poor economic performance. In the year or two after adoption, companies typically experience a lift from improvements in working capital management and asset productivity, but underlying structural or strategic deficiencies that contributed to unsatisfactory performance may not have been fully addressed. In other words, while incentives for value-creating behavior have been strengthened, flaws in the strategic vision and intent of senior management seriously impair the ability of the company to deliver superior value to its shareholders. As a result, EVA stagnates or even deteriorates. Frustration inevitably sets in and, not surprisingly, the system is blamed.

Of course, EVA heralds the disappointing performance; it doesn't cause it—just as EVA does not substitute for the strategies and actions that deliver superior performance. All the same, it is easy to see how managers in underperforming companies confuse cause and effect.

COMPETITIVE COMPENSATION ANALYSIS

The aim of competitive compensation analysis is to determine an executive's *opportunity cost*—that is, the compensation level the executive could obtain from a competitor in a position requiring comparable skills. Such analysis is indispensable in promoting two important goals of management compensation: reducing retention risk and limiting shareholder cost. It helps companies pay enough to attract and retain talented managers, but it also helps them to avoid paying too much.

To determine competitive compensation for a company's executives, we need to

+ Identify labor market competitors ("peer companies").
+ Match jobs.
+ Determine the elements of compensation to be considered, and calculate the value of each element for the peer company executives.
+ Annualize "lumpy" elements of compensation (e.g., large stock option grants).
+ Adjust for pay inflation.
+ Adjust for size, and then prepare a final pay distribution.

To illustrate how a company determines management compensation, in the next section we'll outline the process for the CEO of Hershey Foods.

Peer Group

The purpose of the peer group is to represent the company's labor market competitors. Identification normally begins with the company's product market competitors and may expand to include companies that are not direct competitors, but that require managers with skills and knowledge that are readily transferable to the company's product markets. While size and (occasionally) performance affect compensation, we prefer to statistically adjust for differences in size and performance, rather than exclude companies from the peer group simply because their size or performance is different from that of the target company.

All but three of the companies in our EVA sample provide a description of their peer group in compensation committee reports. As shown in Table 8–6, most of these companies select their peers, at least in part, on the basis of industry. About two-thirds select peer companies partly on size.

In some companies—including ADC Telecommunications, Case, Coca-Cola, Rubbermaid, Silicon Valley Bank, and Whirlpool—the selection of peers is influenced by performance. Three companies—Calmat, Centura Bank, and Johnson Worldwide—use geographic location as a selection criterion. Hershey defines its peer group as "food industry competitors and general industry companies, adjusted for size." For our analysis of Hershey, we define the peer group as the 39 food and beverage companies in

T A B L E   8—6

Peer Groups Used by EVA Companies

Company	Peer Group
Acxiom Corp.	Information technology industry
ADC Telecommunications Inc.	Comparably sized and performing companies in the communications industry
Armstrong World Inds Inc.	20 leading manufacturing companies with comparable sales
Becton Dickinson & Co.	Product line competitors
Boise Cascade Corp.	53 paper and forest products companies + 270 manufacturing companies
Briggs & Stratton	Companies in same size range and broad industry sector
Heist (C. H.) Corp.	Similarly sized companies
Calmat Co.	Industries tied to the construction industry + similarly sized California companies
Case Corp.	22 similarly sized manufacturing companies + 23 manufacturing companies with strong financial performance
Centura Banks Inc.	3 North Carolina banks + 37 similarly sized U.S. banks
Coca-Cola Co.	Large public companies with superior profit growth and ROE
Columbus Mckinnon Corp.	Manufacturing companies adjusted for size
Crane Co.	Companies of similar size, complexity, and industrial category
EG&G Inc.	Similarly sized companies
Lilly (Eli) & Co.	Global pharmaceutical companies of comparable size and stature
Equifax Inc.	Service companies with $1+ billion revenue
Federal-Mogul Corp.	Similarly sized auto parts companies, 38 metal fabricating companies, and 18 similarly sized industrials
Furon Co.	Similarly sized companies
GC Companies Inc.	Similarly sized companies
Georgia-Pacific Group.	Industrial companies similar in size and complexity
Guidant Corp.	Global medical device companies of comparable size and stature
Harnischfeger Industries Inc.	Comparable companies
Hershey Foods Corp.	Food industry competitors and general industry companies adjusted for size
Insteel Industries	Companies in the same industry

T A B L E   8-6

Peer Groups Used by EVA Companies

Company	Peer Group
Intl Multifoods Corp.	Similarly sized companies
Penney (JC) Co.	Retailers and selected Fortune 200 companies
Johnson Worldwide	Recreation and sporting goods companies and leading mfg cos. in Wisconsin
Kansas City Power & Light	Similarly sized companies in the same industry
Knape & Vogt Mfg. Co.	Companies in comparable industries
Manitowoc Co.	Durable goods manufacturing companies of similar size
Material Sciences Corp.	Similarly sized companies in general industry
Millennium Chemicals Inc.	Commodity, intermediate, and specialty chemical companies
Monsanto Co.	Several hundred pharmaceutical, food, and other manufacturing companies adjusted for size
Montana Power Co.	Utility companies of similar size, other specific industry groups, and general industry
Noble Drilling Corp.	Companies in the same industry
Olin Corp.	Chemical, metals, and metals products companies of similar size
Polaroid Corp.	Ten company cross section of general industry, focus on consumer products
Quaker Oats Co.	Comparable companies
Donnelley (R. R.) & Sons Co.	A broad array of companies in various industries
Rubbermaid Inc.	Similarly sized high performing consumer products companies
Ryder System Inc.	Similar companies
Safety-Kleen Corp.	Similarly sized companies
Silicon Vy Bancshares	Similarly sized companies screened for performance
Sprint Fon Group	Similarly sized telecommunications companies, companies in other industries
SPX Corp.	Middle market industrial companies
Tenet Healthcare Corp.	Health companies adjusted for size and other similarly sized companies
Vulcan Materials Co.	Similarly sized companies
Grainger (W. W.) Inc.	Similarly sized companies
Webster Finl Corp.	Similarly sized financial institutions
Wellman Inc.	Similarly sized companies
Whirlpool Corp.	Blue chip companies similar in size, scope, or lines of business

the Standard & Poor Execucomp database with $100 million or more in sales. These companies, along with their sales and market capitalizations, are listed in Table 8–7.

Matching Jobs

The aim here is to ensure that compensation data are truly comparable. Otherwise, the observed pay levels may relate to executives with very different responsibilities than those of the target executives. Job matching issues are straightforward for the CEO position because all CEOs have similar responsibilities. Strong matches can also be found in "top of function" positions, such as chief financial officer or general counsel. Business unit heads also tend to be a strong match because responsibilities are highly similar across a large group of companies. But job matching can be more difficult and less certain for other managers.

Elements of Compensation

We limit the elements of compensation to those reported in the proxy statement filed with the SEC: base salary, bonus, other annual compensation, stock grants, stock options, long-term incentive plan payouts, and other compensation.[10] Normal retirement benefits are excluded because they are difficult to value based on the data reported in the proxy. Except for stock options, we value the elements of compensation based on the values that appear in the proxy statement. Our stock option values are based on the Black-Scholes option pricing model.

The Black-Scholes model says that the value of an option depends on six factors:

- The current price of the stock
- The exercise price of the option
- The term of the option
- The "risk-free" rate of interest

10. Unfortunately, outside the United States, public disclosure on corporate compensation practices is less extensive, which naturally imposes limits on competitive compensation analysis. Still, recent trends on corporate disclosure, especially in Western Europe, are promising.

T A B L E 8–7

Peer Group of Companies in the Food and Beverage Industry*

Company	CEO	Sales	Market Cap.
Conagra Inc.	Rohde	23,841	17,972
Sara Lee Corp.	Bryan	20,011	29,711
Coca-Cola Co.	Ivester	18,813	170,339
Coca-Cola Enterprises	Schimberg	13,414	25,146
IBP Inc.	Peterson	12,849	3,408
Anheuser-Busch Cos. Inc.	Busch III	11,246	35,995
Heinz (H.J.) Co.	O'Reilly	9,209	22,914
Bestfoods	Shoemate	8,374	18,008
Tyson Foods Inc.	Tollett	7,414	6,716
Kellogg Co.	Langbo	6,762	16,057
Campbell Soup Co.	Morrison	6,696	26,766
General Mills Inc.	Sanger	6,033	12,623
Quaker Oats Co.	Morrison	4,843	9,060
Ralston Purina Co.	McGinnis	4,653	11,608
Hershey Foods Corp.	Wolfe	4,436	10,184
Dole Food Co Inc.	Murdock	4,424	2,989
Smithfield Foods Inc.	Luter III	3,867	1,556
Flowers Industries Inc.	McMullian	3,776	3,772
Suiza Foods Corp.	Engles	3,321	3,457
Interstate Bakeries CP	Sullivan	3,266	2,659
Hormel Foods Corp.	Johnson	3,261	2,604

351

T A B L E 8-7

Continued

Company	CEO	Sales	Market Cap.*
Dean Foods Co.	Dean	2,736	2,548
International Multifoods Corp.	Costley	2,297	564
Wrigley (Wm.) Jr. Co.	Wrigley	2,005	10,399
Coors (Adolph)	Coors	1,900	2,214
McCormick & Co.	Lawless	1,881	2,834
Earthgrains Co.	Beracha	1,719	1,210
Brown-Forman	Brown II	1,669	4,065
Whitman Corp.	Chelberg	1,558	3,744
Vlasic Foods International	Bernstock	1,357	1,378
Canandaigua Brands	Sands	1,213	1,470
Breyer's Grand Ice Cream Inc.	Rogers	1,022	692
Michael Foods Inc.	Ostrander	1,020	799
Coca-Cola Bottling Cos.	Harrison III	929	1,002
Universal Foods Corp.	Manning	857	1,409
Triarc Cos Inc.	Peltz	815	1,174
Ralcorp Holdings Inc.	Micheletto	583	444
Lance Inc.	Stroup III	486	598
J&J Snack Foods Corp.	Shreiber	262	224

* In millions of dollars.

Note: Sales figures are from 1997, and market capitalization is as of 31 December 1997.

- The volatility of the underlying stock
- The dividend yield of the underlying stock

Volatility is a measure of the variability of a stock's rate of return. Theoretically, the model calls for expected future volatility, but historical volatility is used instead because expectations cannot be directly observed. Historical volatility is measured as the annualized standard deviation of the stock's rate of return (expressed in logarithms) for some historical period. Our estimate of Hershey's stock price volatility, based on five years of monthly returns ending in December 1998, is 0.20.

A typical executive option is exercisable at the market price of the stock on the date of the grant (in this case, $62.08) and has a 10-year term. For Hershey, with a volatility of 0.20 and a dividend yield of 2.0 percent, the value of a 10-year option exercisable at the 1998 grant price of $62.08 is $18.59, or about 30 percent of the market price. The following table shows the sensitivity of option value to changes in each of the parameters, holding the current stock price constant:

	Initial Value	New Value	Change in Option Value
Exercise price	Market price	Market price + 50%	−43%
Option term	10 years	5 years	−27%
Risk-free rate	5.1%	6.1%	+11%
Stock volatility	0.20	0.30	+26%
Dividend yield	2.0%	1.0%	+23%

An option provides more compensation leverage than the stock itself because a given percentage change in the value of the stock causes an even greater change in the value of the option. For example, if the price of Hershey stock doubles from $62.08 to $124.16, the value of a 10-year option exercisable at $62.08 increases from $18.59 to $64.65, a 248 percent increase. This makes the option's leverage ratio 2.48, nearly two and one-half times the leverage of the underlying stock. The option also has more leverage on the downside than the stock. If the price of Hershey stock declines by 50 percent to $31.04, the value of the option declines by 84 percent from $18.59 to $3.06.[11]

Total Direct Compensation

Total direct compensation in 1997 for the 39 food and beverage company CEOs ranges from a high of $19.247 million for Morrison of Quaker Oats to a low of $295,000 for Coors of Coors Brewing. Total direct compensation includes base salary, bonus, "other annual" compensation, the grant date value of restricted stock grants, the Black-Scholes value of stock option grants, long-term incentive cash plan payouts, and "other" compensation. Total compensation for Wolfe, the CEO of Hershey Foods, was $3.901 million, well above the median figure of $2.305 million. This does not mean, however, that Wolfe's compensation is high by industry standards. Among the 39 sample companies, Hershey ranks thirteenth in market capitalization and fifteenth in sales. In other words, Hershey's size is above average. As we will see later, when size and other relevant factors are accounted for, Wolfe's compensation is actually below average. The compensation figures for all 39 industry CEOs are summarized in Table 8–8.[12]

The Problem of Lumpy Pay

Total direct compensation for a given year might not be representative because option grant levels and long-term incentive plan

---

11. An important assumption underlying the Black-Scholes model is that expected shareholder returns follow a lognormal distribution, which means that the logarithm of shareholder returns is normally distributed (i.e., it follows a bell-shaped distribution). This implies that actual shareholder wealth equal to 200 percent of expected shareholder wealth is just as likely as actual shareholder wealth equal to 50 percent of expected shareholder wealth, because ln (2) = 0.69 = − ln (.5), and that actual shareholder wealth equal to 1000 percent of expected shareholder wealth is just as likely as actual shareholder wealth equal to 10 percent of expected shareholder wealth. Managers and directors already know this intuitively, because they realize that while a stock can increase in value by 200 percent, it can't decline by more than 100 percent.
12. At this writing, the S&P Execucomp database had 1998 compensation data for some but not all of the peer group executives. We show 1997 total direct compensation to provide a comparison of all peer group CEOs.

T A B L E   8–8

1997 Total Compensation for Food and Beverage Industry CEOs*

Executive	Compensation
Morrison	19.247
Ivester	12.873
Shoemate	9.958
Morrison	8.629
Engles	7.835
Peterson	5.726
Dean	5.700
Sanger	5.444
Busch III	5.358
Rohde	5.114
Bryan	4.975
Langbo	4.411
Peltz	4.323
Wolfe	3.901
O'Reilly	3.489
Tollett	3.443
Bernstock	3.390
Chelberg	3.068
Luter III	2.474
Schimberg	2.305
Costley	2.105
Murdock	2.066
McGinnis	2.060
Sullivan	1.933
Rogers	1.898
Brown II	1.884
Wrigley	1.736
Sands	1.407
Beracha	1.388
Manning	1.379
Harrison III	1.274
Lawless	1.256
Micheletto	1.202
Ostrander	1.127
McMullian	1.011
Johnson	0.988
Shreiber	0.831
Stroup III	0.591
Coors	0.295

* In millions of dollars.

payouts can vary substantially from one year to the next. For example, the total direct compensation of Quaker Oats' Morrison, the highest paid CEO in 1997, declined by 63 percent in 1998. Meanwhile, Schimberg of Coca-Cola Enterprises and Bryan of Sara Lee received substantial increases in total direct compensation in 1998. Schimberg's pay increased by 460 percent, from $2.305 million to $12.906 million, while Bryan's increased by 207 percent, from $4.975 million to $15.297 million (see Table 8–9).

We use a multiyear average to get a better estimate of "normal" compensation, although this approach is not without its problems. As we increase the number of years included in the average, we increase the likelihood of capturing all significant special grants, but we also tend to understate the current rate of pay. Prior years tend to have lower pay because of general pay inflation and the inclusion of more years of pre-CEO service. From 1992 to 1998, the median annual increase in total direct compensation for continuing CEOs in the Execucomp database has ranged from 8.0 percent to 16.3 percent, with an average of 12.5 percent. To limit the impact of prior position pay, we use a three-year compensation average, but make two adjustments for special grants.

To capture large option grants made before the three-year period that is used to calculate average pay, we compare the three-year average grant rate with the total number of options held and make an upward adjustment when the number of options held is more than 10× the average grant rate (see Tables 8–10 and 8–11). For executives who hold more than 10 years of grants, based on their three-year average, we increase their average grant until it equals one-tenth of total options held. In effect, we are averaging the excess options over their assumed 10-year life. For Ivester of Coca-Cola, whose three-year average grant is zero, we increase his average grant by 240,000 shares to bring his average grant up to one-tenth of the 2,400,000 shares held. To estimate the expected value at grant of the additional option shares, we assume that the market and exercise price of the additional option shares is equal to the average exercise price of Ivester's exercisable options, $22.63. This gives a Black-Scholes value of $8.67 a share (based on a Black-Scholes ratio value of 0.383) and increases Ivester's average total direct compensation by $2.079 million. We made similar adjustments for five other CEOs in the 39-company sample.

T A B L E   8-9

Three-Year Average Total Compensation for Food and Beverage Industry CEOs*

Executive	3-Year Avg.	1998	1997	1996	1995
Ivester	14.513	20.470	12.873	10.196	9.725
Morrison	13.151	7.055	19.247	—	—
Schimberg	10.845	12.906	2.305	17.325	7.992
Shoemate	10.082	13.219	9.958	7.068	4.639
Bryan	8.327	15.297	4.975	4.709	4.093
Rohde	6.652	—	5.114	8.190	—
Busch III	6.309	8.707	5.358	4.862	5.222
Peterson	5.730	6.249	5.726	5.214	7.229
O'Reilly	5.219	—	3.489	9.069	3.101
Morrison	5.041	5.170	8.629	1.324	1.810
Sanger	5.019	—	5.444	5.174	4.438
Langbo	4.996	5.330	4.411	5.247	4.235
Engles	4.671	5.429	7.835	0.748	—
Beracha	4.658	—	1.388	7.928	—
Bernstock	4.534	5.679	3.390	—	—
McGinnis	3.573	5.444	2.060	3.215	1.976
Wolfe	3.435	3.616	3.901	2.789	1.958
Dean	3.033	—	5.700	2.388	1.012
Chelberg	2.866	—	3.068	3.639	1.890
Peltz	2.414	0.580	4.323	2.339	1.799
Murdock	2.263	1.764	2.066	2.959	2.134
McMullian	2.210	4.190	1.011	1.430	736
Sullivan	1.989	—	1.933	2.824	1.211
Brown II	1.843	—	1.884	1.710	1.935
Tollett	1.805	1.320	3.443	0.651	0.656
Luter III	1.706	—	2.474	1.822	0.823
Rogers	1.678	1.446	1.898	1.690	1.551
Johnson	1.553	2.027	0.988	1.644	1.335
Costley	1.530	1.189	2.105	1.298	—
Sands	1.506	—	1.407	2.241	0.870
Manning	1.446	1.856	1.379	1.103	1.071
Wrigley	1.340	0.665	1.736	1.619	1.528
Harrison III	1.297	1.522	1.274	1.096	0.991
Lawless	1.160	1.558	1.256	0.667	0.366
Ostrander	1.008	1.318	1.127	0.579	0.699
Micheletto	1.000	1.423	1.202	0.376	0.638
Shreiber	0.877	1.044	0.831	0.755	0.753
Stroup III	0.496	0.400	0.591	0.496	0.217
Coors	0.302	0.307	0.295	0.305	0.319

*In millions of dollars

T A B L E   8–10

Three-Year Average Option Grant and Total Option Shares Held by Food and Beverage Industry CEOs*

Executive	3-Year Avg.	Total Option Shares Held	1998	1997	1996	1995
Luter III	0	1200	—	0	0	0
Ivester	0	2400	0	0	0	500
Harrison III	0	150	0	0	0	0
Peltz	117	3516	26	325	0	150
Peterson	30	330	30	30	30	60
Shreiber	25	257	25	25	25	25
Schimberg	200	1897	600	0	0	175
Rogers	107	809	85	120	116	131
Johnson	57	380	70	0	100	40
Sullivan	50	326	—	0	150	0
Murdock	68	446	75	40	90	56
McGinnis	234	1467	402	0	300	195
Manning	80	498	73	76	90	70
Chelberg	111	647	—	135	148	49
Sanger	234	1358	—	208	270	225
Wolfe	55	314	57	48	61	50
Busch III	300	1703	400	300	200	390
Langbo	316	1570	354	274	320	300
Ostrander	56	254	36	89	45	40
Bryan	740	2936	1500	400	320	300
Shoemate	382	1438	427	420	300	90
Dean	120	451	—	216	119	25
Stroup III	20	75	14	18	29	0
Morrison	149	545	200	200	48	70
Lawless	54	179	84	53	25	12
Tollett	100	319	0	300	0	0
O'Reilly	250	750	—	0	750	0
Brown II	19	58	—	27	30	0
Sands	36	107	—	17	90	0
Micheletto	65	196	100	96	0	20
Costley	118	355	30	125	200	—
Engles	162	478	120	353	14	—
McMullian	141	198	198	0	225	0
Wrigley	0	0	0	0	0	0
Coors	0	0	0	0	0	0

*In thousands of dollars.

T A B L E   8–11

Three-Year Average Total Compensation after Option Adjustment for Food and Beverage Industry CEOs*

Executive	3-Year Average	Option Adjustment
Ivester	16,592	2,079
Schimberg	10,845	0
Shoemate	9,801	−281
Bryan	8,292	−35
Busch III	6,309	0
Peterson	5,758	28
Sanger	5,019	0
Langbo	4,996	0
Morrison	4,844	−197
O'Reilly	4,720	−500
Peltz	4,397	1,983
Engles	3,707	−964
McGinnis	3,573	0
Wolfe	3,435	0
Dean	2,942	−91
Chelberg	2,866	0
Murdock	2,263	0
McMullian	2,210	0
Sullivan	1,989	0
Luter III	1,988	282
Brown II	1,843	0
Tollett	1,805	0
Rogers	1,678	0
Johnson	1,553	0
Costley	1,530	0
Sands	1,506	0
Manning	1,446	0
Harrison III	1,423	126
Wrigley	1,340	0
Lawless	1,160	0
Ostrander	1,008	0
Micheletto	1,000	0
Shreiber	881	4
Stroup III	496	0
Coors	302	0

* In thousands of dollars.

To keep recent special grants from overstating the normal grant levels, we make a downward adjustment for executives who (1) hold less than four years of their average annual grant and (2) have an average annual grant value that is greater than the job average annual grant value, expressed as a percent of base salary. For these executives, we reduce their average annual grant until it equals the greater of one-fourth of their total options held or the job average annual grant value, expressed as a percentage of base salary. These rules result in negative option adjustments for 6 of the 39 CEOs. As shown in Table 8-11, three-year average total direct compensation, with adjustment for option grant holdings greater than 10 times the average annual grant or less than 4 times the average annual grant, ranges from $16,592,000 for Ivester of Coca-Cola to $302,000 for Coors of Coors Brewing.[13] No adjustment is required for Wolfe of Hershey Foods. To illustrate the calculations, Ivester's three-year average total direct compensation equals the sum of total compensation for 1996, 1997, and 1998 ($10.196 million + $12.873 million + $20.47 million), divided by 3, plus the option adjustment of $2.079 million. We should note, however, that this does not yield the final total compensation figure because we have not adjusted for pay inflation or differences in company size.

Pay Inflation

To avoid understatement caused by inflation, we adjust prior-year pay figures to current-year equivalents (as of August 1999) and then calculate an inflation adjusted three-year average (see Table 8–12). Our estimate of pay inflation for each year is the average annual total direct compensation increase among all continuing CEOs in the Execucomp database: 16.3 percent for 1996, 15.3 percent for 1997, 11.8 percent for 1998, and 8.2 percent for the first eight months of 1999. The 1999 adjustment is based on the average annual pay inflation since 1992, 12.5 percent. We use the average pay inflation for the entire Execucomp universe, not just food and beverage companies, because the larger sample tends to give a

---

13. For most companies, three-year averages are based on data from 1996 to 1998. For those companies without published 1998 data as of the time that we conducted this analysis, averages are based on 1995 to 1997.

T A B L E   8 – 1 2

Three-Year Average Total Compensation Adjusted for
Pay Inflation for Food and Beverage Industry CEOs*

Executive	3-Year Unadjusted	3-Year Adjusted	1998	1997	1996	1995	Infl.-Adj. Option Adj.
Ivester	16,592	20,680	22,142	15,567	14,217	15,770	3,371
Schimberg	10,845	13,635	13,960	2,787	24,157	12,960	0
Shoemate	9,801	11,729	14,299	12,043	9,856	7,522	−336
Bryan	8,292	10,257	17,550	6,382	6,965	7,040	−42
Busch III	6,309	7,559	9,419	6,480	6,779	8,469	0
Peterson	5,758	7,031	6,760	6,925	7,270	11,723	46
Sanger	5,019	6,664	—	6,269	6,869	6,852	0
O'Reilly	4,720	6,347	—	4,057	12,159	4,834	−670
Peltz	4,397	6,254	627	5,227	3,262	2,918	3,215
Langbo	4,996	6,139	5,766	5,335	7,316	6,868	0
Morrison	4,844	6,016	5,873	10,960	1,939	3,084	−241
McGinnis	3,573	4,416	6,064	2,566	4,617	3,300	0
Engles	3,707	4,342	5,873	9,475	1,044	—	−1,121
Wolfe	3,435	4,172	3,911	4,718	3,889	3,176	0
Chelberg	2,866	3,950	—	3,710	5,074	3,065	0
Dean	2,942	3,655	—	6,563	3,170	1,563	−110
Murdock	2,263	2,844	1,908	2,499	4,126	3,460	0
Luter III	1,988	2,675	—	2,877	2,443	1,283	475
Sullivan	1,989	2,615	—	2,225	3,749	1,869	0
McMullian	2,210	2,583	4,532	1,223	1,993	1,194	0
Brown II	1,843	2,500	—	2,190	2,293	3,018	0
Tollett	1,805	2,231	1,471	4,288	934	1,095	0
Rogers	1,678	2,072	1,564	2,296	2,356	2,516	0
Sands	1,506	2,038	—	1,668	3,065	1,383	0
Johnson	1,553	1,931	2,236	1,219	2,338	2,208	0
Costley	1,530	1,844	1,261	2,496	1,774	—	0
Manning	1,446	1,790	2,067	1,718	1,583	1,788	0
Harrison III	1,423	1,776	1,646	1,541	1,528	1,606	205
Wrigley	1,340	1,692	719	2,100	2,257	2,478	0
Lawless	1,160	1,391	1,702	1,534	939	599	0
Micheletto	1,000	1,208	1,586	1,497	540	1,066	0
Ostrander	1,008	1,199	1,425	1,363	808	1,134	0
Shreiber	881	1,102	1,163	1,035	1,085	1,257	7
Stroup III	496	613	433	715	691	352	0
Coors	302	371	332	356	425	518	0

*In thousands of dollars.

more complete and reliable estimate of true pay inflation in the executive labor market.

The following table shows the calculation of inflation-adjusted total direct compensation for Ivester of Coca-Cola (dollar amounts in thousands):

Year	Pay Inflation	Actual TDC	Inflation Adjusted TDC
1996	16.3%	$10,196	$14,217
1997	15.3%	12,873	15,567
1998	11.8%	20,470	22,142
1999	8.2%		

The 1996 actual total direct compensation is increased for pay inflation in 1997, 1998, and 1999. The calculation of inflated adjusted total direct compensation for 1996 is $14.217 million [$10,196 $\times$ (1.153) $\times$ (1.118) $\times$ (1.082)]. We also inflate the previous option adjustment for pay inflation in 1996 and after, because the additional option shares were granted in 1995 or earlier.

Size-Adjusted Compensation

The final step in competitive compensation analysis is to normalize the pay figures for size. Two issues are raised here. First, how do we define size, and second, how do we define the relationship between size and compensation. Sales is the most commonly used size measure in compensation analysis, but sales comparisons can be distorted by differences in the legal structure of the distribution chain. For example, Coca-Cola's sales do not include the full sales of its bottling companies (only the value of the concentrate sold to its bottlers) because Coca-Cola owns less than 50 percent of its bottlers. Coca-Cola's market capitalization (i.e., market equity value plus debt), on the other hand, does reflect the economic value of Coke's interest in its bottlers' sales. For the peer group CEOs, sales and market capitalization both explain 59 percent of the variation in total direct compensation. For all top five executives reported in the proxy, market capitalization (and pay rank) explain 74 percent of the variation in total direct compensation, while sales (and pay rank) only explain 69 percent. For this reason, we use market capitalization in the analysis that follows even though sales is the more traditional size measure.

The next issue is to define the relationship between size (market value) and pay. The simplest relationship is a linear one between dollars of compensation and dollars of company size, which implies that each additional dollar of company size increases CEO total compensation by a fixed amount. But while this relationship may be simple, it does a poor job of explaining the actual relationship between company size and CEO pay. The reason is that each additional dollar of company size tends to add a diminishing amount to executive compensation. For example, if a company is worth $5 billion and its CEO receives pay of X, a CEO of a company with a market value of $10 billion doesn't receive 2X, but usually a smaller amount.

A linear relationship between the logarithm of pay and the logarithm of company size provides a better fit:

$$Ln \text{ (pay)} = a + b \times Ln \text{ (size)}$$

When we take the antilog of this equation, the relationship becomes

$$\text{Pay} = e^a \times (\text{size})^b$$

From this expression, we can see that a doubling in size (i.e., new size = 2 × size) increases pay by a ratio of 2^b:

$$\text{New pay} = e^a \times (2 \times \text{size})^b = 2^b \times e^a \times (\text{size})^b = 2^b \times \text{Old pay}$$

Defining the relationship in this way implies that any given percentage change in size results in a constant percentage change in compensation. Our statistical analysis for the food and beverage industry, using conventional least-squares regression, implies that a 100 percent increase in market capitalization results in a 37 percent increase in total compensation. To adjust the actual compensation of a peer company CEO for the size difference between the peer company and Hershey Foods, we multiply the CEO's actual compensation by (Hershey size/peer-company size)^b. When Hershey is larger than the peer company, the peer company's size-adjusted compensation is greater than its actual compensation, and when Hershey is smaller than the peer company, the peer company's size-adjusted compensation is less than its actual compensation. Using this technique, we can get normalized compensation figures for each CEO in our sample. Table 8–13 shows the actual and size-adjusted total compensation for each of the 34 peer companies adjusted to Hershey's market value of $10.184 billion.

The median size and inflation-adjusted average total direct compensation (adjusted to Hershey's size) is $4.981 million. For Hershey's CEO, this size-adjusted figure is closer to a meaningful "market rate." Of the 34 cases (excluding Hershey), 22 fall within 30 percent of the median and only one executive (Peterson of IBP) has a size-adjusted compensation level that is more than double the median. The average total direct compensation for Wolfe (Hershey's CEO), $4.172 million, is about 16 percent below the median and ranks 24th among the 35 companies. Interestingly, we find that the level of stock ownership of the peer company CEOs has no statistically significant effect on compensation. Nor does firm performance, measured by the five-year total shareholder return.

The median CEO salary, adjusted for size (to Hershey's market capitalization) and pay inflation, is $932,000, and the median CEO cash compensation (i.e., salary plus bonus) adjusted for size and pay inflation is $1.768 million, about 90 percent of salary.

TOTAL WEALTH LEVERAGE OF CORPORATE OFFICERS IN EVA COMPANIES

In our discussion of EVA bonus calibration, we saw that the wealth leverage of cash compensation was a weighted average of the leverage of base salary (which is zero) and the leverage of the EVA bonus (1.56 for the Hershey calibration). We also saw that by changing the mix of cash compensation from 50 percent salary/50 percent bonus to 36 percent salary/64 percent bonus, we could raise cash compensation leverage from 0.78 to 1.00, or entrepreneurial wealth leverage. In this section, we extend our analysis to incorporate all elements of total compensation as well as stock owned and options held. Our total wealth leverage estimate is a weighted average of the leverage of

- Stock owned
- Options held
- Current year realized compensation

T A B L E   8–13

Inflation and Size-Adjusted Total Compensation for
Peer Companies of Hershey

Executive	Market Value ($000,000)	3-Year Average, Infl.-Adjusted ($000)	Infl. and Size Adjusted Average ($000)
Peterson	3,408	7,031	11,582
Shoemate	18,008	11,729	9,045
Schimberg	25,146	13,635	9,029
Engles	3,457	4,342	7,107
Rogers	692	2,072	7,062
Costley	564	1,844	6,900
Dean	2,548	3,655	6,876
Luter III	1,556	2,675	6,301
Bryan	29,711	10,257	6,295
Shreiber	224	1,102	6,283
Peltz	1,174	6,254	6,254
Chelberg	3,744	3,950	6,234
Sanger	12,623	6,664	6,042
Ivester	170,339	20,680	5,724
Harrison III	1,002	1,776	5,113
Micheletto	444	1,208	5,039
Langbo	16,057	6,139	4,988
Murdock	2,989	2,844	4,974
Sands	1,470	2,038	4,928
Sullivan	2,659	2,615	4,823
Manning	1,409	1,790	4,410
O'Reilly	22,914	6,347	4,385
Busch III	35,995	7,559	4,250
Wolfe	10,184	4,172	4,172
McGinnis	11,608	4,416	4,160
McMullian	3,772	2,583	4,063
Morrison	26,766	6,016	3,872
Ostrander	799	1,199	3,826
Brown II	4,065	2,500	3,800
Johnson	2,604	1,931	3,596
Tollett	6,716	2,231	2,698
Lawless	2,834	1,391	2,493
Stroup III	598	613	2,233
Wrigley	10,399	1,692	1,676
Coors	2,214	371	744

- Expected future compensation for years 1 to 5
- Expected future compensation for years 6 to 10

Our estimates ignore two components of wealth: expected future compensation beyond year 10 and pensions. We ignore compensation beyond year 10 because expected job tenure for most CEOs is unlikely to exceed 10 years. We ignore pensions because of the difficulty of estimating pension wealth leverage from public disclosures.

Wealth Leverage of Stock and Options Held

The wealth leverage of stock owned is 1.00, since any percentage change in shareholder wealth causes an equal percentage change in the value of stock owned. We calculate the leverage of options held using the Black-Scholes model and a 25 percent stock price change. The Black-Scholes value of a 10-year Hershey option exercisable at the 1998 grant price of $62.08 is $18.59 (assuming the current market price is also $62.08). If the stock price increases 25 percent to $77.60, the Black-Scholes value of the option increases by 56.7 percent to $29.14. This makes the wealth leverage of the option 2.27 (56.7 percent/25 percent). For options held, we estimate wealth leverage based on a 25 percent increase over the 1998 year-end stock price, using the actual exercise price and remaining term of the options. We assume a five-year remaining term for exercisable options and an eight-year remaining term for unexercisable options. For the CEOs of the EVA companies, the median leverage of exercisable options is 1.91, while the median leverage of unexercisable options is 1.86.

The leverage of an option differs from the leverage of the stock in two important ways. The leverage of an option can be much greater than 1.0 (and never less than 1.0), while the leverage of the stock is always 1.0. In addition, unlike the leverage of the stock, the leverage of the option changes as the stock price changes and the option comes closer to expiration. The leverage of an option declines as the option comes into the money and increases as the option falls out of the money and comes closer to expiration. The following table shows the leverage of several different options for a company with Hershey's volatility (0.20) and dividend yield (2 percent):

Exercise Price	Market Price	Option Term	Option Leverage
$50	$50	10	2.3
$50	$50	5	3.3
$50	$50	1	8.4
$50	$40	1	20.2

The high leverage of options and the EVA bonus plan play a critical role in designing strong total wealth incentives because they make it possible to design a total compensation program that offsets the effect of base salary (which has zero leverage) and provides total wealth leverage that equals or even exceeds that of an entrepreneur. If 30 percent of the executive's total wealth is the present value of future salary, but the remaining 70 percent is held in options or an EVA bonus with a leverage of 1.45, total wealth leverage is 1.02 [(0.3 × 0) + (0.7 × 1.45)].

Wealth Leverage of Current-Year Compensation

To estimate the wealth leverage of current-year compensation, we make the following assumptions and calculations:

♦ The leverage of base salary, "other annual," and "other compensation" is zero.
♦ The leverage of bonus and long-term incentive (LTI) cash compensation is 1.56 (an assumption based on the leverage of the EVA bonus plan we calibrated for Hershey earlier in this chapter).
♦ The leverage of current-year stock grants is 1.0.
♦ The leverage of current-year option grants is calculated from the Black-Scholes model using a 25 percent stock price change.

The wealth leverage of current-year compensation for the EVA company CEOs ranges from 0.26 for Insteel CEO Howard Woltz III to 1.97 for Sprint CEO William Esrey. As one would expect, Woltz' compensation is heavily weighted on salary, while Esrey's is heavily weighted on options:

Pay Components	Woltz Pct. of Comp.	Woltz Leverage	Esrey Pct. of Comp.	Esrey Leverage
Salary and other	87%	0.00	7%	0.00
Bonus	0%		6%	1.56
LTI cash	0%		8%	1.56
Options	13%	2.09	79%	2.21
Average		0.26		1.97

Wealth Leverage of Future Compensation

The wealth leverage of future compensation depends on how targets and opportunities are adjusted in response to performance. If a company has a competitive pay policy—that is, a policy of recalibrating targets and opportunities each year to maintain the expected value of current compensation at a competitive level—the wealth leverage of future compensation is zero. A company with a competitive pay policy for options uses a target grant value and annually adjusts the number of option shares to maintain the target grant value.

For example, suppose that the target option value is $100,000 and that the Black-Scholes value of the company's options is 30 percent of the grant price. To provide the target option value when the stock price is $10, the company needs to provide an option on 33,333 shares. If the stock price doubles to $20, the company only needs to provide an option on 16,667 shares. This means that an increase in shareholder wealth has no effect on the value of future option grants (it remains at $100,000), and hence, the wealth leverage of future option grants is zero. A company with a competitive pay policy resets the operating performance target each year to reflect current expected performance, usually budgeted performance, and does not use a bonus bank (which makes current bonus payouts depend on prior performance). Such a policy means that the expected bonus is always equal to the target bonus regardless of changes in shareholder wealth, and hence, the wealth leverage of future bonus payments is zero.

An EVA bonus plan with multiyear targets and a bonus bank links future compensation to current performance. If the stock price doubles because investors expect increased EVA, future bonus payouts increase because expected EVA improvement is not recalibrated. For the Hershey EVA bonus calibration, the multiyear wealth leverage of the EVA bonus is 1.56. Three types of option grant guidelines also link future compensation to current performance: fixed-share, front-loaded, and "bonus purchase" grant guidelines. Fixed-share grant guidelines provide an option on a fixed number of shares each year. If the stock price doubles from $10 to $20, the Black-Scholes value of the annual option grant also doubles. This means that the wealth leverage of future option grants under fixed-share grant guidelines is 1.00. Front-loaded option grant guidelines provide a single up-front grant in lieu of two or more years of regular annual grants. If the stock price doubles, the front-loaded option grant (including the shares granted in lieu of subsequent annual grants) more than doubles in value. Bonus purchase grant guidelines use an operating performance bonus to determine the size of the annual option grant. A special case of such guidelines is found in leveraged stock options, or LSOs, which allow managers to use EVA bonus awards to "purchase" shares.

Many EVA companies use formula bonus targets, negative bonus banks, bonus purchase grant guidelines, fixed-share option grant guidelines, and front-loaded option grants to strengthen their wealth leverage. Table 8–14 provides some examples.

To estimate the wealth leverage of future compensation for years 1 to 5, we make the following assumptions and calculations:

- The leverage of future base salary, "other annual" and "other compensation" is 0.0.
- The leverage of future bonus and long-term incentive cash compensation is 1.56 (this assumption is based on the leverage of the EVA bonus plan we calibrated for Hershey earlier in this chapter).
- The leverage of future stock grants is 1.0.
- The leverage of future option grants is 1.0.

On this basis, the wealth leverage of years 1 to 5 future compensation for the EVA company CEOs ranges from 0.13 for Insteel CEO Howard Woltz III to 1.16 for Pulte CEO Burgess:

T A B L E   8–14

Wealth Leverage Enhancement Policies Used
by EVA Companies

Company	Policies
Heist (C. H.) Corp.	Formula bonus targets, LSOs
Centura Banks Inc.	Formula bonus targets, LSOs, indexed LSO purchase price
Miller (Herman) Inc.	Formula bonus targets, negative banks, bonus purchase grant guidelines
SPX Corp.	Formula bonus targets, negative banks, fixed-share options, special grants
Penney (JC) Co.	Formula bonus targets, negative banks, three-year front-loaded options
Furon Co.	Formula bonus targets, negative banks, fixed-share options
Harnischfeger Industries Inc.	Formula bonus targets, negative banks, front-loaded options
Knape & Vogt Mfg. Co.	Formula bonus targets, negative banks, LSOs
Briggs & Stratton	Formula bonus targets, negative banks, LSOs
Crane Co.	Formula bonus targets, negative banks
Lilly (Eli) & Co.	Formula bonus targets, negative banks
Federal-Mogul Corp.	Formula bonus targets, negative banks
GC Companies Inc.	Formula bonus targets, negative banks
Johnson Worldwide	Formula bonus targets, negative banks
Manitowoc Co.	Formula bonus targets, negative banks
Montana Power Co.	Formula bonus targets, negative banks
Donnelley (R. R.) & Sons Co.	Multiyear bonus targets
Kansas City Power & Light	Negative banks
Bausch & Lomb Inc.	Negative bonus banks
Intl Multifoods Corp.	Bonus purchase grant guidelines
Tenet Healthcare Corp.	Front-loaded option grants
Ball Corp.	Front-loaded options in 98 for 99-01
CDI Corp.	Front-loaded stock and option grants
Equifax Inc.	Multiyear option grants
Becton Dickinson & Co.	Performance based option grant guidelines
Whirlpool Corp.	Special career stock grants
Sprint Fon Group	Special option grants
Webster Finl Corp Waterbury	Special option grants
ADC Telecommunications Inc.	Special premium option grant in 97

Pay Components	Woltz % of Comp.	Woltz Leverage	Burgess % of Comp.	Burgess Leverage
Salary and other	87	0.00	10	0.00
Bonus	0		14	1.56
LTI cash	0		33	1.56
Options	13	1.00	43	1.00
Average		0.13		1.16

We assume that the wealth leverage of years 6 to 10 future compensation is zero because we anticipate that few EVA companies will maintain their EVA bonus parameters or option grant guidelines for more than five years without recalibration.

Total Wealth Leverage

The total wealth leverage of the EVA company CEOs ranges from 0.27 for Drew Jennings of Kansas City Power & Light to 1.36 for William Esrey of Sprint:

	Jennings % of Wealth	Jennings Leverage	Esrey % of Wealth	Esrey Leverage
Stock	11	1.00	12	1.00
Options held	0		53	1.86
Current year comp	10	0.37	4	1.97
Yrs 1–5 comp	44	0.27	17	1.01
Yrs 6–10 comp	35	0	14	0
Total/weighted average	100	0.27	100	1.36

Table 8–15 shows the total wealth leverage of the 50 EVA company CEOs with sufficient data in the Execucomp database to permit wealth leverage calculations.

The Importance of Option Grant Guidelines

Assuming fixed-share option grant guidelines and the leverage of the Hershey EVA bonus calibration, the median total wealth leverage of the EVA company CEOs is 0.85, or 85 percent of entrepreneurial wealth leverage. If we assume competitive option grant

T A B L E 8-15

Total Wealth Leverage of EVA Company CEOs

Executive	Wealth Leverage	Stock % of Wealth	Options % of Wealth	Current Comp. % of Wealth	Years 1-5 Compensation % of Wealth	Years 6-10 Compensation % of Wealth	Old Option Leverage	New Option Leverage	Current Compensation Leverage	Years 1-5 Comp Leverage
Esrey	1.36	12	53	4	17	14	1.86	2.21	1.97	1.01
Shapiro	1.14	28	26	5	23	18	2.11	2.01	1.76	0.99
Taylor	1.07	13	20	8	34	27	2.38	2.66	1.46	1.10
Castellini	1.07	5	50	5	22	17	1.45	1.94	1.59	0.93
Barbakow	1.06	1	58	5	20	16	1.36	1.78	1.40	0.94
Stratton, Jr.	1.05	59	11	3	15	12	2.61	2.46	1.47	0.79
Taurel	1.03	25	41	4	17	13	1.34	1.91	1.50	1.03
James	1.00	23	24	6	26	21	1.83	2.53	1.51	0.90
Burns	1.00	14	20	8	33	26	2.67	2.14	1.28	0.73
Morgan, Jr.	0.98	82	9	1	4	4	1.33	1.46	0.99	0.74
Burgess	0.98	1	28	8	35	28	1.58	1.72	1.47	1.16
Ivester	0.96	42	23	4	17	14	1.38	1.96	1.21	1.02
Correll	0.96	13	25	7	31	24	2.01	1.79	1.26	0.75
Wolfe	0.96	17	20	7	31	25	1.74	2.27	1.39	1.10
Ringler	0.94	8	38	6	27	21	1.39	1.80	1.28	0.98
Chapman	0.94	13	20	8	33	26	1.83	2.09	1.39	1.03
Whitwam	0.92	18	12	8	34	27	2.44	2.05	1.31	0.99
Evans	0.92	57	4	4	19	15	2.00	1.94	1.28	1.10
Gerstell	0.91	2	27	8	35	28	2.23	2.11	0.99	0.58

Executive	Wealth Leverage	Stock % of Wealth	Options % of Wealth	Current Comp. % of Wealth	Years 1–5 Compensation % of Wealth	Years 6–10 Compensation % of Wealth	Old Option Leverage	New Option Leverage	Current Compensation Leverage	Years 1–5 Comp Leverage
Oesterreicher	0.89	29	7	7	31	25	2.69	2.17	1.33	0.99
Lorch	0.89	7	13	9	40	31	2.27	1.93	1.44	1.01
Sissel	0.87	10	19	8	35	28	1.87	2.03	1.22	0.90
Volkema	0.86	41	5	6	26	21	1.64	1.60	1.19	1.10
Nemirow	0.86	2	15	9	41	32	1.95	1.75	1.35	1.02
Sokol	0.86	12	12	9	38	30	1.81	1.70	1.58	1.03
Harad	0.85	1	21	9	39	31	2.04	1.68	1.14	0.82
Dollens	0.85	9	44	5	23	18	1.02	1.58	1.43	0.99
Sewell, Jr.	0.84	31	15	6	27	21	1.65	2.06	1.32	0.76
Griffin	0.83	10	9	9	40	32	2.56	2.11	1.32	0.93
Couch	0.83	22	8	8	34	27	3.59	2.63	1.05	0.66
Lockhart	0.82	9	12	9	39	31	2.28	2.03	1.24	0.88
Carpenter	0.80	5	18	9	38	30	1.81	1.76	1.24	0.85
Keyser	0.77	12	11	9	38	30	2.09	2.10	1.07	0.85
Rosso	0.77	6	13	9	40	32	1.80	1.57	1.24	0.92
Cadogan	0.77	3	23	8	37	29	1.28	1.22	1.16	0.96
Day	0.75	5	17	9	39	31	1.37	1.28	1.11	0.95
Schmitt	0.71	13	8	9	39	31	2.51	1.98	1.03	0.72
Kucharski	0.67	13	12	8	37	29	1.87	1.99	0.89	0.64
Costley	0.67	3	6	10	45	36	2.06	1.80	1.42	0.84

T A B L E   8–15

Continued

Executive	Wealth Leverage	Stock % of Wealth	Options % of Wealth	Current Comp. % of Wealth	Years 1-5 Compensation % of Wealth	Years 6-10 Compensation % of Wealth	Old Option Leverage	New Option Leverage	Current Compensation Leverage	Years 1-5 Comp Leverage
Growcock	0.67	4	13	9	41	32	1.57	1.67	1.00	0.80
Dean	0.67	41	3	6	27	22	1.64	1.47	0.66	0.59
DiCamillo	0.65	1	4	11	47	37	2.15	1.82	1.41	0.86
Snell	0.65	2	8	10	44	35	1.53	1.65	1.17	0.86
Grade	0.61	12	6	9	41	32	1.79	1.53	0.88	0.75
Gannon	0.60	22	9	8	34	27	2.43	3.59	0.62	0.29
Duff	0.58	22	6	8	35	28	1.77	1.46	0.66	0.56
Nadig	0.44	9	0	10	45	36	0.00	1.54	0.78	0.60
Woltz III	0.44	31	3	8	33	26	2.51	2.09	0.26	0.13
Viets	0.33	19	0	9	40	32	0.00	3.79	0.28	0.28
Jennings	0.27	11	0	10	44	35	0.00	4.92	0.37	0.27

guidelines and the leverage of the Hershey EVA bonus calibration, the median total wealth leverage of the EVA company CEOs drops to 0.68. This shows that option grant guidelines have a significant effect on total wealth leverage even for a group of CEOs who hold a quarter of their wealth in stock owned and options already granted. If we assume competitive option grant guidelines, annual recalibration of bonus plan targets, and current bonus leverage equal to half the Hershey EVA bonus calibration, the median total wealth leverage of the EVA company CEOs drops to 0.52. This shows that the leverage of the EVA bonus plan also has a significant effect on total wealth leverage for a group of CEOs who hold a quarter of their wealth in stock owned and options held. Finally, if we assume that current and future compensation has zero wealth leverage, so that wealth leverage comes solely from stock owned and options already granted, the median total wealth leverage of the EVA company CEOs drops to 0.46.

We can summarize these findings as follows. Stock owned and options already granted account for more than half of the wealth leverage of EVA company CEOs. The remainder of their wealth leverage comes, in roughly equal parts, from fixed-share option grant guidelines and EVA bonus plan leverage. This shows that stock and option incentives are much more important for EVA company CEOs than EVA bonus plan incentives.

The Impact of Stock Compensation on Business Unit Wealth Leverage

While stock and options make a major contribution to the wealth leverage of EVA company CEOs, they make a much weaker contribution to the wealth leverage of business unit executives. For a business unit executive who runs a quarter of the company, a 100 percent increase in the value of his or her business unit only increases the price of the stock by 25 percent. This means that stock and option compensation provides far less wealth leverage for a business unit manager than an EVA bonus plan based on business unit performance. Despite the weak wealth leverage of stock and options for business unit managers, most EVA companies continue to use stock and option grants for such managers. We suspect that this practice endures, at least in part, because an accounting expense does not have to be recognized for the typical executive option. EVA companies that want to build shareholder value through stronger incentives need to replace corporate stock options granted to business unit executives with greater EVA bonus opportunities and to explain to their investors why the additional bonus expense does not represent additional economic cost.

CONCLUSION

In this chapter we detailed the calibration of an EVA bonus plan using Hershey Foods as an example and demonstrated how capital market expectations for EVA improvement can be used as the basis for determining management bonuses. We also demonstrated the importance of understanding the influence of non-EVA factors on future growth value to more accurately determine expected EVA improvement.

In addition, we examined a sample of companies that have used, or continue to use, EVA-based compensation, and we noted that companies are more likely to stick with the EVA plan when they incorporate other critical elements of value-driven compensation, such as multiyear bonus plans and high levels of managerial wealth leverage. Companies that compromise on these critical elements tend to be disappointed in the results, falsely blaming EVA for their failure to improve corporate performance. Several such companies have abandoned EVA in frustration.

Finally, we showed how to use competitive compensation analysis to determine appropriate types and levels of compensation for managers. Most successful EVA companies use a combination of compensation elements, including but not limited to EVA-linked bonuses, to create a total compensation package, including stock and/or option grants. Without such elements, it is difficult to construct pay plans with the degree of entrepreneurial wealth leverage required to elicit aggressive value-creating behavior from managers.

We do not claim that our approach "solves" the dilemmas that inevitably arise as policymakers try to balance the four key objectives of compensation: strong alignment, high wealth leverage, acceptable retention risk, and reasonable shareholder cost. However, we are confident that our approach goes further than any known alternatives in helping board members and top managers to better understand, and better quantify, the nature of the trade-offs they must consider in designing their companies' pay plans. In short, this approach shows how to produce both (a) the strongest possible alignment between shareholder and managerial interests (by tying management bonuses directly to investor expectations of EVA improvement) and (b) the high degrees of wealth leverage to strengthen the value-creating incentives of management, while keeping retention risk and shareholder cost to manageable levels.

In the next chapter, we will contrast EVA with its most talked-about competitor, CFROI, or cashflow return on investment.

APPENDIX
CALCULATING HERSHEY'S EVA INTERVAL

The following steps are used to calculate an EVA interval that yields a 5 percent probability of zero bonus:

1. Estimate the volatility of Hershey's investor returns using Hershey's stock volatility and leverage.

We assume that the volatility of Hershey bondholder returns is zero, so that the volatility of Hershey's investor returns (at the end of 1992) is its stock volatility × (market equity/market capitalization), or $0.195 \times 0.88 = 0.172$.

2. Estimate Hershey's fifth percentile three-year excess return:

- Calculate Hershey's expected third-year investor wealth using Hershey's initial market value and cost of capital:

$$\text{Expected third-year investor wealth}$$
$$= \$5148 \text{ M} \times (1.1159)^3 = \$7153 \text{ M}$$

- Calculate Hershey's fifth percentile third-year investor wealth using Hershey's cost of capital, investor return volatility and the log-normal distribution assumption:

The log-normal distribution assumption says that Hershey's log return follows a normal distribution:

$$\text{Three-year log return} = 3 \times u + \sqrt{3} \times Z_{.05} \times \sigma$$

where u is Hershey's "mean logarithmic" return, σ is Hershey's investor return volatility (0.172) and $Z_{.05}$ is the fifth percentile value of a standard normal distribution, -1.645.

Hershey's mean logarithmic return u is derived from its cost of capital and investor return volatility, $u = ln\ (1 + WACC) - \sigma^2/2 = ln\ (1.1159) - (0.172^2/2) = 0.0949$, and implies that Hershey's fifth percentile three-year log return is $3 \times 0.0949 - 1.645 \times \sqrt{3} \times 0.172 = -0.2054$.

Hershey's three-year log return is ln (third year investor wealth/beginning wealth), so:

ln (third-year investor wealth/beginning wealth) $= -0.2054$

Third-year investor wealth
$=$ beginning wealth $\times\ e^{-.2054} = \$4192$ M

♦ Calculate Hershey's fifth percentile excess return:

Excess return = actual wealth − expected wealth
$= \$4192 - \$7153 = -\$2961$ M

3. Calculate Hershey's fifth percentile annual excess EVA improvement assuming that the excess investor return is fully reflected in operating performance:

♦ Our assumption that the excess investor return is fully reflected in operating performance implies that the excess return is equal to the cash and perpetuity value of the excess EVA improvement; for simplicity, we will assume that there is a constant annual excess EVA improvement, $x\Delta EVA$.

♦ The year 3 cash value of the first year $x\Delta EVA$ is $x\Delta EVA \times (1 + WACC)^2$, and the year 3 cash value of the first, second, and third year $x\Delta EVA$ is as follows:

$$x\Delta EVA \times [(1 + WACC)^2 + (1 + WACC) + 1]$$

The year 3 perpetuity value of cumulative excess EVA improvement is the year 3 cash value divided by WACC:

$$x\Delta EVA \times [(1 + WACC)^2 + (1 + WACC) + 1]/WACC$$

♦ The sum of the year 3 cash and perpetuity value of the cumulative excess EVA improvement is as follows:

$$x\Delta EVA \times [(1 + WACC)^2 + (1 + WACC) + 1]$$
$$\times [1 + (1/WACC)]$$

or

$$x\Delta EVA \times [(1 + WACC)^2 + (1 + WACC) + 1]$$
$$\times [(1 + WACC)/WACC]$$

or

$$x\Delta EVA \times [(1 + WACC)^3 + (1 + WACC)^2$$
$$+ (1 + WACC)]/WACC = x\Delta EVA \div 0.0309$$

This implies that the fifth percentile annual excess EVA improvement is as follows:

$$0.0309 \times \$2961 \, M = \$91 \, M$$

4. Set the EVA interval equal to Hershey's fifth annual excess EVA improvement to ensure a zero bonus for fifth percentile performance.

In our discussion of expected EVA improvement, we said that the valuation multiple on EVA improvements from a positive base was 12.15 (1 + 1.292/0.1159), while the valuation multiple on EVA improvements from a negative base was 2.73 (1 + 0.201/0.1159). Both of these multiples capture the expected effect of EVA improvement on future growth value, but in one case (improvement from a positive base), the effect is positive, while in the other case, the effect is negative. In calculating the EVA interval, we need a single EVA interval (and, hence, a single assumption about the effect of EVA improvement on future growth value) that can be used across the entire range of EVA performance. This forces us to make the assumption that EVA improvement has zero effect on future growth value. This assumption implies a valuation multiple of (1 + WACC)/WACC, or 9.63.

CHAPTER 9

The Metric Wars

EVA versus Cashflow Return on Investment

In recent years, scores of consulting firms have entered the value-based measurement arena, competing aggressively for the hearts and minds of corporate executives. Journalist Randy Myers has dubbed it the "Metric Wars."[1] To differentiate their services, these firms promote their own value-based metrics, some of which are merely variants of EVA. A.T. Kearney's *Economic Earnings* and McKinsey's *Economic Profit* are examples. Other firms, however, prefer rate-of-return measures such as cashflow return on investment (CFROI).

CFROI is EVA's most formidable competitor in the Metric Wars. Developed by HOLT Value Associates, a Chicago-based consultancy, it is now used by several prominent consulting firms, including Boston Consulting Group (BCG), Price Waterhouse Coopers, Deloitte and Touche, and several others. Bennett Stewart of Stern Stewart & Company, a leading EVA consultancy, calls it "a technology in search of a problem . . . a consultant's concoction . . . not well grounded in the basic elements of corporate finance theory."[2] But plenty of consultants and executives swear by it.

---

1. R. Myers, "Metric Wars," *CFO*, October 1996.
2. R. Myers, p. 41.

CFROI is the centerpiece of a distinctive approach to valuation, performance measurement, and incentive compensation. CFROI advocates believe that the measure provides both:

◆ An operating return measure that is equal to a company's economic, or internal, rate of return on investment

◆ A more accurate estimate of the market value of a business than alternative approaches, such as EVA

CFROI is not, by itself, a measure of market value or investor return. CFROI advocates believe that the proper measure of market value is the present value of future cashflows and that the proper measure of investor return is total shareholder return, or TSR.[3] Of course, EVA proponents also believe that market value is driven by future cashflows. But CFROI users argue that their approach provides better estimates of these cashflows, both at corporate and business unit levels. At the corporate level, market value estimates calculated from CFROI can help investors identify overvalued and undervalued shares. At the business unit level, market value estimates can be used to calculate total business return, or TBR, a business unit surrogate for TSR. In this way, a divisional performance measure can be developed that is, according to CFROI users, directly tied to shareholder returns.

In this chapter, we will explain the CFROI concept with a case study of a simple transport company. We also will show the use of CFROI in valuation, and the calculation of CFROI from publicly reported data. Finally, we present our evaluation of CFROI as a valuation tool, our response to the criticisms leveled against EVA by CFROI advocates, and an evaluation of TBR as a performance measure.

WHAT IS CFROI?

As the term implies, CFROI is a rate of return; it is not expressed in monetary terms, as is EVA. CFROI compares the after-tax, inflation-adjusted cashflows available to a company's investors with

---

3. TSR in a given period equals stock price appreciation (expressed as a percentage), plus dividend yield (dividends paid as a percentage of beginning share price).

the inflation-adjusted gross cash investment made by those investors. This cash-on-cash ratio is then converted into a rate of return
by estimating the economic life of the company's depreciable assets and a residual value based on nondepreciable assets.

If it sounds complicated, it is. The most important facts to
note are that:

- CFROI is calculated in the same way as the internal rate
  of return (IRR), although it cannot be interpreted in the
  same way as IRR.
- CFROI is based on cashflows and therefore goes even
  further than EVA calculations in removing the influence
  of accrual accounting.
- CFROI is an inflation-adjusted (i.e., real) rate of return,
  not a nominal rate of return.

CFROI is normally calculated on an annual basis and is compared to an inflation-adjusted cost of capital to determine whether
the company has earned returns superior to its cost of capital and
thus created value for its shareholders. In this sense, it bears an
important similarity to EVA. Both measures assume that management creates value by earning returns on invested capital greater
than the cost of capital.

HOW IS CFROI CALCULATED?

To illustrate the basic calculations, consider a simple transport
business. Late in 1996, the company buys ten minivans for $25,000
each, for a total of $250,000. In addition, it invests $25,000 in inventory (such as spare parts). The minivans are expected to last
four years, producing $7500 annually per minivan in net operating
cashflows. The minivans are expected to have no salvage value;
each will be scrapped at the end of its four-year service period.
The entire investment of $275,000 ($250,000 for the minivans +
$25,000 for inventory) will be financed with equity, the inflation
rate is 0, and no taxes will be paid. To summarize:

Initial investment = $250,000 (10 minivans)
Residual value   = 0
Service life   = 4 years for each truck

Financing   = All equity
Tax rate   = 0
Inflation rate   = 0
Net cashflows = $7500 per year per minivan ($75,000 for 10 minivans)

We can calculate the IRR for the 10 minivans as shown in Figure 9–1. As shown in the figure, the IRR for the investment is 6.71 percent.

Of course, we cannot observe future cashflows. In fact, if we are outsiders, we don't even know the company's expectations for future cashflows. This means that CFROI has to be estimated from historical financial statements. From this perspective, we can see an important difference between CFROI and IRR. IRR is forward-looking in that it measures the *expected* cashflow return on a prospective investment. CFROI, on the other hand, is a historical measure. It is calculated in precisely the same way as IRR, but the cashflows in question are not projected, but actual.

When the transport company started at the end of 1996, its balance sheet looked like this:

		Shareholders'	
Inventories	$25,000	equity	$275,000
Property, plant, and equipment	$250,000		
Total	$275,000	Total	$275,000

The company began operations in 1997. Let's assume that profitability in that year was exactly as expected. Net income for

F I G U R E   9–1

IRR Calculations

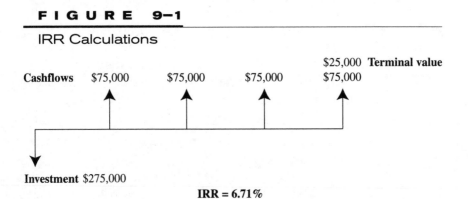

IRR = 6.71%

the year would equal the operating cashflows of $75,000, net of the depreciation expense of $62,500 ($250,000 ÷ 4), or $12,500. Net property, plant, and equipment is reduced by the depreciation expense for the year. Shareholders' equity would increase by $12,500, or the amount of net income for the year, assuming no dividend payments. The balance sheet at the end of 1997 would thus appear as follows:

		Shareholders'	
Cash	$ 75,000	equity	$287,500
Inventories	$ 25,000		
Property, plant, and equipment	$187,500		
Total	$287,500	Total	$287,500

We can now calculate CFROI from the financial statements, a process that involves four steps.

Step 1. *Estimate the economic life of the company's depreciable assets.* To calculate CFROI, we need to estimate the number of years that the company is expected to generate its operating cashflows. In our example, we know this period must be four years, but if CFROI is estimated from the financial statements, we would have no way of knowing this apart from trying to deduce it. We make this deduction by dividing depreciation expense for the current year into gross (depreciable) property, plant, and equipment (PP&E). For example, if gross PP&E is $100, and depreciation expense for the year is $20, we would assume that the assets have an economic life of five years ($100 ÷ $20). Gross PP&E is calculated by adding accumulated depreciation (in this case, $62,500) to net PP&E, and subtracting any investment in land, because land is not a depreciable asset. In the example, all of the investment in fixed assets is in depreciable assets.

Net PP&E	$187,500
+ Accumulated depreciation	62,500
Depreciable gross PP&E	$250,000
÷ Depreciation expense	$ 62,500
Economic life of assets	4 years

We therefore assume that the economic life of the depreciable assets is four years, which means that, for the purpose of calculating CFROI, we assume that the company's assets will generate its current level of operating cashflows for four years. It is important to note that we do not really know, or even expect, that the same level of operating cashflows will be generated over each of the next four years. This assumption is made for computational purposes only.

Step 2. *Estimate the gross, inflation-adjusted cashflows.* Because CFROI is a real rate of return, our estimate of cashflows must be adjusted for any gains and losses caused by holding monetary assets or bearing monetary liabilities in periods of inflation (or deflation). In this example, we assume an inflation rate of 0, and so no adjustment for monetary gains or losses is required. To estimate the cashflows, we add depreciation expense to net income:

Net income	$12,500
+ Depreciation expense	62,500
Gross cashflows	$75,000

We already knew that cashflows would be $75,000. If we had access only to the company's balance sheet and income statement, however, this figure would have to be calculated (although the operations section of a cashflow statement would also reveal the number).

Step 3. *Estimate the gross cash investment.* To calculate an IRR for any capital project, we need to know the initial investment. Because CFROI is calculated in the same way as IRR, an estimate is needed for the investment that must be undertaken (or, more accurately, has already been undertaken) to generate the cashflows identified in step 2.

The gross cash investment equals gross PP&E plus inventories.

Gross PP&E	$250,000
+ Inventories	25,000
Gross cash investment	$275,000

We assume that this amount is the gross cash invested by the company as of the end of 1997.

Step 4. *Calculate the nondepreciating assets.* For CFROI calculations, nondepreciating assets such as land and inventories are assumed to be released at the end of the economic life of the depreciable assets. In short, these assets represent the terminal value of the company's investments. In this case, we have inventories of $25,000, but no land. We therefore assume that the terminal value of the company's assets is $25,000.

To recap:

Economic life of the depreciable assets =   4 years
Gross cashflows = $ 75,000
Gross cash investment = $275,000
Terminal value = $ 25,000

As shown in Figure 9–2, the result is the same CFROI at year-end 1997, 6.71 percent, as the projected IRR calculated as of year-end 1996. Notice that we exclude the cashflow generated in 1997 from the gross cash investment. In fact, we should include it, but if so we must also include any returns received from investing those cashflows. The most likely assumption is that the operating cashflows, when invested, will earn the same rate of return as the company's other assets, 6.71 percent. If so, not only should we add $75,000 to the gross cash investment but also $5032.50 ($75,000 × 6.71 percent) to gross cashflows. If these adjustments are made, the CFROI would still be 6.71 percent, as shown in Figure 9–3.

F I G U R E   9–2

CFROI calculations

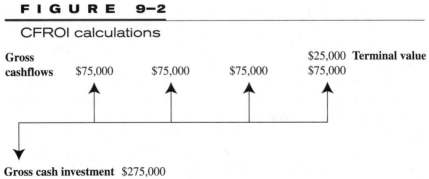

Gross cash investment $275,000

CFROI = 6.71%

F I G U R E   9–3

CFROI calculations

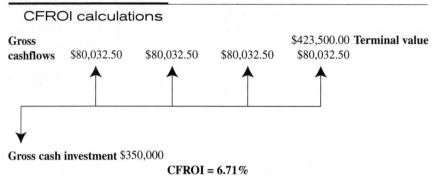

Gross $423,500.00 **Terminal value**
cashflows $80,032.50 $80,032.50 $80,032.50 $80,032.50

Gross cash investment $350,000
                    CFROI = 6.71%

THE CFROI VALUATION MODEL

Although CFROI is expressed as a percentage return, it can also be used to value businesses in monetary terms. This is CFROI's most popular application among portfolio managers. The valuations that emerge from CFROI are discounted cashflow valuations, just like those using the free cashflow or EVA models. In fact, with the same cashflow forecasts and discount rates, all three models should give the same result. However, the use of a different model often leads to different cashflow forecasts (and sometimes to different discount rates), and, hence, to different valuation estimates. In other words, while the three models should, in theory, yield equivalent values, on a practical level significant differences can arise.

The CFROI in the transport company is derived from the cashflows earned by assets already in place. It is tempting to think that we need to forecast cashflows for these same assets, then discount them back to a present value, to derive an estimated value for the firm. Reality is more complicated. The value of a firm depends not only on the value of the assets already in place, but also on the cashflows expected from *future* investments. In other words, the value of a firm is a function of both the cashflows expected from investments already made *and* the cashflows from investments that the company has not made yet. It is not unusual for the value of these future investments to constitute 70 percent, 80 percent, or even more of a firm's total value. In the case of some Internet stocks, for example, the value assigned by the capital markets to future, anticipated investment accounts for over 95 percent of the firm's total value.

The value of any firm can be expressed as follows:

$$\text{Value of the firm} = \underbrace{\sum_{t=1}^{EL} \frac{\text{net cashflows}_t}{(1 + COC)^t}}_{\text{EXISTING ASSETS}} + \underbrace{\sum_{t=1}^{RL} \frac{\text{net cashflows}_t}{(1 + COC)^t}}_{\text{FUTURE INVESTMENTS}}$$

where *net cashflows* equals after-tax operating profit + depreciation; COC is the cost of capital; EL is the economic life of existing assets; and RL is the remaining life of the firm.

If the company is publicly traded, and we can generate reliable estimates for the value of its existing assets, it is a matter of simple arithmetic to estimate the value that the capital markets have attached to the company's future investments:

Value of future investments =

value of the firm − value of existing assets

This figure can provide company managers and investment analysts with valuable insights because it quantifies the markets' beliefs regarding a company's value-creating potential. Many corporate users of CFROI rely on this formulation to improve their understanding of how their firms are viewed by the investing community. In general, the better a company is managed and the greater its growth opportunities, the larger the role that future investments play in the total value of the firm.

Similar insights can also be gained from EVA valuations, but instead of defining value as the sum of the value of existing assets and the value of future investments, we define it in terms of current operations value (invested capital plus the capitalized value of current EVA) and future growth value (the capitalized value of expected EVA improvements, whether from assets in place or new investments). Remember that

MVA = market value − invested capital

Therefore:

Market value = invested capital + MVA

Because MVA equals the present value of future EVAs, we can express the value of the firm as follows:

Market value = invested capital
            + present value of future EVAs from assets
              in place
            + present value of future EVAs from
              future investments

This formulation is easily reconciled to current operations value (COV) and future growth value (FGV). The present value of future EVAs from assets in place is composed of both a continuing value component (which is based on the assumption that current EVA performance is sustained into perpetuity) and the present value of EVA improvements expected from those assets (i.e., an FGV component). Invested capital plus the continuing value component equals COV. The FGV of the firm equals the FGV component from assets already in place plus the present value of future EVAs from future investments.

The CFROI Valuation Model: A Case Study

We illustrate the CFROI valuation model using data from Briggs & Stratton, an American engine producer, drawn from the work of Bartley Madden of HOLT Value Associates.[4] This model is presented uncritically at first, but later in the chapter, we will discuss its shortcomings.

The top panel in Figure 9–4 displays the company's CFROIs over the period 1950 to 1995. Notice that the company enjoyed high returns throughout the 1950s and 1960s. In the late 1970s, CFROI hovered around 10 percent, then dipped sharply in the 1980s and was even negative in 1989. The company underwent a major restructuring program, and from 1992 onward, it showed year-on-year improvement in CFROI.

The long-term average level of CFROI for American companies is about 6 percent. If this seems low, remember that CFROI is a *real* return; the effects of inflation are removed. When a com-

---

4. B. J. Madden, "The CFROI Valuation Model," *Journal of Investing*, Spring 1998.

F I G U R E   9–4

Briggs & Stratton—Historical life cycle, 1950 to 1995

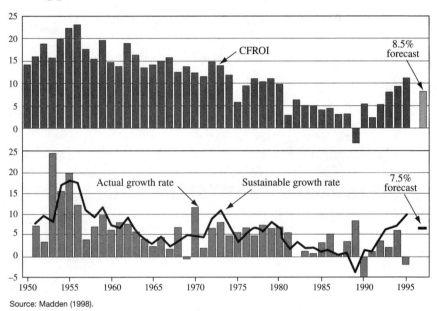

Source: Madden (1998).

pany earns a CFROI far greater than 6 percent, competition intensifies, eventually forcing CFROI down to the long-run average. (See Figure 9–5.) Above-average CFROIs attract competition, resulting in gradual reductions in CFROI. Above-average returns regress toward the long-run mean, but so too do below-average returns. When companies underperform, investors pressure the company to improve. Sometimes these efforts fail, and the company falls ever deeper into loss. In such cases, bankruptcy looms. Yet competitive pressures to restructure combined with the influence of merger and acquisition activity often bring performance back to market standards.

A study by the Boston Consulting Group provides evidence of a CFROI fade.[5] BCG looked at a sample of 3300 American companies between 1987 and 1993. The companies in the bottom 10

5. *Shareholder Value Metrics,* Boston Consulting Group, Shareholder Value Management Series, Booklet 2, 1996, pp. 39–41.

F I G U R E   9—5

Competitive life cycle

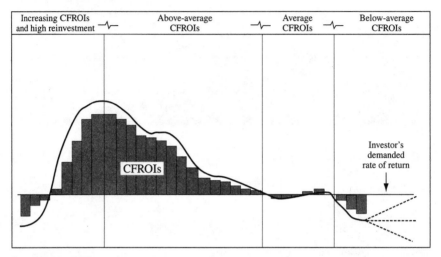

| Increasing CFROIs and high reinvestment | Above-average CFROIs | Average CFROIs | Below-average CFROIs |

Source: Madden (1998).

percent according to CFROI in 1987 have an average CFROI of −7.02 percent, while the top 10 percent have an average CFROI of 19.90 percent. By 1993, the CFROI of the same firms in the bottom 10 percent had improved to an average of 2.54 percent. In fact, 90 of those firms achieved a CFROI of 10 percent or better, well above average for all firms. None of these firms had earned a positive CFROI six years earlier. For the top performers in 1987, the average CFROI declined to 14.94 percent in 1993, with 135 of the firms earning a CFROI below the long-run average of 6 percent. Later in this chapter, we will show that a similar pattern of performance changes can also result from fluctuations around average performance levels, without any fade to an economywide average.

In the case of Briggs & Stratton, we can see that by the early 1980s, performance fell below the long-run mean and stayed there until the company's restructuring efforts began to bear fruit in the early 1990s. By 1994, the company's CFROI was well above average, exceeding 10 percent by the following year.

The second panel of Figure 9–4 shows actual growth rates and sustainable growth rates for total assets over the same period.

Both figures are expressed in real terms (i.e., inflation-adjusted). The large fluctuation in actual growth rates is common because of the erratic nature of acquisitions and divestitures, both of which can dramatically alter total assets from one year to the next. The sustainable growth rate is based on CFROI and measures how fast the company's asset base can grow while holding dividends, external equity financing, and capital structure policy constant. Of course, a company can grow faster than its sustainable growth rate in any given year by cutting the dividend, issuing new shares, or increasing the company's leverage. However, none of these actions is sustainable because eventually dividends cannot fall below zero, endless share issues are not possible, and there are limits to how much leverage a company can bear.

Figure 9–6 shows the elements required to estimate the value of Briggs & Stratton at time *t*, which in this example is set at August 1996. In this version of CFROI, based on the model developed by HOLT Value Associates, security analysts' forecasts for

F I G U R E   9–6

Briggs & Stratton—Forecast life cycle as of August 1996

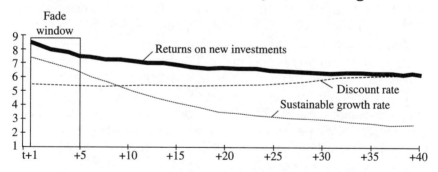

	(t + 1)	(t + 5)	Fades to
CFROI existing assets	8.5	7.6	
ROI new investments	8.5	7.6	6.3
Sustainable growth rate	7.5	6.5	2.7
Real discount rate	5.8	5.8	6.3

Fade Window

Source: Madden (1998).

earnings per share (EPS) are used to derive estimates of CFROI in the next period ($t + 1$) for *existing* assets. These forecasts are available for American firms from the Institutional Brokerage Estimation Service (IBES) or Zack's Investment Services. Of course, analysts can substitute their own estimates and derive their own estimates of company value.

The net cashflows from *future* investments are based on the expected returns from new investments and the sustainable growth rates. We assume that the return on new investment in the following period ($t + 1$) will equal the CFROI on existing assets in that same period. In this case, based on analysts' estimates of EPS, CFROI on existing assets is forecast to be 8.5 percent. New investments undertaken in year $t + 1$ (1997) are also expected to earn 8.5 percent.

Based on Briggs & Stratton's expected CFROI of 8.5 percent, the sustainable growth rate is 7.5 percent. Sustainable growth is important for this model because it represents the rate at which the company's total assets are expected to grow (and therefore determines the magnitude of new investments). When combined with expected CFROI, it can help us derive a value for the company's future investments.

This valuation of future investments requires estimates of CFROI and sustainable growth not just one period into the future but also for all future periods (1998 and beyond). In the case of Briggs & Stratton, the expected CFROI and the sustainable growth rate in period $t + 1$ are well above economywide averages. The long-run average for CFROI is about 6 percent (6.3 percent to be exact). Research by HOLT shows that the average sustainable growth rate is 2.7 percent. We assume that competitive forces will gradually cause both rates to converge to their long-run means. The only questions remaining are how long this convergence will take (what we call the *competitive advantage period* in Chapter 2) and the mathematical process by which the convergence will occur (the *fade rate*).

Specific CFROIs and sustainable growth rates are forecast only over the next five years (a period of time known as a *fade window*). Beyond that, a constant exponential fade rate is normally assumed. Although the extent of the fade window seems arbitrary, empirical studies conducted by HOLT show that there is some improvement in the accuracy of the valuation if specific yearly forecasts are made over the first five years, but broad assumptions such as an exponential decline to a long-run mean are likely to do just as well as specific yearly forecasts of CFROI made more than five years into the future. In other words, extending the fade window does not improve the accuracy of the valuation.

In the case of Briggs & Stratton, the CFROI on both existing assets and new investments is expected to decrease from 8.5 percent in $t + 1$ to 7.6 percent in $t + 5$. Beyond year $t + 5$ (i.e., for the ensuing 35 years), CFROI will converge to a long-run economywide mean of 6.3 percent, as shown in Figure 9–6. A similar procedure is employed for the sustainable growth rate. In this case, the rate is expected to decrease from 7.5 percent in year $t + 1$ to 6.5 percent four years later. After that, the rate declines in a nearly exponential function, reaching the long-run mean of 2.7 percent in year $t + 40$.

The final piece of data needed to value the company is the *discount rate*, which here represents the company's *real* cost of capital, assumed in the long run to equal the long-run average CFROI of 6.3 percent, but over the five-year fade window assumed to be only 5.8 percent. (See the appendix at the end of this chapter for a detailed discussion of the estimation of discount rates for CFROI-based valuations.) Because the CFROI is expected to be 6.3 percent in $t + 40$ and beyond, and the cost of capital is also expected to be 6.3 percent, there is no value creation beyond $t + 40$.

Given the above information and formulas, the value of Briggs & Stratton's existing assets as of August 1996 was $1133 million, while the value of future investments was $347 million, for a total firm value of $1480 million. The value of the company's debt (in this case, $154 million) can be subtracted from the value of the firm to arrive at a value for the company's equity ($1326 million). The value of the equity is then divided by the number of shares outstanding (28.9 million) to calculate a theoretical pershare value ($46). This value can then be compared with the existing share price to determine if the company's shares are over- or underpriced.

Figure 9–7 shows the results of this exercise repeated for the 10 previous years (1986 to 1995), as well as the results for 1996. The vertical line in each year represents the trading range for Briggs & Stratton stock. Note that in each year, the value of the company's equity according to the CFROI model lies within the

F I G U R E   9–7

Briggs & Stratton—Stock prices and forecast CFROIs

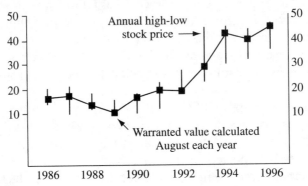

Source: Madden (1998).

trading range. CFROI proponents cite examples like this as evidence that their model works better than competing valuation models in explaining stock prices. In reality, however, a more conventional cashflow valuation model would yield identical results had the same assumptions been made regarding future returns, reinvestment (i.e., sustainable growth) rates, the competitive advantage period (CAP), and fade rates.

The Briggs & Stratton example shows just how complex CFROI can be. Not only must CFROI itself be estimated, but to use it for valuation, estimates are also required for the CAP and the fade rate. HOLT normally assumes a 40-year CAP (which may seem odd, given that sustainability of competitive advantage is known to vary widely among business firms), but this factor can be largely captured in the fade rate used over the five-year fade window. For example, companies that combine above-average CFROIs with low variability in CFROI have shown themselves over time to be more capable than other firms of sustaining any competitive advantage they may acquire. In such cases, the fade rate over the fade window ($t + 1$ to $t + 5$) is slower than for other firms, which in turn translates into higher estimates of company value.

Madden (1998) constructs 20 fade classes based on a long-term historical analysis of the impact of the magnitude of the spread between CFROI and the cost of capital, the variability of

CFROI, and a company's growth potential on the speed of the convergence of CFROI to the long-run mean. The results are shown in Table 9–1. A large universe of stocks is divided into CFROI quintiles over the period 1966 to 1993. For any given year, the companies with CFROIs in the top 20 percent are placed in quintile 1, the next 20 percent in quintile 2, and so on. Within each quintile, firms are sorted according to variability, as measured by the standard deviation of past CFROIs, and growth potential, as measured by the proportion of earnings retained. It is assumed that companies retaining a high proportion of earnings have greater growth potential than firms retaining a low proportion of

T A B L E   9–1

CFROI Fade Rates

CFROI Quintile	Variability	Growth	Approximate CFROI Fade Factor
Highest 1	H	H	0.60
1	H	L	0.50
1	L	H	0.40
1	L	L	0.20
2	H	H	0.50
2	H	L	0.40
2	L	H	0.30
2	L	L	0.20
3	H	H	0.40
3	H	L	0.40
3	L	H	0.40
3	L	L	0.40
4	H	H	0.40
4	H	L	0.40
4	L	H	0.40
4	L	L	0.40
5	H	H	0.40
5	H	L	0.40
5	L	H	0.40
Lowest 5	L	L	0.40

Source: Madden (1998)

earnings. Firms in the top half of each quintile on the basis of standard deviation of past CFROIs are designated as high (H) variability; the remaining firms are designated as low (L). A similar procedure is followed for growth potential; the top half within each quintile are designated high and the bottom half low.

Fade rates are then approximated according to what happened to CFROI from the ensuing year ($t + 1$) to the final year of the fade window ($t + 5$). The approximate fade factor (the final column in Table 9–1) reflects the percentage drop in the spread between CFROI and the long-run economywide CFROI over the fade window. For example, Briggs & Stratton places in the third quintile, according to its 1996 CFROI. All companies in that quintile have a fade factor of 40 percent. This factor indicates that the spread between CFROI and the long-run average CFROI (6.3 percent) is expected to be 40 percent lower in year $t + 5$ than it will be in year $t + 1$. This 40 percent fade factor is based on what happened to third-quintile firms in previous years. For Briggs & Stratton, CFROI in $t + 1$ is expected to be 8.5 percent, for a spread of 2.2 percentage points (8.5 percent – 6.3 percent). Therefore, the expected CFROI in year $t + 5$ is: 8.5 percent – 0.4 (8.5 percent – 6.3 percent), or 7.6 percent. The CFROI is then expected to converge to 6.3 percent over the following 35 years (until year $t + 40$) in the exponential manner shown in Figure 9–6. This process can be seen in Figure 9–8.

CALCULATING CFROI USING FINANCIAL STATEMENTS: HARNISCHFEGER INDUSTRIES

In the Briggs & Stratton example, the CFROIs are given. But how do we calculate CFROI for a real company using public financial disclosures? To show this, we use the financial statements of Harnischfeger Industries, the company featured in Chapter 2 to illustrate the calculation of EVA and MVA. Relevant data from the company's financial statements are shown in Table 9–2.

Besides the financial statement data, we need additional information. Some of this is disclosed in the company's annual report, and the rest is from estimates provided by HOLT Value Associates (all amounts in thousands of dollars):

F I G U R E   9–8

Briggs & Stratton—CFROI fade (All amounts in percent)

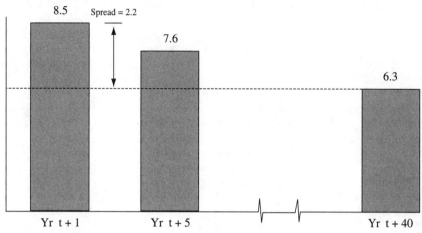

Source: Madden (1998).

- The 1996 annual report reveals a depreciation and amortization expense of $89,270. The problem with this figure is that it includes amortization of intangibles in addition to the depreciation expense for tangible assets. It is the latter figure that we need in order to estimate the economic life of the depreciable assets. Amortization of goodwill and other intangibles is approximated by calculating the average balance of $330,318 for goodwill and $52,985 for other intangibles. (Averages equal beginning balances plus ending balances, divided by 2.) Given disclosures in Harnishchfeger's annual report, it is assumed that goodwill is amortized over a 30-year period and other intangibles over a five-year period. These assumptions yield an estimate for amortization expense of $21,608. The remainder, $67,662, is assumed to be the depreciation expense for tangible assets.

- LIFO reserves (i.e., the difference between the current cost of inventory and its accounting book value) are reported to be $8022.

- Rental expense in 1996 is $27,887. The present value of operating leases is estimated to be $350,226.

T A B L E   9-2

Harnischfeger Industries, Inc., Selected Elements from the Balance Sheet and Income Statement of the 1996 Annual Report*

Current assets	
Cash and cash equivalents	$36.936
Accounts receivable—net	667.786
Inventories	547.115
Businesses held for sale	26.152
Other current assets	132.261
Property. plant. and equipment (gross)	
Land and improvements	48.371
Buildings	301.010
Machinery and equipment	776.332
Investments and other assets	
Goodwill	512.693
Intangible assets	39.173
Other assets	93.868
Current liabilities	
Short-term notes payable	49.633
Trade accounts payable	346.056
Employee compensation and benefits	160.488
Advance payments and progress billings	155.199
Accrued warranties	50.718
Other current liabilities	315.033
Long-term obligations	657.765
Other liabilities	
Liability for post-retirement benefits	78.814
Accrued pension and related costs	39.902
Other liabilities	14.364
Deferred income taxes	54.920
Minority interest	93.652
Restructuring charge	43.000
Operating income	244.019
Interest expense—net	(62.258)
Income before taxes and minority interest	181.761
Provision for income taxes	(63.600)
Minority interest	(3.944)
Net income	114.217

*In millions of dollars.

- The corporate tax rate is 35 percent, although the effective rate in 1996 was slightly lower.
- The company's *real* cost of debt (i.e., after adjusting for expected inflation) is 3 percent.

We can now estimate Harnischfeger's CFROI as of October 31, 1996 (amounts in thousands of dollars).

Step 1. *Calculate the economic life of the company's depreciable assets.*

Gross property, plant, and equipment	$1,125,713
− Land	48,371
Depreciable gross assets	$1,077,342
÷ Depreciation expense	67,662
Estimate of economic life	16 years

Step 2. *Estimate the gross cashflow.*

Net income after tax	$114,217
+ Depreciation	67,662
+ Interest expense	62,258
+ Minority interest	3,944
+ Restructuring cost	43,000
− Tax adjustment for restructuring cost	15,050
+ Operating rental expense	27,887
− Reduction in LIFO reserve	8,022
Gross cashflow	$295,896

Step 3. *Estimate the gross cash investment.*

Gross property, plant, and equipment (excluding land and improvements)	$1,077,342
+ Goodwill and intangibles	551,866
+ Present value of operating leases	350,226
+ Net monetary assets	
Monetary assets	

Cash	$ 36,936	
Accounts receivable	667,786	
Other current assets	158,413	
	$ 863,135	

Monetary liabilities (excluding provisions and interest-bearing debt)

Trade accounts payable	$ 346,056	
Other current liabilities	680,353	
	$1,026,409	
	−163,274	

+ Inventories	547,115
+ Land and improvements	48,371
+ Other assets	93,868
Gross cash investment	$2,505,514

Step 4. *Calculate the nondepreciating assets.*

Net monetary assets	$−163,274
Inventories	547,115
Land and improvements	48,371
Other assets	93,868
Terminal value	$526,080

We now have all the inputs necessary to calculate CFROI. See Figure 9–9. As shown, the resulting CFROI is 9.52 percent.

WHY DON'T WE JUST CALCULATE A SIMPLE RETURN?

Looking at the time line, one might ask, why not divide the gross cashflows of $295,896 by the cash investment of $2,505,514 and measure cashflow returns this way? In other words, why isn't the cashflow return 11.81 percent instead of 9.52 percent? The problem with this approach is that it would ignore the terminal value of

F I G U R E   9–9

CFROI calculations

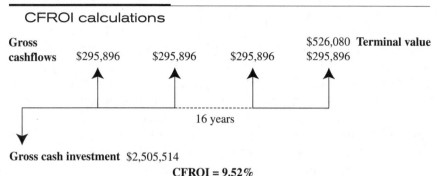

Gross $526,080 **Terminal value**
cashflows $295,896 $295,896 $295,896 $295,896

16 years

Gross cash investment $2,505,514
CFROI = 9.52%

any assets that might be released in future periods (such as land), as well as ignore the fact that the gross cash investment consists of wasting assets. CFROI corrects both of these deficiencies by incorporating the nonwasting assets as a terminal value and by recognizing that the cashflows generated by the assets cannot last forever because the assets (i.e., the gross cash investment) are depreciable. This is why CFROI is calculated in the same way as IRR, even though none of the cashflows in the time line is a forecast.

CFROI AND INFLATION

Thus far, we have assumed no inflation, avoiding the need for an inflation adjustment. Adjusting for inflation is one of the distinctive selling features of CFROI, however, because it facilitates comparison of the return measure across time (inflation rates change) and across borders (inflation rates vary from country to country).

Inflation affects the CFROI calculations in three major ways. First, gains and losses from holding monetary assets and liabilities are taken into consideration. For example, if a company holds cash or receivables in a period of inflation, a monetary loss results because inflation erodes the purchasing power of the assets. The converse is that gains arise in periods of inflation from holding monetary liabilities, such as accounts payable, because debts are repaid with a devalued currency.

The second major inflation adjustment is for fixed assets. For example, suppose that we invested $10 million in PP&E two years ago. Since then, inflation has been running at an annual rate of 3 percent. Gross cash investment as of today would be understated if we were to use the $10 million figure, because the investment was made when the purchasing power of the dollar was greater. To convert the investment to today's purchasing power, we should multiply $10 million by 1.03^2 to reflect the two years of 3 percent inflation, which yields an adjusted figure of $10.609 million.

The final way that inflation affects the calculation of CFROI is in the treatment of inventory. LIFO reserves are added to gross cash investment to reflect the impact of inflation on the value of inventories. Changes in LIFO reserves will also affect gross cash-flows. This adjustment is similar to the one that is made for EVA calculations (see Chapter 6).

Supplemental information on Harnischfeger Industries was provided by HOLT Value Associates (all amounts in thousands of dollars):

- Interest expense in 1996 was $62,258. It is estimated that $11,000 of that interest comes from the company's finance subsidiary. Interest expense for Harnischfeger's manufacturing operations is thus $51,258.
- The company has a monetary holding gain of $6000, which arose because Harnischfeger held a net monetary *liability* position during fiscal year 1996. If the company had held a net monetary *asset* position, a holding loss would have been recognized.
- Finance subsidiary receivables are estimated to be $174,000. The receivables are removed from the gross cash investment, yielding a balance of $493,786 (versus $667,786 on a consolidated basis).
- The inflation adjustment for PP&E, including land, is 15 percent.
- HOLT Value Associates imposes an industry upper bound of 14 years (based on asset lives for Harnischfeger's competitors).
- Because the economic life of the assets is now 14 years, the present value of the operating leases is also reduced.

The four steps for calculating Harnischfeger's CFROI are repeated to reflect this new information. Changes are highlighted in bold.

Step 1. *Calculate the economic life of the company's depreciable assets.*

	Gross property, plant, and equipment	$1,125,713
−	Land	48,371
	Depreciable gross assets	$1,077,342
÷	Depreciation expense	67,662
	Estimate of asset life	16 years

But the industry upper bound reduces the estimated asset life to 14 years.

Step 2. *Estimate the gross inflation-adjusted cashflows.*

	Net income after tax	$ 114,217
+	Depreciation	67,662
+	**Interest expense**	**51,258**
+	Minority interest	3,944
+	Restructuring cost	$ 43,000
−	Tax adjustment for restructuring cost	15,050
+	Operating rental expense (note 11, 1996 annual report)	27,887
+	**Monetary holding gain**	**6,000**
−	Reduction in LIFO reserve (note 5)	8,022
	Gross cashflow	**$ 290,896**

Step 3. *Estimate the gross cash investment.*

	Gross property, plant, and equipment (excluding land and improvements)	$1,077,342
+	**Inflation factor—PP&E (15%)**	**161,601**
+	Goodwill and intangibles	551,866
+	**Present value of operating leases**	**314,955**
+	Net monetary assets	
	Monetary assets	
	Cash	$ 36,936
	Accounts receivable	**493,786**
	Other current assets	158,413
		$ 689,135

Monetary liabilities (excluding provisions and interest-bearing debt)		
Trade accounts payable	$ 346,056	
Other current liabilities	680,353	
	$1,026,409	
	−337,274	
+ Inventories		547,115
+ **LIFO reserves**		**64,164**
+ Land and improvements		48,371
+ **Inflation factor—land (15%)**		**7,256**
+ Other assets		93,868
Gross cash investment		**$2,529,264**

Step 4. *Calculate the nondepreciating assets.*

Net monetary assets	**$−337,274**
Inventories	**611,279**
Land and improvements	**55,627**
Other assets	$ 93,868
Terminal value	**$ 423,500**

We can now reestimate Harnischfeger's CFROI. (See Figure 9–10.) The result of the adjustments reduces Harnischfeger's CFROI by 1.44 percentage points, although the adjusted CFROI is still higher than the long-run average for publicly traded American companies of 6.3 percent. Therefore, Harnischfeger's CFROI

F I G U R E   9—10

CFROI calculations

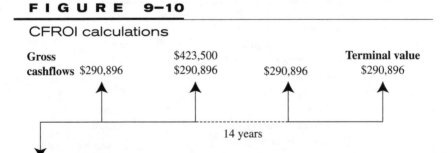

CFROI = 8.08%

suggests that the company is a value creator, earning inflation-adjusted returns on capital in excess of what investors would normally expect to earn. A valuation of Harnischfeger would assume that the company's CFROI converges to the long-run average of 6.3 percent.[6]

As you can see from this example, calculating CFROI is a complicated process. And unlike EVA, which provides a high degree of flexibility in deciding which accounting adjustments to make (if any), the CFROI metric *requires* a comprehensive set of adjustments, some of which are complex and difficult for line managers to understand. Remember that CFROI is a cash-on-cash measure: the return provided by gross, inflation-adjusted cashflows on gross cash investment. Without the adjustments, CFROI is not really a cashflow measure.

In promotional literature on CFROI, one consulting firm claims that

> Companies that have adopted CFROI as their performance yardstick do not find the measure of its calculation mysterious or complex. The adjustments in their basic accounting data are relatively straightforward and become routine.[7]

We find this claim surprising, and not entirely credible. While the adjustments may seem "straightforward" and "routine" to accountants, finance professionals, and consultants, there is no way we can say this for operating managers. Because there are complex adjustments required to produce CFROI figures, companies that have adopted the metric tend to limit its use to the corporate level or to large strategic business units, and then only for planning and resource allocation decisions. EVA's relative simplicity gives it important advantages over CFROI as a divisional performance measure.

Most CFROI advocates concede this point, arguing that its major advantage is not as a performance measure but rather because it provides better estimates of future cashflows. Future cashflows are derived from estimates of future returns on investment

---

6. In the following year, Harnischfeger began experiencing a sharp decline in its fortunes. In mid-1999, the CEO was forced to resign and the company filed for protection from its creditors.
7. *Shareholder Value Metrics,* Boston Consulting Group, Shareholder Value Management Series, Booklet 2, 1996, pp. 35–36.

and future investment levels. Better estimates of future cashflows allegedly arise because the CFROI fade model provides the most reliable estimate of the future returns on investment, and the sustainable growth rate provides the most reliable estimates of future investment levels.

THE CFROI FADE: THE EVIDENCE ISN'T CONVINCING

HOLT and other CFROI advocates claim that there is clear evidence of a fade in CFROI. The fade is measured by the changes in historical, four-year median CFROIs. Madden explains:

> At each of six points in time—1969, 1973, 1977, 1981, 1985, and 1989—the largest 1,000 firms by equity market value were selected. Median CFROIs were calculated for past and future CFROIs at the specified times. For the six points in time, the 1000 firms were ranked high to low on past CFROI. Each firm received a normalized rank score ranging from 1 (lowest) to 100 (highest). An advantage to normalized ranks, for homogenous firms, is that observations across time can be pooled. Fade classes were constructed based on firms' past CFROI level (quintiles) and, for a given CFROI level, further classification was based on past CFROI variability and on growth opportunities, measured by dividend payout ratio.[8]

HOLT summarizes its fade research with tables showing the average changes in rank for companies in each quintile:[9]

Quintile	Change in CFROI Rank over four Years
1	−15
2	−9
3	0
4	9
5	15

8. B. Madden (1999), p. 165.
9. B. Madden (1999), p. 167.

The problem with this evidence is that it is also consistent with the *absence* of fade. To illustrate this point, suppose that each company's CFROI fluctuates around its average CFROI, but there is no fade, i.e., each company's average is stable and does not converge to an economywide average. In this situation, the HOLT data show an apparent fade even though none exists. The reason there appears to be a fade is that the companies in the upper quintiles include a disproportionate number of companies that are temporarily above their average, while the bottom quintiles include a disproportionate number of companies that are temporarily below their average.

To illustrate the problem with the HOLT evidence, we created a database of 500 hypothetical companies with average CFROIs ranging from 1 percent to 25 percent. In the database, 20 companies have an average CFROI of 1 percent, 20 have an average CFROI of 2 percent, and so on. We assume each company's actual CFROI fluctuates around its average with a standard deviation of 10 percent. Each year for eight years, we determine each company's actual CFROI by drawing from a random sample:

$$\text{Actual CFROI} = \text{Average CFROI} + (z \times 10\%)$$

where z is a normally distributed random variable. We then calculate the same measures HOLT uses to estimate the fade: the median CFROI for the first four years and the median CFROI for the second four years. We group the companies into quintiles based on their CFROI performance in the first four years and then calculate the average change in rank from the first four-year period to the second:

Quintile	HOLT Data	Authors' Simulation of No Fade Data
1	−15	−16
2	−9	−6
3	0	0
4	9	8
5	15	15

The apparent fade is not the result of companies converging to an economywide average (nor is it the result of companies converging to their own average—the standard deviation around the company averages is the same, 10 percent, for every year of our data simulation). The fade simply reflects the fact that above-average years are more likely to be followed by poorer performance, and below-average years are more likely to be followed by better performance. In our simulation, 84 percent of the companies in the top quintile have a four-year median CFROI that is above their true average CRFOI, while 91 percent of the companies in the bottom quintile have a four-year median CFROI that is below their true average CFROI. If a company has a 75th percentile year, the probability its performance will be worse in the next period is 75 percent, but this does not prove that the company's performance is becoming less volatile nor that the company's average performance is converging to an economywide average.

The HOLT data give the appearance that performance in the second four-year period is closer to average than performance in the first four-year period. This outcome is entirely an artifact of grouping the data by performance in the first four-year period. If we group the data by performance in the second period, the data now shows that performance in the second four-year period is further from average than performance in the first period:

Second Four-Year Period Quintile	Change in CFROI Rank over Four Years
1	18
2	2
3	1
4	−5
5	−16

HOLT assumes, without proof, that the quintile performance changes from the second to the third four-year period will match those from the first to the second period. In effect, they assume that the passage of time is causing the performance changes from the first period to the second and will continue to produce a similar result from the second period to the third. Our simulation shows that the performance changes from the second period to the third are very different from the earlier changes:

First Four-Year Period Quintile	Change in CFROI Rank over First Four-Year Period	Change in CFROI Rank over Second Four-Year Period
1	−16	0
2	−6	2
3	0	−1
4	8	1
5	15	−1

If a company has 75th percentile performance (relative to its own long-run average) in the first four-year period, there is a 75 percent chance that it will do worse in the second four-year period, because we would expect 50th percentile performance in the second period (as we would in any period). But there is no longer a 75 percent probability of decline as we move from the second period to the third. The company's performance in the second period is, on average, at the 50th percentile (relative to its own long-run average). Since the company's performance in the third period will also be at the 50th percentile, the expected change from the second to the third period is zero. And, in fact, that is just what our simulation shows.

To prove that a predictable fade really exists, CFROI advocates need to measure performance periods of different durations—for example, one-year changes, two-year changes, . . . , five-year changes, and so on—and show that the magnitude of the performance changes are related, in a statistically significant way, to the length of the performance period. As of this writing, no such evidence exists.

ANOTHER PROBLEM WITH THE FADE: IT MAY IMPLY NEGATIVE NPV INVESTMENTS

The HOLT fade model projects a fade in the *average* CFROI, not the marginal CFROI. This approach often implies that the marginal CFROI is below the cost of capital and, hence, that managers will knowingly invest in negative NPV projects. To illustrate, consider the following example of a company with a CFROI of 18 percent, an investment base of $1000, a WACC of 6.3 percent (equal to the long-run, economywide average for CFROI), and a four-year fade rate of 60 percent:

	Year				
	0	**1**	**2**	**3**	**4**
CFROI	18.0%	15.6%	13.7%	12.2%	11.0%
Investment base	1000	1180	1364	1551	1740
Cashflow	180	184	187	189	191
Incremental cashflow		4	3	2	2
Incremental investment		180	184	187	189
Incremental ROI		2.3%	1.5%	1.1%	1.1%
EVA (6.3% WACC)	117	110	101	91	81
EVA improvement		−7	−9	−10	−10

The 60 percent fade means that the spread of CFROI over the cost of capital (i.e., CFROI − WACC) falls by 60 percent, from 11.7 to 4.7 percent, over the four-year fade window. Each year, the company reinvests its cashflow to maintain its investment growth at the sustainable growth rate. At this level of investment growth, the decline in the average CFROI implies a marginal return on investment (ROI) of under 3 percent, well below the 6.3 percent cost of capital. In other words, the fade assumes that the company will knowingly take on negative NPV investments, which is hardly a reasonable basis for valuation.

If we had developed the forecast using EVA, we would have seen immediately that the forecast implies negative EVA improvement. This highlights one of the great benefits of EVA analysis: It focuses on the return on *incremental* capital.

WHERE THE FADE DOESN'T APPLY

A fade to the cost of capital is a more sophisticated approach to forecasting than a simple extrapolation of historical return levels, but even if it is generally accurate (which CFROI advocates have never really proven), there are common situations in which it is not a useful model because investors might expect CFROI to fade *up to and beyond* the cost of capital. For example, as Madden notes,

"CFROIs have limited use with start-up operations, where the portfolio of projects as a whole is still being penalized by very substantial expenses and limited revenues."[10]

Acquisitions are another common situation where fade to the cost of capital does not work well. Consider a company that has a 15 percent NOPAT margin on sales and needs $0.60 in beginning operating capital for every $1 of revenue. With a 10 percent cost of capital, the company has a 9 percent EVA margin on sales (because the capital charge is 6 percent of sales), which makes growth highly valuable. If we buy the company for $3\times$ revenue (or $20\times$ NOPAT), the company will have $2.40 in goodwill per *initial* revenue dollar. The goodwill initially reduces the company's EVA margin on sales (ignoring any tax benefit of goodwill amortization) from 9 percent to -15 percent and its return on invested capital from 25 percent to 5 percent. Fading this 5 percent return on investment up to the 10 percent cost of capital is not likely to provide an accurate valuation of the acquired company. If we can grow the company's revenue by a factor of five, the initial goodwill expenditure declines to $0.48 per current revenue dollar and the company's EVA margin on sales increases to 4.2 percent. If we can grow the company's revenue by a factor of 10, the initial goodwill expenditure declines to $0.24 per current revenue dollar and the company's EVA margin on sales increases to 6.8 percent. While the company's return on operating capital may decline, it would be quite a coincidence if the decline exactly offset the benefit of spreading the initial goodwill expenditure over a larger revenue base. Acquisitions will commonly lead to returns fading back up to *and over* the cost of capital, a pattern that doesn't fit the HOLT and BCG fade models.

In light of this problem, it is not surprising that CFROI advocates are somewhat schizophrenic about the proper treatment of goodwill:

> Goodwill is important to include in TBR cashflows when assessing management—which incurred the financial cost of the acquisition—but it should be excluded when assessing the performance of the business for benchmarking or resource allocation purposes."[11]

---

10. B. Madden (1999), p. 80.
11. Boston Consulting Group, *Shareholder Value Metrics*, 1996, p. 37.

THE SUSTAINABLE GROWTH RATE

The HOLT and BCG valuation models estimate future cashflows from projected CFROI and the projected investment base. The projected investment base is derived from the assumptions that companies (1) maintain a constant debt/equity ratio (measured on a book value basis), (2) maintain a constant dividend payout ratio, and (3) reinvest 100 percent of available cashflow after interest and dividend payments. The growth rate in the investment base is called the *sustainable growth rate* because the required equity investment is covered by current cashflow without any need for external equity financing.

The use of the sustainable growth rate to forecast the future investment base is a simplification that is designed to eliminate the need for a sales forecast. Our preferred valuation approach is based on forecast assumptions or models for sales growth, NOPAT margin on sales, and capital intensity (as measured by invested capital ÷ sales). We develop sales growth models, based on regression analyses of peer company data, for internal and acquisition sales growth. We develop a separate forecast for acquisition sales, because acquisition sales growth typically has much greater capital requirements than internal sales growth. The internal sales growth model generally shows a declining sales growth rate as the company gets bigger. In some industries, however, we find that all companies above a certain size have similar growth rates—in other words, there is no negative size effect within the big company group.

Projected NOPAT margin is generally built up from models of major expense categories such as cost of goods sold, selling, general and administrative (SG&A) expenses, R&D, depreciation, and stock option expense. Our NOPAT models use peer company data to predict how expense ratios will change as a company gets bigger or as capital intensity changes. These models generally show that some expenses—for instance, R&D and stock option expense—decline with company size, while other expenses—for instance, cost of goods sold and SG&A—decline with capital intensity. Our projected capital intensity is generally built up from models of major capital components such as working capital, PP&E, goodwill, and capitalized R&D. We use peer company data to test whether capital intensity declines with size.

The major advantages of a sales-driven forecast are that (1) it makes it easier to determine if the product market assumptions underlying the valuation are reasonable and (2) it gives more insight into the sources of value and how management decision making could impact value. If the sales forecast is derived from assumptions about industry growth and company market share, the forecast can be evaluated for the reasonableness of the projected market share as well as the reasonableness of the absolute sales volume. Such an approach is particularly helpful in valuing acquisitions. A sales forecast can show what level of internal sales growth is required post-acquisition to make an acquisition value-enhancing.

The sustainable growth rate approach to forecasting is far simpler than a sales forecast in deriving future levels of capital investment, which offers important advantages to portfolio managers trying to value hundreds or thousands of companies at the same time. However, the predictive accuracy of this approach is an open question. In addition, such a "black box" simplification imposes serious limitations on the corporate user because it provides no insight on the business-related drivers of expected investment or on whether the assumptions that underlie the forecasts are consistent with economic reality.

THE HOLT/BCG CRITIQUE OF EVA

HOLT and BCG have leveled several criticisms against EVA. They argue that EVA

- Is biased against growth
- Ignores dividend payments
- Is biased by size and difficult to interpret or benchmark
- Is not adjusted for inflation

The argument that EVA is biased against growth is based on the assumption that EVA is calculated using straight-line depreciation. As we saw in Chapter 6, straight-line depreciation makes the accounting return on invested capital (or RONA) rise over the life of a project and differ from the economic, or internal, rate of return. This practice results in understating EVA in the early years of the project, while overstating it in later years. Even if the project is value-creating, the understatement of EVA in the early years might discourage managers with EVA-linked bonuses from undertaking the project.

The problem with this argument is that the source of the antigrowth bias is straight-line depreciation, not EVA. With sinking-fund and economic depreciation, the accounting return on capital equals the economic return. Because EVA equals [(RONA − WACC) × Invested capital], the EVA for a value-creating project (i.e., RONA > WACC) will decline as the capital base is recovered through depreciation. To increase EVA, the company must invest in additional value-creating projects. With proper depreciation, EVA is pro-growth, not anti-growth.

As we saw in Chapter 2, MVA is not a correct measure of shareholder value because it does not properly adjust for dividends. However, this argument does not apply to EVA. Excess return is equal to the sum of capitalized excess EVA improvement plus the excess future growth value (if any). Because excess return includes dividends, it now becomes clear that EVA does *not* ignore dividends. HOLT and BCG do not appear to be aware of the concept of expected EVA improvement and do not appear to understand that shareholder return is related to capitalized excess EVA improvement, not absolute EVA.

In addition, capitalized excess EVA improvement is easy to interpret. It is a proxy for excess return. If excess future growth value is zero, it is a perfect proxy. If excess future growth value is not zero, it is a less-than-perfect proxy.

The charge that EVA is biased by size reflects a confusion about measurement objectives. As we showed in Chapter 2, excess return is the proper measure of a company's contribution to shareholder wealth. It is also a highly useful measure of management's contribution to shareholder wealth, although it may, in part, reflect market and industry factors that are beyond management's control. It is not a perfect measure of management talent—that is, the ability to produce superior returns in the future. A company looking for a new CEO may be much more inclined to hire a manager who achieved a 30 percent excess return in a $100 million company than one who achieved a 5 percent excess return in a $1 billion company, even though the latter has created more wealth in absolute terms.

While TSR may be more predictive of future management performance, it does not make sense to argue, as BCG does, that:

When the TSR produced by a strategy is above the cost of capital, it becomes management's prerogative to focus on maximizing TSR or total market value, with the choice depending on circumstances and strategic considerations. Ideally, both measures should be considered in such decisions.[12]

The goal of management should always be to maximize excess return.

CORPORATE USES FOR CFROI

What does CFROI offer that EVA does not? In our view, not much, but one perceived advantage is that CFROI is expressed as a percentage. While this point may seem trivial, many corporate executives find percentage measures more descriptive than monetary measures such as EVA, especially when comparing companies, divisions, and investments of different size. This helps to explain why most managers prefer IRR to net present value in evaluating capital investments, despite the slight theoretical superiority of the latter. But the principal case for CFROI versus EVA rests on the assertion that it has a stronger conceptual link to total shareholder return (TSR). We find this argument questionable at best, especially in the debate over whether EVA or CFROI is a better value-based measure. The problem that characterizes much of the debate in the Metric Wars is confusion of historical performance measurement with forward-looking valuations.

As we discussed in Chapter 2, TSR is the most direct measure of changes in shareholder wealth over a given period, expressed in percentage terms (remembering, of course, that excess return is the best *monetary* measure of wealth created over a given period). Also, TSR can be easily compared from company to company, and benchmarked against industry or market returns, without having to worry about size bias. TSR is a function of dividends and stock price appreciation or depreciation (i.e., capital gains or losses).

By *dividends*, we mean not only regular dividend payments, but also any cash payments to shareholders, including special (one-time) dividends and share buybacks. Price appreciation is a function of expected profitability on existing assets and the profits expected by the capital markets from future growth. The value of

---

12. Boston Consulting Group, *Shareholder Value Metrics*, 1996, pp. 2–3.

the future cashflows expected from this growth is also a function of the company's cost of capital. The lower the cost of capital, the greater the value of expected future cashflows. Dividends and share buybacks are functions of free cashflow, net of interest and principal payments made to bankers and bondholders. The greater the free cashflow available to shareholders, the greater the amount that companies can devote to dividends and share buybacks.

TSR is driven by

♦ Profitability of assets in place
♦ Growth
♦ Cost of capital
♦ Free cashflow

No one would argue with this logic so far. Clearly, value-based companies want to achieve the highest TSR possible, and there is little controversy over the factors that drive returns. But TSR cannot be observed for privately held firms, or for divisions of public companies. For this reason, companies seek proxies that are both measurable and closely related to shareholder returns. The debate centers on which proxy does best in promoting value-creating behavior in companies or divisions.

According to CFROI advocates, the key to good performance measurement is to select a metric that directly incorporates all four TSR drivers. RONA, for example, does a good job of capturing the first TSR driver—the profitability of assets already in place. But it ignores growth and free cashflow, and it does not directly incorporate the cost of capital. EVA does better than RONA because it incorporates not only the profitability of assets in place but also the cost of capital. As a historical performance measure, however, it does not directly address growth or free cashflow. How does CFROI do better? After all, historical measures of CFROI ignore growth. Also, the cost of capital is not directly incorporated in the measure. How, then, can we develop a measure that incorporates *all* four TSR drivers?

The answer, according to CFROI proponents, is to use a forward-looking measure of CFROI called *total business return* (TBR). Of course, at this point we no longer have an historical performance measure. Employing the same valuation methodology used in the Briggs & Stratton example, TBR is designed to emulate the way capital markets determine TSR, but for an internal business unit or company plan. When CFROI is used in this way, it becomes, in effect, a forward-looking internal rate of return, and not a measure of the performance already achieved.

The parallels between TSR and TBR can be seen in Figure 9–11. To calculate TSR over, say, a three-year period, the actual price of a company's stock at the beginning of the period (in this case, the end of 1995) represents the initial investment. Returns are then a function of the dividends paid over the next three years and the actual price of the stock at the end of the period (in this case, the end of 1998). This return is equivalent to an IRR, and it is calculated in precisely the same way.

F I G U R E   9–11

Total shareholder return (TSR) and total business return (TBR)

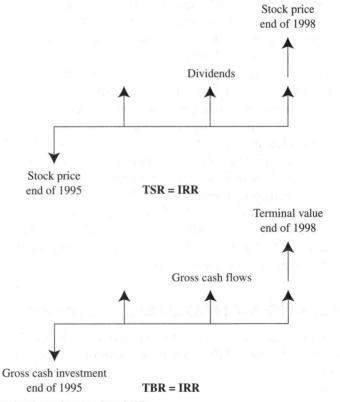

Source: Adapted from Boston Consulting Group (1995).

Now assume that instead of calculating TSR at the *end* of the three-year period, we attempt to estimate an IRR at the *beginning* of the period (as of the end of 1995). This is what we would do if, for example, we want to evaluate a proposed business strategy in one of our operating divisions. The value of the division is estimated as of the beginning of the period. This estimate is a substitute for the initial investment in the IRR calculation. The free cashflows expected in the division, assuming the strategy is undertaken, substitute for the dividends in the TSR calculation. The estimated terminal value of the division, which is based either on the present value of future free cashflows or on the value of nondepreciating assets, is a proxy for the stock price as of the end of the period. The result is a forward-looking IRR, which CFROI users call TBR.

TBR is calculated for any company, division, or strategy by using the inputs from CFROI: the economic life of depreciable assets; gross, inflation-adjusted cashflows; gross cash investment; and terminal value. Returning to Figure 9–11, gross cash investment represents the estimated value at the beginning of the period; gross cashflows substitute for the free cashflows (and, in fact, are calculated in much the same way); the terminal value represents the expected value at the end of the period; and the economic life of the depreciable assets describes the length of the investment horizon. The terminal value is a function of both the CFROI expected in the final year of the investment horizon and a fade rate at which the CFROI converges to a long-run, economy-wide average. In a manner similar to that described in the Briggs & Stratton example, these fading CFROIs are converted into a cashflow stream and discounted at a real cost of capital (i.e., inflation-adjusted). As a result of these calculations, TBR incorporates all four TSR drivers: the return on existing assets, growth, the cost of capital, and free cashflows.

CFROI AND MANAGEMENT COMPENSATION

Although CFROI advocates have yet to publish a detailed description of how to use CFROI for management compensation, BCG argues that[13]

---

13. BCG, 1996, pp. 24–25.

The TBR measure can be used for incentive compensation in two ways. For long-term-incentive programs, it can be used directly as a comprehensive measure of value creation by a business over several years (typically three to five). It can also be used to set annual targets for traditional measures (e.g., what earnings improvement is required to reach a target TBR if capital spending is held to budget or replacement levels) . . . TBR can also be accurately benchmarked against peer or market TSR performance as an objective way to set compensation targets using external standards. . . . The TBR achieved by the business can then be compared with either the TSR of a peer group, the TSR of the S&P 500 index, or a preset TSR target to determine compensation payouts. This feature avoids the need for extensive and often counterproductive negotiations around budgets and subsequent compensation targets.

BCG's description does not articulate a precise relationship between TBR and management compensation. Because TBR is a percentage, it cannot directly determine the dollar amount of management incentive compensation. If management's compensation is equal to the product of TBR (assuming it's greater than zero) and a target bonus, management compensation is equivalent to a phantom option with a percentage interest equal to the ratio of the target bonus to the estimated market value of the company.

Phantom option plans are a common approach to management compensation at the business-unit level. These plans give management a fixed percentage of the increase in business-unit shareholder wealth. The increase in shareholder wealth is the difference between ending shareholder wealth—that is, the terminal value of the business plus the future value of free cashflow over the measurement period—and beginning shareholder wealth. The incentive created by these plans depends on the NOPAT multiple used in the terminal value calculation. If the terminal value is $(1/\text{WACC}) \times \text{NOPAT}$, the incentive is equivalent to a bonus plan based on EVA improvement. A manager is better off reinvesting a dollar of NOPAT if the expected return on the investment is greater than the WACC—in other words, if the present value of expected EVAs from the investment is greater than zero. If the dollar is not reinvested, shareholder wealth is $1 + \text{WACC}$. If the dollar is reinvested and earns a return of r, shareholder wealth is $r + (r/\text{WACC})$. The manager is better off reinvesting the dollar as long as $1 + \text{WACC} < r + r/\text{WACC}$

$$1 + \text{WACC} < r \times [(1 + \text{WACC})/\text{WACC}]$$

$$\text{WACC} < r$$

If the terminal value is greater than $1/\text{WACC} \times \text{NOPAT}$, the phantom option plan provides an incentive to make investments that earn less than WACC. If the terminal value multiple is $2/\text{WACC}$, the manager is better off reinvesting a dollar as long as

$$1 + \text{WACC} < r + (2 \times r/\text{WACC})$$

$$1 + \text{WACC} < r \times [(2 + \text{WACC})/\text{WACC}]$$

$$[(1 + \text{WACC})/(2 + \text{WACC})] \times \text{WACC} < r$$

If the cost of capital is 10 percent, a manager is better off reinvesting a dollar as long as it earns a return of 5.2 percent.

Does it make sense to reward operating investments that only earn 5.2 percent, when the WACC is 10 percent? If current investments with an economic return in excess of the cost of capital only provide a current cash return of 5 percent, it may well make sense to reward investments that only earn 5 percent. In theory, it is possible to recognize negative economic depreciation and insist on a 10 percent (cost of capital) return, but, in practice, it may be more effective to use conventional accounting and reward investments that only earn 5 percent. However, if investments with an economic return in excess of the cost of capital normally provide a current cash return of 10 percent, then it does not make sense to reward investments that only return 5 percent. The company may well have an enterprise value of $20 \times \text{NOPAT}$, but this multiple may be due entirely to future investments that provide a current cash return of 10 percent. In this case, an EVA bonus plan makes more sense.

CONCLUSION

In this chapter, we've looked at the major battle in the so-called "Metric Wars," CFROI versus EVA. We showed how to calculate and interpret CFROI and how to use it to value businesses. The advocates of CFROI argue that it yields better estimates of corporate value; however, we demonstrated that the CFROI approach depends on a set of assumptions that either have an insufficient empirical basis (e.g., CFROI rates tend to fade to an economy-wide average) or are based on faulty logic (e.g., managers may knowingly invest in value-destroying capital projects). In addition, the calculations required for CFROI are complex and not easily understood by operating managers. Overall, CFROI offers few if any attractions as a measure of historical performance, and unlike EVA, it is generally unsuitable as the foundation for a value-driven compensation plan.

In the next chapter, we'll extend our analysis of the "Metric Wars" by examining several other important financial metrics.

APPENDIX: THE COST OF CAPITAL UNDER CFROI

CFROI proponents reject the capital asset pricing model as a tool for deriving a company's cost of equity and, through the weighted-average cost of capital formula, its cost of capital. Instead, discount rates are derived from current market prices for publicly traded shares, a process that can be seen from the following formula:

$$\text{Aggregate market value} = \frac{\text{forecasted aggregate net cashflows}}{1 + \text{market discount rate}}$$

The first step in calculating the market discount rate is to identify a universe of firms representing a large cross-section of the market, and then sum their market values (including debt and equity) at a particular time. Forecasts of net cashflows in the next period are derived from analysts' forecasts of earnings per share. These forecasts are then summed to provide a forecast of aggregate net cashflows. If two of the three variables in the equation are known, the third (in this case, the market discount rate) can be derived. The market discount rate is the rate of interest that equates the capitalized value of the aggregate net cashflows to the aggregate market value.

Madden (1998) uses this procedure to estimate a real market discount rate as of August 1996, based on market values and net cashflow forecasts for 1284 firms. The derived rate is 5.8 percent. In the Briggs & Stratton example, the forecast cashflows over the five-year fade window are discounted at 5.8 percent, while all subsequent cashflows (year $t + 6$ to year $t + 40$) are discounted at 6.3 percent, the long-run average CFROI. This assumption assumes that after year $t + 40$, no value is created because CFROI

T A B L E 9–3

Median Risk Differentials: 10,350 Observations, August 1986 to August 1996

		Largest									Smallest	
	All	1	2	3	4	5	6	7	8	9	10	
Highest 1	1.34	1.00	1.02	1.04	1.15	1.15	1.21	1.39	1.48	1.65	1.64	
2	0.92	0.64	0.53	0.95	0.82	0.76	0.70	1.01	1.15	1.19	1.60	
3	0.65	0.26	0.43	0.47	0.72	0.45	0.71	0.72	0.76	1.11	1.06	
4	0.38	0.21	−0.19	0.18	0.28	0.35	0.37	0.50	0.90	0.82	1.18	
Financial 5	0.16	0.07	−0.46	−0.12	0.10	0.13	0.45	0.25	0.98	0.64	0.88	
Leverage 6	−0.02	−0.60	−0.69	−0.20	−0.46	−0.11	0.14	0.14	0.49	0.76	0.38	
Deciles 7	−0.29	−0.81	−0.68	−0.33	−0.49	−0.45	−0.11	−0.17	0.08	0.19	0.73	
8	−0.47	−1.25	−0.74	−0.70	−0.78	−0.57	−0.05	−0.24	−0.26	0.05	0.19	
9	−0.77	−1.47	−1.23	−1.09	−1.14	−0.95	−0.43	−0.77	−0.36	−0.57	0.05	
Lowest 10	−0.99	−1.32	−2.09	−1.61	−0.99	−0.74	−1.52	−0.81	−0.44	−0.43	−0.56	
All	0.16	−0.19	−0.23	−0.06	−0.15	−0.02	0.18	0.22	0.51	0.64	0.90	

Size (Equity Market) Deciles

Sources: Madden (1998).

will have converged to the cost of capital. Value creation is possible only when CFROI is greater than the cost of capital.

Although the Briggs & Stratton example uses the market-wide discount rate, company-specific discount rates can also be used. The HOLT CFROI approach assumes that company-specific risk is a function of financial leverage and size, two risk factors that cannot be eliminated through diversification and therefore should be reflected in discount rate differentials. It is assumed that small firms and highly levered firms are riskier than larger companies and those with low levels of debt. Therefore, high-leverage companies and small companies will tend to have company-specific discount rates that exceed the market discount rate. Madden (1998) reports the results of a test for discount rate differentials based on size and leverage. A universe of firms is selected starting in August 1986 and ending in August 1996. The number of firms in the sample grows from 732 in the first year to 1284 in the last as the necessary data become available for more companies. The final sample consists of 10,350 observations. In each year, each company is placed in a decile based on size and financial leverage. The firms in the top 10 percent based on size are placed in the first-size decile, the next 10 percent in the second decile, and so on. An implied discount rate is then calculated based on forecast net cashflows (as usual, derived from analysts' forecasts of earnings per share) and the market value of the firm.

Finally, a risk differential is calculated on the basis of the implied discount rate for the company, minus the market discount rate at that time (market rates varied from 5.2 percent to 6.7 percent over the 10-year period). The risk differentials are then averaged over the 10 years in each of the size/leverage categories. The results are reported in Table 9–3. Companies in the top-size decile and the lowest-leverage decile have a risk differential of −1.32 percent. This means that the company-specific rate used to discount future cashflows for valuation purposes would equal the market discount rate *minus* 1.32 percent. As of August 1986, when the market discount rate was 5.8 percent, companies in this category would have company-specific discount rates of 5.8 percent − 1.32 percent, or 4.48 percent.

CHAPTER 10

Understanding the Metric Wars

As we've stressed throughout this book, even the most ardent supporter of any performance metric, including EVA, will undoubtedly concede that no single performance measure should be used for every situation. Most companies rely on a number of measures, with each providing varying benefits and serving a different purpose. In this chapter, we will compare the advantages and disadvantages of the most widely used performance metrics. Such an understanding is indispensable to designing management systems—in the areas of performance measurement, incentive compensation, operating budgets, and internal and external communications—that promote the creation of shareholder value.

Before we begin our assessment, let's break the metrics down into categories to aid our analysis. Although measures of corporate performance can be distinguished along many dimensions, we believe that a useful first step is to sort them into five basic categories:

- Residual income measures
- Residual income components
- Market-based measures
- Cashflow measures
- Traditional income measures

1. *Residual income measures,* such as economic value added, are derived by subtracting capital costs, including debt *and* equity, from operating profit, whether measured on the basis of accounting accruals or cashflows. Economic profit (or what we refer to earlier as "unadjusted EVA") and cash value added (CVA) are also residual income measures.

2. *Residual income components* are elements of residual income, but typically do not include capital costs. Because they are more detailed, or disaggregated, measures than residual income and can be tied more directly to the responsibilities of middle managers, their use is popular below business-unit level. Examples include earnings before interest and tax (EBIT); EBITDA (EBIT, with depreciation and amortization added back); net operating profit after tax (NOPAT); and return on net assets (RONA).

3. *Market-based measures* are derived from the capital markets and include total shareholder return (TSR), market value added (MVA), excess return, and future growth value (FGV). Because market-based measures require reliable estimates for the value of equity, these measures are available only for publicly traded entities.

4. *Cashflow measures* are designed to sidestep the influence of accrual accounting, and include cashflow from operations (CFO), free cashflow, and cashflow return on investment (CFROI).

5. *Traditional income measures* include the metrics that corporate executives and external analysts have focused on for decades, such as net income and earnings per share (EPS).

Of course, some measures do not slot conveniently into just one category. For example, CVA, which is a residual income measure, and EBITDA, a residual income component measure, can also be considered measures of cashflow. EBIT is both a residual income component and a traditional income measure. Nevertheless, we find this classification scheme useful in our work and believe it to be a convenient and logical way of comparing the most popular metrics.

What distinguishes each of these five categories of performance metrics from the others is how they differ according to whether they

- Are denominated in monetary terms (e.g., dollars) or in percentage terms
- Include the cost of debt
- Include the cost of equity
- Are measurable at divisional level
- Are easy to calculate
- Are inflation-adjusted
- Include the value of future investments

The differences among 16 of the most important financial metrics are summarized in Table 10–1. We focus on these characteristics not only because they help us to differentiate competing metrics but also because these are the characteristics that consultants, finance specialists, and corporate users typically cite to describe the relative advantages and disadvantages of the metrics.

All residual income measures, including EVA, are denominated in monetary terms and include the effects of all capital costs, both debt and equity. Another attractive feature is that they are measurable at the divisional level, thereby providing a better line of sight than market-based measures, such as TSR and MVA, which can be measured only for publicly traded entities. However, unlike market-based measures, residual income measures do not incorporate the market's opinion on the value of future growth opportunities. In other words, EVA and its sister metrics are short-term in nature, as are all metrics apart from those that are based on market values.

EVA is distinguished from other residual income measures in that it is not bound by generally accepted accounting principles (GAAP). This difference offers the potential advantage of producing more economically valid figures, but at the cost of added computational complexity. This is why we consider economic profit and CVA easier to calculate than EVA. CVA does require some adjustment, however, because accounting accruals must be reversed. Therefore, CVA calculations are more complicated than those of economic profit, or unadjusted EVA.

TABLE 10-1

Comparison of Performance Metrics

Measure	Measure Type	$ or %	Includes Cost of Debt	Includes Cost of Equity	Measurable at Divisional Level	Ease of Calculation	Inflation-Adjusted	Includes Value of Future Investments
EVA	RI	$	Yes	Yes	Yes	Medium	Possibly	No
Economic profit	RI	$	Yes	Yes	Yes	High	No	No
CVA	RI/CF	$	Yes	Yes	Yes	Medium/high	Usually no	No
EBIT	RIC/TI	$	No	No	Yes	High	No	No
EBITDA	RIC/CF	$	No	No	Yes	High	No	No
NOPAT	RIC	$	No	No	Yes	High	No	No
RONA	RIC	%	No	No	Yes	High	Usually no	No
TSR	MB	%	*	*	No	High	No	Yes
MVA	MB	$	*	*	No	High	No	Yes
Excess return	MB	$	Yes	Yes	No	Low/medium	No	Yes
FGV	MB	$	*	*	No	High	No	Yes
CFO	CF	$	No	No	Yes	High	No	No
Free cashflow	CF	$	No	No	Yes	High	No	No
CFROI	CF	%	No	No	Yes	Low	Yes	No
Net income	TI	$	Yes	No	Yes	High	No	No
EPS	TI	$	Yes	No	No	High	No	No

Note: RI = residual income; RIC = residual income component; MB = market-based; CF = cashflow; TI = traditional income.
* Capital costs are not explicitly included in market-based measures but are reflected indirectly in the discount rates the market inputs to the expected stream of future cashflows or EVAs.

The principal attraction of residual income components, such as RONA and EBITDA, is that while their links to residual income (or EVA) are unmistakable, they are easier to calculate and observe at divisional and subdivisional levels of the firm. In many companies, residual income measures are reserved for corporate level, and perhaps major sector, division, or business-unit levels. But below these levels, where discretion over resource allocation is highly limited, the general preference is for RONA and similar measures. The most important potential drawback of RONA—namely, that managers in high-RONA divisions turn down value-creating projects because RONA may decrease—is less of a concern at levels of a company in which major investment decisions are made by the unit manager's bosses.

Market-based measures have the important advantage that they incorporate market expectations of future growth and, apart from excess return, are easy to calculate. Their main drawback, of course, is that they can only be measured for publicly traded entities and therefore are unusable at divisional levels.

Cashflow measures are also easy to calculate, apart from CFROI, and offer the additional (perceived) advantage that they tie performance measurement to the factor that capital markets prize most: the ability of a business to generate cashflow. They also cater to a common bias among finance professionals that accounting earnings simply cannot be trusted to guide the evaluation of corporate performance. Cashflow metrics are seen as a means of liberating companies from the tyranny of GAAP. We question whether this really is an advantage and have more to say on this point later in the chapter.

Finally, traditional income measures, such as net income and EPS, have the important virtue that they are already available through the normal financial reporting process. Also, despite the critiques of cashflow advocates, they are closely scrutinized by the capital markets and have been shown through empirical research to be surprisingly resilient in terms of explaining stock price performance (at least when compared to other measures). The downside is their failure to directly consider the cost of equity, and the relative ease with which they can be manipulated, which can sometimes lead to value-destroying decisions on the part of managers who are evaluated and paid on the basis of these measures.

COMPARING THE METRICS: A CASE STUDY

To further illustrate the key features of the competing metrics, we demonstrate how to calculate all the most commonly used measures of performance from a common set of data. Table 10–2 reports selected financial data from Hewlett-Packard, the American computer firm, covering a five-year period from the end of fiscal year 1993 to the end of fiscal year 1998.[1] Most of the data comes directly from the company's annual reports. All other data, such as end-of-year share price, is in the public domain. The cost of capital for each year is based on estimates from Stern Stewart & Company, while the figures related to operating lease expense and the present value of operating leases are based on our own estimates (using public information).[2]

This example not only allows us to show how all of the metrics are calculated but also provides an opportunity to compare and contrast the key features of these metrics.

Four of the most popular measures are available directly from the financial statements and require no further calculation: operating income, sometimes known as EBIT (Table 10–2, line 2); net income (line 6); cashflow from operations (CFO, line 21); and earnings per share (line 31). All these measures, apart from CFO, are conventional measures of accounting profit, although EBIT can also be viewed as a residual income component. The main difference between net income and operating income is that the former includes the effects of interest expense, interest income, and taxes, while the latter does not. EPS converts net income to a per share basis, incorporating the effects of potential share dilution owing to convertible securities, stock options, and the like.

In the case of Hewlett-Packard, the three noncash measures tell a similar story (see Table 10–3). The level of profits increases over the first four years, especially from 1994 to 1995, but declines in 1998. CFO, which eliminates the influence of accrual accounting, tells a somewhat different story. Operations actually generated less cash in 1995 than in 1994, despite a sharp rise in accounting profits. Also, CFO increased in 1998, despite a fall in profits.

---

1. Hewlett-Packard's fiscal year runs from November 1 to October 31.
2. Operating lease expense is based on the projected minimum lease payments for that year, as of the end of the previous year.

T A B L E 10-2

Hewlett-Packard Selected Financial Data

		1998	1997	1996	1995	1994	1993
(1)	Net revenue	$47,061	$42,895	$38,420	$31,519	$24,991	
(2)	Operating income	3,841	4,339	3,726	3,568	2,549	
(3)	Interest income	485	331	295	270	29	
(4)	Interest expense	235	215	327	206	155	
(5)	Income taxes	1,146	1,336	1,108	1,199	824	
(6)	Net income	2,945	3,119	2,586	2,433	1,599	
(7)	Depreciation and amortization	1,869	1,556	1,297	1,139	1,006	
(8)	Cash + short-term investment	4,067	4,569	3,327	2,616	2,478	1,644
(9)	Other current assets	17,517	16,378	14,664	13,623	10,031	8,592
(10)	Gross property, plant, and equipment (PPE)	12,570	11,776	10,198	8,747	7,938	7,527
(11)	Accumulated depreciation	6,212	5,464	4,662	4,036	3,610	3,347
(12)	Land	450	468	475	485	508	514
(13)	Other long-term investments (including intangibles)	5,731	4,490	4,172	3,477	2,730	2,320
(14)	Total assets	33,673	31,749	27,699	24,427	19,567	16,736
(15)	Short-term debt	1,245	1,226	2,125	3,214	2,461	2,190

TABLE 10-2

Continued

		1998	1997	1996	1995	1994	1993
(16)	Other current liabilities	12,228	9,993	8,498	7,730	5,761	4,678
(17)	Long-term debt	2,063	3,158	2,579	663	547	667
(18)	Other long-term liabilities	1,218	1,217	1,059	981	864	690
(19)	Shareholders' equity	16,919	6,155	13,438	11,839	9,926	8,511
(20)	Number of shares outstanding (adjusted for stock splits)	1,015*	1,041*	1,014*	1,020*	1,019*	1,011*
(21)	Cashflow from operations	5,442	4,321	3,456	1,613	2,224	
(22)	Net investment (PPE + other investments, net of disposals)	2,346	2,005	2,619	1,615	1,298	
(23)	Share buybacks, net of new issues	1,957	305	726	325	25	
(24)	Dividends	625	532	450	358	280	
(25)	Effective tax rate (in %)	28.0	30.0	30.0	33.0	34.0	
(26)	Closing share price (in $)	60.25	61.625	50.25	46.313	24.469	18.406
(27)	PV of operating leases	598	598	482	442	406	498
(28)	Operating lease expense	182	182	162	157	179	
(29)	WACC (in %)	15.0	15.0	15.7	15.5	16.5	
(30)	Cost of equity (in %)	16.08	16.08	17.05	17.06	18.21	
(31)	EPS (diluted)	2.77	2.95	2.46	2.31	1.54	

* In billions.

Notes: Amounts in millions of dollars unless otherwise noted.
Fiscal year ends October 31.

T A B L E   10–3

EBIT, Net Income, CFO, and EPS for Hewlett-Packard*

	1998	1997	1996	1995	1994
(2) Operating income (EBIT)	3841	4339	3726	3568	2549
(6) Net income	2945	3119	2586	2433	1599
(21) Cashflow from operations (CFO)	5442	4321	3456	1613	2224
(31) Earnings per share (EPS)	2.77	2.95	2.46	2.31	1.54

* In millions of dollars.

The other metrics are not directly revealed in the financial statements, but they can be calculated from data provided either in the financial statements or in the notes to the financial statements, or from other public disclosures. All calculations are based on the data in Table 10–2.

Residual Income Components

We begin the calculations with residual income components, because without one such component—net operating profit after tax (NOPAT)—EVA and the other residual income measures cannot be calculated. NOPAT is calculated by adding interest income (Table 10–2, line 3) to operating income (line 2), or EBIT, then multiplying the result by [1 – the effective tax rate (line 25)]. In our model (see Method 1 of Table 10–4), interest income is included in NOPAT because cash balances are included in invested capital. If management is to be charged for the use of cash, any returns generated on the cash, such as interest on government bonds, should also be included in NOPAT. When residual income measures are brought into divisions, cash is normally excluded from invested capital, because it is nearly always managed centrally by a corporate treasurer. In such cases, interest income should not be included in NOPAT.

T A B L E   10–4

Calculating NOPAT for Hewlett-Packard*

NOPAT	1998	1997	1996	1995	1994
Method 1					
(2) Operating income	3841	4339	3726	3568	2549
+ (3) Interest income	485	331	295	270	29
	4326	4670	4021	3838	2578
× [1 − (25) effective tax rate]	72%	70%	70%	67%	66%
= NOPAT	3115	3269	2815	2571	1701
Method 2					
(2) Operating income	3841	4339	3726	3568	2549
+ (3) Interest income	485	331	295	270	29
− (5) Income taxes	1146	1336	1108	1199	824
− Tax shield on interest expense					
[(4) Interest expense × (25) effective tax rate]	66	65	98	68	53
= NOPAT	3114†	3269	2815	2571	1701

* In millions of dollars.
† Rounding difference.

Alternatively, NOPAT can be calculated by subtracting the income tax expense from the income statement (line 5), then subtracting the tax shield on interest expense (see Method 2 of Table 10–4). In this way, the amount of tax expense reflected in NOPAT is based only on operating income (including interest income), which is equivalent to multiplying the corporate tax rate by the sum of operating income and interest income. Any differences between the two approaches to calculating NOPAT are attributable to rounding errors.

Hewlett-Packard's NOPAT increased sharply from 1994 to 1995, then increased steadily over the following two years, and fell slightly in 1998. As we will see in Table 10–5, this deterioration in operating profitability helps to explain the sharp drop in the company's EVA from 1997 to 1998. EBITDA exhibits a similar pattern to NOPAT, as we would expect assuming consistent tax rates and depreciation policies. (NOPAT is essentially EBITDA, minus

T A B L E   10–5

Calculating EBITDA and RONA for Hewlett-Packard*

	1998	1997	1996	1995	1994
EBITDA					
(2) Operating income	3,841	4,339	3,726	3,568	2,549
+ (7) Depreciation and amortization	1,869	1,556	1,297	1,139	1,006
= EBITDA	5,710	5,895	5,023	4,707	3,555
RONA					
NOPAT	3,115	3,269	2,815	2,571	1,701
÷ Invested capital [(14) total assets − (16) Other current liabilities]	21,756	19,201	16,697	13,806	12,058
= RONA	14.32%	17.03%	16.86%	18.62%	14.11%

*In millions of dollars.

taxes and depreciation.) RONA tells a slightly different story. Because it incorporates invested capital, unlike NOPAT and EBITDA, RONA can decrease even with higher operating profits because of higher capital. This is exactly what happened from 1995 to 1996. RONA decreased by nearly 2 percent because modest increases in NOPAT were more than offset by a nearly $3 billion increase in capital. Even strong profit improvement in 1997 did little to RONA as a result of still further investment. In 1998, invested capital increased by another $2.5 billion. When this is combined with lower operating profits, RONA decreases by nearly 3 percent.

Residual Income Measures

Residual income is the generic term describing any profit measure that charges for the use of capital resources, including equity. Economic profit, EVA, and cash value added (CVA) are residual income measures.

Our definition of economic profit is identical to the unadjusted, or shortcut, version of EVA introduced in Chapter 2. With *economic profit*, at least as defined here, a company's accounting policies are taken as given, without adjustment for potential biases or distortions caused by the application of generally accepted accounting principles (GAAP). The more generic term residual income is sometimes used in place of economic profit.

The calculation is straightforward (Method 1 of Table 10–6), using the NOPAT figure derived earlier. Capital charges are based on invested capital at the beginning of each year (although averages can be used too, as they are in Chapter 2), multiplied by WACC (Table 10–2, line 29). Invested capital is calculated by subtracting short-term, non-interest-bearing liabilities, or what Hewlett-Packard calls "other current liabilities" (line 16), from total assets (line 14).

Economic profit can also be calculated by multiplying the spread between RONA and WACC by invested capital (Method 2 of Table 10–6). The two approaches yield the same answer (apart from rounding errors).

The (adjusted) EVA calculations are based on the economic profit figures, adjusted for operating leases.

Although many more adjustments could be made, our intent (see Table 10–7) is to contrast the approach of calculating adjusted

T A B L E   10–6

Calculating Economic Profit for Hewlett-Packard*

	1998	1997	1996	1995	1994
Method 1					
NOPAT	3,115	3,269	2,815	2,571	1,701
− Capital charges [invested capital × (29) WACC]	3,263	2,880	2,621	2,140	1,990
= Economic profit	(148)	389	194	431	(289)
Method 2					
Invested capital	21,756	19,201	16,697	13,806	12,058
× [RONA − (29) WACC]	(0.0068)	0.0203	0.0116	0.0312	(0.0239)
= Economic profit	(148)	388†	194	431	(288)†

* In millions of dollars.
† Rounding difference.

T A B L E   10–7

Calculating Adjusted and Unadjusted EVA for Hewlett-Packard*

	1998	1997	1996	1995	1994
Unadjusted NOPAT	3,115	3,269	2,815	2,571	1,701
+ Changes in other long-term liabilities	1	158	78	117	174
+ Interest portion of operating lease payments (net of tax shield on interest)	43	34	31	27	33
= Adjusted NOPAT	3,158	3,303	2,846	2,598	1,724
− Capital charges [adjusted invested capital × (29) WACC]	3,353	2,952	2,691	2,203	2,072
= EVA	(195)	351	155	395	(338)
(27) PV of operating leases (beginning)	598	482	442	406	498
× Pretax interest rate on leases	10%	10%	10%	10%	10%
= Interest portion of lease payments	60	48	44	41	50
× [1 − (25) effective tax rate]	72%	70%	70%	67%	66%
= Interest portion, net of tax shield	43	34	31	27	33
Unadjusted invested capital (beginning)	21,756	19,201	16,697	13,806	12,058
+ PV of operating leases	598	482	442	406	498
= Adjusted invested capital	22,354	19,683	17,139	14,212	12,556

*In millions of dollars.

and unadjusted EVA, and to show how both NOPAT and invested capital are affected.

Cash value added, or CVA, is an alternative residual income measure designed to produce a profit figure even closer to cash-flow than the adjusted version of EVA, while retaining EVA's advantage of accounting for all capital costs. The most important difference between CVA and EVA is that the latter is net of depreciation, while the former is not.

Under CVA (see Table 10–8), NOPAT does not include charges for depreciation or amortization. Also, invested capital is reported gross, and not net, of depreciation. In other words, invested capital is "grossed up" by the amount of accumulated depreciation. According to CVA advocates, its main advantage is that it cannot be influenced by depreciation policy.

For example, if two companies are similar in terms of performance but depreciate their assets at different rates, huge differences in EVA may result. Similar problems can arise when attempting to compare divisions of the same company. For example, one division may have fully depreciated assets, while another has largely undepreciated assets because of recent investments. The former will have far less invested capital than the latter, resulting in lower capital charges and higher EVA. In such cases, and they are common, divisions report different levels of EVA, not necessarily because of different levels of performance

T A B L E   10–8

Calculating Cash Value Added for Hewlett-Packard*

	1998	1997	1996	1995	1994
NOPAT	3,115	3,269	2,815	2,571	1,701
+ (7) Depreciation and amortization	1,869	1,556	1,297	1,139	1,006
+ (18) Changes in other LTLs	1	158	78	117	174
= Cash-basis NOPAT	4,985	4,983	4,190	3,827	2,881
− Capital charges [cash-basis invested capital × (29) WACC]	4,083	3,579	3,255	2,699	2,542
= Cash value added	902	1,404	935	1,128	339
Invested capital (unadjusted)	21,756	19,201	16,697	13,806	12,058
+ (11) Accumulated depreciation	5,464	4,662	4,036	3,610	3,347
= Cash-basis invested capital	27,220	23,863	20,733	17,416	15,405

* In millions of dollars.

but because depreciation policy has led to wildly different capital bases.

Because CVA is a cash-based measure, we must add back depreciation to NOPAT and to invested capital, and adjust key elements of accrual accounting such as provisions and deferred taxes (both of which comprise other long-term liabilities). Of course, just as with EVA, users of CVA can choose from a broad range of other adjustments; our version ignores these. Our CVA is calculated by adjusting the NOPAT and invested capital figures used for the unadjusted version of EVA. Depreciation and amortization (Table 10–2, line 7) and changes in long-term liabilities (the ending balance minus the beginning balance, from line 18), encompassing provisions and deferred taxes, are added to NOPAT to produce a cash-basis NOPAT. No tax adjustment is required for depreciation because the tax effects of depreciation have cashflow consequences. We want those consequences, already included in the NOPAT used for EVA, to be reflected in the calculation of CVA. The capital charges are based on the same WACC (line 29) as before, but invested capital is grossed up for accumulated depreciation (line 11). Further adjustment is not required for provisions and deferred taxes because these balances are already included in the unadjusted version of invested capital.

The time series of Hewlett-Packard's CVA is similar to that of EVA, in that the years with the highest EVA (1995 and 1997) also have the highest CVAs. Of course, the CVA figures are higher than EVA because of the depreciation add-back. Although EVA is negative in 1994 and 1998, the CVA for 1998 is noticeably higher than that of 1994 because large investments in the interim led to high depreciation charges in 1998. These charges ($1.869 billion) depress EVA but have no effect on CVA.

In our view, the perceived advantages of CVA over EVA— namely, that it removes the effect of depreciation on results and that it more directly measures cashflow—are somewhat spurious. First, the problem that divisions can report different *levels* of EVA because of different asset bases (because of depreciation) is of little consequence as long as the company focuses attention on, and rewards performance on the basis of, *improvement* in EVA. Also, for companies that continue to rely on levels of EVA as a performance measure, the use of economic depreciation (discussed in

Chapter 7 as sinking fund or annuity depreciation) effectively solves the problems sometimes caused by conventional accounting depreciation.

The major drawback of the CVA metric is that it fosters the potentially dangerous illusion that if cashflow is what matters in the capital markets, we should base performance measurement systems on cashflows. We have gone to great lengths in this book to show why this thinking is wrong. Cash may be king, but only in the form of *expected future free cashflow*. It does not necessarily follow that performance measurement and management compensation (both based on the recent past) should be based on historical cashflows. We elaborate on this point later in the chapter.

Market-Based Measures

Market-based measures reflect company performance from a capital markets perspective. In this section, we focus on market value added (MVA), total shareholder return (TSR), and excess return.

MVA equals the difference between the market value of the firm and invested capital, which is typically measured at the end of each year. Because market values for debt are not available, we assume that the market value of debt equals the book value of debt (Table 10–2, line 15 for short-term debt; line 17 for long-term debt). The market value of equity equals the number of shares of common stock outstanding (line 20) times the share price at the end of each year (line 26). Invested capital is calculated in the same manner as before, but using end-of-year balances in place of beginning balances (as we do with the EVA calculations). See Table 10–9.

Hewlett-Packard's MVA rose sharply in 1995, thanks mainly to a near doubling of the company's share price. MVA rose again in 1996, although more modestly, followed by a larger increase in 1997. It then declined by nearly $4 billion in 1998. Given the strong stock market returns of the late 1990s, Hewlett-Packard was clearly an underperformer.

TSR is estimated by adding annual dividends per share [dividends (line 24) ÷ average number of shares outstanding (line 20)] to the change in share price (i.e., capital appreciation or depreciation) during the year [the ending share price – the beginning share price (from line 26)], divided by the beginning share price.

T A B L E   10–9

Calculating Market Value Added for Hewlett-Packard*

	1998	1997	1996	1995	1994
(15) Short-term debt	1,245	1,226	2,125	3,214	2,461
+ (17) Long-term debt	2,063	3,158	2,579	663	547
+ (18) Other long-term liabilities	1,218	1,217	1,059	981	864
+ Market value of equity	61,154	64,152	50,954	47,239	24,934
= Market value of the firm	65,680	69,753	56,717	52,097	28,806
− Invested capital (ending)	21,445	21,756	19,201	16,697	13,806
= MVA	44,235	47,997	37,516	35,400	15,000
(20) # of shares outstanding	1.015	1.041	1.014	1.020	1.019
× (26) Closing share price	60.25	61.625	50.25	46.313	24.469
= Market value of equity	61,154	64,152	50,954	47,239	24,934

* In millions of dollars.

For Hewlett-Packard, TSR tells a similar story as MVA (see Table 10–10), but then it should, because changes in share price are the major influence on both metrics. The major difference, of course, is that TSR is expressed as a percentage, while MVA is expressed in monetary terms. Hewlett-Packard registers strongly positive TSRs in three of the four years from 1994 through 1997, but turns slightly negative in 1998.

Excess return measures the difference, in dollars, between *actual* shareholder wealth and the *expected* shareholder wealth as of a particular date. This calculation requires a starting point from which both components can be calculated. In theory, this starting point is the time the firm was established, because excess return is designed as a measure of cumulative wealth creation. As a practical matter, data limitations require selection of a more recent date, at least for a long-established company such as Hewlett-Packard. In this example, beginning wealth is defined as of the end of 1993.

The principal advantage of excess return as a performance measure becomes apparent when we contrast it with MVA. Like excess return, MVA purports to be a measure of cumulative wealth

T A B L E   10–10

Calculating Total Shareholder Return for
Hewlett-Packard*

	1998	1997	1996	1995	1994
Dividends per share [(24) dividends ÷ (20) average no. of shares outstanding]	0.608	0.518	0.442	0.351	0.276
+ (26) Ending share price − (26) Beginning share price	(1.375) (0.767)	11.375 11.893	3.937 4.379	21.844 22.195	6.063 6.339
÷ (26) Beginning share price × 100	61.625	50.25	46.313	24.469	18.406
= TSR	(1.24%)	23.67%	9.46%	90.71%	34.44%
[(20) Beginning no. of shares outstanding + (20) Ending no. of shares outstanding]					
÷ 2	2	2	2	2	2
= Average no. of shares outstanding	1.028	1.028	1.017	1.020	1.015

*In millions of dollars.

creation, but, in fact, it is not. The reason MVA is misleading as a cumulative measure of wealth is that it ignores distributions to and contributions from shareholders. Only in the highly restrictive case in which all positive EVAs are treated as reductions to invested capital and all negative EVAs are treated as increases does MVA equal excess return and thus provide an accurate indication of the wealth created over a measurement period. Excess return, on the other hand, is always an accurate measure of cumulative wealth creation, regardless of dividend policy, share buybacks, or new equity issues. The reason is that excess return charges companies for the opportunity cost of the equity capital tied up in the firm over the measurement period, and it credits the company for the returns its shareholders should have received from reinvesting cash distributions.

Excess return does have one important disadvantage. The calculations are far more involved than those for MVA, which helps to explain why MVA is still the dominant, dollar-denominated measure of corporate wealth creation. Even so, we believe that the conceptual superiority of excess return is well worth the effort. And, as we will show with Hewlett-Packard, the calculations are not quite as complex as one might think. As long as we know the value of equity at the beginning and the end of the measurement period, distributions to shareholders (dividends + share buybacks), net of new equity contributions, and the cost of equity, we can calculate excess return.

Excess return is calculated as follows:

Ending market capitalization of equity
    [no. of shares outstanding (Table 10–2, line 20)
    × share price (line 26)]

+

Future value of distributions to shareholders
    [dividends (line 24) + share buybacks,
    net of new share issues (line 23) × annual cost of equity
    (line 30) for each year since the start of the measurement period]

−

Expected shareholder wealth [capitalized value of equity
    at the beginning of the measurement period (line 20 × line 26)
    × annual cost of equity (line 30)
    for each year since the start of the measurement period]

Adding the future value of dividends and share buybacks, net of new share issues, to the ending market capitalization of equity yields the ending shareholder wealth. Excess return is the difference between this level of wealth and the wealth that investors would expect if they receive a cost-of-equity return on the beginning market value of their investment (see Table 10–11).

The future value of dividends and share buybacks, net of stock issues, is calculated as follows. Beginning in 1994, Hewlett-Packard returned $25 million in cash via share buybacks, net of

T A B L E   10–11

Calculating Excess Return for Hewlett-Packard*

	1998	1997	1996	1995	1994
Ending market value of equity†	61,154	64,152	50,954	47,239	24,934
+ Future value of dividends and share buybacks, net of new share issues	6,722	3,566	2,351	1,040	305
= Ending shareholder wealth	67,876	67,718	53,305	48,279	25,239
− Expected shareholder wealth	40,612	34,987	30,140	25,750	21,997
= Excess return	27,264	32,731	23,165	22,529	3,242

*In millions of dollars.
†See MVA calculations.

the cash contributions made that year by shareholders for newly issued shares (Table 10–2, line 23). The company also made $280 million in dividend payments (line 24), bringing the total of net cash distributions to $305 million. We assume that the future value of these distributions in 1994 is equal to the nominal amount of the distribution. In other words, we assume that investors would not have expected returns from these cash payments in the year in which the payments were made. This means that shareholder wealth at the end of 1994 is $25,239 million, or $305 million + the market capitalization of Hewlett-Packard's equity.

The calculations become slightly more complex in later years. Given Hewlett-Packard's cost of equity in 1995 of 17.06 percent, an investor in Hewlett-Packard stock would rightly have expected to earn this rate of return on the cash distributions made in 1994. The value of these distributions now becomes $305 million × 1.1706, or $357 million. In addition, there are further cash distributions in 1995 of $683 million ($325 million in share buybacks, and $358 million in dividends). The value of these cash distributions at the end of 1995 is thus $1,040 million ($357 million + $683 million). When added to the market capitalization of equity as of the same date, ending shareholder wealth becomes $48,279 million.

For 1996, the ending value of distributions equals $1040 million (the ending value from the previous year) × 1.1705 (the cost of equity for 1996), plus the cash distributions made in 1996 ($726 million in buybacks and $450 million in dividends), for a total of $2351 million. When added to the year-end market capitalization ($50,954 million), ending shareholder wealth is $53,305 million.

The value of the cash distributions at year-end 1996 is multiplied by 1.1608 (the cost of equity in 1997) to derive the value of those distributions at the end of 1997 ($2729 million). When the share buybacks ($305 million) and dividends ($532 million) of the current year are added, the ending value of cash distributions becomes $3566 million. Adding the value of cash distributions to the ending market capitalization ($64,152 million) provides an ending shareholder wealth of $67,718 million.

The ending cash distributions have an ending value for 1998 of $3566 million (the value at the end of 1997) × 1.1608 (the cost of equity in 1998), plus the share buybacks ($1957 million) and dividends ($625 million) made in 1998, for a total of $6722 million. When added to the year-end market capitalization ($61,154 million), ending shareholder wealth is $67,876 million.

To calculate excess return, expected shareholder wealth is subtracted from ending, or actual, shareholder wealth. Expected shareholder wealth is calculated by taking the capitalized market value of equity at the beginning of the measurement period (1.011 billion shares outstanding × the share price at the end of 1993, or $18.406) and multiplying by the cumulative costs of equity.

To illustrate, expected shareholder wealth at the end of 1994 is $18,608 million (the market capitalization of Hewlett-Packard's equity as of the end of 1993, the beginning of the measurement period) × 1.1821 (1 + the cost of equity for 1994), or $21,997 million.

Expected shareholder wealth at the end of the following year equals $21,997 million × 1.1706 (reflecting that year's cost of equity), or $25,750 million. Expected wealth at the end of 1996 is $25,750 × 1.1705 (that year's cost of equity), or $30,140 million; for 1997, $30,140 million × 1.1608, or $34,987 million; and for 1998, $34,987 million × 1.1608, or $40,612 million.

The excess return figures for Hewlett-Packard are substantially lower than those for MVA, mainly because the former charges the company for the opportunity cost of equity capital used over the measurement period, while the latter does not.

Future growth value (FGV) is another market-based measure. Although few companies calculate it, we are confident that this situation will change. FGV is an important metric for two reasons. First, it tells senior executives what the capital markets think about their firm, but in a way that has more managerial relevance than total market value. FGV equals the difference between total market value and current operations value, thus revealing the level of EVA improvement already impounded in the company's share price. FGV is also important because, as we showed in Chapter 4, it can be used to tie EVA targets directly to stock price. To put it another way, by knowing FGV and linking it to required improvements in EVA, companies can provide strong incentives for managers to reach and exceed capital market expectations.

The calculation of FGV begins by capitalizing the current year's EVA. For this purpose, we use the adjusted EVAs reported earlier, and the WACCs reported in Table 10–2. The capitalized value of EVA is added to invested capital, which we take from the ending figures used to calculate MVA. The result is current operations value, which is subtracted from market value (also reported in the MVA calculations) to arrive at the future growth value.

FGV as a percentage of total value steadily rises throughout the period, starting at 54 percent in 1994 ($15,130 million ÷ $27,942 million) and reaching 69 percent in 1998 (see Table 10–12). These results indicate that by the end of the observation period, more than two-thirds of Hewlett-Packard's stock price was based on expected EVA improvements, versus little more than half in 1994. This means that Hewlett-Packard management must deliver large improvements in financial performance in the future just to provide a cost-of-equity return on the end-of-1998 stock price. EVAs returns would require even better performance.

Cashflow Measures

In addition to cash value added (discussed as a residual income measure), two other cashflow measures are examined here: free cashflow and cashflow return on investment (CFROI). We define free cashflow as:

T A B L E   10–12

Calculating Future Growth Value for Hewlett-Packard*

	1998	1997	1996	1995	1994
Economic value added	(194)	509	233	512	(164)
÷ (29) WACC (in %)	15.0	15.0	15.7	15.5	16.5
= Capitalized value of EVA	(1,293)	3,393	1,484	3,303	(994)
+ Invested capital (ending)	21,445	21,756	19,201	16,697	13,806
= COV	20,152	25,149	20,685	20,000	12,812
Market value	64,462	68,536	55,658	51,116	27,942
– COV	20,152	25,149	20,685	20,000	12,812
= Future growth value	44,310	43,387	34,973	31,116	15,130

Note: COV = current operations value.
* In millions of dollars.

EBIT $(1 - T)$ + depreciation and amortization

Changes in the working capital requirement

Net investment in fixed assets

where T is the corporate tax rate, and net investment in fixed assets equals new investment net of proceeds from asset disposals. Cashflow from operations (Table 10–2, line 21) approximates the first three lines of this formula (because depreciation and amortization are added back to net income in calculating it, and changes in the working capital requirement are subtracted), as long as the interest expense (line 4) included in net income is added back. When net investment (line 22) is subtracted, the result is free cashflow (see Table 10–13).

The calculation of Hewlett-Packard's CFROI (see Table 10–14) follows the four-step procedure outlined in Chapter 11. Land (line 12), which is a nondepreciable asset, is subtracted from gross property, plant, and equipment (line 10) to yield depreciable gross assets. This figure is then divided by depreciation (line 7) to derive the estimate for the economic life of Hewlett-Packard's depreciable assets. In its financial disclosures, Hewlett-Packard does not distinguish between depreciation (of tangible

T A B L E   10–13

Calculating Free Cashflow and Cash-Basis Invested
Capital for Hewlett-Parkard*

	1998	1997	1996	1995	1994
(21) Cashflow from operations	5,442	4,321	3,456	1,613	2,224
+ (4) Interest expense	235	215	327	206	155
− (22) Net investment	2,346	2,005	2,619	1,615	1,298
= Free cashflow	3,331	2,531	1,164	204	1,081
Invested capital (unadjusted)	21,756	19,201	16,697	13,806	12,058
+ (11) Accumulated depreciation	5,464	4,662	4,036	3,610	3,347
= Cash-basis invested capital	27,220	23,863	20,733	17,416	15,405

*In millions of dollars.

assets) and amortization (of intangible assets), but because the
level of intangibles is modest, we assume that the entire amount
shown in line 7 of Table 10–2 is depreciation.

Gross cashflow is then estimated by adding depreciation and
amortization (line 7), interest expense (line 4), and operating lease
expense (line 28) to net income (line 6).

The third step is to estimate the gross cash investment. To
the depreciable gross assets, calculated in Step 1, we add other
long-term investments (line 13), cash and short-term investments
(line 8), other current assets (line 9), land (line 12), and the present
value of operating leases (line 27), and then subtract other current
liabilities (line 16).

The final step is to estimate a terminal value composed of
nondepreciable assets (on the assumption that these assets can be
recovered at the end of the economic life of the company's depreciable assets). To derive this figure, we add cash and short-term
investments, other current assets, land, and other long-term investments, and subtract other current liabilities.

The CPROI calculation is graphically presented for the final
year (1998) in Figure 10–1. The most striking aspect of the CFROI
time series (1994–1998) shown in Table 10–14, in contrast to the
other performance measures, is that it appears to be less volatile.

T A B L E   10—14

Calculating CFROI for Hewlett-Packard*

	1998	1997	1996	1995	1994
Step 1					
(10) Gross PP&E	12,570	11,776	10,198	8,747	7,938
− (12) Land	450	468	475	485	508
= Depreciable gross assets	12,120	11,308	9,723	8,262	7,430
÷ Depreciation†	1,869	1,556	1,297	1,139	1,006
= Economic life	6 years	7 years	7 years	7 years	7 years
Step 2					
(6) Net income	2,945	3,119	2,586	2,433	1,599
+ (7) Depreciation and amortization	1,869	1,556	1,297	1,139	1,006
+ (4) Interest expense	235	215	327	206	155
+ (28) Operating lease expense	182	182	162	157	179
= Gross cashflow	5,231	5,072	4,372	3,935	2,999
Step 3					
Depreciable gross assets					
[(10) Gross PPE − (12) Land]	12,120	11,308	9,723	8,262	7,430
+ (13) Other long-term investments (including intangibles)	5,731	4,490	4,172	3,477	2,730
+ (8) Cash + short-term investments	4,067	4,569	3,327	2,616	2,478
+ (9) Other current assets	17,517	16,378	14,664	13,623	10,031
+ (12) Land	450	468	475	485	508
+ (27) PV of operating leases	598	598	482	442	406
− (16) Other current liabilities (including trade payables)	12,228	9,993	8,498	7,730	5,761
= Gross cash investment	28,255	27,818	24,345	21,175	17,822

T A B L E   10–14

Continued

	1998	1997	1996	1995	1994
Step 4					
(8) Cash + short-term investments	4,067	4,569	3,327	2,616	2,478
+ (9) Other current assets (including inventories)	17,517	16,378	14,664	13,623	10,031
+ (12) Land	450	468	475	485	508
+ (13) Other long-term investments	5,731	4,490	4,172	3,477	2,730
− (16) Other current liabilities	12,228	9,993	8,498	7,730	5,761
= Terminal value	15,537	15,912	14,140	12,471	9,986
CFROI	13.12%	14.28%	14.06%	14.85%	13.44%

* In millions of dollars.
† Assumes no amortization.

F I G U R E   10–1

CFROI calculations.

While EVA increases from −$338 million to $395 million in the following year, a change equal to 5.3 percent of 1995 invested capital, CFROI improves by only 1.4 percentage points. Similarly, the sharp decline in performance from 1997 to 1998 barely registers with CFROI. Despite steep declines in several other indicators, CFROI declines by barely more than 1 percentage point. CFROI often has this normalizing effect on performance measurement.[3] While this may be an advantage in cyclical industries, it can also obscure genuine, and significant, year-on-year differences in performance.

One obvious disadvantage of CFROI is the complicated nature of the calculations, even in the relatively simplified version reported here. A more sophisticated CFROI measure would include an adjustment for inflation. This adjustment is seen as providing a measure that better facilitates comparison of business performance across time, because changing rates of inflation can sometimes result in significant impacts on traditional earnings or return measures. Most of the other measures explored in this chapter are not inflation adjusted. EVA, CVA, and RONA can be prepared on an inflation-adjusted basis but usually are not.

A PERSPECTIVE ON THE PERFORMANCE MEASUREMENT ALTERNATIVES

No company relies entirely on a single measure of performance; different measures serve different purposes. For example, some measures help us understand what the capital markets think about the company, including the quality of its management and its potential for value-creating growth. Other measures might be used to communicate with investors, to evaluate the yearly, quarterly, or monthly performance of the corporate group, or to drive the value-creating imperative deep into the organization.

Consider EPS and net income. An important reason for their enduring popularity is that analysts continue to use them in their valuation models. Hence, these measures continue to be the most widely used, along with EBITDA, in corporate communications with investors. EVA is also used as a tool for communicating

---

3. One reason for the relatively low volatility of the CFROI time series, in contrast to EVA, is that the former, being a rate of return, hides the growth of the asset base and its contribution to EVA volatility. Another reason is the leveraging effect that comes from measuring EVA as a return in excess of the WACC. By contrast, CFROI is an absolute return measure, and is not calculated net of a cost of capital. If CFROI is calculated as an excess return, and if both CFROI and EVA are standardized by beginning invested capital, the volatilities of the two times series should be similar.

with analysts, but most companies, even in the United States, continue to focus on more conventional metrics.

We believe that EVA will play an increasingly important role in communication as more companies implement it and as analysts become more comfortable in using EVA for valuation purposes. As of this writing, however, analyst attention, and therefore corporate attention, is focused more on EPS. Our preference for EVA is based on a simple idea: EVA more directly communicates company performance from a shareholder value perspective than EPS or net income. Also, because EVA is usable at divisional levels, it allows companies to pursue an internal measurement program more in line with the factors that ultimately drive value in the capital markets.

Market-based measures—TSR, MVA, excess return, and future growth value—serve several purposes. First, they indicate to managers how successful they have been in communicating the value-creating potential of their businesses to investors. Second, market measures can provide performance benchmarks for management bonus plans, so that managers are given incentives to reach and to exceed the targets already set for the company by investors. For example, if the value of a company includes a significant future growth value component, EVA improvement targets can be derived that tie management bonuses to capital market expectations for improvement. Market measures are the only ones that can capture the value of growth.

One problem shared by all such measures, and also by EPS, is that they are unobservable at the divisional level. For division performance measurement, the primary choices are residual income measures (e.g., EVA), residual income components (e.g., EBIT or RONA), and cashflow measures (e.g., CFO or free cashflow). Net income is usually not used for divisions because it mixes operating performance with financing (interest charges are included). Unless efforts are made to equalize the influence of debt levels on interest expense, variations in profit among divisions of the same firm can be driven not just by differences in operating performance but also by differences in capital structure. Because capital structure is nearly always beyond the control of division managers, there is a strong preference for measures that ignore the interest component.

One advantage of EVA in this regard is that capital charges are assessed on the basis of total capital, whether that capital is in the form of debt or equity. Therefore, differences across divisions in the way that assets are financed will not create cross-divisional differences in EVA. A capital structure policy can be set at the corporate level, which then feeds into divisional WACC calculations. Divisions might have different WACCs, but only because they have different levels of operating risk. Meanwhile, EVA does charge division management for the use of capital, unlike EBIT.

EBIT is a popular measure of division performance. One reason for its popularity is that it measures only operating performance, ignoring both taxes and financing costs, two factors generally thought to be beyond the control of division managers. By measuring performance in this way, corporate managers signal to division managers that they should focus their efforts on growing sales and controlling expenses. But there is a serious flaw to this logic. While it is true that division managers typically have no say in major capital structure decisions, and with good reason (there are strong economies of scale in corporate finance, and division managers nearly always lack the expertise to adopt wise financing policies), they can certainly influence financial charges. Their influence comes not from the mix of debt and equity in their balance sheets, but from the level of assets they have under their control. The problem with EBIT is that it ignores capital and asset efficiency.

Predictably, in companies that evaluate unit managers on the basis of operating profits, requests for capital budgets will far exceed the ability of the corporate group to supply capital. The reason is that managers may seek to grow operating profits by expanding capacity, whether this growth creates value or not. The one great advantage of RONA over EBIT is that it forces managers to think about capital and asset productivity, in addition to operating profits.[4]

EBITDA has become an immensely popular measure, especially in the analyst community. Many analysts in New York, London, and other financial centers base their stock recommendations on price-to-EBITDA multiples. Because EBITDA incorporates EBIT, it serves as a residual income component but is also thought (wrongly we believe) to provide a link to cashflow measurement.

---

4. Although the RONA we report here is net of tax, it can just as easily be reported pre-tax.

One of its attractions is that it controls for differences in depreciation policies across firms, presumably making cross-company comparisons easier. Also, because it adds back depreciation and amortization to operating income, analysts view it as a rough proxy for cashflow.

As a measure of cashflow, though, EBITDA has one serious flaw: It ignores changes in the working capital requirement (WCR). As we showed in Chapter 2, increases in the WCR consume cash, while decreases release cash. This means that for fast-growing companies, which must increase their WCR to sustain high rates of sales growth, EBITDA seriously overstates pretax operating cashflow.

Cashflow from operations (CFO) avoids this problem because, unlike EBITDA, it adjusts for changes in the components of the WCR (receivables, inventories, and payables). In fact, it adjusts for *all* noncash expenses (and revenues). A period measure of cashflow performance should focus on a company's success in extracting cashflow from its operating cycle. Because of its adjustment for changes in the WCR, CFO provides such a measure. EBITDA does not.

In Chapter 2, we asserted that corporate value is driven by capital market expectations of future free cashflows, discounted at the cost of capital. If so, why not use free cashflow as a primary measure of performance? Although we find free cashflow (and CFO) to be interesting, and even indispensable, measures for understanding and interpreting a company's performance, there are serious dangers to relying on any cashflow measure to evaluate historical performance. In short, while free cashflow may be king in the world of valuation, it does not necessarily follow that it plays a similar role in the world of performance measurement.

To illustrate this point, and to show why any historical cashflow measure must be interpreted with great caution, consider the information shown in Table 10–15, which includes five years of data from the cashflow statements of three prominent U.S. firms— Sun Microsystems, Wal-Mart, and Merck.

Over the observation period, 1986 to 1988, the three companies exhibit profoundly different cashflow profiles. For example, Sun Microsystems failed to generate significant CFO despite fast growing net income, while both Wal-Mart and Merck earned large and growing CFO. Another important difference is that while Wal-

T A B L E   10–15

Selected Cash Flow Data for Sun Microsystems,
Wal-Mart, and Merck*

	1986	1987	1988
Sun Microsystems			
Net income	$ 12	$ 36	$ 66
Depreciation	6	25	51
Changes in WCR	(36)	(53)	(114)
Cashflow from operations	(18)	8	3
Cashflow from investing	(38)	(99)	(149)
Wal-Mart			
Net income	$ 450	$ 628	$ 837
Depreciation	124	166	214
Miscellaneous adjustments	7	(1)	1
Changes in WCR	(316)	(334)	(318)
Cashflow from operations	265	459	734
Cashflow from investing	(679)	(808)	(788)
Merck			
Net income	$ 676	$ 906	$ 1207
Depreciation	194	210	205
Miscellaneous adjustments	37	(66)	(245)
Changes in WCR	187	272	220
Cashflow from operations	1094	1322	1387
Cashflow from investing	(337)	(460)	(111)

*In millions of dollars.
Note: WCR = working capital requirement.
Sources: Sun Microsystems, Wal-Mart, and Merck.

Mart was able to generate a fast-growing CFO, its free cashflow (CFO, net of investing cashflows) was negative in each of the three years. Of course, one might argue that these different cashflow profiles are primarily a function of performance, with Merck outperforming the other two companies.

However, keep in mind that we selected these companies for a reason. In hindsight, we know that all three were immensely successful over this period. Each company was truly world class in its field. Sun Microsystems, then a producer of computer workstations, became the industry leader by 1988, only six years after it was founded. Wal-Mart practically reinvented the way discount retailing is done in the United States, sustaining high rates of growth throughout the 1980s. Meanwhile, Merck was the standard by which pharmaceutical companies were judged in that era. So, here we have three companies that were arguably the best in the world at what they did. And yet their cashflow profiles are so radically different. Why?

The answer is surprisingly simple. These companies at the time were in very different stages of development. Sun Microsystems was in a super high-growth phase, having recently emerged from its start-up phase; Wal-Mart was also a growth company, but more mature than Sun and in a more mature and developed market; Merck was by far the most mature of the three companies, although it continued to enjoy growth rates above those of the national economy. This means that all three companies could be world-beaters and yet exhibit sharply different patterns in their cashflows.

Sun's rapid growth required a sharp increase in receivables and inventories. Logically, if the company was to sell more computer workstations, it needed to produce more, which required more inventory. Also, because workstations are expensive, the company would have to extend more credit to get customers to buy them. This is why Sun's net income grows so fast over the three years, from $12 million to $66 million, and yet CFO hovers around zero. In other words, the company became increasingly profitable but was not yet able to generate cash from the business. Meanwhile, it continued to invest in fixed assets; investing cashflows go from −$38 million in 1986 to $149 million in 1988. In short, free cashflows were negative, and increasingly so.

One problem with free cashflow as a measure of performance, despite its supremacy in the world of valuation, is that its level in any year may be dictated more by growth opportunities in a company's industry than by operating performance in that year. Returning to the example of Hewlett-Packard (Table 10–16), free cashflow was lowest in 1995, which happened to be an excellent year in terms of EVA, and highest in 1998, the worst year in terms of EVA. Which figures do we believe?

The low free cashflow in 1995 should not be interpreted as an indication of poor performance, but rather as an indication that

T A B L E   10–16

Summary of Performance Measures for Hewlett-Packard, 1994–1998*

	1998	1997	1996	1995	1994
EVA	(195)	351	155	395	(338)
Economic profit	(148)	388	194	431	(288)
CVA	902	1,404	935	1,128	339
EBIT	3,841	4,339	3,726	3,568	2,549
EBITDA	5,710	5,895	5,023	4,707	3,555
NOPAT	3,114	3,269	2,815	2,571	1,701
RONA (in percent)	14.32	17.03	16.86	18.62	14.11
TSR (in percent)	(1.24)	23.67	9.46	90.71	34.44
MVA†	44,235	47,997	37,516	35,400	15,000
Excess return (from end of 1993)†	27,263	32,731	23,165	22,530	3,242
Future growth value†	44,310	43,387	34,973	31,116	27,942
Cashflow from operations	5,442	4,321	3,456	1,613	2,224
Free cashflow	3,331	2,531	1,164	204	1,081
CFROI (in percent)	14.37	15.13	14.89	15.66	13.44
Net income	2,945	3,119	2,586	2,433	1,599
Earnings per share (in $)	2.77	2.95	2.46	2.31	1.54

* All amounts in millions of dollars unless otherwise noted.
† Calculated as of the end of the year.

growing profits stimulated Hewlett-Packard management to increase its investment in what were, *ex ante*, value-creating capital projects. Free cashflow was higher in the previous year, not because of superior performance, but because of lower levels of investment. By contrast, high levels of free cashflow in 1998 may reflect fewer profitable investment opportunities. Viewing other performance measures from that same year—EVA, CBA, EBIT, and RONA—we certainly couldn't attribute the higher cashflows to superior performance.

Although Wal-Mart's CFO figures were already positive, and growing, its WCR grew sharply over the period, just like Sun's. In Wal-Mart's case, this is due mainly to increases in inventory, as each new store (and there were hundreds of them in those days) had to be stocked with merchandise. Trade payables increased over the three years but did not come close to keeping pace with increases in inventory, which means that Wal-Mart had to finance most of the increases itself. This is why CFO is lower than net income, which is the opposite of what we would expect for more mature firms. In companies like Merck, for example, the depreciation add-back, combined with a steady or even declining WCR, leads to CFO figures substantially higher than net income.

In evaluating the performance of Sun Microsystems and Wal-Mart, which figures do you think are most useful? Net income, CFO, or free cashflow? In hindsight, the answer is obvious: net income.

What this example shows us is that while historical cashflow information may be of great interest, it sometimes obscures more than enlightens, especially in fast-growing firms. Of course, low CFO figures might indicate that a company is not managing its working capital properly, in which case CFO may tell us something about performance that net income does not (because robust net income figures might mask problems in collecting receivables or selling inventories). But what if low, or negative, CFO results from the company investing for future (value-creating) growth and not from sloppy management? In such cases, CFO understates management performance and could, if used as a basis for determining bonuses, discourage managers from investing.

Similar issues arise when using free cashflow as a benchmark for performance. Are negative figures bad and positive figures good? Not necessarily. For relatively mature companies like Merck, we would expect positive free cashflow. The most successful of such companies, and Merck certainly numbers among them, generate far more cash from their day-to-day business operations than they can profitably invest, providing a lot of cash for shareholders. And that is exactly what happened in Merck's case. CFO, net of investment, averaged over $1 billion per year over the period. Although we don't show the relevant figures in Table 10-15, all this cash was returned to shareholders, in dividends and in share buybacks. But what are we to make of the negative free cashflows in the other two companies?

Negative free cashflow simply means that a company is unable to finance all of its investment from internally generated cashflow. In short, the company takes in capital from investors, instead of returning it as Merck does. This is exactly what we would

expect in a high-growth company in which profitable growth opportunities exceed the company's ability to finance those opportunities from CFO. Of course, negative free cashflows could signal
poor performance, but evaluating managers on this basis is subject
to the same risk as relying on CFO: It may discourage investment
that would reduce free cashflow in the short term, even if it would
increase free cashflows in the future and create shareholder
wealth. One virtue of EVA is that the cost of such investment is
charged gradually, in the form of depreciation and capital charges,
and not all at once as with free cashflow.

The criticisms we direct at CFO and free cashflow apply
equally to other cashflow measures, including CVA and CFROI.
CVA is proposed as a metric that combines the virtues of residual
income measures, such as EVA, with cashflow; for this reason,
it has an undeniable surface appeal. But in our view, CVA's advantages are illusory. As a residual income measure, it is inferior
to EVA.

One of the supposed advantages of CVA over EVA is that it
does not include depreciation and amortization charges. By adding back depreciation to net income, not only does CVA produce
a residual income measure closer to cashflow, but it also eliminates
the potentially distorting influence of arbitrary depreciation policies. First, as we note above, cashflow measures can seriously bias
the measurement of short-term, or single-period, performance.
Also, as we showed in Chapter 7, if management perceives the
distortions as serious enough, accounting- (or GAAP-) based depreciation can be replaced with economic (or sinking fund)
depreciation, which effectively eliminates any potential distortion
from including depreciation charges. In other words, the perceived advantages of CVA over EVA are either dubious (as in the
case of producing a cashflow measure) or easily overcome with
an accounting adjustment.

Another reason that EVA is better than CVA as a period
measure of performance comes from the latter's elimination of
accounting accruals. A central aim of all cashflow measures, including CVA, is to remove the influence of accruals on the
measurement of results. The problem is that while reversing accruals does produce figures closer to actual cashflows, it can also
remove from profits information that the capital markets find useful in predicting future profits and cashflow. A large academic

literature has firmly established that investors price accruals, such
as those related to taxes, receivables, and provisions. Eliminating
these items will almost certainly reduce the statistical association
between the performance measure and shareholder returns. As the
relationship between the measure and shareholder wealth is reduced, value-destroying actions by management are more likely,
especially if compensation plans are tied to the measure.

A further advantage of EVA becomes evident when we think
back to the discussion on EVA-based compensation in Chapter 4.
In that chapter, we argued that EVA bonus plans can substitute
for MBOs, providing strong wealth incentives and closer alignment of management and shareholder interests at reasonable levels of retention risk and shareholder cost. At the same time, the
company can obtain these advantages without assuming the pun-
ishing levels of debt that characterize the typical MBO. In short,
the incentives that EVA bonus plans offer are inspired by the MBO
model, but they offer a degree of financial flexibility that MBOs
generally do not.

An important aspect of this EVA-MBO equivalence is that the
charges imposed on managers under EVA mimic those of an MBO.
The capital charges are EVA's substitute for the interest expense
paid to the MBO's debt providers, while depreciation charges are
EVA's proxy for the principal payments on the debt. Yet one of
the virtues of EVA, in contrast to the MBO model, is that depreciation is charged to managers over the economic life of the acquired assets. In a typical MBO, debt must be repaid more quickly
(usually within five years). If the assets cannot generate sufficient
cashflows quickly enough, the company could face bankruptcy,
even if the present value of the company's expected EVAs over
the long term is positive. In this way, if a company needs to grow
quickly to capture value-creating opportunities in its sector, sacrificing cashflow generation in the short term, EVA-based incentives can accommodate the change, while the MBO typically
cannot. To put it another way, EVA bonus plans are more patient
than MBOs and do not require the immediate delivery of cashflow
to bankers if investment opportunities suggest that the cashflow should be reinvested.

In other words, EVA offers many of the advantages of an
MBO while allowing the firm a degree of financial flexibility that

more easily allows for the exploitation of profitable growth opportunities. For these conditions to hold, and for EVA to impose discipline on managers in much the same way as an MBO, managers must be assessed *all* the charges that would pertain in an MBO setting, which include not only the capital charges but also the depreciation. Because it eliminates depreciation from the profit calculation, CVA weakens the conceptual link between residual income and the MBO.

CONCLUSION

In the metric wars, there is no single measure that is perfect for all corporate functions that rely on financial measurement. In our view, however, EVA has proven to be remarkably versatile, with important uses in a broad range of corporate functions and settings. Still, there are important roles to be played by market-based measures (especially excess return and future growth value), cash-flow measures, and even traditional income measures. Residual income components, such as RONA, are indispensable for driving EVA-type incentives deep into companies.

In the next and final chapter, we'll summarize our key findings on EVA implementation, and will also give our views on the important trends that appear to be emerging in value-based management.

PART THREE

Conclusions

CHAPTER 11

Lessons Learned, and the Future of Economic Value Added

The ideas behind EVA and value-based management have been around for a long time, but only within the last few years have we seen a large number of companies implement formal value-based systems. Good managers have always had a sound, intuitive grasp of these ideas and have employed them, sometimes informally, in the way they ran their companies. Great business leaders, past and present, have always known about EVA without calling it that.

But as globalization and deregulation have swept the corporate world, and the pressure for shareholder returns has intensified, a much larger group of managers has sought to attain the same insights that make it possible for the most successful managers to deliver superior performance year after year. EVA and the value-based management movement have evolved in recent years to help managers in any company anywhere incorporate the systems and thinking required to create value for their own shareholders. Think of EVA as a means of revealing to the rest of us the insights that Jack Welch, Percy Barnevik, and other great managers have always had at a deep intuitive level.

Of course, EVA is not a strategy and should never be thought of as a substitute for one. What EVA can do is put the proper incentives and monitoring systems in place to increase the chances that managers will run the firm in a manner consistent with the creation of shareholder value.

Thousands of companies have implemented value-based ideas to some extent, but the experience is still recent. Although many managers testify to the improvements in corporate performance that they see with the adoption of EVA and value-based management, the cause-and-effect relationships between such practices and corporate performance are still sketchy.

Most companies that have adopted formal EVA and value-based management systems have done so since the early 1990s. Combine this lack of experience with the sharp competition among the world's largest consulting firms, each with a growing value-based management practice and its own differentiated product offerings, and it becomes easy to see why businesses have not yet coalesced around standards and accepted best practice.

In the grand historical sweep of things, our experience with EVA is limited. Encouragingly, however, so much has been learned in the short time that these ideas have gained popularity among business managers. We certainly know much more today about EVA than we did a few years ago, and we will know much more a few years from now. Still, the experiences thus far, combined with the arguments and experiences laid out in this book, suggest several crucial lessons for any company that truly seeks to capture the benefits that EVA and value-based management practices have to offer. These lessons include the following:

1. *The starting point of any value-based management system is the acceptance that value is ultimately determined by the capital markets, and what the markets want is cashflow.* This notion is most conveniently expressed in the free cashflow model of valuation. When we say, "cash is king," this is what we mean. Value is a function of capital market expectations of a company's ability to deliver free cashflow in the future. One practical consequence of this intuition is that before capital is invested, managers should believe that the present value of the future cash inflows expected from the investment will exceed the amount of capital invested. In this way, investment contributes to excess return, the ultimate arbiter of management's success in creating shareholder value.

2. *However, the central role of cashflow in determining value does not mean that cashflow is always an appropriate benchmark for analyzing historical performance.* While undeniably important, the emphasis on cashflow for performance measurement can obscure other factors related to current performance that may provide crucial links to future cashflow generation. Free cashflow has important limitations as a performance measure, despite the vital role it plays in company valuation. Negative free cashflow in a given year may simply reflect an abundance of profitable growth opportunities, and not management's failure to deliver good financial results.

3. *Implementation of EVA must begin at the very top of the organization.* The board of directors, the CEO, and other members of the top management team must buy into the concept wholeheartedly. The EVA story goes far beyond measuring profits in a different way. It is about changing attitudes and behavior. Such change must be driven from the top.

4. *The company should have a formal implementation plan that addresses key strategic issues, beginning with perhaps the most important issue of all: How will EVA be used?* A thorough value-based orientation requires that EVA become a part of the strategic planning process, capital allocation, operating budgets, compensation, and investor relations. Does this mean that if we are already using discounted cashflow techniques for capital allocation decisions, we should switch to EVA and frame all analyses in those terms? Not necessarily. The most important lesson here is to incorporate the insights of EVA and value-based thinking into all of the company's key processes and systems. If these insights are already used for capital investment decisions by means of discounted cashflow techniques, so much the better. That means the company already has some experience in working with value-oriented concepts.

5. *Implementing EVA will have only a modest impact unless (a) efforts are made to measure EVA at least two rungs below*

the corporate level and (b) EVA is used to create strong wealth incentives at the business unit level. Managers must think like owners, not like employees, but such a change is not possible unless managers are paid to think this way.

6. *EVA is designed to provide the line of sight at division levels that is lacking when share price is used as the key indicator of performance.* However, calculating meaningful EVA numbers at different levels of the corporate hierarchy is fraught with difficult measurement problems. A first pass at EVA measurement will probably parallel the profit center reporting that already exists in the company, although there may be benefits to defining EVA centers in ways that don't correspond exactly to organizational boundaries. As to bringing EVA into service departments, there are techniques for transforming cost centers into profit centers, which would then allow the calculation of unit EVAs. However, few CFOs consider such practices to be worth the effort. The arbitrariness of pricing products or services bought in or sold by such units will lead to arbitrary EVA figures that confuse more than enlighten. In such cases, line of sight can be achieved by using EVA drivers instead of EVA itself. Applying the balanced scorecard can help managers identify these drivers. A similar approach can be used to identify EVA drivers for lower-level employees.

7. *EVA calculations are highly sensitive to estimates of the cost of capital.* Unfortunately, we can never precisely know our company's cost of capital because we cannot directly observe the cost of equity. However, this inability does not excuse us from having to try. In addition, if divisions within the company face very different risk levels, either because they operate in different sectors or in different parts of the world, divisional costs of capital should also be calculated. Here, the exercise becomes even harder than when estimating the cost of capital at the corporate level. Still, we must make the effort, and a set of best-practice

rules has emerged in recent years to guide companies in this difficult task.

8. *Capital structure can create value, and it can destroy it.* Nevertheless, while the debt-equity choice is an important one, corporate strategy is more important. In other words, capital structure should be only a second-order concern. Real value creation comes from having the right strategies, as well as the right processes and systems in place to deliver the economic benefits of these strategies.

9. *Remember that EVA is above all else a measurement system.* By measuring value creation more directly than conventional accounting measures, it can help companies to better motivate their managers to do right by their shareholders. But EVA can never be a substitute for good strategy. No one understood this lesson better than General Motors' Alfred Sloan, the first executive known to have implemented an EVA-type system for divisional management bonuses (and he did so over 75 years ago). Sloan was a great believer in managerial incentives, but his most lasting contribution to the firm was establishing a clear understanding of what GM was trying to do, then communicating that vision throughout the organization. He practically invented the modern multidivisional corporation, revitalized the company's many brands, and in the process led his company to market supremacy over arch rival Ford. Ultimately, it was Sloan's strategic vision and his ability to translate that vision into concrete actions that delivered the high returns that GM's shareholders enjoyed under his leadership.

10. *Remember too that success is generally built around the things a company is uniquely able to do.* Sometimes a company's distinctive capabilities are based on cost leadership and operating efficiency, sometimes on customer service and reputation, and sometimes on product innovation. But in any case, sustained value creation is not possible without first identifying the

company's capabilities (or, as we say in the modern management parlance, its "core competencies"). These competencies must then be matched with the external environment to determine which markets the company should be in and how to serve them. Only by serving markets in ways that others cannot duplicate, or at least cannot do so easily, is it possible for a firm to add value and produce returns greater than its cost of capital. In short, companies must determine where they can add value and where they cannot. EVA is an especially helpful analytical tool in carrying out this vital task, but it is only a financial metric. It can never tell us whether, for example, to position ourselves up-market or down-market from our competitors, or how we should respond to competitors' initiatives in product innovation, pricing, or marketing.

11. *The EVA message requires continuous reinforcement by top management.* Making EVA an important part of the compensation system helps, but the CEO and other members of the top management team must take every opportunity to drive home the value creation story.

12. *Accounting issues are important, and adjustments to EVA should be carefully evaluated.* Under GAAP, value-creating investments (including R&D and corporate acquisitions) can be negative EVA for many years. As a result, managers may be reluctant to undertake them. Adjustment techniques, such as negative economic depreciation, can overcome such problems, but adjustments increase the complexity of EVA measurement. Because the number of adjustments must be kept small, those that are chosen should have a significant, and positive, influence on managerial decision making.

13. *However EVA is calculated, bonuses should be geared to improvements in EVA.* Emphasizing improvements, as opposed to levels, offers several advantages. First, it reinforces the imperative in competitive markets for continuous improvement. Second, measurement issues become less important when evaluation is based on

change. For example, managers sometimes wonder why EVA calculations are not based on market or replacement values for assets, instead of book values. "Won't that provide better estimates of invested capital?" they ask. Perhaps, but when the emphasis shifts from levels of EVA to changes in EVA, such issues become less important. Also, emphasizing change reduces the possibility that managers who are given control of underperforming divisions will believe that the EVA bonus system is unfair. Again, it is improvement in EVA that counts. When managers understand this, they are less reluctant to take on difficult assignments.

14. *For senior managers, don't pay out the entire EVA bonus in the year in which it is earned; instead, establish bonus banks.* These banks encourage longer-term thinking by giving managers a direct economic stake in medium-term EVAs (i.e., EVAs over the next three to five years). They can also improve retention because bank balances are normally forfeited when managers leave a firm voluntarily. Because of frequent job shifts, the large number of people involved, and administrative complexities, bonus banks are impractical and should be avoided for middle managers, however.

15. *Stock options must still play an important role.* Stock options bind managers and employees to the firm, strengthening the feeling nurtured by EVA bonus plans that as shareholders get richer, they will too. Stock options also provide long-term incentives for value creation, to augment the short-term and medium-term incentives provided by frequent EVA measurement and the bonus bank. In addition, stock options are indispensable when trying to create ownerlike wealth leverage for senior managers (to ensure that manager wealth is highly sensitive to changes in shareholder wealth).

16. *Employees must be trained in the meaning and use of EVA.* Reinforce the training with follow-up workshops in which employees can share experiences and discuss

concrete actions they have taken to boost EVA in their
units. However, we do not believe that it is necessary
to train *all* employees in EVA, as some users in the
United States have done. EVA may even prove
distracting for lower-level employees.

WHAT NEXT?

In recent years, we have seen major changes in the ways that
companies implement, and try to sustain, value-based practices.
What will the future look like for EVA and value-based management? Attempts to predict change in such a fast-moving area are
risky, of course, but we can already observe certain trends that
should persist in the coming years. We are already trying to incorporate these important trends in the work we do with our clients, and we urge others to do likewise. Following are the major
forces and practices that we believe are likely to shape EVA and
value-based management over the next 10 years:

1. *Now that many companies have implemented value-based*
   systems, at least to some extent, increased emphasis will be
   given to value creation as a dynamic process. VBM and EVA
   professionals can learn a valuable lesson from the total
   quality management (TQM) and reengineering
   movements. Most implementers of process improvement
   programs, for example, have struggled to maintain initial
   successes. One possible reason for this problem is that
   improvement programs are highly dependent on links to
   various other functions and processes in the firm, and to
   key external constituents such as customers and
   suppliers. The same can be said for TQM programs.
   Failure to account for feedback and the dynamic
   character of relationships among these various activities
   and groups leads to unexpected and costly side effects.
   Implementers of EVA face potentially similar problems,
   unless proper emphasis is given to understanding the
   organizational capabilities required to deliver superior
   performance year after year, and to creating management
   systems, including performance measurement, that can

respond quickly and decisively to important changes in a company's environment.

2. *Nonfinancial performance measurement will grow in importance as the emphasis in many companies, especially the early implementers of EVA, shifts toward developing organizational capabilities and executing strategy.* The balanced scorecard, and similar frameworks for identifying nonfinancial value drivers, give senior managers a way to describe their strategy, putting it at the center of the performance measurement system.

3. *External analysts too will devote more attention to nonfinancial drivers.* With future growth value often encompassing most of the total enterprise value of the firm, analysts need to look beyond current-period financial results to other metrics that may be better predictors of future EVA.

4. *The increased emphasis on nonfinancial metrics will result in greater capital market pressure on companies to release more such information to the investing public.* In other words, demands for public disclosure will grow, not only for information of a financial nature, but also for "soft" information relating to a company's customers, its internal processes, and its people. Because of the internal and external demands for such information, standards will evolve with the aim of improving the reliability of scorecard-type measures. Recent work by A.C. Nielsen on customer ratings and J.D. Power on quality are examples. Similar efforts are underway to gauge performance in the Internet sector. This trend will likely intensify in the coming years.

5. *Performance measurement, both financial and nonfinancial, will focus less on discrete organizational boundaries, such as business units (although these will continue to be important), and more on processes, such as new product introduction, order fulfillment, and supply chain management.* As companies continue outsourcing, increased emphasis will be given to improving integration of external partners. While activities may be getting pushed outside the formal legal boundaries of the organization, managers

should never be excused from ensuring that these separate legal entities (comprising suppliers, distributors, service providers, etc.) are managed as one economic entity. In other words, we can take certain functions outside of the company, but we can never outsource responsibility for integration. Increasingly, performance measurement systems will be called on to help managers perform this crucial task.

6. *Transparency will become a key theme of performance-based information.* As we noted earlier, companies will be expected to provide more detailed information to investors on both the financial and nonfinancial drivers of EVA. But transparency will increase internally too. We hear a lot these days about the "knowledge economy" and "knowledge workers." It should go without saying that knowledge workers cannot function without access to information. In addition, strategy execution requires cooperation and teamwork, which in turn require knowledge sharing. Traditionally, senior managers have been reluctant to share detailed data on strategy implementation, mainly out of fear that competitors might learn valuable corporate secrets. The problem is that if important elements of strategy are kept confidential, not only are competitors kept in the dark, so too are employees. Even if the performance metrics used by a company are in the public domain, and therefore can be copied by competitors, competitors cannot so easily copy the management and working relationships of the company.

7. *Companies will sharply increase the amount of resources devoted to training on EVA and other value-oriented themes.* Our experience has taught us that if companies skimp on training, an integrative, value-based approach to management is not possible. Implementation becomes haphazard, because too many key employees do not really understand what is expected of them. A growing number of companies are starting to learn this lesson.

BIBLIOGRAPHY

Allen, J., "Capital Markets and Corporate Structure: The Equity Carve-Outs of Thermo Electron," *Journal of Financial Economics*, 1998.

Amelio, G., with W. Simon, *On the Firing Line*, New York: HarperBusiness 1998.

Anders, G., *Merchant of Debt: KKR and the Mortgaging of American Business*, New York: Basic Books, 1992.

Andrade, G. and S. N. Kaplan, "How Costly Is Financial (Not Economic) Distress? Evidence from Highly Leveraged Transactions that Became Distressed," *Journal of Finance*, October 1998.

Andrews, E. L., "Boran's Chief Executive Quits Amid Big Losses," *International Herald Tribune*, January 5, 2000, p. 4.

Bacidore, J. M., J. A. Boquist, T. T. Milbourn, and A. V. Thakor, "The Search for the Best Financial Performance Measure," *Financial Analysts Journal*, May/June 1997.

Banker, R. D., G. Potter, and D. Srinivasan, "An Empirical Investigation of an Incentive Plan That Includes Nonfinancial Performance Measures," *The Accounting Review*, January 2000, pp. 65–92.

Barr, S., "Misreporting Results," *CFO Magazine*, December 1998.

Biddle, G. C., R.M. Bowen, and J. S. Wallace, "Does EVA Beat Earnings? Evidence on Associations with Stock Returns and Firm Values," *Journal of Accounting & Economics*, 1997, pp. 301–336.

Boston Consulting Group, *Shareholder Value Metrics*, Shareholder Value Management Series, Booklets 1 and 2, 1996.

Deutsch, C. L., "A Lesson in Hatching Businesses," *International Herald Tribune*, June 8, 1999, p. 16.

Dolven, B., "Taiwan's Trump," *Far Eastern Economic Review*, August 6, 1998, pp. 12–15.

Epstein, M. and J. F. Manzoni, "Implementing Corporate Strategy: From Tableaux de Bord to Balanced Scorecards," *European Management Journal*, April 1998, pp. 190–203.

Ehrbar, A., *EVA: The Real Key to Creating Wealth*, New York: John Wiley & Sons, 1998.

Fama, E. F. and K. R French, "The Cross-Section of Expected Stock Returns," *Journal of Finance*, 1992, pp. 427–466.

Fama, E. F. and K. R. French, "Common Risk Factors in the Returns on Stocks and Bonds," *Journal of Financial Economics*, 1993, pp. 3–56.

Freher, E. W., "Designing the Annual Management Incentive Plan," in *Paying for Performance: A Guide to Compensation Management*, P. T. Chingos, ed., New York: John Wiley & Sons, 1997, pp. 161–175.

Glassman, J. K. and K. A. Hassett, "Stock Prices Are Still Far Too Low," *Wall Street Journal Europe,* March 18, 1999, p. 12.

Hall, B. J. and J. B. Liebman, "Are CEOs Really Paid Like Bureaucrats?" *The Quarterly Journal of Economics,* August 1998, pp. 653–691.

Hodak, M., "The End of Cost Allocations as We Know Them," *Journal of Applied Corporate Finance,* Fall 1997, pp. 117–124.

Hofstede, G. and M. H. Bond, "The Confucius Connection: From Cultural Roots to Economic Growth," *Organizational Dynamics,* 1988, pp. 4–21.

Hulburt, H., J. Miles, and R. Woolridge, "Value Creations from Equity Carve-Outs," working paper, Penn State University, 1998.

Ittner, C. D., D. F. Larcker, and M. V. Rajan, "The Choice of Performance Measures in Annual Bonus Contract," *The Accounting Review,* April 1997, pp. 231–255.

Jabonsky, S. F. and P. J. Keating, *Changing Roles of Financial Management: Integrating Strategy, Control, and Accountability,* Morristown, N.J.: Financial Executives Research Foundation, 1998.

Jackson, T., "The Fat Cats Keep Getting Fatter," *Financial Times,* August 1–2, 1998, p. 7.

Kamm, T., "Market Forces Push France's Elite Corps Out of Top Sinecures," *Wall Street Journal Europe,* May 7, 1998, pp. 1–8.

Kaplan, R. and D. Norton, "The Balance Scorecard—Measures that Drive Performance," *Harvard Business Review,* January–February 1992.

Kaplan, R. and D. Norton, "Putting the Balanced Scorecard to Work," *Harvard Business Review,* September–October 1993.

Kaplan, R. and D. Norton, "Using the Balanced Scorecard as a Strategic Management System, *Harvard Business Review,* January–February 1996.

Kaplan, R. and D. Norton, *The Balanced Scorecard: Translating Strategy into Action,* Boston: Harvard Business School Press, 1996.

Kaplan, R. and D. Norton, "Linking the Balance Scorecard to Strategy," *California Management Review,* July 1996.

Kaplan, S., "Effects of Management Buyouts on Operations and Value," *Journal of Financial Economics,* October 1989, pp. 217–254.

Kaplan, S. "The Staying Power of Leveraged Buyouts," *Journal of Financial Economics,* October 1991, pp. 287–314.

Kaplan, S. and J. Stein, "How Risky Is Debt in Highly Leveraged Transactions?" *Journal of Financial Economics,* October 1990, pp. 215–246.

Kersnar, J., "Europe's Corporate Cash Machine," *CFO Europe,* June 1998.

Knight, J. A., *Value-Based Management,* New York: McGraw-Hill, 1998.

Lynch, R. L. and K. F. Cross, *Measure UP!,* 2d ed., Cambridge, MA: Blackwell Publishers, 1995.

Madden, B. J., "The CFROI Valuation Model," *The Journal of Investing,* Spring 1998.

Madden, B. J., *CFROI Valuation: A Total System Approach to Valuing the Firm.* : Butterworth-Heinemann Finance, 1999.

Malkiel, B. G., "Tracking Stocks Are Likely to Derail," *The Wall Street Journal Europe,* February 15, 2000, p. 42.

Mintz, S. L. "Inside the Corporate Cash Machine," *CFO Magazine,* June 1997.

Myers, R., "Metric Wars," *CFO Magazine,* October 1996, pp. 41–50.

O'Byrne, S., "EVA and Market Value," *Journal of Applied Corporate Finance,* Spring 1996.

O'Byrne, S., "EVA and Shareholder Return," *Financial Practice and Education,* Spring/Summer 1997, pp. 50–54.

O'Byrne, S., "EVA and Its Critics," *Journal of Applied Corporate Finance,* Summer 1999, pp. 92–96.

Pfeffer, J., "Six Dangerous Myths About Pay," *Harvard Business Review,* May–June 1998, pp. 109–119.

Schuler, R. S. and N. Rogovsky, "Understanding Compensation Practice Variations Across Firms: The Impact of National Culture," *Journal of International Business Studies,* October 1998, pp. 159–177.

Sirower, M. L. and S. F. O'Byrne, "The Measurement of Post-Acquisition Performance: Toward a Value-Based Benchmarking Methodology," *Journal of Applied Corporate Finance,* Summer 1998, pp. 107–121.

Solomons, D., *Divisional Performance: Measurement and Control,* New York: Financial Executives Research Foundation, 1965.

Stewart III, G. B., *The Quest for Value,* New York: Harper Collins, 1991.

Stewart III, G. B., "EVA: Fact or Fantasy?" *Journal of Applied Corporate Finance,* Summer 1994.

Tully, S., "The Real Key to Creating Wealth," *Fortune,* September 20, 1993, pp. 38–50.

Vijh, A. M., "Long-Term Returns from Equity Carveout," *Journal of Financial Economics,* February 1999, pp. 273–308.

Wallace, J. S., "Adopting Residual Income-Based Compensation Plans: Do You Get What You Pay For?," *Journal of Accounting & Economics,* 1997, pp. 275–300.

Zimmerman, J. L., "EVA and Divisional Performance Measurement: Capturing Synergies and Other Issues," *Journal of Applied Corporate Finance,* pp. 98–109.

INDEX

INDEX

Note: locators in **bold** indicate full-page tables and charts

AB Volvo, 225
ABC (activity-based costing), 104
Accounting and accounting adjustments:
    accrual accounting method, 108–110,
      428, **430**
    adjustment process, 255–260
    capital charges, 253–255
    clean surplus accounting, 238
    deferred taxes, 218–222
    depreciation, 229–236
    EVA implementation, 107–111
    EVA principles, 5, 475–476
    goodwill, 236–248, **242**
    LIFO reserves, 226–227
    operating leases, 247–251
    recommended adjustments, 268
    refined EVA, 260–263
    R&D, 210–217, **218**
    restructuring charges, 252–253
    stock market return explanation, 263–
      267
    successful efforts accounting, 208–210
    warranty and bad debt provisions,
      223–226
    (*See also* Generally accepted accounting
      principles)
Activity-based costing (ABC), 104
Agency costs, capital structure, 195–197
Akers, John, 129
Allen, Jeffrey, 150–152
Amelio, Gil, 47
Amortization:
    discounted cashflow, 24
    goodwill, 239–248, **242**
    R&D capitalization, 212–217, **218**
    (*See also* Earnings before Interest,
      Taxes, Depreciation, and
      Amortization)
Andrade, Gregor, 194–195
APM (asset pricing model), 181–184, 185
Apple Computer, 46–47
Arbitrage, 181

Arbitrage pricing model (APM), 181–184,
    185
Arbitrage pricing model (APM)
    alternative, 181–185
Assets:
    CAPM, 165–166, 170–172, 179–181
    deferred taxes, 218
    depreciation, 232, 384–386
    EVA implementation, 93, 97
    fixed, 48, 53–55, 276
    goodwill, 240
    intangible, 211
    intellectual and human capital, 110
    net assets, 45, 48
    tangible, 43
    turnover, 84–85, 276–277
    (*See also* Return on net assets)
Asymmetric information, capital structure,
    197–198
AT&T, 115, 155

Baan NV, 190–191
Bad debt provisions, accounting
    adjustments, 223–226
Balance sheet, 44–46, **52–53,** 89, 107, 206–
    208
Balanced scorecard, value drivers, 289–301
Banker, R. D., 284
Beatrice, 119, 121, 125
Berle, Adolf, 115–116
Beta:
    asset pricing model, 183–184
    cost of capital, 164–165, 166–173, 176–
      179
    defined, 166–168
    divisional product line organization,
      177–178
    (*See also* Weighted-average cost of
      capital)
Biddle, G. C., 263
Black-Scholes methods, 125–126, 127, 350,
    353, 356, 369

ABOUT THE AUTHORS

S. DAVID YOUNG, PH.D., is a professor at INSEAD, one of the world's leading graduate business schools. A consultant on EVA and value-based management for several American, European, and Asian companies, Dr. Young's research has appeared in many academic and professional journals. He can be reached at david.young@insead.fr.

STEPHEN F. O'BYRNE is president and co-founder of Shareholder Value Advisors Inc., a consulting firm that helps companies increase shareholder value through better performance measurement, incentive compensation, and valuation analysis. O'Byrne was formerly senior vice president at Stern Stewart & Co., and his articles have appeared in a wide variety of journals. He can be reached at sobyrne@valueadvisors.com.